Diminished Parties

Many contemporary party organizations are failing to fulfill their representational role in contemporary democracies. While political scientists tend to rely on a minimalist definition of political parties (groups of candidates that compete in elections), this volume argues that this misses how parties can differ not only in degree but also in kind. With a new typology of political parties and diminished subtypes, the authors provide a new analytical tool to address the role of political parties in democratic functioning and political representation. The empirical chapters apply the conceptual framework to analyze seventeen parties across Latin America. The authors are established scholars expert in comparative politics and in the cases included in the volume. The book sets an agenda for future research on parties and representation, and it will appeal to those concerned with the challenges of consolidating stable and programmatic party systems in developing democracies.

Juan Pablo Luna is Professor of Political Science at the Pontificia Universidad Católica de Chile. He is the author of *Segmented Representation: Political Party Strategies in Unequal Democracies* (2014) and co-author of *Latin American Party Systems* (Cambridge, 2010).

Rafael Piñeiro Rodríguez is Associate Professor at the Universidad Católica del Uruguay. With Verónica Pérez Bentancur and Fernando Rosenblatt, he has coauthored *How Party Activism Survives: Uruguay's Frente Amplio* (Cambridge, 2020), which won the APA's Leon Epstein Outstanding Book Award.

Fernando Rosenblatt is Associate Professor of Political Science at the Universidad Diego Portales, Chile. He is the author of *Party Vibrancy and Democracy in Latin America* (2018) and co-author with Verónica Pérez Bentancur and Rafael Piñeiro of *How Party Activism Survives: Uruguay's Frente Amplio* (Cambridge, 2020), which won the APA's Leon Epstein Outstanding Book Award.

Gabriel Vommaro is Professor at the Universidad Nacional de San Martín, Argentina, and researcher in the Argentinian Consejo Nacional de Investigaciones Científicas y Técnicas (CONICET). His books include *La larga marcha de Cambiemos* (2017), Mundo PRO (2015; with S. Morresi and A. Bellotti) and *Sociologie du clientélisme* (2015; with H. Combes).

Diminished Parties

Democratic Representation in Contemporary Latin America

Edited by

JUAN PABLO LUNA

Pontificia Universidad Católica de Chile

RAFAEL PIÑEIRO RODRÍGUEZ

Universidad Católica del Uruguay

FERNANDO ROSENBLATT

Universidad Diego Portales

GABRIEL VOMMARO

Universidad Nacional de San Martín/CONICET

CAMBRIDGE
UNIVERSITY PRESS

CAMBRIDGE
UNIVERSITY PRESS

Shaftesbury Road, Cambridge CB2 8EA, United Kingdom

One Liberty Plaza, 20th Floor, New York, NY 10006, USA

477 Williamstown Road, Port Melbourne, VIC 3207, Australia

314–321, 3rd Floor, Plot 3, Splendor Forum, Jasola District Centre, New Delhi – 110025, India

103 Penang Road, #05–06/07, Visioncrest Commercial, Singapore 238467

Cambridge University Press is part of Cambridge University Press & Assessment, a department of the University of Cambridge.

We share the University's mission to contribute to society through the pursuit of education, learning and research at the highest international levels of excellence.

www.cambridge.org
Information on this title: www.cambridge.org/9781009073233

DOI: 10.1017/9781009072045

First published 2022
First paperback edition 2023

A catalogue record for this publication is available from the British Library

ISBN 978-1-316-51318-7 Hardback
ISBN 978-1-009-07323-3 Paperback

Contents

Figures

Tables

Contributors

DIEGO ABENTE BRUN is Professor and Director of the Latin American and Hemispheric Studies Program at the Elliott School of International Affairs, The George Washington University since 2019. Previously, he was Professor of Political Science at Miami University of Ohio (1984–93). He has authored and edited more than forty books, chapters, and articles in academic journals such as *Comparative Politics*, *Latin American Research Review*, *Journal of Latin American Studies*, and *Journal of Inter-American Affairs*. During the period between his two academic positions, he spent ten years in government as Senator, Ambassador, and Minister of Justice and Labour in Paraguay and over a decade in democracy promotion and the OAS.

RONALD ALFARO-REDONDO received his PhD in political science from the University of Pittsburgh and is Associate Professor, Department of Political Science, University of Costa Rica. His research emphasizes electoral politics, electoral systems, political parties, voter turnout, public opinion, and political culture. His research has been published in *Electoral Studies*, *Revista de Ciencia Política*, *Revista Uruguaya de Ciencia Política*, and *Revista de Ciencias Sociales*. His book *Divide y votarás* was published in 2019 by the University of Costa Rica and Programa Estado de la Nación.

SANTIAGO ANRIA is Assistant Professor of Political Science and Latin American Studies at Dickinson College. His research focuses on social movements and parties in Latin America and has appeared in journals including *Comparative Politics*, *Comparative Political Studies*, *Journal of*

Democracy, *Studies in Comparative International Development*, and *Latin American Politics and Society*. He is the author of *When Movements Become Parties: The Bolivian MAS in Comparative Perspective* (Cambridge University Press 2018).

MARÍA CLAUDIA AUGUSTO earned a degree in political science and government at Pontificia Universidad Católica del Perú, where she is a teaching assistant. From 2017 to 2019 she worked as a research assistant at Universidad del Pacífico, Perú. Her research focuses on state capacity, political representation, and subnational politics.

HÉLÈNE COMBES earned a PhD in political science from Université la Sorbonne Nouvelle and is CNRS researcher at Sciences Po's Centre for International Studies (CERI). Since 2017, she has been Editor-in-Chief of the academic journal *Critique Internationale*. Her research focuses on political parties and social movements in Latin America, particularly in Mexico. She has authored and coedited several books, including *Faire parti: Trajectoires de gauche au Mexique* (Karthala 2011); *Pensar y mirar la protesta* (coedited with Sergio Tamayo and Michael Voegtli, Ediciones de la UAM 2015); *Les lieux de la colère: Occuper l'ñce pour contester de Madrid à Sanaa* (coedited with David Garibay and Camille Goirand, Karthala 2016); and *El clientelismo político* (with Gabriel Vommaro, Siglo XXI 2017).

CATHERINE M. CONAGHAN is Professor Emerita of Political Studies and an Andean specialist at Queen's University in Kingston, Ontario. Her research on parties, interest groups, and regimes has included extensive fieldwork in Ecuador, Peru, and Bolivia. She has been a visiting scholar at Princeton University, the University of Notre Dame, the Woodrow Wilson International Center for Scholars, the Instituto de Estudios Peruanos, American University, and the Facultad Latinoamericana de Ciencias Sociales-Ecuador. She was appointed as the visiting Knapp Chair at the University of San Diego in 2000 and as the Sir Edward Peacock Professor of Latin American Politics at Queen's University (2013–18).

JENNIFER CYR is Associate Professor of Political Science and Latin American Studies at the University of Arizona. She examines representation, identity, and institutional change in Latin America and studies the integration of qualitative methods into mixed-methods research. She has published two books with Cambridge University Press: *The Fates of Political Parties: Institutional Crisis, Continuity, and Change in Latin America* (2017) and *Focus Groups for the Social Science Researcher*

(2019). She has also published in *Comparative Political Studies*, *Comparative Politics*, *PS: Political Science and Politics*, *Quality & Quantity*, *Studies in Comparative International Development*, *Sociological Methods and Research*, and *Revista de Ciencia Política*.

STEFFAN GÓMEZ-CAMPOS received his MSc in transition studies at Giessen University, Germany, and is Assistant Professor of Political Science at the University of Costa Rica. His research focuses on democracy and development, political parties, elections, data mining, and data visualization. His research has been published in *Revista de Ciencia Política*, *Revista Uruguaya de Ciencia Política*, and *Revista de Ciencias Sociales*.

JONATÁN LEMUS is currently a PhD student in political science at the University of Texas at Austin. From 2016 to 2019 he was a lecturer at the Universidad Francisco Marroquin, where he taught courses on comparative politics. He graduated from Harvard University with a BA in government in 2012 and holds a Master's degree in business administration from UNIS Business School. He previously worked as Director of Research at the CACIF business association (2014–16), consultant at Rafael Landívar University (2014) and as a researcher at the Association for Research and Social Studies (ASIES) in Guatemala (2012–13). His publications include "The private sector and political parties: Guatemala, a case study" which appeared in the *Journal of Politics and Society*. His academic interests focus on political parties and judicial politics. Mr. Lemus frequently provides political analysis and opinion to various Guatemalan newspaper and television outlets.

JUAN PABLO LUNA is Professor of Political Science at the Pontificia Universidad Católica de Chile. He received his PhD in political science from the University of North Carolina at Chapel Hill. He is the author of *Segmented Representation: Political Party Strategies in Unequal Democracies* (Oxford University Press 2014) and co-authored *Latin American Party Systems* (Cambridge University Press 2010). In 2014, he coedited along with Cristobal Rovira *The Resilience of the Latin American Right* (Johns Hopkins University).

BIBIANA ORTEGA is Assistant Professor of Political Science at Pontificia Universidad Javeriana in Bogotá, Colombia. She received her Master's degree and PhD in political science from Universidad de los Andes, her Master's in sociology and Bachelor in political science from Universidad Nacional de Colombia, and her Master's in public administration and management from the INAP-Universidad de Alcalá, Spain. Her research interests include the relationship between politics and religion, especially the evangelical political parties, as well as political participation of women, elections and political parties, and Colombian politics.

VERÓNICA PÉREZ BENTANCUR received her PhD in political science at the Universidad Torcuato Di Tella, Argentina, and is Assistant Professor of Political Science at the Departamento de Ciencia Política, Universidad de la República, Uruguay. Her research focuses on Latin American politics, political parties, and gender and politics. Her research has been published in *Comparative Political Studies*, *Gender and Politics*, *Revista de Ciencia Política*, *Revista Uruguaya de Ciencia Política*, and *Revista Debates*. In collaboration with Rafael Piñeiro Rodríguez and Fernando Rosenblatt, she has coauthored *How Party Activism Survives: Uruguay's Frente Amplio*, published in 2020 by Cambridge University Press. This book received the Leon Epstein Outstanding Book Award from the Political Organizations and Parties section of the American Political Science Association.

RAFAEL PIÑEIRO RODRÍGUEZ received his PhD in political science from Pontificia Universidad Católica de Chile and is Associate Professor at the Departamento de Ciencias Sociales, Universidad Católica del Uruguay. His research focuses on transparency, party financing, and party organizations. He has published in *Governance*, *Comparative Political Studies*, *Party Politics*, *Government Information Quarterly*, *Latin American Politics and Society*, *Latin American Research Review*, *Journal of Democracy*, *Política y Gobierno*, and *Revista de Ciencia Política*, among others. In collaboration with Verónica Pérez Bentancur and Fernando Rosenblatt, he has coauthored *How Party Activism Survives: Uruguay's Frente Amplio*, published in 2020 by Cambridge University Press. This book received the Leon Epstein Outstanding Book Award from the Political Organizations and Parties section of the American Political Science Association.

FERNANDO ROSENBLATT received his PhD in political science from Pontificia Universidad Católica de Chile and is Associate Professor of Political Science at the Universidad Diego Portales. He has published in *Perspectives on Politics*, *Governance*, *Comparative Political Studies*, *Party Politics*, *Latin American Politics and Society*, *Latin American Research Review*, *Democratization*, *Política y Gobierno*, and *Revista de*

Ciencia Política. His book *Party Vibrancy and Democracy in Latin America* was published in 2018 by Oxford University Press. In collaboration with Verónica Pérez and Rafael Piñeiro, he has coauthored *How Party Activism Survives: Uruguay's Frente Amplio*, published in 2020 by Cambridge University Press. This book received the Leon Epstein Outstanding Book Award from the Political Organizations and Parties section of the American Political Science Association.

OMAR SANCHEZ-SIBONY is Associate Professor of Political Science at Texas State University. He received his PhD in political science from the University of Oxford and holds Master's degrees from the London School of Economics and Georgetown University. His research focuses on the politics of economic reform, taxation, party systems, and competitive authoritarianism in Latin America. He has published on these topics in journals such as *Party Politics*, *Democratization*, *World Development*, *Latin American Politics and Society*, *Journal of Politics in Latin America*, and others. His first book was *Mobilizing Resources in Latin America: The Political Economy of Tax Reform* (Palgrave Macmillan 2011) and his recently completed book *Democracies without Parties: the Case of Peru* is forthcoming from Palgrave Macmillan. He is the editor of a two-volume work in progress on Guatemala's democratic institutions and state-society relations.

VIVIANA SARMIENTO works as a researcher at *Congreso Visible*, the legislative observatory of the Universidad de Los Andes in Bogotá, Colombia. She received a BA in political science, from Universidad de los Andes, and an MSc in politics and communications from the London School of Economics (2018). Her research focuses on elections, political parties, and legislative studies.

SERGIO TORO MAUREIRA is Associate Professor and President of the Information Center for Democracy at the Universidad de Concepción, Chile. He studies the logic of representation in Latin American political systems and the science of information for public policies and has directed nationally (FONDECYT, FONDEF, etc.) and internationally (UNDP, IDB) funded projects on both subjects. His work has been published in the *Journal of Legislative Studies*, *Electoral Studies*, *European Journal of Political Economy*, *Latin American Research Bulletin*, and *World Political Science Review*, among others. From 2014 to 2016 he served as the elected president of the Chilean Association of Political Science.

ALBERTO VERGARA teaches in the Department of Social and Political Sciences at the Universidad del Pacífico in Lima, Peru. He holds a PhD in political science from the University of Montreal. His two most recent books are *Acercamientos al Perú de hoy desde las ciencias sociales*, coedited with Felipe Portocarrero (Fondo editorial de la Universidad del Pacífico 2019), and *Politics after Violence: Legacies of the Shining Path Conflict in Peru* coedited with Hillel Soifer (Texas University Press 2019).

GABRIEL VOMMARO is Full Professor at the Instituto de Altos Estudios Sociales, University of San Martín and researcher in the Argentinian National Research Council. He received his PhD from the Ecole des Hautes Etudes en Sciences Sociales, Paris. He has published on political activism and political parties, political clientelism and the state, and political communication. His books include *La larga marcha de Cambiemos* (Siglo XXI 2017), *Mundo PRO* (Planeta 2015) with S. Morresi and A. Bellotti; and *Sociologie du clientélisme* (La découverte 2015; with H. Combes). His research has been published in *Actes de la Recherche en Sciences Sociales*, *Party Politics*, and *Journal of Latin American Studies*, among others.

LAURA WILLS-OTERO is Associate Professor in the Department of Political Science at the Universidad de los Andes in Bogota, Colombia. She received her PhD from the University of Pittsburgh. Her research interests include institutional change, political parties' internal features and electoral trajectories, subnational politics, and legislative studies. She focuses on Latin American politics, and particularly on Colombian politics. Her work has been published in the *Oxford Research Encyclopedia of Politics* (2020) and in the journals *Party Politics*, *Latin American Politics and Society*, *Journal of Politics in Latin America*, *Revista de Ciencia Política*, and *Colombia Internacional*, among others.

Acknowledgments

This book was possible thanks to the invaluable commitment of all the contributors. We are grateful for the various sources of funding that we received for this project. Fernando Rosenblatt acknowledges support from ANID Fondecyt #1190072 and ANID REDI #170101. Juan Pablo Luna acknowledges support from ANID Fondecyt #1190345; the Millennium Institute for Research on Violence and Democracy – VIODEMOS; and the Center for Applied Ecology and Sustainability (CAPES), Pontificia Universidad Católica de Chile, Santiago, Chile. Fernando Rosenblatt and Juan Pablo Luna also acknowledge the support they received from the Millennium Institute for Foundational Research on Data – Code ICN17_002. Rafael Piñeiro thanks the Sistema Nacional de Investigadores of the Agencia Nacional de Investigación e Innovación of Uruguay (ANII) for financial support associated with the Sistema Nacional de Investigadores (SNI_2015_2_1006237). Gabriel Vommaro acknowledges support from the Agencia Nacional de Promoción Científica y Tecnológica, PICT 2010047 and from the Consejo Nacional de Investigaciones Científicas y Técnicas (CONICET) of Argentina.

We also express our deepest gratitude to Sara Doskow, our editor at Cambridge University Press. Her guidance and support throughout the process was invaluable in moving the project forward and to completion. Chapter 1 was published in the journal *Party Politics* as an article entitled, "Political Parties, Diminished Sub-types and Democracy," 2021, Vol. 27 (2) 294–307. We are thankful to the journal's editor, Paul Webb, for permission to reproduce the paper here. David Schwartz provided valuable editing services and help with many aspects of the book, all of which greatly improved our work. The editors also want to thank Ursula Acton for her excellent professional work during the copy editing stage.

The project has been enriched by thoughtful comments contributed by many generous colleagues. In 2018, for example, we organized a workshop at the Universidad Diego Portales, Chile. We are deeply grateful to Santiago Anria, Laura Wills-Otero, and Verónica Pérez Bentancur for the time they devoted to helping us develop our theoretical framework. We presented early versions of different chapters of this book at the 2019 annual conference of the Latin American Studies Association, where we received thoughtful remarks from Kenneth Roberts. In 2019, we also presented our framework at the seminar of the Observatorio de Partidos Políticos, Facultad de Ciencias Sociales, Universidad de Buenos Aires, Argentina, organized by Juan Manuel Abal Medina, Gerardo Scherlis, and Carlos Varetto. In 2021, Gerardo Munck organized a mini-workshop to discuss the introduction and conclusion to this book. Besides Munck's own comments and critiques, we benefited from comments and reactions by Ana Arjona, Agustina Giraudy, Aníbal Pérez-Liñán, Andreas Schedler, Alisha Holland, Candelaria Garay, Daniel Brinks, Deborah Yashar, Kent Eaton, Lucas González, María Paula Saffon, Maritza Paredes, Paula Muñoz, Richard Snyder, Sandra Ley, Sebastian Mazzuca, and Silvia Otero-Bahamon. We also thank the two anonymous reviewers of the book and two anonymous reviewers of the paper published in *Party Politics* Volume 27 #2. Their comments helped us to streamline the theory and improve the empirical analysis.

Finally, we thank our families and friends, too numerous to mention, for the many ways they have supported us throughout this project.

Abbreviations

AD	Acción Democrática (Democratic Action)
ALDF	Asamblea Legislativa del Distrito Federal (Legislative Assembly of the Federal District)
AMLO	Andrés Manuel López Obrador
ANAPO	Alianza Nacional Popular (National Popular Alliance)
ANN	Alianza Nueva Nación (New Nation Alliance)
ANR	Asociación Nacional Republicana (National Republican Association)
AP	Movimiento Alianza PAIS (PAIS Alliance Movement)
APRA	Alianza Popular Revolucionaria Americana (American Revolutionary Popular Alliance)
ARI	Argentina por una República de Iguales (Argentina for a Republic of Equals)
AU	Asamblea Uruguay (Uruguayan Assembly)
CC	Coalición Cívica (Civic Coalition)
CCT	Conditional Cash Transfer
CEN	Comité Ejecutivo Nacional (National Executive Committee)
CEO	Chief Executive Officer
CICIG	Comisión Internacional contra la Impunidad en Guatemala (International Commission against Impunity in Guatemala)
CIDOB	Confederación de Pueblos Indígenas del Oriente Boliviano (Bolivian Confederation of Eastern Indigenous Peoples)

CNE	Consejo Nacional Electoral (National Electoral Council)
CNI	Congreso Nacional Indígena (National Indigenous Congress)
CNMCIOB-BS	Confederación Nacional de Mujeres Campesinas Indígenas Originarias de Bolivia – Bartolina Sisa (Bartolina Sisa National Confederation of Campesino, Indigenous, and Native Women of Bolivia)
CNOC	Coordinadora Nacional de Organizaciones Campesinal (National Coordinator of Peasants Organizations)
CNT	Convención Nacional de Trabajadores (National Workers Convention)
COMUDE	Consejos Municipales de Desarrollo Urbano y Rural (Municipal Councils of Urban and Rural Development)
CON	Congreso Nacional Ordinario (Regular National Congress)
CONAIE	Confederación de Nacionalidades Indígenas del Ecuador (Confederation of Indigenous Nationalities of Ecuador)
CONAMAQ	Consejo Nacional de Ayllus y Markas del Qullasuyu (National Council of Ayllus and Markas of the Qullasuyu)
CONIC	Coordinadora Nacional Indígena y Campesina (National Indigenous and Peasants Coordinator)
COS	Colectivo de Organizaciones Sociales (Social Organizations Collective)
CRC	Comités de la Revolución Ciudadana (Citizens' Revolution Committees)
CREO	Movimiento Creando Oportunidades (Creating Opportunities Movement)
CSCIB	Confederación Sindical Intercultural de Comunidades de Bolivia (Syndicalist Confederation of Intercultural Communities of Bolivia)
CSO	Civil Society Organizations
CSUTCB	Confederación Sindical Única de Trabajadores Campesinos de Bolivia (Unique Confederation of Rural Laborer of Bolivia)

CUC	Comité de Unidad Campesina (Peasants' Unity Committee)
CUT	Confederación Unitaria de Trabajadores (Unitary Workers' Confederation)
DC	Partido Demócrata Cristiano (Christian Democratic Party)
DEA	Drug Enforcement Agency
DGEEC	Dirección General de Estadística, Encuestas y Censos (General Office of Statistics, Surveys and Census)
DSV	Double Simultaneous Vote
EDE	Encuentro por la Democracia y la Equidad (Meeting for Democracy and Equity)
EFA	Equipo Federal de Activistas (Federal Team of Activists)
EMA	Equipos Municipales de Activistas (Municipal Teams of Activists)
ENA	Equipo Nacional de Activistas (National Team of Activists)
EPA	Equipos Parroquiales de Activistas (Parrish Teams of Activists)
ERA	Equipo Regional de Activistas (Regional Teams of Activists)
FA	Frente Amplio (Broad Front)
FAES	Fundación para el Análisis y los Estudios Sociales (Foundation for Social Analysis and Studies)
FAP	Frente Amplio Progresista (Broad Progressive Front)
FARC-EP	Fuerzas Armadas Revolucionarias de Colombia-Ejército Popular (Revolutionary Armed Forces of Colombia)
FEI	Federación de Indios (Indigenous Federation)
FENACLE	Confederación Nacional de Organizaciones Campesinas, Indígenas y Negras (National Confederation of Peasants, Indigenous, and Black Organizations)
FLS	Frente Líber Seregni (Líber Seregni Front)
FMLN	Frente Farabundo Martí para la Liberación Nacional (Farabundo Martí National Liberation Front)
FN	Frente Nacional (National Front)

FONAPAZ	Fondo Nacional para la Paz (National Fund for Peace)
FP	Fuerza Popular (Popular Strength)
Frepaso	Frente País Solidario (Solidary Country Front)
FRG	Frente Republicano Guatemalteco (Guatemalan Republican Front)
GANA	Gran Alianza Nacional (Grand National Alliance)
INE	Instituto Nacional Electoral (National Electoral Institute, Mexico)
IRI	International Republican Institute
LGBT	Lesbian, Gay, Bisexual, and Transgender
MAS	Movimiento al Socialismo (Movement toward Socialism)
MAS-U	Movimiento al Socialismo – Unzaguista (Movement toward Socialism – Unzaguista)
MIFAPRO	Mi Familia Progresa (My Family Progresses)
MNC	Multinational Corporation
MODIN	Movimiento por la Dignidad Nacional (Movement for the National Dignity)
MORENA	Movimiento de Regeneración Nacional (National Regeneration Movement)
MPD	Movimiento Popular Democrático (Popular Democratic Movement)
MPP	Movimiento de Participación Popular (Popular Participation Movement)
MRL	Movimiento Revolucionario Liberal (Liberal Revolutionary Movement)
MUD	Mesa de la Unidad Democrática (Democratic Unity Roundtable)
MUP	Movimiento Urbano Popular (Popular Urban Movement)
MVR	Movimiento Quinta República (Fifth Republic Movement)
NGO	Nongovernmental Organization
OTAC	Oficina Técnica de Atención al Candidato (Technical Office of Candidate Support)
PAC	Partido de Acción Ciudadana (Citizen Action Party)
PAIS	Movimiento Patria Altiva y Soberana (Proud Sovereign Country Movement)
PAN	Partido Acción Nacional (National Action Party)

PC	Partido Conservador (Conservative Party)
PCCh	Partido Comunista de Chile (Communist Party, Chile)
PCU	Partido Comunista del Uruguay (Communist Party)
PDC	Partido Demócrata Cristiano de Uruguay (Christian Democratic Party)
PdelT	Partido del Trabajo (Party of Work)
PDVSA	Petróleos de Venezuela Sociedad Anónima (Venezuelan Oil Company)
PEMEX	Petróleos Mexicanos (Mexican Oil Company)
PEN	Programa Estado de la Nación (State of the Nation Program)
PIT-CNT	Plenario Intersindical de Trabajadores – Convención Nacional de Trabajadores (Interunion Workers Plenary – National Workers Convention)
PJ	Primero Justicia (Justice First)
PL	Partido Liberal (Liberal Party)
PLN	Liberación Nacional (National Liberation Party)
PLRA	Partido Liberal Radical Auténtico (Authentic Radical Liberal Party)
PMDB	Partido do Movimento Democrático Brasileiro (Party of the Brazilian Democratic Movement)
PN	Partido Nacional (National Party)
PND	Plan Nacional de Desarrollo (National Development Plan)
PPD	Partido por la Democracia (Party for Democracy)
PRD	Partido de la Revolución Democrática (Party of the Democratic Revolution)
PRI	Partido Revolucionario Institucional (Institutional Revolutionary Party)
PRN	Partido Restauración Nacional (National Restoration Party)
PRO	Propuesta Republicana (Republican Proposal)
PSC	Partido Social Cristiano (Social Christian Party)
PSCh	Partido Socialista de Chile (Chilean Socialist Party)
PSD	Partido Socialista Democrático (Democratic Socialist Party)
PSFA	Partido Socialista-Frente Amplio (Socialist Party-Broad Front)

PSOE	Partido Socialista Obrero Español (Spanish Socialist Workers' Party)
PSU	Partido Socialista del Uruguay (Socialist Party of Uruguay)
PSUV	Partido Socialista Unido de Venezuela (United Socialist Party of Venezuela)
PT	Partido dos Trabalhadores (Workers Party)
PUSC	Partido Unidad Social Cristiana (United Social Christian Party)
PVP	Partido por la Victoria del Pueblo (Party for the Victory of the People)
Recrear	Recrear para el Crecimiento (Recreate for Growth)
RED	Asociación Red de Maestros y Maestras (Teachers' Network Association)
RENAP	Registro Nacional de las Personas (National People's Registry)
RN	Renovación Nacional (National Renewal)
SDL	Fortalecimiento y Transparencia de la Democracia (Strengthening and Transparency of Democracy Law)
SERVEL	Servicio Electoral (Electoral Service, Chile)
SOCMA	Macri Societies Corporation
TIPNIS	Territorio Indígena y Parque Nacional Isiboro Sécure (Isiboro Sécure Indigenous Territory and National Park)
TSJE	Tribunal Superior de Justicia Electoral (Supreme Electoral Justice Court)
UAM	Universidad Autónoma Metropolitana (Autonomous Metropolitan University, México)
UASP	Unidad de Acción Sindical y Popular (Popular and Union Action Unity)
UCeDe	Unión del Centro Democrático (Union of the Democratic Centre)
UCR	Unión Cívica Radical (Radical Civic Union)
UDI	Unión Demócrata Independiente (Democratic Independent Union)

UNE	Unidad Nacional de la Esperanza (National Unity of Hope)
UNT	Un Nuevo Tiempo (A New Time)
URNG	Unidad Revolucionaria Nacional Guatemalteca (Guatemalan National Revolutionary Unity)
VP	Voluntad Popular (Popular Will)

1

Introduction

Juan Pablo Luna, Rafael Piñeiro Rodríguez, Fernando Rosenblatt, and Gabriel Vommaro

More often than not, contemporary works on political parties start by referring to Schattschneider's now-famous dictum concerning democracy's need for political parties. At the same time, many authors have identified parties that, in democratic contexts, fail in various ways to fulfill the function of democratic representation. Mainstream political science has defined a political party as a group of candidates who compete in elections (Downs 1957 and Schlesinger 1994, among many others). This minimal definition has important analytical implications. When analyzing electoral politics, we run the risk of looking for parties – and thus, finding them – without realizing that what we have found, empirically, is only weakly related to democratic representation. In this introduction to the edited volume we present a thick definition of political parties to provide a conceptual framework for classifying different diminished subtypes of political parties in democratic regimes. The volume builds upon the rich literature concerning political parties that highlights the ways in which many party organizations are failing to fulfill their representational role in contemporary democracies. The empirical chapters that follow this introduction apply our conceptual framework to analyze seventeen parties in twelve Latin American countries.

Minimalist definitions of political party (i.e., Schlesinger's 1994) seem disconnected from reality, that is, the proliferation of electoral vehicles that do not function as parties. The sole attribute of the minimalist definition of a political party is not theoretically linked to a central aspect of democracy, namely the representation of social interests and values. As Kitschelt (2000) claims, parties "in the institutional sense" can be defined as in the minimalist definition. However, parties in the "functional sense" are those that "solve problems of collective action and of collective choice" (848). The conventional minimalist definition of political party fails to capture two main attributes of parties: horizontal coordination of ambitious politicians and vertical interest aggregation. However, the party politics literature has emphasized the horizontal coordination of ambitious politicians (Aldrich 1995)[1] while the vertical aggregation of collective interests has been problematized in the political sociology literature (Lipset and Rokkan 1967; Schwartz 1990). Vertical interest aggregation is also related to parties' expressive function (Sartori 1976).

The mainstream definition of political party assigns the same analytical category (political party) to very different empirical objects. This approach does not distinguish between different kinds of political parties. Recent empirical research conflates political organizations that a thicker theoretical perspective would consider dissimilar entities that have different effects on the democratic process. As Sartori (1976) stresses, the minimalist definition does not suffice to adequately differentiate the various kinds of political organization. The minimalist definition of political party also lacks predictive or explanatory capacity. In this edited volume, we seek to analyze Latin America's recent party trajectories as an empirical reference for exploring a new conceptual framework for studying political parties, one that includes diminished subtypes. Although we draw our empirical examples from Latin America, our framework is applicable to any region.

There is a recent body of research that has sought to unpack the black box of party organizations (Anria 2018; Bolleyer and Ruth 2018; Calvo and Murillo 2019; Cyr 2017; Levitsky et al. 2016; Luna 2014; Madrid 2012; Pérez Bentancur, Piñeiro Rodríguez, and Rosenblatt 2020; Rosenblatt 2018; Vommaro and Morresi 2015). Notwithstanding this renewed interest in the study of party organizations in Latin America, there remains a significant lack of theorized mechanisms and attributes of the concept of political party that connect parties to democratic representation. In her *Annual Review* article, Stokes (1999) claims that it remains unsettled whether parties are good for democracy or instead a necessary evil (244). The author rightly notes that this relationship heavily depends on the definition of democracy: "Do parties reveal and aggregate voters' preferences such that governments are responsive to citizens? Or do

[1] Aldrich (1995) emphasizes that parties, as political institutions, solve collective action and social choice problems within the government and for electoral mobilization.

parties form oligopolies of competitors with interests and preferences at odds with those of voters?" (Stokes 1999, 248–249).

The literature has identified various pitfalls party organizations encounter in various contexts and thus has highlighted the fact that many parties do not fulfill the expectation of contributing to democratic representation. However, the weak conceptualization of diminished political party subtypes lessens the analytical value of the study of parties. These problems of conceptualization neglect an important way in which political parties differ not simply in degree but in kind.[2] Moreover, the literature tends to conflate the age of a party with its degree of consolidation qua political party. An electoral vehicle might emerge as a political party and over time lose its ability to either coordinate horizontally or to vertically aggregate interests. Conversely, an electoral vehicle might gain those capacities over time. The minimalist conceptualization implies a static view that omits consideration of the changes organizations undergo over time. While the literature on democratic regimes has developed the notion of diminished subtypes of democracy (Collier and Levitsky 1997; Goertz 2006), there exists no such parallel in the party politics literature. In this introductory chapter we suggest a new typology of political parties that combines the two main attributes mentioned here: horizontal coordination of ambitious politicians, and vertical aggregation to electorally mobilize collective interests and to intermediate and channel collective demands – for example, by simplifying and clarifying political preferences for the citizens.

Our work is an attempt to remedy the lack of conceptualization of diminished subtypes in the political parties' literature. This helps to clarify analytical differences between failed parties that other authors have already described (and even explained) but have not yet conceptualized. In so doing, we revise the concept of political party in relation to its contributions to democratic accountability. On that basis, we propose a typology of political parties that includes diminished subtypes – with each type having different implications for democratic accountability – and we propose analytical strategies to empirically distinguish between them. The ultimate goal of our framework is to highlight how not all electoral vehicles – not even those with stable labels – are theoretically

[2] The reliance on an operationalization that measures changes in degree is not inconsistent with a conceptual view that identifies thresholds below (above) which causes qualitative change. Indeed, our measurement attempt, presented in Table 1.1, relies on a set of indicators that track differences in degree.

equivalent and thus do not contribute equally to democratic representation. While the absence of stable parties hinders democratic representation, the presence of stable electoral vehicles cannot fully guarantee the smooth operation of representation. Thus, our theoretical and conceptual contribution has concrete analytical consequences that reshape the debate concerning political parties.

PARTIES AND DEMOCRACY: A NECESSARY REASSESSMENT

What is the theoretical and empirical relationship between political parties and democracy? If democracy is simply the competition between groups of people for votes and access to government (i.e., a vision that some associate with Schumpeter's vision of democratic competition), then defining a political party as a group of individuals who compete in elections to access office and receive a handful of votes – the minimal definition of "political party" employed in mainstream postwar political science (c.f. Downs 1957; Sartori 1976; Schlesinger 1994) – would suffice to ensure a positive relationship between parties and democracy. This implies functions that are necessary for democracy, such as the recruitment and nomination of candidates that fosters elite-level socialization. Thus, if electoral competition, in and of itself, automatically engenders the representation of citizens' preferences, the type of party is irrelevant. As agents in such competition, parties are automatically functional to democratic representation.[3]

If, however, one proceeds from Dahl's (1971) definition of polyarchy, the competition for votes does not necessarily lead to representation of citizens' preferences. Dahl's perspective requires that, for citizens to have equal influence in politics, certain conditions and guarantees must exist; competition among groups does not suffice for there to be a positive relationship between parties and democracy. Not all electoral vehicles that compete in elections are functional to interest representation. The types of electoral vehicles that compete in elections determine how democracy works. A party system can exist without representing or distorting citizens' preferences (Gilens 2012). Only under very specific (and unrealistic) conditions, as in the Downsian perfect information competition

[3] The notion of representation we pursue in our conceptualization is, to be sure, not the only possible one; some alternative views to the one we follow are articulated in prominent works in the literature (e.g., Pitkin 1967; Przeworski, Stokes, and Manin 1999). Moreover, the concepts of representation and democracy are not necessarily compatible (Pitkin 2004).

model, can it be the case that any group that competes for votes represents citizens' preferences. Yet, as Downs stressed, democracy does not function in these conditions and representation does not automatically derive from the existence of competition. In practice, in different democracies, electoral vehicles might or might not function as channels for citizen representation. Thus, according to Dahl's logic, some electoral vehicles facilitate democratic representation, while other vehicles are less sensitive to citizens' demands and interests and so channel them less effectively. This complex relationship between electoral vehicles and citizen representation has been studied extensively in the party politics literature (as will be discussed).

Democratic representation in modern societies can be analyzed as a principal-agent relationship (Michels 1999 (1911)). Different types of electoral vehicles structure the principal-agent relationship differently, with some being unable to structure it at all, given their detachment from their principals. The latter occurs in contexts where citizens can vote for a given electoral vehicle without having the ability to monitor the vehicle's actions in the aftermath. The inability to hold electoral vehicles accountable can derive from exogenous factors; that is, it may be contingent on socioeconomic conditions – poverty, inequality, or economic crises – or institutional settings, such as more autocratic contexts (Kitschelt and Wilkinson 2007; Luna 2014; Taylor-Robinson 2010). Here, however, we are interested in analyzing whether party organizations channel the principals' preferences. We claim that there are endogenous constraints that relate to the specific characteristics of each political party.

The literature has systematically argued that there exists a much more nuanced relationship between existing parties (and party systems) and democratic representation (Hicken 2009; Kitschelt and Wilkinson 2007; Lawson and Merkl 1988; Levitsky 2003; Luna 2014; Luna and Zechmeister 2005; Mainwaring 2018; Mainwaring and Scully 1995; Piñeiro Rodríguez and Rosenblatt 2020; Roberts 2014b). The party politics literature has extensively considered the exogenous conditions that determine levels of representation. Developing societies, where the structural conditions for channeling citizens' preferences are unfavorable, have a wide variety of electoral vehicles with differing capacities to channel citizens' preferences (Bartolini 2000; Kitschelt 1994; Kitschelt et al. 2010; Luna 2014; Mainwaring and Zoco 2007; Samuels and Shugart 2010; Stoll 2013; Taylor-Robinson 2010). Yet, even developed societies, with more favorable exogenous conditions, have also witnessed the emergence of various types of political organizations that seek to perform the political representation function, and not all succeed in doing so.

The literature on party politics in developing countries in general, and in Latin America in particular, has identified various kinds of agents that compete in elections but do not contribute to democratic representation. However, this literature has not provided a conceptual discussion that theorizes the existence of diminished political party subtypes (with some exceptions, e.g., Mustillo 2007). While there exists abundant empirical evidence concerning the various failures of different party organizations in modern democracies and several theoretical arguments regarding the causes and effects of such failings, there remains a lacuna in the conceptualization of the type of parties that function as channels of democratic representation. This lack of theoretical debate concerning diminished party subtypes derives from the minimalist definition of political party. There has been little discussion in the literature as to whether this minimalist definition is useful for differentiating the various ways an agent can compete for power in a democratic process. While the minimalist definition is efficacious for encompassing different electoral vehicles, it obscures the debate about which vehicles contribute to the functioning of democracy. This is especially critical because the minimalist definition of political party works better in dialogue with a definition of democracy that privileges electoral competition as the main attribute of the regime, but it does not fit a more demanding perspective, such as Dahl's. When electoral competition does not suffice as a defining attribute of democracy, the minimalist definition of political party makes it difficult to articulate a clear-cut relationship between parties and democracy. The minimalist definition grants the label "party" to electoral vehicles that compete in elections but do not hold the status of party.

In fact, for much of the twentieth century, the relationship in Latin America between parties and democracy was problematized in terms of the acceptance of electoral competition: the movement-parties and the "illiberal" parties did not support democracy. However, in the twenty-first century, parties accept democratic competition, but they do a poor job of fulfilling their representation function. In several countries – for example, Bolivia, Peru, Venezuela, and Argentina – many of the traditional parties have been weakened or have disappeared. Their social bases were transformed or became more heterogeneous (e.g., weakening of the industrial working class, crisis of the farming sector, emergence of new middle classes and pauperization of others, emergence and consolidation of an informal sectors). New electoral vehicles emerged in turbulent times around electorally successful leaders (e.g., Alberto Fujimori in Peru, Mauricio Macri in Argentina, or Hugo Chávez in Venezuela), who, in some cases, exited from traditional parties (e.g., Álvaro Uribe in Colombia).

Confronting that emerging reality, several scholars turned their attention to causal factors and theories about party building, failure, and success including Anria (2018); Cyr (2017); Hunter (2010); Levitsky (2001; 2003); Levitsky et al. (2016); Lupu (2016); Madrid (2012); Tavits (2005; 2008; 2013); Samuels (2004; 2006); and Vommaro and Morresi (2015). However, the resurgence of party politics research in the last decade has not been adequately matched by a conceptual reanalysis of the empirical objects that we label as political parties. To address this gap in the literature, we reanalyze the concept of political party and its diminished subtypes, by adding or subtracting attributes to its definition. Specifically, we propose to distinguish between diminished subtypes by adding to the current mainstream minimalist definition two dimensions: horizontal coordination and vertical aggregation.

CONCEPTUALIZATION, OPERATIONALIZATION, AND MEASUREMENT

Following Goertz (2006), our conceptual analysis assumes the existence of specific links or associations between the existence of parties and democracy. Electoral vehicles that exhibit both dimensions (horizontal coordination and vertical aggregation) positively influence democratic representation. Political organizations that exhibit high levels of both dimensions reduce transaction and informational costs for citizens, who are the principals in the representation relationship.

An electoral vehicle is an association of candidates, that is, office-seekers, whose members compete in elections under the same label. Although the coalition seeks to win office, not all electoral vehicles fulfill the two basic functions necessary for a political party to be an effective means of democratic representation. A political party is, then, an electoral vehicle subtype, a more intense and less extended concept (Sartori 1970): it coordinates the activities of ambitious politicians (during campaigns and between elections) and vertically aggregates collective interests. "Electoral vehicle" is a more general concept than "political party," which occupies a lower level of abstraction (Sartori 1970). More specifically, political parties want to access office and promote policies (Strom 1990). Parties seek to win state power and impose an allocation of resources through policies and state institutions. This is achieved by crafting social coalitions, which involves coordination during campaigns and between elections.

Parties can accomplish the two functions in very different ways and with very different organizational forms (Gunther and Diamond 2003). The literature has extensively documented different types of parties in different historical and geographical settings (i.e., with an evolutionary logic), including cadre and mass-based parties (Duverger 1954), catch-all parties (Kirchheimer 1966), professional-electoral parties, and cartel parties (Katz and Mair 1995), among others. As opposed to these typologies, our conceptualization is independent of organizational form and assumes that different organizational arrangements can fulfill both conditions. Moreover, our framework does not imply that the linkages between the party and its constituency must necessarily be programmatic. In this vein, our idea of interest aggregation is broad. Because clientelistic politics can represent groups, it is possible to aggregate collective interests in a clientelistic manner. The horizontal coordination can be based on party members' adherence to shared rules or on a personalistic leadership. In this regard, very different parties, at different periods, such as the Radical Party in the early twentieth century, and the Unión Demócrata Independiente (Independent Democratic Union, UDI) in Chile, the Partido dos Trabalhadores (Workers' Party, PT) in Brazil, and the Partido Conservador (Conservative Party, PC) in Colombia (see Wills-Otero, Ortega, and Sarmiento this volume) throughout the twentieth century (until 1991), differ in their organizational structure and in their linkages with voters, though all accomplished the two defining functions.

Our concept of political party comprises five levels. The basic level constitutes the concept of political party itself. The secondary level introduces its main attributes. We identify two necessary and sufficient conditions that qualify an electoral vehicle as a political party in terms of democratic representation: the horizontal coordination of ambitious politicians and vertical interest aggregation. Figure 1.1 presents the structure of the concept of political party and its attributes (indicators will be presented in subsequent figures). Horizontal coordination denotes the role of parties in facilitating the coordination of ambitious politicians during campaigns and between electoral cycles. Vertical interest aggregation denotes the role of parties in the electoral mobilization and intermediation (or channeling) of collective interests and demands between elections. There is low substitutability between these two main attributes. They are separately necessary and are jointly sufficient conditions; thus,

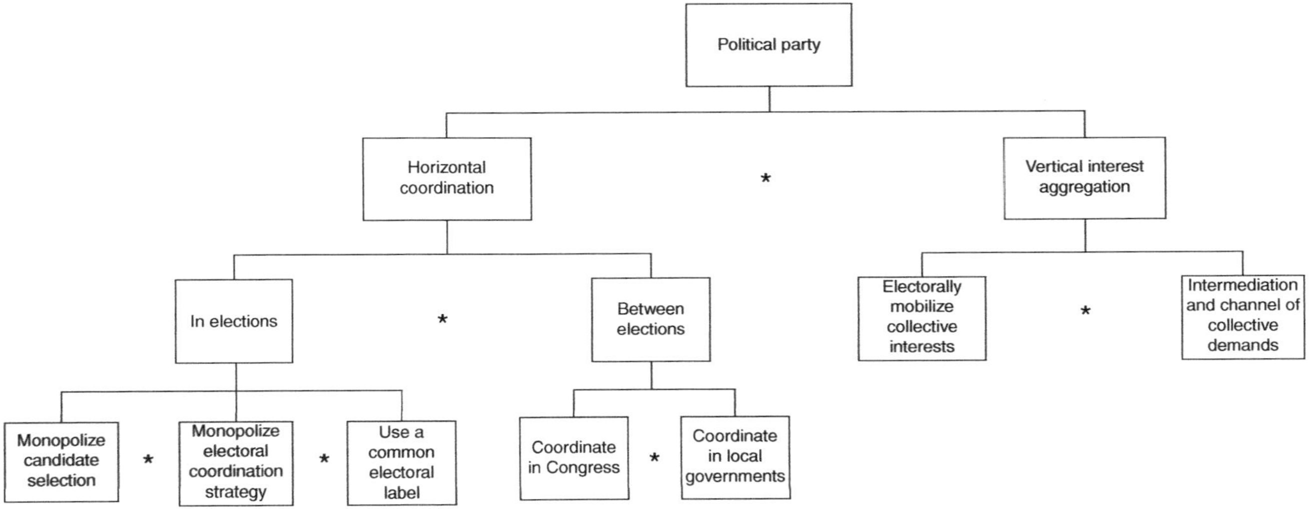

FIGURE 1.1 Political party attributes

they interact, and both need to be present to warrant labeling a given electoral vehicle as a political party.

These two dimensions (horizontal coordination and vertical interest aggregation) are functional to the idea of democratic representation. Horizontal coordination implies that political parties solve collective action problems of ambitious politicians, and this benefits democratic representation by helping stabilize electoral vehicles. Many electoral vehicles can support horizontal coordination between politicians; yet this function can be achieved without considering any societal preferences. This occurs, for example, in political systems where the competition between parties is stable but does not incorporate citizen preferences and thus alienates important portions of the electorate, as Luna and Altman (2011) show for the Chilean case. Therefore, electoral vehicles should also perform vertical interest aggregation to function as a channel for democratic representation. Conversely, electoral vehicles that aggregate collective interests but do not support horizontal coordination tend to be fragmented, undisciplined, and unstable organizations.

At the third level, following Aldrich (1995), we stipulate that horizontal coordination implies coordination during electoral campaigns and between elections (i.e., in Congress and in office). During campaigns, a political party is an electoral vehicle capable of monopolizing the candidate selection process, monopolizing the electoral coordination strategy (i.e., deciding the number of candidates that will compete in each district), and providing a common electoral label. These three capabilities are necessary and sufficient attributes for coordination during elections and entail the existence of a minimum common platform. In political parties, thus, candidates must be personally or collectively validated. These attributes enable parties to propose a uniform and coherent electoral offer. This coordination can be achieved in very different ways; for example, the candidate selection process can be centralized or decentralized, and can be carried out through open primaries or by a commission (Hazan and Rahat 2010; Rahat and Hazan 2001; Siavelis and Morgenstern 2008a). The crucial point is that a political party has the ability to coordinate action to avoid electoral losses. Between elections, a political party coordinates activity in Congress and in local governments. A political party establishes formal and informal obstacles to prevent its leaders from proposing contradictory public policies at different levels of government, and generates incentives to favor a certain amount of discipline among their legislators regarding whether to support or oppose given policies. Coordination both during and between elections is necessary and sufficient; that is, there is low substitutability between the two instances of horizontal coordination.

Also at the third level, the electoral mobilization of collective interests and the intermediation and channeling of collective demands are the two attributes that compose vertical interest aggregation. Both are necessary and sufficient attributes of the vertical dimension and, thus, there is low substitutability between them. To serve as agents for democratic representation, political parties need to aggregate preferences during campaigns (by mobilizing collective interests) and between elections (providing a channel for articulating collective interests). Parties must be valid options for citizens and collective actors (classes, movements, social groups) in democratic elections and must channel citizens' and collective actors' demands between elections. Voters must know that by voting for a particular label they are voting for a certain type of bias in public policies and especially in distributive policies. This dimension highlights the crucial role of vertical accountability in contemporary democracies (Adams 2001; Downs 1957; Przeworski, Stokes, and Manin 1999) and both attributes, the electoral mobilization of collective interests and the intermediation and channeling of collective demands, are needed to promote what Dahl (1971) considered an essential attribute of democracy: "the continuing responsiveness of the government to the preferences of its citizens" (1).

Figure 1.2 presents the complete conceptual tree for one of the two secondary-level attributes of a political party: horizontal coordination. It shows the two necessary and sufficient second-level attributes (coordination must occur both in elections and between elections) and it introduces a set of indicators. The figure also specifies the relationship between dimensions (or attributes) at each level and their indicators. During electoral campaigns, a party must monopolize the process of candidate selection and the electoral coordination strategy and candidates must use the common party label. We introduce two indicators, each necessary and both jointly sufficient, to determine the presence of the party's monopoly control of the candidate selection process: (1) a party authorizes candidate nomination at all levels and (2) prospective candidates accept nomination processes and the results of those processes. Parties must enforce horizontal coordination among ambitious politicians throughout a candidate selection process. This implies that the party has the power to define who can run under the party's label. Also, all prospective candidates should respect the results of the candidate selection process; for example,

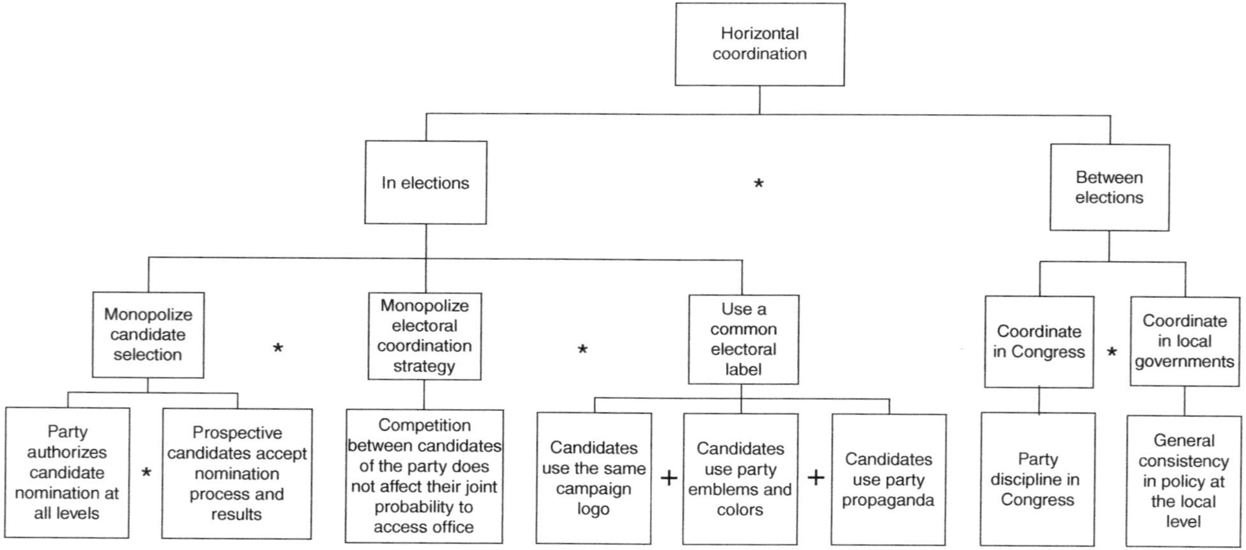

FIGURE 1.2 Indicators of horizontal coordination

there should be no defections by those who were not selected. This is not related to how open or closed the rules are.

The indicator of the party's monopoly control of the electoral coordination strategy is that the party considers the restrictions of the electoral system and enforces electoral coordination among candidates. More specifically, the party must control the number of candidates to avoid a situation that might affect the party candidates' joint probability of accessing office. On some occasions, candidates have more influence in the selection processes than does the party. When this happens, candidates might end up failing to coordinate and, thus, may hinder the party's electoral performance.

Finally, the indicators for the use of a common label are: (1) candidates use the same campaign logo; or, (2) candidates use party emblems or colors; or, (3) candidates use the party's propaganda (i.e., campaign literature). In this case, there is substitutability between the different indicators as each is functionally equivalent to the other (i.e., each one captures different ways to observe the use of a common label).

Between elections, a party must coordinate in Congress and in the different local-level governments, including in local-level legislative bodies. The indicator for horizontal coordination in Congress is the observation of significant party discipline. The indicator for coordination in local-level governments is the observation of a general consistency of public policies across different units; that is, in general terms, a party must have a similar policy orientation throughout the country and while voting in Congress. This coordination distinguishes parties from electoral vehicles that only coordinate different autonomous agents for the election (national or local). An environmentalist party, for example, should consistently promote a "green" agenda in all the governmental institutions in which it has representatives. Similarly, labor-based parties oppose deregulatory labor reforms even in times of policy convergence promoting economic liberalization and state retrenchment (Murillo 2001).

Figure 1.3 presents the complete operationalization of vertical interest aggregation. The figure shows the two necessary and sufficient attributes of vertical interest aggregation: a party electorally mobilizes collective interests and it intermediates and channels collective demands. A party mobilizes collective interests when its electoral platform includes general demands of one or several of the party's constituencies or when the party has a stable core constituency. A party might not have developed a core constituency (or it might have lost it), but its electoral platform has unequivocal references to a clear constituency. These parties have

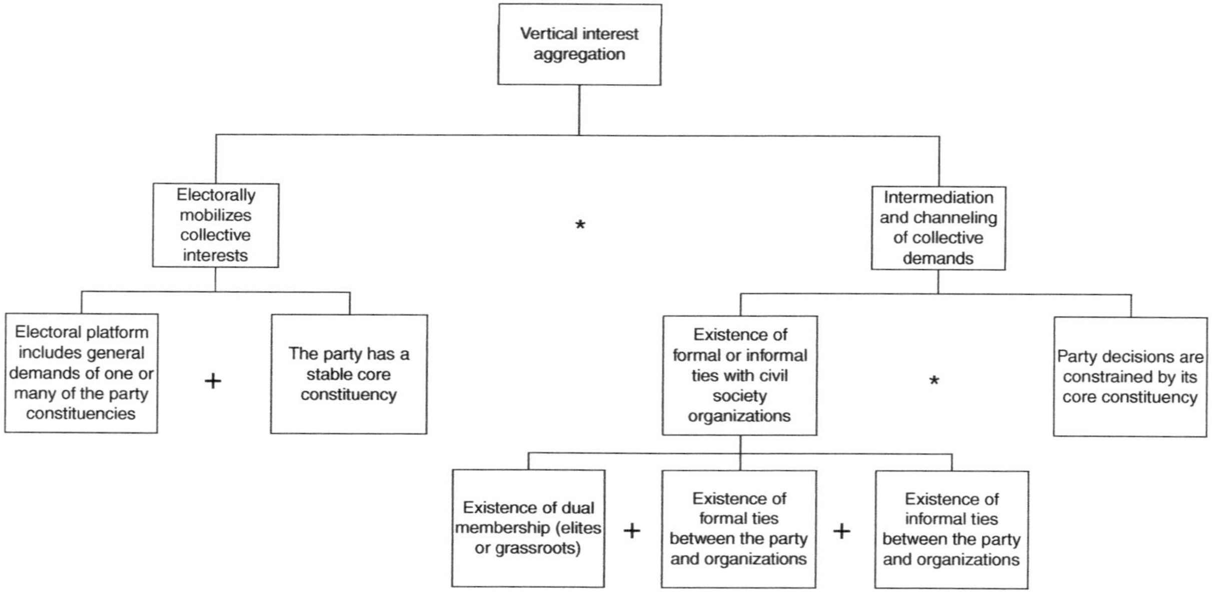

FIGURE 1.3 Indicators of vertical interest aggregation

a platform that is oriented toward formal workers but many times those workers do not vote for these parties. The family resemblance structure in this case (i.e., complete substitutability between the indicators) helps to capture these situations.

The intermediation and channeling of collective demands has two indicators: the existence of formal or informal ties with civil society organizations and the observation that party decisions are constrained by its core constituency. Both are necessary and sufficient, that is, there is low substitutability between them. Also, the attribute "existence of formal or informal ties with civil society organizations" itself has three indicators: the existence of dual membership (elites or grassroots), the existence of formal ties between the party and civil society organizations, or the existence of informal ties between the two. We allow complete substitutability between the three indicators, because each represents a different path to the same result. For example, the Movimiento al Socialismo (Movement toward Socialism, MAS) and the Frente Amplio (Broad Front, FA) both have strong ties with social movements. However, the two parties build their ties in dissimilar ways. Social movements are organically part of the MAS (Anria 2018 and Anria this volume) whereas the FA's ties with social movements are informal and FA members often have dual membership in both the party and social movements (Pérez Bentancur, Piñeiro Rodríguez, and Rosenblatt 2020 and Pérez Bentancur, Piñeiro Rodríguez, and Rosenblatt this volume).[4]

To measure each indicator, we propose using a five-point scale where values on the scale indicate the degree to which a particular condition is satisfied, with the scale values 1–5 corresponding to 0 percent, 25 percent, 50 percent, 75 percent, and 100 percent fulfillment of a given condition, respectively. For example, when a party has rules for nominating candidates, but half of the time prospective candidates do not comply with the rules, the case should receive a score of "3" on the indicator "Prospective candidates accept nomination processes and results," indicating 50 percent fulfillment of the condition. If there is no rule at all and candidates can nominate themselves, the case should receive a score of "1" on this indicator, corresponding to 0 percent fulfillment of the condition. Each

[4] Our proposed indicators of the concept should not be reified, and thus, fused with the concept and its dimensions. In other words, the indicators we have proposed and explored here should be subjected to revision and improvements in the future. For each of our indicators, there may be functional equivalents that can better capture each conceptual dimension in a different context.

indicator is normalized on a scale from 0 to 1. The overall index is computed by the aggregation rule reflecting the conceptual structure at each level. The overall index varies from 0 to 1, where "0" signifies that the case lacks any and all characteristics of a political party and "1" signifies that it exhibits all of them.

Consistent with our conceptualization of political party, we aggregated the component indices as follows. When there is complete substitutability between the indicators of an attribute, we used the maximum value. For example, the attribute "Existence of formal or informal ties with civil society organizations" has three indicators that we consider functionally equivalent measures of the attribute observed in different contexts, that is, each indicator captures a different way to fulfill the attribute (see Figure 1.3). Therefore, in a given case, the degree of fulfillment of the attribute will be determined by the highest value of the three indicators. In cases where the relationship between indicators or attributes, at different levels, is one of necessity and sufficiency, we use the geometric mean.[5] This aggregation rule allows for low substitutability. A low level of one indicator is partially compensated for by a high level of another indicator. Nonetheless, it emphasizes the necessary and sufficient conceptual structure and implies lower levels of compensation than does using the average or the maximum (Goertz 2006). Using the geometric mean mitigates the loss of additional information associated with using the minimum, and thus captures the multi-dimensionality of the concept. For example, vertical interest aggregation has two dimensions: "Electorally mobilizes collective interests" and "Intermediation and channeling of collective demands." If a case has a score of 2 on the former dimension, representing a 0.25 degree of fulfillment, and a score of 4 on the latter dimension, representing a 0.75 degree of fulfillment, the case will have an aggregate score of 0.43[6] for vertical interest aggregation.

We asked the authors of each case study in this edited volume to categorize their cases according to our conceptual scheme.[7] In the online appendix we include the codebook and the value of each indicator for

[5] The geometric mean is the nth root of the product of n numbers,

$$\overline{x} = \sqrt[n]{\pi_{i=1}^{n} x_i}.$$

[6] This value is lower than the average (0.50) and higher than the minimum (0.25). The average allows for greater substitutability, while the minimum precludes it.

[7] We also asked Germán Lodola to categorize the Argentinean Justicialist Party.

each case.[8] We considered the following cases: Propuesta Republicana, (Republican Proposal, PRO, Argentina), Partido Justicialista (Justicialist Party, Argentina), MAS (Bolivia), the Partido por la Democracia (Party for Democracy, PPD, Chile), the Partido Liberal (Liberal Party, PL, Colombia), PC (Colombia), Partido Acción Ciudadana (Citizen Action Party, PAC, Costa Rica), Liberación Nacional (National Liberation Party, PLN, Costa Rica), Movimiento Alianza PAIS (PAIS Alliance Movement, AP, Ecuador), Unidad Nacional de la Esperanza (National Unity of Hope, UNE, Guatemala), Partido de la Revolución Democrática (Party of the Democratic Revolution, PRD, Mexico), Movimiento Regeneración Nacional (National Regeneration Movement, MORENA, Mexico), Partido Colorado (Colorado Party, Paraguay), Partido Liberal Radical Auténtico (Authentic Radical Liberal Party, PLRA, Paraguay), Fuerza Popular (Popular Strength, FP, Peru), the FA (Uruguay), Primero Justicia (Justice First, PJ, Venezuela) and Voluntad Popular (Popular Will, VP, Venezuela).[9]

Table 1.1 shows each party's score on the two dimensions of the political party concept as well as on the overall party index. The scores vary across almost the entire range of the measure, showing that it is sensitive to differences between cases. Overall, the cases exhibit higher ratings on the horizontal coordination dimension than on the vertical interest aggregation dimension. The former is an easier property to achieve because a party's basic raison d'etre is to solve collective action problems for politicians. However, the different cases show variance in both dimensions and this variance is independent. These results show that each dimension captures different aspects of the concept and are not redundant.

TYPOLOGY OF POLITICAL PARTIES AND DIMINISHED SUBTYPES

To capture the existence of political organizations that lack one or more of the necessary dimensions in our conception of political party, we develop a typology of electoral vehicles: political parties and diminished subtypes. While the literature has analyzed the effects of the existence of independent candidates, flash parties, etc., it has been relatively silent on

[8] See https://journals.sagepub.com/doi/suppl/10.1177/1354068820923723.

[9] For the Venezuelan cases, evidence for vertical interest aggregation was drawn primarily from party statutes and interviews. Thus, the ranks were confirmed formally (in party statutes) and rhetorically (in interviews), but are difficult to assess in the Venezuelan authoritarian political context.

TABLE 1.1 *Component and overall party index scores*

Party	Horizontal coordination	Vertical interest aggregation	Party index
AP (Ecuador)	0.84	0.42	0.59
Colorado Party (Paraguay)	0.45	0.87	0.62
FA (Uruguay)	1.00	1.00	1.00
FP (Peru)	0.11	0.11	0.11
MAS (Bolivia)	0.74	0.93	0.83
MORENA (Mexico)	0.73	0.68	0.70
PAC (Costa Rica)	0.59	0.57	0.58
PC (Colombia)	0.49	0.51	0.50
Justicialist Party (Argentina)	0.35	0.93	0.57
PJ (Venezuela)	0.98	0.13	0.36
PL (Colombia)	0.47	0.35	0.41
PLN (Costa Rica)	0.87	0.68	0.77
PLRA (Paraguay)	0.18	0.39	0.27
PPD (Chile)	0.47	0.25	0.34
PRD (Mexico)	0.78	0.93	0.85
PRO (Argentina)	0.83	0.68	0.75
UNE (Guatemala)	0.10	0.13	0.12
VP (Venezuela)	0.91	0.93	0.92

Source: Authors' own construction.

diminished subtypes, in which one of the two attributes of the political party concept is absent (Collier and Levitsky 1997; Goertz 2006). Thus, these diminished subtypes are not subsets of a more general category of political party. On the contrary, these are theoretically possible variant forms of electoral vehicle, that is, political party diminished subtypes. Diminished subtypes are neither more nor less abstract than the concept of political party (Goertz 2006; Sartori 1970). The absence of one or more attributes does not imply greater abstraction or greater extension; rather, it indicates a diminished subtype. Thus, the different types in our taxonomy occupy the same level of abstraction, but diminished subtypes are cases that lack one or more of the attributes of a political party.

We identify the various possible electoral vehicles to understand the different types of political organizations and groups that compete in elections in contemporary democracies and their effects on democratic representation. If we treat the two attributes identified in our definition of political parties as binary variables that can be either present or absent, we create a 2 × 2 conceptual space, which yields four different types of political organization, as shown in Figure 1.4.

In our framework, the political party denotes an electoral vehicle that accomplishes two essential functions: it coordinates ambitious politicians and aggregates collective interests vertically. This category encompasses long-standing parties such as the PLN in Costa Rica and the Partido Acción Nacional (National Action Party, PAN) in México; more recently established parties such as the FA in Uruguay, the PT in Brazil, the PRD in Mexico, and the UDI in Chile; and new parties like the PRO in Argentina, the MAS in Bolivia, and VP in Venezuela. These examples illustrate that the two attributes, horizontal coordination and vertical interest aggregation, can be fulfilled with different organizational structures. The PT and the FA resemble mass organic parties, while the PAN, the PRO, and the UDI resemble cadre and professional electoral parties. Also, the age of a party, an indicator commonly used to assess a party's stability, does not define its capacity to fulfill the functions associated with a political party, as we define it. For example, a political organization can be vibrant at the time of its origin, showing robust horizontal coordination and vertical aggregation of interests, such as the PRO in Argentina, but lose one or both of those attributes over time as a consequence of endogenous or exogenous crises, such as the Partido Socialista de Chile (Chilean Socialist Party, PSCh). Studies of adaptation and party collapse provide accounts of this phenomenon (Levitsky 2003; Lupu 2016), while recent works have analyzed the factors that determine political organizations' degree of vibrancy over time (Rosenblatt 2018).

A political organization can achieve harmonious coordination between its elites (both during campaigns and between elections), without having a consistent capacity to articulate collective interests. We designate this

FIGURE 1.4 A typology of political parties and diminished subtypes

		Horizontal coordination	
		No	Yes
Vertical interest aggregation	Yes	Uncoordinated party	Political party
	No	Independents	Unrooted party

electoral vehicle an unrooted party. This kind of electoral vehicle can contribute to the stability of democratic institutions, but they are weak in terms of channeling the electoral and congressional representation of social groups/interests. In Latin America, there are cases of established political groups that have a high capacity for horizontal coordination among their elites, but have substantially lost (or never developed) stable linkages with any social base. This type of vehicle generally appeals to the "citizen" and espouses a negative vision regarding the representation of different social sectors in the political arena. Usually, they are centrist vehicles but not all centrist vehicles lack a constituency. The clearest example is the Partido Demócrata Cristiano (Christian Democratic Party, DC) in Chile; at the time of its origin, it was a centrist party with a clear constituency.

Unrooted party elites coordinate during campaigns and between elections. These vehicles can coordinate between elections because the agreements between individual leaders are also kept in the parliamentary arena, or because one of these leaders stands as primus inter pares (e.g., by being elected president, prime minister, mayor, or because of the leader's electoral appeal), and manages to retain coordination mechanisms for incumbents based on the distribution of selective incentives and/or collective incentives associated with the persistence of the vehicle. This type of vehicle fails to build effective channels for aggregating collective interests. These are usually traditional electoral labels, such as the Partido do Movimento Democrático Brasileiro (Party of the Brazilian Democratic Movement, PMDB) in Brazil, activated during election season. However, the reference to a unified electoral list reflects an alliance between individual ambitious political leaders rather than the existence of a political party.

There are electoral vehicles that develop persistent ties with loyal constituencies but lack horizontal coordination mechanisms; they usually lack congressional discipline and they have problems coordinating during elections. Sometimes this lack of coordination implies uncoordinated electoral strategies between different leaders. We label this diminished subtype an uncoordinated party. The Peronists in Argentina, in the absence of strong national leaders, lack congressional discipline and are unable to coordinate in the electoral arena. However, as Levitsky (2003) shows, this diminished subtype has informal negotiation channels with mobilized groups, such as trade unions. Also, this type of diminished party subtype is more common in organizations built or developed by regional leaders, linked to local interests, who have difficulty establishing common strategies outside the electoral arena, as happens with traditional parties in Colombia (Wills-Otero 2015).

Ambitious politicians can operate without coordinating political activity, running for office based on enabling electoral rules and/or their prestige or popularity (Levitsky and Zavaleta 2016; Zavaleta 2014). This diminished subtype tends to proliferate in the context of a party system crisis, when the cost of entry to the competition is low, as occurred in Argentina during the financial and economic collapse of 2000 and 2001, in Ecuador during the emergence of Rafael Correa in 2006, or in Peru in 1990 when Fujimori won the election with Cambio 90, his electoral vehicle (Cyr 2017; Dietz and Myers 2007; Levitsky and Zavaleta 2016; Seawright 2012; Zavaleta 2014). This subtype also proliferates in party systems where traditional parties have declined, opening electoral competition to individuals who have access to valuable campaign resources (money, fame, prestige) that render them competitive. In federal systems, and in systems with strong regional identities, this type of electoral vehicle often exists at the subnational level. To a certain extent, the subtype Independents represents the extreme case of stretching the party concept that we want our typology to amend.

Unpacking the different types of electoral vehicles better equips researchers to assess electoral vehicles' effects on democratic representation. In a recent edited volume, Levitsky et al. (2016) identify different cases of successful party building. The authors classify successful party building (i.e., parties that "take root") simply by considering the stability of a party label in successive elections: "We score party-building as successful when a new party wins at least 10 percent of the vote in five or more consecutive national legislative elections" (Levitsky et al. 2016, 8). Temporal bounds, while easy to measure, neglect to consider how or whether party organizations accomplish both essential functions described previously. In our conceptualization, however, the Renovación Nacional (National Renewal, RN) and the PPD of Chile do not constitute true parties but are instead diminished subtypes. In the former, there is no coordination of activity during the elections, while the "party" represents defined interests – business and rural sectors. It is thus an uncoordinated party within our conceptual framework. The latter (PPD) is a coalition of independent politicians who struggle to accomplish either of the two functions (see Piñeiro Rodríguez, Rosenblatt, and Toro Maureira this volume). Conversely, new parties such as the MAS in Bolivia (see Anria this volume) and the PRO in Argentina (see Vommaro this volume) are, indeed, successful cases of party building. In both cases, horizontal coordination mechanisms are observed and there are vertical representation channels – with social movements or business sectors – that have been robust and persistent over time. Both new political party organizations managed to incorporate collective demands. Thus, for example, for the first time in history, the Bolivian peasantry managed to build its own party (Anria 2018), while a center-right pro-market party managed to compete for power in Argentina (Vommaro and Morresi 2015).

Figure 1.5 presents the observed values for the analyzed cases on each of the two dimensions (horizontal coordination and vertical interest aggregation) of the party index. We divide the panel to illustrate the classification of cases into each subtype. The classification follows the description presented here. In the upper right cell of the table, we find parties such as the FA, VP, MAS, and PRO, among others. These parties perform both functions, though to varying degrees. For example, while the MAS and the PRD are rated more highly on vertical interest aggregation, the PRO and the PLN are rated more highly on horizontal coordination. In the bottom left cell, we find Independents, such as the FP and the UNE. The Chilean PPD and the Colombian PL are borderline cases that have characteristics of both unrooted parties and independents. The Colombian PC, the Argentinean Justicialist Party, and the Paraguayan

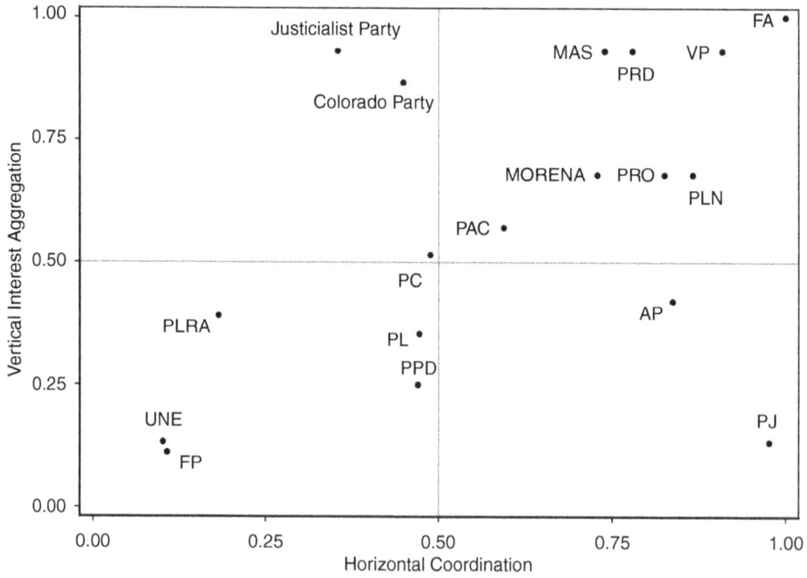

FIGURE 1.5 Empirical distribution of types Source: Authors' own construction.

Colorado Party most closely resemble the uncoordinated party type. Finally, the Venezuelan PJ is a typical example of an unrooted party. It exhibits high levels of horizontal coordination but lacks vertical interest aggregation. Finally, the distribution of our cases seems to indicate that organizations rarely exhibit the capacity to vertically aggregate social interests without also exhibiting the capacity for horizontal coordination.

Given our emphasis on the functions parties should fulfill to satisfy horizontal coordination and vertical aggregation, our definition might be seen as a functionalist one. Yet, our argument is not functionalist because electoral vehicles can and often do fail to fulfill one or both functions. Our conceptualization is, thus, adequate to make such normatively and substantively consequential variance visible to those interested in exploring it empirically. Indeed, we identify diminished subtypes precisely in order to characterize cases that fail to fulfill one or both functions. Diminished subtypes, which are empirically pervasive in contemporary democracies, exist without fulfilling the functions our conceptualization assigns to political parties (i.e., diminished subtypes are not different forms of a political party, and they exist despite not fulfilling the functions we use to demarcate diminished subtypes from political parties). When identifying diminished subtypes, we are not moving up or down a conceptual ladder of abstraction; rather, we identify a positive pole (political party) and a negative pole (an electoral vehicle that is not a political party). Thus, for example, the absence of the two necessary dimensions – horizontal coordination and vertical aggregation – in the "independents" diminished subtype does not render "independents" a more abstract notion than that of political party. By the same token, political parties are not conceptualized as a subset of a more abstract notion of independents.

OVERVIEW

This edited volume includes chapters describing seventeen parties in twelve countries in Latin America. The case studies describe and analyze how different electoral vehicles perform or fail to perform horizontal coordination and vertical interest aggregation. The empirical chapters also offer a variety of cases to illustrate political parties and diminished subtypes. The volume seeks to encompass variation in the two theoretically relevant dimensions (vertical interest aggregation and horizontal coordination). The case selection also aims to include regional, organizational, and ideological variation. Additionally, the chapters provide an overview of the evolution of each case over time. This overview is particularly instructive because it provides a dynamic perspective showing that there is no single inevitable developmental trajectory; parties that persist over time do not necessarily improve their ability to perform horizontal coordination and vertical interest aggregation, nor does this ability necessarily deteriorate over time.

In Chapter 2, Pérez Bentancur, Piñeiro Rodríguez, and Rosenblatt analyze the case of the FA in Uruguay as an unusual organization. Since its foundation, the FA has exhibited a dual structure: the coalition (manifested in the factions of the party) and the movement (comprising a common grassroots structure of *Base Committees*). The FA fulfills both essential functions required to qualify as a political party: vertical interest aggregation and horizontal coordination. The coalition structure of the FA fulfills the criterion of horizontal coordination, while the grassroots activist structure accomplishes vertical interest aggregation and, in crucial decisions, promotes and ensures horizontal coordination. More critically, the coalition and the grassroots structure influence the most important policy decisions of the party's parliamentary caucus and, when the FA was in government (2005–20), the decisions of the Executive. In terms of vertical interest aggregation, the FA has developed strong and informal ties with social actors, especially with labor unions, based on leaders' and grassroots activists' dual membership.

Chapter 3 analyzes the case of the Argentinean PRO. Vommaro's analysis highlights the fact that the PRO has been able to perform both functions in the districts where the party was born (mainly in the Ciudad de Buenos Aires) but has had greater difficulty fulfilling them in the rest of the country. This shows that parties can vary across districts in how well they perform the defining attributes. The PRO established horizontal coordination through a division-of-labor mechanism. PRO leaders maintain control of the party's electoral strategy and candidate selection and allow its allies from traditional parties to capture and distribute resources to their clients. This division of labor also implies that PRO leaders rule and the allied parties mobilize voters, especially from popular sectors and from districts in the countryside. In exchange, allied party leaders receive selective incentives, such as important slots in the party lists, access to public resources, and positions in the public administration. These two groups bring different constituencies to the party. PRO leaders have strong linkages with the upper-middle- and upper-class sectors of Argentinean society. Middle- and working-class sectors are incorporated by politicians from traditional parties who joined the PRO. This produces a logic of segmented representation (Luna 2014).

Chapter 4 develops the case of the MAS. Anria's chapter shows how a loosely organized structure can still achieve horizontal coordination and vertical interest aggregation. This is based on the interaction between the strong leadership of Evo Morales and the social movements and social organizations that formally integrate the party. As Anria stresses, "[The MAS] operates as a hybrid organization that combines top-down leadership by a dominant personality, weak bureaucratic development, and the bottom-up power of autonomous social mobilization" (Anria this volume). As in the case of the PRO, the MAS is heterogeneous throughout the territory. In some districts, social movements are stronger and have more influence over the party's decision-making and candidate selection, while in others the party's structure and its leadership prevail. However, in general, party leaders cannot impose their positions and must negotiate with social actors that are part of the MAS. This "contentious bargaining game" (Anria this volume) occurs through informal channels. This interaction is different from that observed in the case of the FA. In contrast to the FA, where social organizations have informal ties with the party but the party's decision-making is grounded in formal rules, social organizations are formally incorporated in the MAS but the party's policy agenda is negotiated through informal channels.

In Chapter 5, Combes analyzes the cases of the PRD and MORENA. This chapter highlights the importance of personalism as a factor that facilitates not only horizontal coordination (as in the case of the AP or the FP) but also vertical interest aggregation (as in the case of the MAS). Candidate selection is highly connected to the complex interaction that both parties have with civil society and social movements. However, the PRD and MORENA did not institutionalize their ties with social movements because they rejected the corporatist model historically observed in the PRI. In both the PRD and MORENA, vertical interest aggregation is based on informal ties linked to the recruitment of activists and candidates from social movements. In the case of the PRD, the party recruited leaders of the mobilizations against neoliberal reforms. Given the territorial concentration of the protests, this strategy limited the territorial expansion of the party. In the case of MORENA, there was an explicit strategy to control recruitment from the center.

In Chapter 6, Alfaro-Redondo and Gómez-Campos present the cases of the PLN and the PAC in Costa Rica, both classified as parties, though the PAC less clearly so. The PLN is a traditional party that has been experiencing a process of organizational decay, especially in its ability to perform the vertical interest aggregation function. Historically, the PLN has had a developed structure and deep ties with specific constituencies, though this has been eroding since the 1990s. The PAC is a new party that also performs both functions but has so far struggled to reproduce the vertical interest aggregation function beyond its core constituency in the middle- and upper-middle-class sectors of the country's capital, San José.

Chapter 7 analyzes the Paraguayan Colorado Party and PLRA parties. Abente Brun's chapter shows how vertical interest aggregation is not necessarily programmatic. In the case of the Colorado Party, vertical interest aggregation is related to the satisfaction of particularistic demands for specific constituencies. The electoral machine of the Colorado Party was consolidated during Stroessner's authoritarian regime and operated as a tool for vertical interest aggregation. This capacity was reduced and had to adapt as the country underwent a transition to democracy. In contrast, the PLRA had operational difficulties during Stroessner's regime that limited its organizational development. Since the 1992 constitutional reform, horizontal coordination has been weakened. The power to coordinate horizontally now lies with party factions rather than with the national party directorates. The weakening of the capacity to perform horizontal coordination was aggravated by the introduction of an open list electoral system in the 2019 reform. The Paraguayan cases highlight the role that political regimes and institutional rules play in the fulfillment of both functions.

In Chapter 8, Wills-Otero, Ortega, and Sarmiento, show the secular process of erosion of the Colombian traditional parties, the PC and the PL. These parties have found it increasingly difficult to achieve horizontal coordination and vertical interest aggregation. The extensive history of both parties enables a long-term analysis of their evolution, and reinforces the idea advanced in this framework that a party's ability to fulfill one or both functions can change over time (this is also analyzed in the Costa Rica and Paraguay chapters). The chapter also shows the positive and negative impacts that various changes in electoral rules have had on the parties' capacity to perform horizontal coordination, as in Paraguay (see Abente Brun this volume). The electoral changes introduced in the 1991 constitutional reform facilitated the personalization of politics, while the electoral reform of 2003 and the 2005 Law that governs political blocs counterbalanced this tendency. The authors claim that the PL and the PC, in contrast to the Colorado Party in Paraguay, have difficulties promoting a programmatic aggregation of interests because of the combination of the pervasive role of clientelism and the power of departmental or local leaders.

Chapter 9 reviews the cases of the PJ and the VP in Venezuela. Cyr's analysis introduces the challenges of party building in contexts of democratic erosion and high polarization based on *chavismo*/anti-*chavismo* logic. This context prevents opposition parties from proactively building ties with different social sectors based on programmatic stances. However, this context does not have the same effect in Cyr's two cases. The PJ developed a limited capacity to vertically aggregate interests. By contrast, the VP established bottom-up channels to incorporate interests from below. Paradoxically, the regime dynamics, that is, polarization and increasing authoritarian tendencies, hinder vertical interest aggregation but, at the same time, facilitate horizontal coordination.

In Chapter 10, Conaghan analyzes the case of the AP in Ecuador, which achieved something rare among Ecuadorian electoral vehicles: it ran candidates in every district. However, the AP did not become a political party. Since its inception, the AP was designed to concentrate power around its leader, Rafael Correa. Conaghan's analysis stresses that the AP performs horizontal coordination, yet this coordination was always imposed from above; compliance with the party's directives was a condition of obtaining access to governmental positions. Vertical interest aggregation, however, is lacking. The grassroots groups that originally supported Correa disappeared. Correa's government instead used clientelism, co-optation, and strategically targeted benefits as the main tactics to relate with civil society organizations or sectors.

In Chapter 11, Piñeiro Rodríguez, Rosenblatt, and Toro Maureira analyze the case of the Chilean PPD. The PPD exhibits horizontal coordination in Congress and in elections. However, the coordination occurs between leaders who control different territories. There is no common party organization that coordinates and integrates social interests. The structure of the party resembles a federation, where a small cadre of leaders dominates different territories and exerts control over nominations, programmatic proposals, and segmented linkages with society. The case of the PPD shows that one cannot infer simply on the basis of electoral results and the existence of partisan discipline in Congress (as a measure of horizontal coordination) that an organization has a common structure capable of developing some kind of partisan identity in society to aggregate of interests at the national level.

Chapter 12 reviews the case of the FP in Peru. Vergara and Augusto question whether vertical interest aggregation and horizontal coordination are necessarily functional to democracy and the rule of law. The FP is an example of this dysfunctionality because, in Peru, horizontal coordination and vertical interest aggregation involve the incorporation of illegal interests in the political process. According to Vergara and Augusto, the FP represents these illegal interests in Congress while it neglects the party's programmatic agenda and does not effectively represent its electoral base. Moreover, the FP's congressional behavior threatens democracy, in both its republican and liberal dimensions. The FP, like the AP in Ecuador (see Conaghan this volume), depends on the power of the party leadership to co-opt candidates and to enforce discipline. This power, in turn, is determined by the electoral power of the leader in the presidential election. When the leadership seems unlikely to win election or is defeated, internal conflicts and coordination problems arise.

Chapter 13 describes the UNE in Guatemala. Sanchez-Sibony and Lemus classify this case as Independents. The UNE, as with all electoral vehicles in Guatemala, relies on local *caudillos* to fulfill the requirement of presenting candidates in every district, set forth by the electoral law. Even though the UNE has a good record of legislative discipline, it suffers from large numbers of defections in all electoral cycles. This is the main indicator of the UNE's inability to carry out horizontal coordination. Sanchez-Sibony and Lemus's chapter shows how structural conditions seriously hamper horizontal coordination and, more critically, vertical interest aggregation. The fragmentation and feebleness of social organizations in Guatemala limit the possibilities of developing programmatic linkages. Therefore, the UNE substituted clientelism in place of vertical interest aggregation to develop a limited popular constituency.

2

The Case of Uruguay's Frente Amplio

Verónica Pérez Bentancur, Rafael Piñeiro Rodríguez, and Fernando Rosenblatt

INTRODUCTION

The theoretical framework of this edited volume establishes that a political party is an electoral vehicle subtype capable of vertically aggregating collective interests and through which ambitious politicians coordinate their strategies during campaigns and between elections. As the literature has extensively documented, parties can accomplish these two functions in very different ways and with very different organizational formats (Gunther and Diamond 2003). The Uruguayan Frente Amplio (Broad Front, FA) fulfills both essential functions and thus qualifies as a political party. In fact, it ranks first in the Party Index introduced in Chapter 1. Even though the FA was born as a coalition of small leftist parties and factions of the foundational Uruguayan parties, it has since its inception satisfied both conditions. The FA so far has exhibited a common organizational structure and a uniquely high level of member engagement and vitality. In fact, Levitsky and Roberts (2011) categorize the FA as the only institutionalized mass-organic leftist party in Latin America.

Until 1971, the Uruguayan party system comprised two major parties: Partido Colorado (Colorado Party) and Partido Nacional (National Party, PN).[1] Although there were other leftist parties (e.g., Socialist and Communist), they were significantly smaller. The two major parties collectively obtained around 90 percent of the votes in every democratic election prior to 1971. Contextual factors help explain the emergence of

[1] From 1931 until 1956, the PN was split in two different parties: the PN and the Partido Nacional Independiente (Independent National Party).

the FA as the unification of the left in Uruguay: the economic stagnation of the 1960s, the political context of an increasingly authoritarian government led by Jorge Pacheco Areco (1968–71), the unification in 1964 of the labor movement under the Convención Nacional de Trabajadores (National Workers Convention, CNT), the unification of grassroots-level popular organizations (in the Congreso del Pueblo – People's Congress – held in 1965), as well as the political negotiations between five important leaders from the various left-of-center parties that existed at the time.

The FA was born in 1971, as a coalition of political organizations and as a movement of self-organized grassroots activists. Thus, FA leaders and activists usually refer to the FA as a combination of "coalition and movement." The FA coalition and movement structures are synthetized in a pyramidal organization with bodies at three levels: the grassroots level, the intermediate level and the national level. This interaction between factions and grassroots activists is peculiar and promotes checks and balances and diffuse power distribution.

The horizontal coordination in the FA is generated through the factions and in the relationship between them and the common structures of the FA. Each faction autonomously conducts candidate selection for election to legislative and executive bodies and competes with other factions for party voters. They coordinate on different issues (e.g., campaign finance) for the presidential election (Acuña, Piñeiro Rodríguez, and Rossel 2018), the party's shared campaign, and the mobilization of activists during the campaign and on election day. In electoral campaigns, the FA factions collaborate in the distribution of resources, and ensure the availability of factions' campaign literature and ballots throughout the country. The FA factions compete among themselves even though they all use a common electoral label. The FA logo is everywhere and the party's colors (red, blue, and white) are part of the electoral campaigns of all factions. More crucially, the party articulates a common platform in the FA Congress, which is essentially FA grassroots activists. To mobilize voters throughout the territory, all factions take advantage of the organizational capacity based on a common grassroots structure.

In office, the horizontal coordination has been a central concern of party leaders. Since its inception, the FA identified unity of action as an imperative mandate for all its members, and this mandate was translated into a uniform legislative caucus. Discipline was enforced by faction leaders, by the FA caucus, and, on some important issues, by the organizational bodies of the FA. In government, the FA has also institutionalized mechanisms to constrain the government, at both national and subnational levels.

The FA performs vertical interest aggregation through the mobilization of collective interests as well as through the intermediation and channeling of collective demands. The latter is achieved through the existence of informal ties with civil society organizations. First, FA elites and grassroots activists have dual membership; they belong to the party as well as to unions, social movements, or civil society organizations. Second, the FA organization has informal ties with these organizations. As we will show in this chapter, the FA's most important decisions must consider the opinion of its core constituency. The FA also electorally mobilizes collective interests. The party's electoral platform reflects issues that are central to unions and to various social movements (e.g., feminist, human rights, LGBT). These social movements and unions have been the core constituency of the party since its inception and remained so after the FA gained the national government.

The FA is a distinctive political party for two main reasons. First, according to Levitsky and Roberts (2011) it is the only institutionalized mass-organic leftist party in Latin America. Second, it is distinctive because it has a peculiar and complex organizational structure that affords grassroots activists a significant role in the decision-making, which affects the decisions of the party in Congress and in government (Pérez Bentancur, Piñeiro Rodríguez, and Rosenblatt 2020). Thus, in terms of Samuels and Shugart's (2010) taxonomy, the FA works as a parliamentary party rather than as a presidential party. That is, the FA's particular organizational structure constrains its leaders because the party's major decisions need the organization's explicit support (or absence of opposition). This logic is not expected under presidential regimes where voters directly elect presidents for fixed periods and, as a result, parties are less able to control them.

Also, the FA has stable informal ties with social actors and movements, especially with the unions, as do the Social Democratic parties in Europe (Kitschelt 1994). However, the FA distinguishes itself from other parties in Latin America that built strong linkages with unions, like the Partido Justicialista (Justicialist Party) in Argentina, and Partido dos Trabalhadores (Workers Party, PT) in Brazil. The FA was born and has always been an ally of the union movement but the union movement is independent of the party (Senatore, Doglio, and Yaffé 2004). The FA also has strong relations with social movements, as does the Movimiento al Socialismo (Movement toward Socialism,

MAS) in Bolivia (Anria 2018). However, the FA is not exactly a movement party in the way that Anria (2018) characterizes the MAS. That is, the FA is not built from the social movements (see Anria this volume). Although the FA's ties with social movements are manifested in the dual membership of many grassroots activists and in the informal linkages FA politicians at all levels have with union leaders and with social movement leaders, the FA and the social movements are entirely independent of one another.

The analysis in this chapter takes advantage of an in-depth case study of the FA. The data we refer to come from an online survey of FA activists that we post-stratified using observational population data from the FA's internal election registries. We also gathered qualitative evidence using in-depth interviews and other secondary sources (for more detail on the methods and sources of data for this research, see Pérez Bentancur, Piñeiro Rodríguez, and Rosenblatt 2020).

This chapter will proceed as follows: We first describe the FA's particular organizational characteristics. We then show how the party accomplishes horizontal coordination and vertical interest aggregation. Throughout the chapter, we show how the peculiar organizational structure of the FA enhances democratic representation and facilitates the party's capacity to adapt to changing societal demands.

THE FA AS A POLITICAL PARTY

The FA emerged in the context of severe political crisis (Astori 2001; Nahum et al. 1993) and throughout the more than forty-eight years since its birth, it has remained a continuously vibrant party with activists (Rosenblatt 2018). Although the FA underwent a process of ideological transformation (Garcé and Yaffé 2005; Yaffé 2005), it retains its leftist ideological identity and remains the only mass-organic institutionalized leftist party in Latin America (Levitsky and Roberts 2011).

At its foundation, the FA was an alliance of small leftist parties (Partido Comunista del Uruguay, Communist Party, PCU; the Partido Socialista del Uruguay, Socialist Party, PSU; the Partido Demócrata Cristiano, Christian Democratic Party, PDC), factions from the traditional parties (like the Movimiento por el Gobierno del Pueblo, Movement for People's Government from the Colorado Party and the Herrerista Movement from the PN), and independent social and union leaders. From its inception, however, the FA was also a movement. This implied, from the very beginning, the presence of strong bottom-up participation that materialized in Comités de Base (Base Committees).[2] Very early in the life of the party, in the national elections of 1971, an army of volunteers was responsible for a significant proportion of the time and money invested in the campaign. Base Committees function as the party's mass movement arm. They comprise grassroots activists who are not necessarily affiliated with factions. Since the party's origin, these grassroots activists have worked as volunteers and have played a key organizational and mobilization role for a party with scant resources and limited access to the media.

Grassroots activists became critical players in the party's early stages of development; they demanded participation in the decision-making structure and the coalition leaders granted it. Immediately after the constitutive act, the FA approved a series of significant documents: the Bases Programáticas de la Unidad (Programmatic Bases of Unity), approved on February 17, 1971; the Reglamento de Organización (Organizational Rules), approved on March 17, 1971; and the Compromiso Político (Political Commitment), approved on February 9, 1972 (Aguirre Bayley 2001). These documents laid the foundations for the significance of the common FA structure beyond each individual faction's organization.

After this initial stage, there occurred a period of dictatorship from 1973 to 1985. The dictatorship banned political parties, and FA's leaders (including Liber Seregni, its presidential candidate in 1971, and the party's main leader until the 90s) were imprisoned, tortured, or had to go into exile. Nevertheless, during the authoritarian regime, grassroots members were crucial to maintaining the party's vibrancy in a clandestine context. In the early years of the transition (1982–85), Base Committees reorganized in private houses and contributed, intensively, to rethinking the party's internal structure and statutes. Due to the central roles Base Committees played in the 1971 elections and in the resistance to the dictatorship, the leaders felt it natural to fulfill the promise of the Political Commitment of 1972; that is, to incorporate the party's grassroots activists within the highest decision-making structures of the FA. This commitment to incorporation materialized in the first statute of 1986.

After the authoritarian regime (1973–85), the two foundational parties (Colorado Party and PN) won the next four national elections, (in 1984,

[2] In 2015, there were over 152 active Base Committees in Montevideo, which is equivalent to one Base Committee for every 10,000 people. According to FA administrative data there were 352 Base Committees in 2015; approximately 40 percent of these were located in Montevideo and the others were located throughout the rest of the country.

1989, 1994, and 1999) and led the processes of structural adjustment and market reform. In close alliance with the union movement, the FA used mechanisms of direct democracy and social mobilization to systematically oppose the reforms (Altman 2010; Monestier 2011; Moreira 2004). The opposition to the neoliberal reforms positioned the party as the single political actor on the center-left of the ideological spectrum, pushing both traditional parties to the right-of-center (Buquet and Piñeiro 2014). Thus, Uruguay is a case of programmatic alignment (Roberts 2014).

In 2004, the FA won the presidential election for the first time. The FA initiated its first term in office (2005–10) in a country that was just overcoming a severe financial and economic crisis and which needed both to achieve financial stability and to address the "social emergency" that resulted from the economic crisis of 2002. The FA addressed these challenges and enacted structural reforms that revitalized the role of the state. These reforms promoted redistribution of income (Huber and Stephens 2012; Padrón and Wachendorfer 2017; Pribble 2013; Rossel 2016). During Tabaré Vázquez's first term (2005–10), social spending increased (Caetano and De Armas 2011). The most iconic example of increased spending was the first measure his government adopted: the enactment of a conditional cash transfer program. It was implemented to address the social emergency that erupted as a consequence of the 1999–2003 economic depression. A few years later, the program turned into a universal family-based transfer program (Pribble 2013).

Also, the first FA administration reinstated collective bargaining at the sectoral level (i.e., within various sectors of economic activity) and collective bargaining was expanded to rural workers and housekeepers. In total, over forty bills concerning workers' rights were approved (Etchemendy 2019; Senatore and Méndez 2011). Unionization rates increased, especially among private-sector employees, and the number of workers in the formal sector also increased (Padrón and Wachendorfer 2017). Additionally, the government implemented a progressive tax reform by adopting an income tax and created a national integrated health care system (Bergara 2015). Finally, the FA implemented the One Laptop Per Child program, "Plan Ceibal." José Mujica's government (2010–15) continued and expanded these policies and advanced other progressive policies. For example, during Mujica's term, the Law of Voluntary Interruption of Pregnancy, same-sex marriage, and the self-cultivation and commercialization of cannabis were approved (Bidegain Ponte 2013).

The reforms enacted by the first FA governments occurred in the context of favorable economic conditions. Similar to many countries in the region, Uruguay experienced a commodity boom. This meant high prices for food and raw materials that made the country's economy grow exponentially over the course of a decade (until 2014). Yet, this economic context changed, affecting the country's economic dynamism. The FA's third government therefore had to deal with more restrictive economic conditions, which imposed a difficult trade-off between macroeconomic equilibria and redistribution (Pérez and Piñeiro 2016).

Forty-eight years after the party's birth – after suffering political severe persecution during the authoritarian regime, after being in the opposition for more than thirty years, and after fifteen years in government – the FA retains its original dual structure. One structure pertains to the coalition of political organizations ("the coalition"), and the other institutionalizes the political role in the party of the grassroots members who are not necessarily affiliated with factions (what the FA calls "the movement"). The emergence of this dual structure in Uruguay is peculiar due to the incentives set by the electoral rules. The double simultaneous vote (DSV) allows members of an electoral alliance, such as the FA, to have complete electoral autonomy, that is, to nominate candidates for the House, Senate and – until the Constitutional Reform of 1996 – the presidency (Buquet, Chasquetti, and Moraes 1998; González 1991; Luján and Moraes 2017; Piñeiro and Yaffé 2004). However, the FA coalition not only nominated a single common candidate for the presidency, but also built a common grassroots structure, parallel to those of each faction. The FA organizational structure has several collective decision-making bodies, where grassroots activists are granted the right to send delegates. The vertical structure connects grassroots-level activism with the decision-making bodies and with the factions – since both the factions and the grassroots activists send representatives to the different bodies (Pérez Bentancur, Piñeiro Rodríguez, and Rosenblatt 2020).

HORIZONTAL COORDINATION

The Party Coordinates in Electoral Campaigns

The FA has been successful in electoral terms, obtaining 18.3 percent of the votes in the 1971 national elections, and reaching 51.7 percent in the national election of 2004. It retained the presidency and the absolute majority in both chambers of Congress in 2009 (49.6 percent of the popular vote) and 2014 (49.4 percent). In 2019, the FA lost both its majority in Congress and the presidency. In the first round

(October 2019) it received almost 10 percent less of the vote share (39.9 percent) than it received in the 2014 national elections. However, the FA remains the largest party (in terms of votes and seats) and retains the capacity to mobilize a large number of adherents in mass rallies. For example, in the last rally before the first round of the 2019 election, the FA mobilized at least 10 percent of its voters (conservative estimates put the number of rally participants at about 100,000, though the actual number of participants was likely much higher). In videos of recent and past campaigns that are easily found on Youtube, one readily observes that the FA factions use a common electoral label. The FA logo is everywhere, and the three colors (red, blue, and white) are part of the electoral campaign of all affiliated groups (factions) – although each also uses its own characteristic colors, such as green for the PSU or red and black for the Movimiento de Participación Popular (Popular Participation Movement, MPP).

The FA developed a unified electoral coordination strategy. The campaign is financed by all factions together and the FA redistributes public subsidies among the factions and the presidential ticket (Acuña, Piñeiro Rodríguez, and Rossel 2018). At the local level, the Base Committees coordinate the campaign in the territory and all the election-day logistics (e.g., providing party delegates to each poll station). Base Committees serve as resources for all the competing factions, including distributing ballots for all FA factions. Also, the Base Committees organize campaign activities with candidates of different factions, and the candidates themselves conceive of the Base Committees as a natural place to stage activities.

In terms of candidate selection, each faction nominates its own candidates for the Senate and the House. Each faction can also nominate a presidential candidate to compete in the party's primary elections. The primary election and the DSV electoral system promote high intraparty competition and reduce the need for coordination between factions or for a common electoral structure. However, the FA developed a common structure and also retained the power to authorize presidential candidates to run in the FA's primary election. The party Congress – which consists almost entirely of grassroots activists – must authorize which candidates are approved to compete in the primary election, thus monopolizing the nomination.

More critically, the FA – as opposed to the foundational parties (Colorado Party and PN) – articulates a common platform in the party Congress. To articulate the programmatic platform for the elections, Base

Committee and faction grassroots activists work on thematic committees months before the Congress, where they discuss and agree on proposals suggested by Base Committees, factions, or leaders. These proposals are then put to a vote in the plenary of the congress. Thus, in the FA, the process of programmatic articulation is deliberative and participative. This platform then constitutes the basic road map of the FA in government and also serves as a powerful tool to keep representatives accountable (see the following).

The Party Coordinates in Office

After 1971, the FA continuously improved its electoral performance until it won in 2004. As previously stated, the party has been electorally successful and has retained both the presidency and the legislative majority for three consecutive national elections. This was the result of a very sophisticated and articulated electoral coordination. This coordination has continued during the party's term in office. The party has power over the government and its legislative caucus. The latter holds regular meetings where legislators coordinate a legislative agenda.

The FA has institutionalized mechanisms to check the government and the legislative caucus. The Plenario Nacional (National Plenary) and the Mesa Política Nacional (National Political Board) have the power to determine the positions of the legislative caucus and the government.[3] The National Plenary is the highest directive body of the FA. It comprises 170 delegates. Factions and Base Committees have the same number of delegates. All delegates are elected in open internal elections with secret voting. The National Political Board, in turn, is the permanent executive body and it convenes on a weekly basis (every Friday).[4] Government authorities regularly attend party decision-making bodies. For example,

[3] Both instances also illustrate the FA's capacity to vertically aggregate interests.

[4] It comprises the president and vice-president of the party, fifteen representatives from the FA factions and eleven delegates from the Base Committees (six from Montevideo, two from Canelones, and three from the rest of the country). Decisions are mostly arrived at by consensus. If there is no consensus, decisions can also be made by majority, as long as fewer than a third of the National Political Board members oppose (article 96, Party Statutes). The National Political Board has a Secretariat where Base Committee delegates also participate. The representatives of the Base Committees to the National Political Board and to the Secretariat are chosen in Montevideo by the Group of 41, in Canelones and in the rest of the country by the delegates that attend the regional Coordinating Group meeting. In general, Base Committee delegates to the National Political Board and to the Secretariat periodically rotate.

government authorities regularly visit the National Political Board – in electoral years the frequency decreases (source: database of National Executive Board minutes). On average, every year there are eleven visits to the National Political Board by government authorities (source: FA administrative data). This is a conservative estimate because, in fact, government authorities regularly visit all the different party organizational structures (source: online survey).

In terms of party discipline in Congress, the FA established a doctrine of "imperative mandate."[5] As a result, dissenting votes in Congress are rare. Those few cases that have occurred are very well documented because, first, they were notable exceptions and, second, because the votes involved sensitive issues. Even though during the FA governments (2005–20) the opposition regularly participated in hearings (i.e., they demanded explanations from government ministers), these instances all ended without consequences for the ministers due to the alignment of the FA majority in Congress.[6]

The party also created the Agrupación Nacional de Gobierno (National Group of Government) and the Agrupación de Gobierno Departamental (Departmental Group of Government) to coordinate political decisions between the government and the party. Even though the National Group of Government was the more regular body, this aspect of the FA in government is a rare instance of coordination for a political party. Finally, the party has coordination mechanisms that come into play when the preferences of the government and of the party diverge or when there are policy disagreements among the different factions (e.g., free trade agreements, budget, tax reform, debt).

VERTICAL INTEREST AGGREGATION

The FA's distinctive trait as a party is its capacity to vertically aggregate a very complex set of interests: this operates in two ways. First, since the FA's inception, the different factions within the FA compete for votes and represent different constituencies. For example, the MPP represents the popular sectors while the different factions that compose the Frente Liber Seregni (FLS) represent the middle sectors; the former is more leftist and the latter more centrist (Luna 2014). The foundational factions came from very different ideological traditions; the PDC, for example, lies at the

[5] This was included in the Political Commitment, approved on February 9, 1972.
[6] Source: https://parlamentosite.wordpress.com/interpelaciones/#more-420.

opposite end of the spectrum from the PCU. Each faction is represented within the different organizational bodies that form the FA's complex structure, with representation based on each faction's performance in competitive internal elections. Although a faction's electoral performance in national elections is less relevant for the party's structure, it influences each faction's role in the legislative caucus and in the cabinet of the Executive.

Second, interest aggregation is also channeled through the grassroots structure. This structure is open and relies on volunteer activists. Activists interact on an ongoing basis with local-level organizations and movements, and many activists have dual membership in unions or local social organizations. These activists can convey societal demands to the very top echelons of the party at the local and national level. Faction leaders do not have the tools to control the discussion or the selection of grassroots delegates. This second form of interest aggregation does not afford direct control of factions, leaders, or party elites because the grassroots structure is not involved in the candidate selection process. Also, grassroots members' delegates in the directorate lack status or the power to distribute positions or resources.

The organizational structure comprises several collective decision-making structures. While factions have representatives throughout the FA's structure, grassroots activists are granted the right to send delegates to all the decision-making bodies. Thus, besides the existence of grassroots activism, the FA has a vertical structure that connects base-level activism with the decision-making authorities and, even more crucially, grassroots activists have a significant presence in all party decision-making organs, including in the most important ones (Congress, National Plenary, and National Political Board). Finally, grassroots activists also have developed informal institutions that complement the formal institutions and through which they coordinate their actions. This development is particularly important because factions' representatives have a structure that facilitates their coordination at the faction level. Without coordination opportunities and mechanism of their own, grassroots delegates would remain atomized and would lose relevance.

The Party Electorally Mobilizes Collective Interests

During electoral cycles, Base Committees are a tool for the FA and its constituent factions to mobilize supporters in the neighborhoods. The Base Committees have deep knowledge of the territory and thus help organize canvassing and provide detailed information about the problems and interests in each zone. They also publicize the party and its candidates (e.g., paint walls, design and produce posters, set up stands in the local street markets, etc.). On election day, they cover many voting locales as party representatives. Although online and TV campaigns are becoming increasingly important and the level of grassroots activism is declining, grassroots activists still play a role during the electoral campaigns. This is a rare trait of party organizations in Latin America. The existence of a network of committed volunteer activists who can deploy an efficient electoral campaign in the territory is evidence of the ability of the FA to electorally mobilize collective interests. However, the suggested indicators of this ability mentioned in the Introduction to this volume can also be observed in the case of the FA.

During the programmatic and electoral realignment of the Uruguayan party system, the FA not only captured more votes, but also changed its electoral base of support (Lanzaro 2004; Luna 2007b; López Cariboni and Queirolo 2015; Moreira 2000; Moreira and Delbono 2016). As in other Latin American countries in which the left accessed government, a class-based vote gradually consolidated (Handlin 2013; Madrid 2012). Since 2009, the FA has been attracting an increasing number of voters from poor sectors, individuals oriented toward voting for the FA not only because of the leftist government's economic performance but also because of the individuals' position in the social structure.[7]

The electoral platform of the FA is defined in the party Congress. It convenes every thirty months, though occasionally the National Plenary will convene a congress outside the normal schedule to address some significant issue. The FA congresses convene many activists. In the 2016 "Rodney Arismendi" congress, more than 1,000 grassroots delegates participated. The 2018 "Compañero General Víctor Licandro y Compañera Susana Dalmás," congress convened 1,143 delegates. This congress discussed the programmatic platform for the 2019 national election.

The programmatic project of the FA was modified through internal deliberative processes and thus it occurred gradually. In fact, the ideological congress is essentially an instance of bottom-up organization. In the platform the party presented for the 2004 national election, which it

[7] Using survey data from 1989 to 2014, López Cariboni and Queirolo (2015) show that class voting models better explain the vote in the last national election than do traditional economic voting models (the latter fare better in explaining election results prior to 2009).

won, the most radical positions of the party were abandoned (Garcé and Yaffé 2005; Yaffé 2005). The organizational attributes already reviewed have also affected the way the FA carried out programmatic adaptation over the years. As opposed to what happens in parties that are mere personalistic vehicles, change for the FA has been gradual and the result of intense debate.

After the authoritarian period, the FA gradually moderated ideologically and programmatically. The late 1980s and early 1990s were years of realignment within the party and the formation of new factions, some of which continue to exist today (e.g., Asamblea Uruguay, Uruguayan Assembly, AU). Garcé and Yaffé (2005) and Yaffé (2005) indicate that the FA gradually moderated starting in 1995, adopting more centrist perspectives compared to the clearly leftist manifesto of 1971. Changes were undertaken through lively debates in party congresses and documents. This gradual and mostly deliberative process indicates a process of party adaptation. Yaffé summarizes this process, which he analyzes in detail based on party documents, as follows: "and that change should not be interpreted as a sheer operation of electoral catch-up, or a last minute opportunist turn, because it has been the result of a long and complex process of programmatic and ideological renovation" (2005, 97).[8] However, it is crucial to emphasize that this process did not involve abandoning the opposition to the neoliberal turn nor a distancing of the party from its grassroots members, the unions (Lanzaro 2008), and the social movement. In this vein, during the 1990s and 2000s, the FA's electoral platform incorporated several issues historically important to the feminist movement, including controversial positions such as support for legal abortion.

In moderating its program, the FA did not imitate the traditional parties' centrist positions or convert the party to a professional electoral machine (Moraes and Luján 2015). The party kept its stances regarding the main economic cleavages in Uruguayan politics. It retained its staunch opposition to the privatization of public utility companies. In the 1990s, as market reform process advanced during Lacalle's term (1990–95), direct democracy mechanisms were intensively used, though with varying success.[9] Notably, given the uncertain prospects of the different referenda

[8] All direct quotes that appear in the chapter were translated from Spanish by the authors. See also Lanzaro (2004).

[9] While the referendum on the Annulment of Privatization of State Companies Law successfully halted the privatization of state-owned companies, other referenda and popular

and popular initiatives and the fact that some of the proposals were not the preferred policies of FA leaders or of its main factions, the FA grassroots activists were the ones who on some occasions advocated for the use of direct democracy mechanisms. This was the case in at least two campaigns, one against allowing private investment in the state-owned petroleum company monopoly (2003) and, second, a campaign in support of a law to annul amnesty for human rights crimes (2009).

Intermediation and Channeling of Collective Demands

The FA distinguishes itself from other leftist parties in Europe and Latin America because it does not have formal ties with the union movement nor is it the political arm of a social movement. However, from the very beginning, the FA developed strong ties with social organizations, especially with the labor union movement. A first indication of this strong bond was the creation of multiple functional committees, that is, non-territorial Base Committees, based in the workplace. These grassroots groups organized workers. Second, the main decision-making body of the party has always included union leaders. For example, Héctor Rodríguez, a key leader of the People's Congress and of the unification of the union movement in Uruguay, served on the first National Political Board. Third, according to Senatore, Doglio, and Yaffé (2004), 10 percent of the first slots on the party's senatorial lists and Montevideo representative lists for the 1971 and 1984 national elections were awarded to union leaders. Fourth, in the 1984 elections (the first after the transition from the authoritarian regime), the FA ticket included for vice-president José D'Elía, the most important leader of the CNT.

At the grassroots activists level, dual membership also characterizes Base Committee attendees who also participate in unions and other civil society organizations – mainly at the local level. Some 33 percent of Base Committee activists participate in unions and 42 percent participate in neighborhood associations such as social or sport clubs, parent-teacher associations, etc. Given that these grassroots activists have a significant role throughout the party structure, their dual membership generates a bottom-up capillarity between the social movements and the party.

The FA, like every political party organization in a democratic context, experiences a tension between choosing policies and candidates that are

initiatives did not fare as well. The success of a direct democracy mechanism required the decisive support of the FA as a whole (Monestier 2011).

closer to the median voter versus those that are closer to members' preferences. The FA organizational structure limits the leaders' and government's room to maneuver. It limits the party leaders' incentives to moderate their positions because major decisions need to have the organization's explicit support or, at least, an absence of opposition. When the FA is in government, the party organization – the combination of the coalitional nature of the FA and its grassroots activist structure – also constrains the government's pursuit of crucial, substantive policies. In this party with activists and powerful (institutionalized) factional leaders, the party's decisions and the policy orientation do not depend on a leader, as in other parties with activists, such as the Justicialist Party (Levitsky 2003). This gives more stability to the party's positions and reduces the likelihood of a dramatic policy switch.

In the institutional setting in which the FA is immersed, the major challenge in the relationship between the party and the government is that the former might control the latter. Even though the party does not have institutional rules, as in parliamentary regimes, to restrict government policies, the FA has been able, directly or indirectly, to limit the FA in government. Most of the time, as expected, the party has supported the government and has taken responsibility for its actions – in theoretical terms, the exception should be the opposite. Yet, on several significant occasions, the FA structure, especially the grassroots structure in combination with the factions that participate in the FA's vertical structure, has clashed with government positions. These controversies engendered changes in government positions and prevented the government from adopting more centrist positions on these policies, positions that could eventually distance the government from the party's platform. Vetoes coming from the organization (and its parliamentary caucus) prevented the implementation of these policies but did not imply a general blockade of the FA's government agenda, nor did these vetoes create long-term conflicts between the organization and the government authorities. The following examples illustrate this phenomenon.

During the FA's first government (2005–10), a group of social organizations (including the PIT-CNT, the student movement, groups of families of people who were detained and disappeared during the dictatorship, some minor groups from the left, and intellectuals) started a campaign to hold a plebiscite to repeal the "Ley de Caducidad" (15,848 Ley de Caducidad de la Pretensión Punitiva del Estado, Law of the Expiration of the Punitive Pretension of the State). The Law was enacted in 1986, during the first democratic government after the authoritarian regime. It resulted from an agreement between the Colorado Party and the PN and established amnesty for crimes committed during the authoritarian regime (1973–84) by the military and the police. Those that supported the bill argued that it was a way to pacify the country. For those opposed (the political left and some minor groups within the traditional parties), the bill gave impunity to those who committed crimes and violated human rights during the dictatorship. In 1989, civil society organizations and the FA convened a call for a referendum to repeal the Law; the referendum failed to receive the necessary votes.

In 2007, in a different political context, civil society organizations argued the need for a plebiscite to repeal the law, because repealing it through Congress (the FA had the necessary majority to do so) would not yield the desired retroactive effects and would not allow the government to put the responsible military personnel on trial. By contrast, annulling the law through a plebiscite that would establish a constitutional amendment included the retroactive effects, among which was the "negation of res judicata." It was politically difficult to argue for the annulment of the law for two main reasons: first, because the Congress of the FA prior to the 2004 national elections decided not to proceed with this since it was a delicate issue at a juncture where the FA had a good chance of winning the national elections for the first time. Second, because Tabaré Vázquez (2005–10) argued against it, claiming that he would respect his campaign promises.[10]

The position of the party on the human rights policy stance of the FA's government toward the Law of the Expiration of the Punitive Pretension of the State changed when the party took office. At the fifth Ordinary Congress of 2007, a motion was approved that called on the population to participate in the campaign, initiated by social organizations, to gather the required number of signatures to annul the Law of the Expiration of the Punitive Pretension of the State. This resolution was approved almost unanimously by the 1,400 grassroots delegates attending the Congress, and resulted from the synthesis of approximately ten different motions, all of which supported the campaign already set in motion by social organizations.[11] The position of the party was consolidated at the

[10] Montevideo Portal: http://www.montevideo.com.uy/auc.aspx?49753 (last accessed in July 20, 2016).

[11] "El FA adhirió a la anulación de la Ley de Caducidad" (The FA adhered to annulation of the Law of the Expiration of the Punitive Pretension of the State) (La República, December 17, 2007).

National Plenary on April 5, 2008 when a majority of eighty-one in favor (fifty-three abstentions and nine against) decided to support the campaign to gather the required number of signatures. The motion was introduced by the grassroots activists' delegates from Montevideo and the delegates from Base Committees from abroad.

The representatives of the grassroots members were decisive in changing the position of the party, putting it in opposition to the President's preferences. In the vote, the only factions that were in favor of supporting the signature collection campaign to repeal the Law were the minor more leftist factions, as well as the PCU and the New Space. The major factions (Mujica's MPP, the FLS of Astori, and the PSU)[12] were aligned with Tabaré Vázquez's position and voted against the FA taking part in the signatures campaign. If the decision had been in the factions' hands – in the hands of their delegates to the National Plenary – the party would have remained in line with the President's position. The grassroots activists' decision, however, made the difference. Even those grassroots delegates who were also part of the MPP or the PSU factions voted against the positions of their respective factions and therefore voted for the FA to participate in the campaign for the Annulment of the Expiration Law.[13] Thus, without the grassroots activists, the decision of the party would have been different.

The ability of the FA to obstruct the government highlights the organizational strength of the party. This distances the FA from other left-of-center parties in Latin America, even from other well-organized parties like the Brazilian PT or the Chilean Partido Socialista de Chile (Chilean Socialist Party, PSCh). Thus, as opposed to the cases of other parties in Latin America, FA party elites do not have the leverage to take the party in any direction they desire (Burgess and Levitsky 2003). In the case of the FA, activists have a significant influence over policy decisions, especially policies to which the left is particularly sensitive. The coalitional structure and the grassroots structure interact such that party decisions are constrained by the party's core constituency.

Even though the FA developed its strongest linkages with the unions, the party also developed other significant bonds with social movements.

[12] Mujica and Astori were the candidates who competed in the party's primary election to determine the presidential candidate for the 2009 national elections.

[13] See "La Ley de Caducidad: comienza campaña masiva para anularla," April 7, 2008, in El Espectador (accessed on July 20, 2016), and "Desafía el Frente Amplio a Tabaré por la amnistía," (The FA challenges Tabaré over amnesty, *Página* 12, April 7, 2008).

These bonds proved crucial in the FA's promotion of gender and sexual orientation equality legislation. For instance, discussion within the party regarding the legalization of abortion illustrates the existence of informal ties with civil society organizations and the role these ties play in constraining party decisions. Feminist activists have had a two-tier relationship with the FA. On the one hand, many feminist activists were grassroots activists in the FA; on the other hand, they had personal ties with FA leaders, especially female leaders. In 1985, during the transition to democracy, many feminists formed Cotidiano Mujer (Everyday Woman), one of the most active NGOs at the time, and they were also activists of the PCU and the Partido por la Victoria del Puebl (Party for the Victory of the People, PVP). Even though these women abandoned active participation in the FA structure, they maintained close ties with (and thus had direct access to) FA politicians, especially to the feminist caucus (Margarita Percovich, Mónica Xavier, Constanza Moreira, and Carmen Beramendi). The pregnancy-interruption law was approved in the FA second government (2010–15, Mujica's administration) and it was one of the toughest laws to approve for the left (for example, Tabaré Vázquez always opposed this bill and he vetoed it during his first government, 2005–10).

CONCLUSIONS: THE FA ORGANIZATIONAL STRUCTURE AND DEMOCRATIC REPRESENTATION

The electoral success of the FA, its capacity to challenge the established Uruguayan foundational parties and its ability to serve as a pole of attraction for social movements was accompanied by the existence of institutionalized channels for *voice*, through which the party activists influence strategic decisions. These channels provide a means for activists to influence the party's agenda and to exercise a veto over party leaders' objectives. Activists participate in the party's strategic discussions and party leaders, when making decisions, consider the potential problems they might face if they deviate far from activists' preferences. Thus, the party grassroots members constitute a potential (or actual) threat to incumbent party elites.

In the case of the FA, activists have an institutionalized role in the decision-making structure. They have institutionalized channels that facilitate participation; more crucially, these channels enable them to exert a significant *voice* (Hirschman 1970), which imbues activists' participation with a strong sense of efficacy. Building on Pizzorno (1970),

Panebianco (1988) analyzed how selective and collective incentives affect individuals' level of engagement with parties. The term "collective incentives" refers to how leaders reproduce a party's identity and satisfy party members' need to identify with ideas and values. Selective incentives, by contrast, concern leaders' ability to distribute positions within the party or in government, or other types of patronage. While collective incentives are crucial for voters, supporters, and members, activists' willingness to continue their activism depends on a combination of both collective and selective incentives. Activists will participate as long as the party leadership provides these two types of incentives.

The FA is a dynamic organization. The coalition and movement that was born in 1971 changed over time. It changed ideologically and programmatically and its social bases broadened. The FA had to adapt to contextual transformations – as did all leftist parties in the region and in the rest of the world – including political violence, the end of the Cold War, the neoliberal turn, the epochal shift that is summarized in the idea of "globalization," financial crises, and economic crises. These processes and events are often cited as factors that in many cases explain the death of parties. The FA, like many other parties, has adapted and survived. This ability to adapt is largely attributable to the existence of a strong organizational structure that facilitates the incorporation of new demands and affords grassroots activists the belief that their engagement matters.

In sum, the FA structure not only distinguishes the party from other leftist parties in Latin America but also (and more crucially) enables the party to efficiently represent the demands of multiple social actors whose policy preferences are not always aligned with those of the main party leaders. In this way, the FA serves as a powerful vehicle to achieve democratic representation of popular interests.

3

Horizontal Coordination and Vertical Aggregation Mechanisms of the PRO in Argentina and Its Subnational Variations

Gabriel Vommaro

INTRODUCTION

During the 2001–2 crisis, new electoral vehicles were created in Argentina. These included, from the center to the left, Argentina por una República de Iguales (Argentina for a Republic of Equals, ARI) and Encuentro por la Democracia y la Equidad (Meeting for Democracy and Equity, EDE), and from the center to the right, Recrear para el Crecimiento (Recreate for Growth, Recrear) and Propuesta Republicana (Republican Proposal, PRO). All these vehicles were built around personalistic leaders. Most split off from preexisting parties and most of them failed to survive much beyond that juncture. In almost all cases, their leaders did not invest in political organization and the vehicles suffered the ups and downs of their leaders' approval ratings, or were absorbed by the traditional parties. The PRO is one of the few relatively successful cases of party-building. In the framework established by the theory developed in this volume, the PRO is a political party that established coordination mechanisms among its leaders and articulates social interests. However, it does not perform these tasks in the same way throughout the country. The PRO was born in the City of Buenos Aires, the epicenter of the 2001–2 crises of the traditional parties; in that district, PRO came to power in 2007. The City of Buenos Aires has remained, since then, its electoral stronghold. The PRO used different strategies to acquire a national anchor, but only through an alliance with one of the traditional parties, the Unión Cívica Radical (Radical Civic Union, UCR), did the PRO manage to be competitive in most of the districts of the country. Thus, the PRO is a case of an electoral vehicle that behaves as a political party in some districts of the country and as an unrooted party in others. The case of PRO therefore helps elucidate the subnational variations of the theoretical model proposed in this volume.

In this chapter, based on long-term research with mixed methods, PRO party-building activity in the City of Buenos Aires is studied in relation to its ability to accomplish the two dimensions proposed in the introduction of this volume:[1] first, horizontal coordination between the heterogeneous party leaders; second, vertical articulation of interests and groups that are part of both the core constituency and the noncore constituency, the latter being necessary for right-wing parties whose core constituency is made up of minority social groups (Gibson 1996). In both cases, in the City of Buenos Aires, the PRO became an organization with some stability over time capable of offering a sociocultural proposal (based on aesthetic and ethical repertoires) (Vommaro 2017) distinguishable from that of its competitors, that is to say, a party brand (Lupu 2016) – as a new, pragmatic party associated with concrete problem solving – capable of creating lasting attachments with a programmatic leaning toward the business sector's preferences.

I argue that the PRO managed to build this coordinated and rooted party by virtue of having established two effective organizational mechanisms. First was a division of labor and incentives within the party that facilitated the incorporation of long-standing politicians and their electoral clientele while a small ruling coalition (Kitschelt 1994), comprising new politicians who were in the PRO from its founding, maintained control of the electoral strategy and the definition of the party brand. The second mechanism was mediating organizational devices adapted to the business and the NGO worlds of the PRO's core constituency – the upper-middle and upper classes and the economic elites (Gibson 1996) – that were used to recruit new politicians and activists aligned with the main features of the party's brand. These two mechanisms, however, failed to solve the challenge of expanding the territorial reach of a party born in the City of Buenos Aires under auspicious historical conditions lacking in other districts of the country (Bril Mascarenhas 2007; Morresi and Vommaro 2014). Centralizing the horizontal coordination of

[1] Our analysis employs mixed methods with a primarily qualitative approach. The data come from longitudinal research (2010–17) on the PRO's party-building efforts – in organizational, sociological, and programmatic terms – in the city of Buenos Aires, its territorial expansion strategies in other districts, and its transformation in recent years (Morresi and Vommaro 2014; Vommaro 2017; Vommaro and Morresi 2014; Vommaro, Morresi, and Bellotti 2015).

a leading coalition located in the City of Buenos Aires hindered the incorporation of long-standing politicians and their constituencies because the centralized electoral strategy did not take into account local interests. After several failed electoral attempts, in 2015 a PRO-led coalition established an electoral alliance with a traditional party, the UCR. This alliance solved the PRO's national anchorage problem in terms of its electoral offer, but it did not help to strengthen party organization and social roots at the subnational level. The PRO remained weak in this regard in many districts of the country, where it behaves as an unrooted party.

This chapter is organized as follows. First, I briefly present the history of the PRO and its break with the tradition of right-wing parties in Argentina since 1983. Second, I address the two dimensions of the theoretical model developed in this volume. Specifically, I describe the coordination among leaders based on the division of labor that the party has developed and I describe how organizational mediation devices vertically aggregate the interests of the party's social core as well as the interests of noncore constituencies traditionally distant from the right-wing parties in Argentina (Gibson 1996). Third, I analyze the challenges the new party has faced in its efforts to extend its reach territorially and I show its varying strength at the subnational level. Finally, I offer concluding remarks about the case of the PRO and its contribution to the theory developed in this volume.

THE DIFFICULT CONSTRUCTION OF A COMPETITIVE RIGHT-WING PARTY IN ARGENTINA

Right-wing parties have traditionally been weak in Argentina (Di Tella 1971; Gibson 1996).[2] This fact was among the factors that explain, for some authors, democratic instability during the twentieth century (Di Tella 1971).[3] In 1983, when the nonelectoral pathway was closed, it

[2] As Kevin Middlebrook notes, "One of the principal legacies of nineteenth-century Argentine history was the absence of a nationally organized conservative party capable of contesting free elections under conditions of mass suffrage. By 1930, Argentine elites had turned to the armed forces as the most reliable defenders of their interests" (Middlebrook 2000, 19).

[3] This electoral weakness of the right coincided with a weak capacity for coordination of business groups, which privileged their direct relationship with the State (lobby, capture of privileged areas of accumulation, participation in government coalitions with reformist objectives) rather than the establishment of centralized organizations with the capacity for interest aggregation and collective action (Schneider 2004).

was expected that a center-right party would emerge seeking to organize the political elites associated with the right side of the political spectrum, as well as the related electorate. However, until 2007, the right-wing political offer was dispersed and unstable.[4] It was dispersed because in only a few cases were the political parties identified with liberal-conservative traditions unified.[5] It was unstable because even the most successful of these forces ended up disappearing or occupying a marginal place in the electoral competition. The crisis or dissolution of right-wing party brands undoubtedly caused a coordination problem for political elites, who abandoned party life or had to rebuild their careers in other parties, but it also caused the defection of the rightist electorate (Lupu 2016).

The 2001–2 crisis provided an opportunity for the emergence of new political forces. This is consistent with Levitsky et al.'s (2016) suggestion regarding the role of conflict situations, as well as with Rosenblatt's (2018) suggestion of the role of shared traumas in creating the heroic founding myth of a party. In Argentina, the rejection of traditional parties and the political class had been more intense among non-Peronist voters (Torre 2003) and was particularly destructive of the party system in districts such as the City of Buenos Aires (Bril Mascarenhas 2007). Center-right political actors saw the social and economic collapse of Argentina as a new opportunity to build their own party that this time would be autonomous from the discredited traditional leaders (Vommaro, Morresi, and Bellotti 2015). The crisis of traditional parties would also function as an opportunity to build new party brands (Lupu 2016) that sought to attract "orphaned" voters (Torre 2003) who had abandoned their prior party identifications.

[4] At the provincial level there were some provincial conservative parties with relative success (such as the Partido Demócrata de Mendoza – Democratic Party of Mendoza), as well as forces led by personnel of the security forces closest to the authoritarian right (Fuerza Republicana – Republican Force – in Tucumán, the Movimiento por la Dignidad Nacional – Movement for the National Dignity, MODIN – in the province of Buenos Aires).

[5] Unlike other Latin American cases, in Argentina there was no sharp separation between liberals and conservatives, either in ideological or partisan terms. This is due in part to the fact that, after the emancipation from Spain, in Argentina the religious question did not occupy a significant place in the conflict among the elites. The liberal-conservative term applies to the political lineage associated with the political order founded in 1880 and with the political and intellectual right-wing groups that, after the crisis of that order at the beginning of the twentieth century, kept it as a reference. Thereafter, conservative political parties consolidated relatively successfully in the provincial arenas but were less successful at the national level (Tato 2013).

Two political formations emerged. One, called Recrear, was a clearly non-Peronist party, led by an orthodox economist, Ricardo López Murphy, and had a strong programmatic character. It maintained the canons of the dominant neo liberal economic discourse of the 1990s. This party managed to attract members of most of the provincial conservative parties and soon became a force that was national in scope (Vommaro 2017). However, by 2007, it showed signs of stagnation in electoral terms, as well as challenges to the leadership of López Murphy. The other party was PRO. Born in a think tank, it was constituted around Mauricio Macri, an heir to one of the country's major business corporations who had been president of the popular football club Boca Juniors. Unlike Recrear, this new party was born with a pragmatic imprint. From the outset, it was viewed as a vehicle to achieve political power and chose to start at the local level and from there build a nationally competitive party. Its epicenter was the City of Buenos Aires, fertile ground for the growth of center-right parties and, at the same time, the district in which both the traditional parties and the new parties that emerged in the 1990s – such as Frente País Solidario (Solidary Country Front, Frepaso) – suffered further weakening (Lupu 2016). The PRO incorporated leaders from different backgrounds. The party is organized into five groups (Morresi and Vommaro 2014): long-standing politicians, Peronists, the UCR, and traditional right-wing forces formed the first three groups. The other groups comprised new politicians, including some from NGOs and professional or international foundations, other entrepreneurs and CEOs from the business world. The amalgam of these heterogeneous leaders presented an organizational challenge for the new party, both in terms of horizontal coordination and in terms of constructing a defined offer that could add interests and social demands in a lasting way.

The competition between the two forces concluded in 2007, when the PRO came to power in the City of Buenos Aires and a group of Recrear leaders challenged López Murphy, imposed internal elections and decided to merge with Macri's party (Vommaro 2017). The goal of the Recrear challengers was to join the country's first competitive right-wing party since 1983. Thus, the PRO managed to unify the center-right and expand its national anchorage, which remained insufficient for the party to be competitive at the national level (Vommaro 2017). With the organizational resources of the richest subnational state in the country, the PRO developed a successful party-building process. It also established high levels of coordination between leaders and an efficient mechanism of interest aggregation. However, while they maintained control of the brand and party strategy, Macri and his inner circle were less successful in their attempt to expand the social anchor of the party to other districts.

In 2015, the PRO finally allied with the UCR, which gave it roots in districts where the PRO had weak support, and with other minor partners including personalistic vehicles (Coalición Cívica, Civic Coalition, CC) and small niche parties (e.g., the neo-Peronist Partido Fe – Faith Party – founded by Gerónimo Venegas, the leader of the rural labor union). This strategy gave birth to the Cambiemos coalition, and – in an environment of increasing rejection of Kirchnerism, which had been in government for twelve years – an electoral alliance led by a center-right party won the presidential elections for the first time in Argentina's history. The contribution of UCR leaders can be seen in the fact that Cambiemos built its electoral stronghold in the center of the country, both in urban centers and in rural areas, traditionally controlled by the UCR (Mangonnet, Murillo, and Rubio 2018). The UCR, founded in 1891, is the oldest political party of the Argentinean party system. It won the presidency on different occasions during the twentieth century and has a nationwide presence and dense organizational structure (Malamud 2011; Persello 2007).

The shortcut chosen to remedy the historical weakness of the forces on the center-right of the political spectrum, which had been successful at the local level but only partially so at the national level, gave PRO territorial coverage and expanded its electorate, but did not imply organizational growth. PRO remained a robust organization in the City of Buenos Aires and a weak one at the national level. In the following section, I consider the factors that explain the strengths and weaknesses of PRO party-building on the two dimensions of the explanatory model developed in this volume: horizontal coordination between ambitious politicians and vertical aggregation of societal interests.

HORIZONTAL COORDINATION: CENTRALIZED CONTROL AND PARTISAN DIVISION OF LABOR

Having learned the lessons of the recent history of right-wing forces in Argentina that had been absorbed by traditional parties, or had experienced crises when allied with those forces, PRO leaders set out from the beginning to build an autonomous political organization. This party has a ruling coalition capable of controlling the party label and the party brand (and a certain identity associated with it) and of selecting candidates compatible with that brand, in order to offer the electorate personalities whose public image was consistent with the party program.

This section analyzes the process of PRO party-building in relation to these challenges, and it explains the mechanisms by which it managed to advance the formation of a party with high levels of horizontal coordination among elites with heterogeneous political origins. It shows that the PRO developed a division of labor mechanism that proved successful in solving the problem of horizontal coordination, because it allowed the original ruling coalition to maintain control of the party's electoral strategy and identity, while selective incentives were distributed among ambitious politicians who came to the PRO from traditional political forces.

The first coordination factor was the leadership of Macri, who managed to overcome internal challenges in the foundational stage of the party – when the PRO lists were used by some free-rider politicians as a platform to win a parliamentary seat (Morresi and Vommaro 2014) – and to impose himself, later, as primus inter pares among the leaders of the allied parties. The second most fundamental coordination mechanism was the division of labor between the ruling coalition, comprising new politicians from the NGO and business worlds as well as leaders of the traditional right, and politicians from traditional parties (Peronism and the UCR). The ruling coalition was relatively stable and controlled the party brand, alliance strategies, as well as the candidate selection process at the national level and, in many cases, also at the subnational level. The fact that a stable and centralized ruling coalition commanded political strategy and party brand building prevented the party from being colonized by free riders or by other political forces. At the same time, politicians from traditional parties received selective incentives, that is, positions on electoral lists and in government, which allowed them to channel resources to their clients. This division of labor made it possible to provide a factor identified by Rosenblatt (2018) as necessary to ensure party vibrancy: namely, the construction of channels for the political careers of its leaders.

A 2011 survey of PRO cadres in the City of Buenos Aires had similar proportions of old and new politicians in the sample: 54 percent came from Peronism, radicalism, or right-wing parties, while 46 percent had recently entered politics from the business and NGO worlds. Right-wing party leaders were linked to federalist groups – the Partido Demócrata de la Capital Federal (Democratic Party of the Federal Capital) – that joined the PRO party early, as well as former Unión del Centro Democrático (Union of the Democratic Centre, UCeDe) leaders (Arriondo 2015), and the most recently formed right-wing parties (Acción por la República – Action for the Republic – and Recrear). They came to the PRO convinced of the importance of building an electorally competitive party, for which they were willing to sacrifice, in most cases, ideological purity. Those who came from the UCR joined the PRO as part of an agreement between mid-level UCR leaders and Macri. They found in the PRO a space to advance their political careers, which had been blocked in the UCR, a party in crisis and dominated by leaders from the 1980s (Persello 2007). Ideologically, they were the furthest from the center-right ideas prevalent among the other PRO factions (Morresi and Vommaro 2014). As for the Peronists, they were mostly mid-level leaders who came to the PRO in its formative years (between 2002 and 2003, when it was still called Compromiso con el Cambio – Commitment to Change). Peronism in the city of Buenos Aires was in crisis at that time. These mid-level leaders found in the new party created by Macri and his group a competitive vehicle to access political positions. Ideologically, they were closer to the PRO core than were the UCR leaders. But, like the latter, the Peronists who joined the PRO maintained the marks of their origin (Vommaro, Morresi, and Bellotti 2015) as well as the political connections to link with their clientele and constituencies, through problem-solving networks (Auyero 2001; Levitsky 2003).

Businessmen and NGO professionals and leaders were newcomers to political activity and although they shared sociocultural features (e.g., socio-occupational positions, worldviews and a detachment from politics) they did not act concertedly as a faction. Instead, they responded directly to the party leader's strategies and decisions. Businessmen, at the beginning, were cadres of the Macri Societies Corporation (SOCMA) who had accompanied Macri during his time as president of Boca Juniors, and who were integrated first into the Fundación Creer y Crecer (Believe and Grow Foundation) and subsequently in positions associated with the management of finances in the government of the City of Buenos Aires. This entry of business cadres into PRO was followed by that of others who joined the local administration after 2007, especially through recruitment support channels such as the Generación 2025 (Generation 2025, G25) foundation (Vommaro 2017). As for NGOs, foundation professionals, and activists, the largest contingent entered in the early years of the PRO. Subsequently, other actors joined the party in response to the call to "get involved in politics" that PRO leaders accompanied with offers of positions in government and on the electoral lists.

The strategy of offering recruited leaders opportunities to satisfy their political ambitions can be seen, for example, in the fact that all factions were represented among PRO local deputies and/or City of Buenos Aires government officials: 14 percent of the people in these positions were UCR, 21 percent were Peronists, 19 percent were right-wing leaders, 17 percent were businessmen, and 29 percent were NGO members. However, some of these factions were more committed to the PRO than were others. Taking formal party membership as a proxy for this engagement, only 14 percent of the UCR leaders and 45 percent of the Peronists were PRO members, as opposed to 70 percent of the right-wing leaders, 66 percent of the businessmen, and the 80 percent of NGO members. One observes a similar pattern of differences in how much time and resources members of the various factions invested in animating the party's internal life: 53 percent of the NGO cadres and 50 percent of the right-wing leaders held party positions, as opposed to 45 percent of the Peronists and 33 percent of the businessmen who held such positions; no UCR leader had a party position in the PRO. Involvement in party life thus was lower among those who came from traditional parties, while new politicians and right-wing leaders were the ones who invested most in building the PRO organization. The interviewees argued that this lesser degree of involvement on the part of the former is explained, first, by the strategy of the PRO ruling coalition to control the internal life of the party as a means to control the political-electoral strategy and brand building. They also attributed it to the fact that the politicians of the traditional parties maintained their original party membership and were not willing to renounce these ties and identify fully with a nascent party.

This division of labor within the party, accepted by both groups, defined clear roles: the PRO ruling coalition did not require cadres who came from traditional parties to formally participate in the party's internal life, and instead excluded them from the work of devising party strategy and controlling the party brand. Conversely, in exchange, the faction received places on electoral lists and government positions were awarded to leaders only weakly engaged with the party. Table 3.1 shows the allocation of positions on the party's electoral lists and appointments to high governmental positions. Fewer than half (48 percent) of the party members with the highest level of engagement (i.e., those serving in leadership roles) were appointed to nonelective positions in government or were ranked high enough on the party's electoral lists to have a reasonable expectation of winning office (i.e., were given expectant elective positions). By contrast, 90 percent of the cadres with less organizational commitment to PRO were rewarded for their participation in the party with either appointment to nonelective office (52 percent) or

TABLE 3.1 *Appointment of PRO leaders to elective and nonelective positions according to level of partisan involvement*

Position	Party Involvement					
	Nonmember		Member without appointment		Member with appointment	
	N	%	N	%	N	%
Nonelective position	11	52	5	50	5	24
Nonexpectant elective position	2	10	1	10	11	52
Expectant elective position	8	38	4	40	5	24

Source: 2011 survey with PRO political cadres in Buenos Aires.

TABLE 3.2 *Appointment of PRO leaders to elective and nonelective positions, by faction*

Position	Faction									
	Right		UCR		Peronist		Business		NGOs	
	N	%	N	%	N	%	N	%	N	%
Nonelective position	2	20	5	71	2	18	7	78	5	33
Nonexpectant elective position	4	40	0	–	4	36	2	22	4	27
Expectant elective position	4	40	2	29	5	45	0	0	6	40

Source: 2011 survey with PRO political cadres in Buenos Aires.

inclusion in the party's electoral lists in an expectant elective position (38 percent).

The analysis based on membership in party factions yields similar results. The businessmen were almost entirely absent from the electoral lists, and those who participated in the lists did so in a manner more symbolic than substantive (Gaxie 1977), because they occupied nonexpectant positions. Conversely, UCR leaders, who, as noted, had the lowest commitment to the party, either held nonelective positions, or participated in elections with a high expectation of being elected (Table 3.2). At the same time, the factions most engaged with the party had the highest percentage of cadres competing in elections in expectant positions. In Siavelis and Morgenstern's (2008b) typology, the PRO distributed its expectant positions on the electoral lists to those who were party loyalists and entrepreneurs. In Panebianco's (1988) terms, the PRO followed a strategy that combined the distribution of collective incentives (to those leaders most involved with the party) and selective incentives (to the least involved leaders).

The success of this division of labor and the incentive distribution strategy associated with it is also a source of cohesion among party leaders. This cohesion can be seen, for example, in the fact that the PRO survived an electoral defeat in the City of Buenos Aires (2003), its stronghold, and a defeat at the national level in 2019. It also survived its leader's exit from the local scene, when Macri was elected president in 2015. The construction of organizational mediation mechanisms also played a crucial role in solidifying the party, by articulating the interests of its core constituency and establishing linkages with noncore constituencies.

VERTICAL INTEREST AGGREGATION: PARTISAN MEANS AND TERRITORIAL IMPLEMENTATION

The PRO mobilized both the right-wing parties' traditional core constituency, associated with the country's social and economic elites (Gibson 1996), and other social segments (noncore constituency). Investment in territorial organization is a component Cyr (2017) and Levitsky et al. (2016) identified in successful party survival and building. It enables a party to establish lasting relations with their electorate, as well as to recruit activists and party cadres. In the case of the PRO, as a new party born with a mission to renew politics from the outside, these bonds also allowed it to incorporate discursive and aesthetic repertoires that nurtured its party brand, which was built around the renewal of traditional politics (Vommaro 2017). As a right-wing party, the PRO faced the additional challenge of establishing lasting links with its core constituency (the upper-middle and upper classes) and with its natural allies – businessmen – in a country where the upper classes had a deficit of party representation (Di Tella 1971; Gibson 1996; Monestier 2017) and the economic elites traditionally established particularistic and informal links with the political sphere, privileging a direct relationship with the State (Schneider 2004). At the same time, to become competitive, the PRO needed to establish organizational connections with secondary electorates, or noncore constituencies (Gibson 1996).

PRO faced these challenges as follows: On the one hand, it established organizational mediations adapted to its core constituency. It did so informally, through foundations associated with the party. This was an efficient approach in the case of the CEOs of companies connected to world markets as well as their social networks, which comprised members of upper-middle and upper classes. On the other hand, depending on the division of labor within the party, the PRO outsourced to the UCR and Peronist leaders the mobilization of those parties' traditional clienteles, which assured it a foothold in the middle classes and urban lower classes, which in Argentina have typically not supported right-wing parties. The activists of these factions depend on the selective incentives that their leaders receive, and they draw on the party's access to public resources by virtue of its control, initially, of the City of Buenos Aires government and, subsequently, the national government. The mechanisms of interest aggregation thus operate according to a similar logic as does the division of party labor analyzed previously, and in line with arguments concerning the segmentation of political linkages that gives rise to right-wing parties (Luna 2010; Thachil 2014).

Informal mediations enabled the PRO to articulate upper- and upper-middle-class interests through NGOs and foundations, which functioned as bridges between the political world and the business and NGO worlds. These mediating organizations include those created by the party or its leaders, such as foundations and think tanks that incorporated entrepreneurs, CEOs, and upper-class activists, and preexisting entities with which the PRO established fluid and permanent bonds, such as international NGOs or university student centers at private and private denominational universities (Grandinetti 2015). Both types of organizations form part of the PRO party environment (Sawicki 1997).

The foundations and think tanks created by the party or by some of its leaders installed subsidiaries throughout the country and recruited and mobilized activists from the business world and from the upper and upper-middle classes. They provided a way to contact, recruit, and mobilize people who otherwise would not have engaged in traditional party activity. The Fundación Pensar (To Think Foundation),[6] for example, is in charge of designing PRO government programs. The G25 was founded in 2008 on the initiative of Esteban Bullrich and Guillermo Dietrich, two

[6] The Pensar Foundation arose from an initiative of intellectuals and center-right political leaders. They considered it necessary, at the end of the 2001 and 2002 crisis, to create a think tank that would propagate conservative ideas, in the mold of the Spanish Fundación para el Análisis y los Estudios Sociales (Foundation for Social Analysis and Studies, FAES), created by José María Aznar in 1989. Following the growth of the PRO, during which many Pensar members joined the party, the Foundation itself joined the party and in 2010 and redefined its objective to be the design of government programs for the PRO national government project. See Echt (2016).

major PRO leaders and former managers. Its objective is to recruit businessmen and managers for the PRO administration (both at the subnational and national levels). G25 is defined as "an autonomous and self-sufficient foundation with respect to the Party, identified with the PRO's values" (G25 2015, 8).[7] The foundations sought to import values associated with efficiency and management into public life. The goal was, in the words of a member of the G25 board, to build a "trusted circle of at least 1,000 or one 1,500 officials" that could surround Macri and his team in the national government.[8] The G25 foundation staff spoke the same language as the people coming from the world of business. Both foundations were friendly territories and at the same time provided tasks tailored to what businessmen could do to contribute to the political project. They used rituals and the logic of sociability taken from the social worlds with which they linked. In fact, much of the G25 organizational format was imported from exclusive CEO clubs such as the Young Presidents Organization: the mentoring of newcomers and the organization of small groups to work on the affective impact of embarking on political activity (Vommaro 2017). PRO leaders asked CEOs for commitments of varying degrees. They managed to articulate different ways CEOs could contribute time and/or money to promote the PRO brand, which, from the activists' point of view, turned their small timely acts (a Facebook post, the organization of a meeting with candidates in their homes) into a coordinated contribution. Hahrie Han's (2014) studies of how civil organizations recruit activists showed that to be successful they must have mobilizers and organizers, that is, those who take on the task of giving newcomers a place in the organization. These two tasks enable the organizational conversion of these newcomers into activists. For example, the PRO leaders who actively participated in these mediation devices established a range of activities that varied widely in terms of the amount of time, resources, and career investment they required of volunteers and in this way adapted these devices to audiences who were not always ready for a more complete conversion into activists or politicians. Also, in provinces where the party had a weak presence, these foundations played the role of local party organizations. G25 Mujeres (G25 Women) played a key role in these activities. Created in 2013, G25 Mujeres enables members of business managers' social environment to become activists. This group enabled members of the upper and upper-middle classes to find

[7] All direct quotes that appear in the chapter were translated from Spanish by the author.
[8] Personal interview with a G25 board member.

a channel for political participation during the time when the Kirchnerist mobilization was dominant.

The PRO's mobilization of managers and CEOs was successful and had two effects: First, it produced the large volume of electoral activism that now forms the core of the PRO party. In 2012, G25 had 800 adherents. By 2013, it had 2,450 adherents, comprising a similar proportion of men and women (G25 2014). By 2014, G25 Women already had three established territorial committees – Capital, North Zone, and West Zone – and claimed to communicate with more than 7,000 women through social networks. By 2008, the PRO had, at the national level, 35,676 adherents. Thus, the volume of activism that G25 added was significant. Second, it produced a massive entry of managers and CEOs into the government: 31 percent of those who occupied senior positions in the government of Cambiemos (initial cabinet) had a senior management role in the private sector before 2015. Among the ministers, in 2017, 50 percent still held positions on the board of directors of private companies (Castellani 2018).

In summary, the PRO provided a variety of opportunities for participation in its core activism, from social media activism to participation in the design of government programs, in proselytizing activities and in electoral control. It combined a permanent – though in many cases a part-time – involvement (Vázquez, Rocca Rivarola, and Cozachcow 2018) with a seasonal activism that was latent in social networks and became particularly intense during electoral campaigns (Vommaro 2017). Thus, the mechanisms of interest aggregation and the social entrenchment of the party generated a permanent infrastructure, of considerable size, but active especially during election season, with the mobilization of all types of volunteers.

SUBNATIONAL VARIATIONS: FROM POLITICAL PARTY TO UNROOTED PARTY

PRO's growth strategy based on experience in local government was successful. However, this strategy posed a challenge for national territorial expansion, which requires combining national appeals and subnational (provincial) anchors (Gibson and Suárez-Cao 2010; Leiras 2007).

The PRO succeeded in establishing mechanisms for coordinating its elites and aggregating interests in the City of Buenos Aires. However, its efforts to build a national party were less successful. According to our argument, the cost of centralized control of the party's brand and electoral strategy by a ruling coalition in the City of Buenos Aires was weak national party building, because the centralized coordination of subnational elites worked as a negative incentive for the recruitment of competitive candidates and grassroots support. The central ruling coalition granted little autonomy to subnational allies. It subordinated representation of subnational interests to its Buenos Aires-based program. In that context, the alliance with the UCR – as a shortcut to building a national anchor that the PRO on its own had failed to accomplish – solved an immediate electoral problem but maintained the organizational weakness of the new party.

Undoubtedly, the nationalization of a party born at the subnational level is critical in a country with a strongly decentralized party system (Gibson and Suárez-Cao 2010; Leiras 2007). As has been observed in other national cases, and with regard to political forces arising from leftist armed groups (Holland 2016), experience in local governance can be a resource for building a party's brand and, if it is successful, demonstrating its efficacy to other districts. It also provides an opportunity to train leaders in the work of governance. Other studies (Muñoz and Dargent 2016) have shown the importance of patronage resources in the establishment of national forces, and in relation to parties' ability to distribute those resources from the national level to the subnational level. Although PRO used local government in both ways, its construction as a national force was less successful, despite the strength of its brand. To a large extent, this is because it did not find in other provinces the same political opportunities that it had in the City of Buenos Aires during its early development, namely an available electorate and weakened traditional parties with social bases whose interests it could articulate and from whom it could recruit ambitious politicians.

Since its beginnings, the new party tried different strategies to nationalize. First, beginning in 2005, and with greater intensity after 2007, it established an alliance with the provincial conservative parties. In part, the PRO inherited this alliance from its merger with the Recrear. With the consolidation of the PRO, the leaders of those parties saw a "historic opportunity" to have a unified national representation, historically a weakness of those forces (Gibson 1996). Likewise, the PRO ruling coalition promised to maintain the autonomy of the new party and protect party boundaries against traditional parties' attempts to colonize it. In a personal interview, a former conservative leader of Córdoba stated,

> the UCeDe never became a political party. And I think the PRO did become one. That is for me the big difference, in addition, UCeDe ended up melting into Peronism, so it never came to power. That is the big difference. . . . It is the first time we have this possibility . . . we never had the possibility of having a national party.[9]

The merger between the PRO and Recrear, which was finalized in June 2010, consolidated Argentina's first national right-wing political force in decades, perhaps since the beginning of the twentieth century. However, beyond Buenos Aires it represented only a minority of politically ambitious conservatives.

The second strategy then consisted of incorporating UCR and Peronist leaders who were dissatisfied with their own parties' strategies. The strategy sought to maintain the division of party labor that existed in the City of Buenos Aires, although in many cases conservative party leaders acted as delegates of the ruling coalition in some districts, by virtue of their bonds of trust with the members of that coalition. To carry out this expansion by incorporating leaders of traditional parties, it was important to have the resources of the government of the City of Buenos Aires. From there, the PRO ruling coalition established a sort of Ministry of Government in charge of the relationship with provincial leaders. They also offered those leaders the use of the PRO brand, associated with management and efficiency. However, this strategy only succeeded at incorporating considerable numbers of leaders in provinces where the traditional parties were strongly divided and/or were not very competitive. In addition, because Macri did not run in presidential elections until 2015, the PRO label was not attractive to subnational politicians without a national reference. For example, in Neuquén, a province governed by a provincial party, some UCR leaders who had approached Macri in 2011 did not run on the PRO lists until 2015.

The third strategy was to recruit prominent figures from the sport, entertainment, business, and NGO worlds who were aligned with the PRO brand. The national party leaders initiated a systematic campaign of scouting to incorporate candidates in different provinces of the country where the party was not well established, or where it needed more socially recognized figures to top their lists. Sports, media, and entertainment

[9] Laura Rodríguez Machado, former conservative leader of Córdoba, then subnational leader of Recrear and finally PRO national senator, personal communication, September 13, 2016.

celebrities topped the PRO electoral lists in districts where the party had a weak presence. The entry of former Boca Juniors footballer Carlos MacAllister and former football referee Héctor Baldassi helped the PRO advance significantly in the 2013 mid-term elections in the provinces of La Pampa (20 percent) and Córdoba (15 percent). Meanwhile the comedian Miguel Del Sel twice came close to winning the governorship of Santa Fe. In that province, a former Peronist leader had organized the PRO party by incorporating anti-Kirchner Peronist leaders, but the party only achieved good electoral results when Del Sel joined. Celebrities from the NGO world, such as Jorge Gronda in Jujuy – a gynecologist and founder of a private health service for low-income people who was named a social entrepreneur by prestigious NGOs – and managers and entrepreneurs publicly known at the local level, such as Facundo Garretón in Tucumán (creator of a financial investment site and board member of the Ashoka social entrepreneurship network), were recruited as candidates. The G25 Foundation played a central role in that task.

The coalition of national leaders tried to maintain high levels of coordination among themselves, as well as centralized control of the party brand, which also enabled them to produce a unified message and image in all districts in which the PRO competed electorally. With this firm control, the party brand remained anchored in its two original components: the party of the newcomers who get involved in politics and management as an action program based on concrete problem solving, that is to say, beyond ideology (Vommaro, Morresi, and Bellotti 2015).

The political communication team commanded by one of the party leaders, the Macri's main collaborator, created manuals for activists and candidates in which criteria for the use of party symbols were established, but which also provided guidelines on how candidates and activists should dress at campaign events and the profiles they should adopt in the photographs taken at those events, which they should then share on social media. They also produced speech manuals and even a periodic summary of what should be said – talking points – on different issues related to the PRO administration and on issues of public debate. The political communication team was also in charge of training the main outsider figures. These people were trained in speaking techniques, sitting for interviews with journalists and face-to-face political communication.

The central ruling coalition also intervened directly in defining the subnational candidates based on opinion polls as well as in their correspondence with the PRO brand. Thus, there were frequent complaints from traditional parties or provincial conservative party leaders who were relegated to lower positions on the electoral lists in order to incorporate outsiders who presented a better image.

The PRO achieved a high degree of homogeneity throughout this process in its public image and discourse, and in the use of the party symbols. However, achieving this level of coordination presented difficulties and produced negative consequences. The difficulties can be seen in the fact that, between 2009 and 2013, the central ruling coalition took control of party subsidiaries in different districts where local leaders ignored instructions sent from the center. These rogue districts included the province of Buenos Aires, where Macri's cousin formed a pattern of alliances that differed from that at the national level, but also Salta, Mendoza, Catamarca, Misiones, Entre Ríos, Chaco, and Tucumán, in all of which an envoy of the central ruling coalition took control of the party at the local level. These interventions displaced rogue leaders but also brought order to the party when it fell into the hands of leaders who had low public prestige or an image inconsistent with the PRO brand.

The negative consequence of these efforts to establish coordination among leaders and between levels via centralized control was the difficulty the PRO encountered advancing the nationalization of the party. Taking PRO participation in federal elections under its own label as an indicator of territorial establishment (Table 3.3), the alliance with Recrear and with provincial conservative parties that took place after 2007 enabled the PRO to increase its degree of nationalization, but left

TABLE 3.3 *Number of districts in which the PRO competed in national elections, according to electoral labels, 2003–2013*

Election	Provinces in which PRO competed	Competed under its own label	Competed with allies under other labels
2003	1	1	0
2005	3	3	0
2007	8	7	1
2009	10	8	2
2011	11	3	8
2013	17	7	10

Source: Author's elaboration based on data from the National Electoral Chamber.

it still short of truly national coverage.[10] The incorporation of Peronist and UCR leaders occurred throughout the period, although with greater intensity after 2009 (when the PRO established an alliance with anti-Kirchner Peronists in some districts). This incorporation gave the party its maximum level of district presence, which decreased as a result of its decision not to participate in the 2011 presidential elections. PRO subsequently maintained its presence in all the districts where it was established, but the number of provinces in which the acronym PRO had low visibility increased, while the number of provinces in which the party controlled its label decreased. In 2013, meanwhile, the two strategies for incorporating cadres – adding leaders of traditional parties and adding outsiders – gave new impetus to the national expansion of the party. Yet after more than ten years of life, the PRO still could not compete in all districts of the country, and only in seven districts did it compete under its own label. The PRO brand maintained its differentiation from the other electoral proposals, but its visibility and national implementation were limited.

Only from 2015 on, with the Cambiemos alliance, did the PRO manage to run candidates in all districts. However, in many districts its subnational presence remained strongly dependent on UCR organization. Although it achieved the degree of electoral growth needed to win a national election by combining forces with its allies, since 2015 the PRO's development as a national party has slowed, leaving certain traditional strongholds in the hands of UCR leaders.

The trajectory of the party in the provinces of the central area of the country (the City of Buenos Aires, the provinces of Buenos Aires, Córdoba, Entre Ríos, and Santa Fe) and, to a lesser extent, in Tucumán, has been an exception to this trend. In the central area of the country, the PRO established political ties with the agricultural sectors, which, according to some studies, became its core constituency (Mangonnet, Murillo, and Rubio 2018). This linkage was consolidated during the Macri administration under the policies developed for that sector. The first measure the Macri government adopted was to eliminate taxes on grain exports that had caused a major conflict between the agricultural sector and Kirchner Peronism in 2008. Even during the financial and fiscal crisis of 2018–19, Macri refused to significantly increase those taxes again (Vommaro and Gené 2019). PRO-Cambiemos enjoys strong electoral support in areas

[10] The PRO was legally recognized as a national party, that is, with the minimum number of affiliates in five or more districts, as of March 6, 2010, after its merger with Recrear.

that are home to intensive grain production (Mangonnet, Murillo, and Rubio 2018), but beyond those areas, PRO failed to establish solid social anchors. Thus, in some provinces, the PRO remains an unrooted party at the local level: a party with a capacity for horizontal coordination among its elites, largely due to the influence of the central ruling coalition, but with a weak capacity to articulate local social demands. In those districts, the UCR or, failing that, some provincial allies, maintain the ties with constituencies socially and culturally related to PRO.

CONCLUSIONS

As a new center-right party, the PRO faced two major challenges. Because it was a new party, it needed to build coordination mechanisms among heterogeneous elites who were recruited in a particular context of (1) the availability of politicians from traditional parties, and (2) interest in party politics on the part of businessmen and NGO activists. The party's ruling coalition, based in the City of Buenos Aires, succeeded in establishing and maintaining party borders (organization, party brand), differentiating the PRO from its competitors and protecting the party from free riders. As a right-wing party, its challenge was to build solid social anchors (to aggregate the interests of its social core constituency) and a broad electorate that extended beyond the traditional core constituency of right-wing political forces (Gibson 1996). Informal mediations and linkage segmentation strategies proved successful in achieving the latter objective. In both cases, the division of labor that allowed the PRO to recruit traditional politicians from other parties without the original ruling coalition losing control of the strategy and the party brand was crucial. The case of the PRO shows, as does that of the UDI in Chile (Luna 2010), that strong cohesion among the ruling coalition is a crucial factor for successful party building. This cohesion is expressed in two central levels of party life: collective moral motivations, associated with both the past and the future (Rosenblatt 2018), and organizational coordination between leaders and factions.

At the time of the PRO's territorial expansion, this sociocultural and organizational cohesion produced divergent effects. Sociocultural cohesion gives the ruling coalition great resilience in the face of internal challenges and external adversity, while maintaining brand consistency (Lupu 2016) in electoral discourse and public policies (Stokes 2001). However, this cohesion creates important difficulties for the party's territorial growth beyond its stronghold and therefore for the establishment of a robust political force.

In countries where multilevel policy involves heterogeneous political traditions, party-building processes require material resources (Muñoz and Dargent 2016) and symbolic resources (Holland 2016) of various kinds. The weaknesses of an organization in its early stages, which are critical in the case of right-wing parties in Argentina, as well as the strategies used to overcome them, can create a path dependence that hinders success. An electoral victory does not necessarily solve those problems. On the contrary, under certain conditions, it can prolong them over time.

The typology proposed in this book thus helps us not only to understand the diachronic variations in the life of an electoral vehicle (its construction as a party, the loss of the capacities associated with a party and its transformation into a diminished subtype), but also its synchronous variations in party systems in which a political force may manifest differently at the local level, depending on the district in which it is observed. In terms of Argentine history, the varying strength of the PRO's social roots in different parts of the country hinder its ability to represent interests beyond its social core in the central agrarian region of the country, consistent with the tradition of the Argentine center-right (O'Donnell 1977).

What were the consequences of the PRO's 2019 electoral defeat on the features of horizontal coordination and aggregation of interests described in this chapter? Although, at the time of writing, it remains too early to draw definitive conclusions, some comments can be made. First, Macri's electoral defeat created a struggle for succession in a strongly top-down party that was built on Macri's unchallenged leadership. The founding leader of the party is no longer the only competitive candidate that PRO can offer to the electorate. Horacio Rodríguez Larreta, mayor of Buenos Aires, now seems to control the PRO's stronghold. Second, the party has embarked upon a process of reorganization that is keeping pace with this competition. Macri appointed a party president to serve as his delegate, while strengthening the presence of provincial leaders to counteract the weight of the City of Buenos Aires – although the growth of the party beyond its core remains an unfinished task. Despite efforts to show a united front to the outside world, these disputes account for a relative weakening of coordination among PRO leaders. Third, the dispute between two sectors within the party has undermined PRO's pragmatic strategy. Macri's party faction now espouses a more openly right-wing and anti-Peronist position, while the pragmatic image that the PRO sought to project seems to have been left in the hands of the group led by Rodríguez Larreta. The probable resolution of the conflict in favor of the moderate wing would entail maintaining the current features of the PRO's party brand as well as its claim to electoral ties beyond its core constituency, but this remains an open question. Finally, during PRO's time in office, the party did not consolidate its organizational capacity to mobilize the business world. Tensions with the internal market-oriented sectors and the economic failure of Macri's administration hinder the possibility of the PRO becoming the main guarantor of business interests in the political arena.

4

Bolivia's Movement toward Socialism

A Political Party Based on and Anchored in Social Movements

Santiago Anria

INTRODUCTION

In Latin America and elsewhere, new political parties rarely succeed (Levitsky et al. 2016). This chapter offers an in-depth account of one of Latin America's rare party-building successes in the contemporary landscape – the Bolivian Movimiento al Socialismo (Movement toward Socialism, MAS) – and explains its organizational development. My central goal is to shed light on current scholarly debates about the internal operations of Latin American parties and, in so doing, draw lessons about party building, political representation, and democratic accountability in the region.

The MAS began as an electoral vehicle for a social movement of coca producers in 1995. It captured the presidency only ten years later, and although the party was forced out of power in 2019, it remains competitive and is Bolivia's only truly national political party. Although the party as a formal bureaucratic organization is weakly developed, and although party leaders often eschew talking about the MAS as a "political party," it meets the two criteria established in this book's theoretical framework at fairly high levels: The MAS does coordinate the behavior of ambitious politicians both in and between election cycles, and it does aggregate collective political preferences. Reflecting its origins in autonomous social mobilization, its main source of organizational power still derives from its close ties to a wide array of popular movements and associations, which provide a formidable mass base.

The MAS is a clear example of what I call "movement-based" parties – parties formed directly by social movements (Anria 2018, 7–11). The ability of movements to transition into political parties, and then to capture national-level government, is remarkable in the contemporary political landscape. Given that their internal politics remain poorly understood and weakly documented, there are great analytical payoffs in studying and drawing lessons from such a paradigmatic example.

The Bolivian MAS shares some similarities with Uruguay's Frente Amplio (Broad Front, FA) (Pérez Bentancur, Piñeiro Rodríguez, and Rosenblatt this volume). They are two of Latin America's most electorally successful and innovative new political parties. Both parties were formed in opposition and created from the bottom up by a wide array of subordinate social actors, including labor and social-movement activists. Both parties became a place of convergence for several actors on the left, and both captured the presidency after spending their formative period in opposition. Both parties, moreover, preserved bottom-up features as they grew territorially, organizationally, and sociologically – and as they exercised national-level power for consecutive terms. Finally, both qualify as political parties on the basis of this volume's theoretical framework.

Yet, despite their similarities, they fulfill the functions of political parties differently. The FA, since early in its formative period, developed strong party organizational structures that boosted the influence of base activists in internal decision-making processes. Thus, the FA case invites us to think about the operation of those channels. The case of the MAS invites us to theorize about the relationships between social movements, party politics, and democratic representation in a more fluid and loose political organization. It illustrates a path whereby the development of weak bureaucratic structures facilitated the concentration of decision-making at the top, enabling the party's top leadership to perform a central role in coordination and interest aggregation, and also provides strong incentives and opportunities for the party's social-movement bases to act autonomously in performing some of the party's functions. The chapter demonstrates, in short, that both the horizontal and vertical components of party building can occur in the absence of major bureaucratization.

This chapter makes two central contributions. First, it deepens our understanding of a "movement path" to successful party building, a path that remains under-theorized. The chapter shows that social movements not only can facilitate the development of new parties, but they also meaningfully shape party organizational models, leadership patterns, and internal operations. Following this book's theoretical framework, the chapter shows that social movements and civic networks – the party's core organizational constituencies – are key actors in processes of horizontal coordination and vertical interest aggregation. Not only does the MAS represent those constituencies in the electoral arena, but those constituencies also coordinate candidate-selection procedures, electoral campaigns, and political strategy. Second, the chapter dissects the most relevant organizational attributes of the MAS. It not only describes how those structures work on the ground, but also links them to broader issues related to democratic representation and accountability.

This chapter is divided into six sections. In the first section, I conceptualize movement-based parties and highlight the distinctive genesis of these parties as organic political expressions of social movements. In the second section, I classify the Bolivian MAS as a movement-based party. In the third section, I explain the origins and organizational evolution of the MAS. I trace, in particular, the transition from being a local movement of coca producers to a national party with strikingly heterogeneous social bases and hybrid organizational features. In the fourth section, I discuss the weakness of formal party structures. In the fifth section, I elaborate on two critical processes of political horizontal coordination and vertical interest aggregation within the MAS – candidate selection and national policymaking – where weak bureaucratic development generates important incentives for the party's bases to operate with independence and shape party decision-making. In the sixth section, I provide some conclusions.

MOVEMENT-BASED PARTIES

As the social-movement literature recognizes, many social-movement activists are hostile toward, or at least wary of, political parties and generally oppose participating in electoral politics. Part of this hostility can be explained by the imperatives of electoral contestation and office seeking – a situation that often leads to a widening gap between the objectives of the party or its leaders and those of the movements. Movements have their own set of goals, and they seek to avoid party co-optation and often reject the horse-trading politics that lie at the heart of coalition building. Parties prioritize vote seeking, and restive social movements can be unreliable partners. Often, then, parties and movements operate independently of one another, and avoid the liabilities associated with trying to broker some sort of alliance. And yet, sometimes movements go as far as to form parties, through which they can gain access to formal electoral and policymaking arenas. These are best described as movement-based parties.[1]

Movement-based parties share two attributes. First, they are parties directly formed by social-movement activists and leaders. This means they have a different logic of party formation than that stipulated in the dominant, Downsian models of party formation (Downs 1957). In the latter influential models, parties are seen as the creation of strategic legislators; they are depicted as electoral vehicles for political elites and as structures largely detached from their social bases (Aldrich 1995, 29–50). By contrast, movement-based parties are the direct creation of militant movement activists and grassroots leaders forged in the heat of social mobilization who decide to enter into the electoral arena and compete for office while sustaining collective action in the streets; they are generally formed as opposition parties or as regime challengers, and they follow a distinctively "bottom-up" logic of party genesis. In short, if in Aldrich's (1995) dominant model the logic of party formation consists of rootless political entrepreneurs in search of social bases, movement-based parties stand out because they follow the reverse logic: they begin life as movements.

Second, movement-based parties are parties with a core constituency of grassroots social movements.[2] This definition parallels Levitsky's (2003) definition of labor-based parties, with grassroots social movements rather than organized labor as the sponsoring organizations and core constituency. Movement-based parties are also different from Kitschelt's (2006) analytical characterization of movement parties, which are almost always the electoral vehicles of a social movement mobilized around a single issue (Kitschelt 2006). By contrast, movement-based parties are broader alliances of various movements and other popular organizations and, as such, they are better prepared to incorporate a broader set of issues, actors, and demands. My conceptualization is also different from della Porta et al.'s (2017) definition of movement parties, which stresses the strength of the associational linkages between parties and movements. In della Porta et al.'s definition, movement parties are those that have particularly strong organizational and external links with social movements. My definition of movement-based parties also considers those connections but emphasizes

[1] This section draws heavily on Anria (2018).

[2] The term "core constituency" refers to specific sectors that provide financial resources, policymaking support, and guidance to a political party (Gibson 1996).

that these parties are the direct creation of social movements. They are, in short, founded directly by movements.

In contemporary Latin America, examples of these parties include, but are not limited to, the Bolivian MAS, the Brazilian Partido dos Trabalhadores (Workers' Party, PT), the Ecuadorian Pachakutik, the Salvadorian Frente Farabundo Martí para la Liberación Nacional (Farabundo Martí National Liberation Front, FMLN), and the Uruguayan and Chilean FA.[3] The rise in popularity of some of these parties, and especially their ascension to national-level power in some countries, generated theoretically relevant questions at the interface of the party–society nexus: How do these parties work internally? How do they perform representative functions? How, in particular, do they coordinate the actions of their multiple constitutive parts so the organization functions as a unit?

Although the aforementioned parties are similar in their emergence as electoral vehicles for social-movement entrepreneurs, they do not have the same starting points in their founding organizational characteristics. For example, while the Brazilian PT developed a bureaucratic, centrally organized party organization with hierarchical leadership structures, the MAS did not develop these kinds of structures and developed instead a looser organizational model. As I discuss in the following, this founding organizational characteristic enabled the party to sustain a great deal of grassroots participation even as the party formed national governments – and it has been strongly resistant to change (Anria 2018).

Movement-based parties offer a unique opportunity to examine the relationships between social movements, party politics, and democratic representation. First, they provide insight into the role that movements can play in facilitating successful party building.[4] Existing studies tend to focus on explaining how the inherited infrastructures of interest associations help to explain variation in party strength. As recent empirical work shows, the presence of a robust associational

[3] Pérez Bentancur, Piñeiro Rodríguez, and Rosenblatt (this volume) do not classify the FA as a movement-based party because the FA, unlike the MAS, was not formed directly by social movements. It still has deep roots and connections with social movements.

[4] Keck (1992) focuses on labor unions in the formation and early expansion of the PT; Pérez Bentancur, Piñeiro Rodríguez, and Rosenblatt (2020) focus on labor unions in the formation of the FA; Van Cott (2005) and Madrid (2012) focus on indigenous movements and the formation of ethnic parties in the Andes; Van Dyck (2016) focuses on urban popular movements and rural unions in explaining the origins of Mexico's Partido de la Revolución Democrática (Party of the Democratic Revolution, PRD). On the Mexican PRD and its ties with social movements, see also Combes's chapter in this volume.

inheritance can provide invaluable resources to emerging political parties that allow them to take off and that contribute to their long-term empowerment (Levitsky et al. 2016). New parties are more likely to establish deep roots, and also to persist over time, where party builders can draw upon the mobilizing structures of preexisting civic organizations (Cyr 2017).

Second, movement-based parties are a crucial channel by which those civil society actors can gain access to and effective representation in formal electoral and policymaking arenas. Because the organizational boundaries of these parties are fuzzy and permeable, they offer unique opportunities to examine a type of political organization that, in recent years, has become common in both new and established democratic regimes (della Porta et al. 2017; Roberts 2019). They offer lessons not only for the comparative study of political parties but also concerning the impact that movements have on political institutions.

THE MAS AS A MOVEMENT-BASED PARTY

The MAS is an especially interesting case because it deviates sharply from the conventional theorizing about this type of party: defying theoretical expectations, the MAS has followed a different organizational trajectory that has facilitated grassroots impact and constrained elite control, even after assuming and exercising power at the national level. The party's social-movement origins not only facilitated successful party building, but also enabled the party to maintain high levels of grassroots participation and to develop structures of accountability where movements continue to influence, constrain, and hold the party leadership accountable. The party achieved, in short, high levels of horizontal coordination and vertical interest aggregation as a governing organization. Although the party did not invest heavily in the development of formal bureaucratic structures (as did Uruguay's FA; Pérez Bentancur, Piñeiro Rodríguez, and Rosenblatt this volume), it represents strongly organized social constituencies, and these play a leading role coordinating party action. As such, the case of the MAS can offer important lessons to key debates articulated in the book's theoretical framework. The case invites us to think about how loose organizational formats may shape modes of horizontal coordination in political campaigns, in the selection of candidates for electoral office, and the vertical aggregation of interests once in power. It can also contribute to our understanding of how mechanisms of social accountability develop and operate on the ground.

This last issue is crucial for democratic politics. When democratic participation within governing parties is deficient, those parties can more easily become vehicles for the unrestrained will of political elites and even dominant single leaders. In such contexts, the voices of regular citizens or even of the party's own social bases may not be heard, thereby hindering the average citizen's participation in political life while enhancing the discretion of the party leadership – a condition conducive to personalistic politics.

At the party level, using Hirschman's (1970) terminology, where groups and individuals that constitute a party's social base have limited opportunities to exert "voice" in party decisions, it is generally much harder to establish and maintain high levels of organizational loyalty, partisan engagement, and mobilization capacity (Anria and Cyr 2017; Pérez Bentancur, Rodríguez, and Rosenblatt 2019; Rosenblatt 2018). At the broader political regime level, where instances for bottom-up input are significantly narrow while in power – or where there is little room for the party's social bases to play a meaningful role in horizontal coordination and vertical aggregation – bait-and-switch policymaking may become more likely (Roberts 2014a). This, in turn, can negatively affect the consistency of the party brand and impact the stability of the overall party system (Lupu 2016).

When governing parties are more open to bottom-up input, by contrast, there are greater opportunities to establish checks on the decisions of their leaders and constrain their strategic behavior and hierarchical control. In such contexts, it is less likely that the party will become a vehicle to advance the goals of a personalistic leader – even if oligarchic temptations are readily available. The presence of channels to exert "voice" provides incentives for the social bases to shape important decisions, as these bases become de facto veto actors within the organization. Developing greater opportunities for bottom-up input, moreover, makes it comparatively easier for these parties to maintain strong grassroots linkages as well as to breed organizational loyalty, partisan engagement, and mobilization (Rosenblatt 2018). At the broader regime level, when a governing party establishes and upholds well-developed opportunities for bottom-up grassroots participation, instances of bait-and-switch policymaking are less likely – a condition conducive to policy stability. This, in turn, makes the consistency of the party brand more likely to stick and the party system more stable (Lupu 2016).

When governing parties – especially those formed by social movements pushing for inclusion – are more open, they may generate opportunities and incentives for the political empowerment of traditionally marginalized groups by boosting the input that those groups have in the political power game. Seen from this angle, then, movement-based parties that remain open and responsive can become effective channels for the integration of interests from excluded groups. Inclusion, in turn, is both a good in itself and also has instrumental value: it enhances participation and empowers citizens to demand better representation.

ORIGINS AND EVOLUTION

The MAS emerged in 1995. It started out as a small, localized party that was initially regarded as an "instrument" of a specific social group, the *cocaleros* in the Chapare. Although the MAS started out small, it experienced very rapid growth to become the electoral vehicle for a broad set of urban and rural grassroots social movements. It expanded to Bolivia's largest cities and in less than a decade became the country's largest party, as its leader, Evo Morales, was elected to the presidency in 2005 and then reelected in 2009 and 2014. The MAS achieved territorial and organizational expansion not so much through the development of an elaborate territorial party infrastructure, but by tapping into the organizational apparatus of existing mass organizations and civic networks and integrating them within the party. It followed a social movement path to party building.

The history of the MAS has been widely documented.[5] It bears noting, however, how truly organic and bottom-up the party and the leadership were at the party's founding. Evo Morales rose to the fore of the *cocalero* movement in the heat of the cycles of contention around coca eradication in the early 1980s (Sivak 2010). Morales had started as the Secretary of Sports for his local union in 1982 – the San Francisco Syndicate – but then worked his way up the union ladder and was elected as the Executive Secretary of the Federation of the Tropics in 1988 (Sivak 2010). His leadership was distinctively bottom-up. Cocalero unionism was Morales' political school. It marked his " ... political origin, and for many years he understood politics as the sum of assemblies, negotiations with politicians and officials, and fights in the streets and roads" (Sivak 2010, 43).

Before the MAS became what is known as "the MAS," Morales and other peasant leaders formed several electoral vehicles based on the idea of

[5] See, e.g., Grisaffi (2018).

self-representation of popular social actors – an idea that had been on the agenda of rural unions since the early 1990s (García Linera, Chávez León, and Costa Monje 2004). Attaining legal registration was not easy, however; it happened only after *cocaleros* borrowed the legal registration of a dying party, the Bolivian Movimiento al Socialismo-Unzaguista (Movement Toward Socialism-Unzaguista, MAS-U), which enabled them to participate in national elections using the MAS's legal registration, its emblems, and its blue, black, and white colors. The union leaders who founded the MAS still reject the party designation and refer to the MAS as a "political instrument" or, better yet, a direct extension of the union organization (Van Cott 2005; Grisaffi 2018).

The MAS won four congressional seats in the 1997 elections. A major turning point for the party was in 2002, when Evo Morales finished second in his presidential bid. Although the MAS did not capture the presidency in 2002, the size of its parliamentary block grew from four to thirty-five representatives. By 2002, the MAS had become Bolivia's main opposition party and significant institutional positions in Congress would then serve as a power base for future elections. The party's major breakthrough was in 2005 when Morales was elected to the presidency in a landslide victory.

The MAS's ascent to national power was meteoric. In its rapid march to power, between 1995 and 2005, the party became a hybrid fusion of party and movements and developed two strikingly distinctive social coalitions. The central coalition – or the party's core constituency – is highly stable and targeted; it is based in Bolivia's rural sector and consists of the *cocaleros* in the Chapare, as well as three national-level peasant associations, which conceive of the MAS as their creation under their tutelage.[6] In this segment, the MAS is organized from the bottom up and relies on the collective, assembly-like (*asambleísta*) style of decision-making utilized in Bolivia's rural social movements – especially those in the country's highlands.

The MAS maintains strong organic links to its core constituency, and there are permanent interactions between grassroots leaders and party

[6] These organizations include the Confederación Sindical Única de Trabajadores Campesinos de Bolivia (Unique Confederation of Rural Laborers of Bolivia, CSUTCB); the Confederación Sindical Intercultural de Comunidades de Bolivia (Syndicalist Confederation of Intercultural Communities of Bolivia, CSCIB); and the Confederación Nacional de Mujeres Campesinas Indígenas Originarias de Bolivia – Bartolina Sisa (Bartolina Sisa National Confederation of Campesino, Indigenous, and Native Women of Bolivia, CNMCIOB-BS).

leaders, who work closely together selecting party candidates and defining party electoral strategy. This often happens in meetings called *ampliados*, which are important spaces for horizontal coordination. From the point of view of the party leadership, *ampliados* and other forms of union meetings, like *cabildos*, serve not only to shape party strategy but also to collect valuable information from the rank and file.[7] In those meetings, there are also strong pressures from below to keep the leadership accountable to the rank and file over aspects of policy, a pattern that is closely associated with the movement origins of the MAS and the legacies of social mobilization that forged the party organization since its inception. However, it bears noting that the idea of strict bottom-up control in this segment is not always empirically accurate. As has been documented, the MAS's top leadership does not always respect the wishes of the social bases, and there are in fact growing tensions and challenges of coordination between the rank and file and the party leadership over aspects of party strategy and policy (Anria 2018; Grisaffi 2018).

The peripheral coalition is broader and more flexible. It relies on a wider set of urban-popular organizations in Bolivia's largest cities, where neighborhood associations, trade unions, cooperatives, and other forms of local collective organization play a key articulatory role. This expansion of the party to urban areas was based, on the one hand, on the ability of the MAS to vertically aggregate interests and bundle issues together by finding common programmatic ground, articulating the claims for a remarkably diverse array of movements that were mobilized in opposition to neoliberalism and extractive policies in the late 1990s and early 2000s – a process by which the MAS became an "instrument" for a broader set of subordinate social actors. On the other hand, the strategy used to attract these more diverse peripheral constituencies combined attempts to co-opt the leadership of local organizations with the pursuit of political alliances with established center-left parties in hopes of reaching middle class segments (Anria 2013).

In this regard, the MAS provides an example of a party that relies on a clearly segmented linkage strategy to mobilize different constituencies (Luna 2014). The different electoral strategies pursued by the MAS to reach core and peripheral constituencies are, at the same time, associated

[7] In my observations during these meetings, Morales, who is often present, usually beings by telling grassroots leaders and the rank and file that he is there "to listen to them," to "inform them about the things that we are doing in government," and "to ask you [affiliates] and your leaders to come up with proposals."

with different organizational formats in each segment. On the one hand, the MAS's rural roots reflect patterns of bottom-up organization and organic movement–party linkages, a pattern that has facilitated some degree of grassroots control over the leadership and is associated with the party's "movementist" origins. On the other hand, this ten-year period of rapid growth and extension into urban areas – and the evolution of the party apparatus in power, with growing access to patronage resources – posed important challenges to the party's original, bottom-up organizational characteristics. The party expansion fostered not only the emergence of top-down mobilization strategies but also the co-optation of community- and social-movement leaders into mid-level government positions – a process that at the same time compromised the autonomy of many civil society groups (Zuazo 2010). Although expansion posed important challenges to the party's bottom-up foundational characteristics, the party's grassroots social bases found ways to preserve relative autonomy and replicate the party's genetic imprint as expansion occurred.

This is in part because the party adopted, from its early days, a loose bureaucratic structure, which facilitated the reproduction over time of the party's DNA. The absence of those structures as transmission belts contributed to the de facto concentration of power in the hands of Evo Morales, whose leadership became increasingly personalistic and plebiscitarian (Madrid 2012). This mode of top-down horizontal coordination is similar to the one described by Conaghan (this volume) in her description of Correa's Alianza PAIS in Ecuador. At the same time, the weak bureaucratic development of the party provided opportunities for the party's social bases to act autonomously, with few bureaucratic constraints. This meant that, as organizational expansion took place, MAS-affiliated movements in Bolivia retained significant degrees of autonomy from Morales and the MAS and continued to influence, constrain, and hold the party's leadership accountable.

To summarize, the MAS was formed over twenty years ago, and it became Bolivia's largest party. After ten years in opposition and thirteen in national power, it is truly remarkable that the party has retained several founding organizational characteristics. The MAS does not function under a purely bottom-up logic, however. Rather, it operates as a hybrid organization that combines top-down leadership by a dominant personality, weak bureaucratic development, and the bottom-up power of autonomous social mobilization. Although party leaders do not refer to the MAS as a party and prefer to call the MAS a "political instrument," it meets the two criteria established in this book's theoretical framework:

The MAS does coordinate the behavior of ambitious politicians both in and between elections, and it does vertically aggregate interests. For both dimensions, formal party structures play a marginal role, as I discuss in the pages that follow, and the bulk of coordination and interest aggregation within the party occurs through nonbureaucratic channels.

WEAK PARTY STRUCTURES

The bureaucracy of the MAS is weakly developed, both nationally and subnationally.[8] The party has limited professional paid staff, equipment, or records of membership and finances. Its headquarters are located in a modest office in La Paz, where members of the Dirección Nacional (National Directorate) meet at least once a month to coordinate activities. However, formal leadership bodies such as the National Directorate and the Direcciones Departamentales (Departmental Directorates) lack independent authority vis-à-vis MAS officeholders, particularly the president and his ministers, and also prominent leaders of allied civil society groups who often have an upper hand in coordinating party activity.[9] Prominent political figures within the MAS see formal leadership bodies as "empty shells" with no real power and little capacity for coordination.

Formal party organs – whether at the local, departmental, or national levels – have little independent power for shaping competitive processes of candidate selection, campaign strategies, and defining overall party strategy in electoral periods. They also have very limited influence in coordinating legislative behavior once in office. Although party organs do not have sufficient decision-making autonomy or even independent capacity to generate decisions, they play an important role in dealing with intra-party conflicts, especially conflicts between MAS-affiliated social movements. Instead of relying on party organs to generate decisions, influential figures within the MAS rely more on *ad hoc* committees for input on specific topics.[10]

[8] This is a difference between the MAS and Uruguay's FA (Pérez Bentancur, Piñeiro Rodríguez, and Rosenblatt this volume).

[9] Positional authority within the party generally does not correspond to "real" authority, legitimacy, or political influence. The exception is Morales, who is both the president of the MAS National Directorate and the Executive Secretary of the overarching union of coca growers in Bolivia's Chapare region.

[10] For example, an ad hoc political committee was formed to design the strategy for the 2005 electoral campaign. Party organs, as independent structures, played no role. Instead, key actors included individuals who would then become ministers under the first Morales government. The tendency to bypass party organs became more pronounced as the MAS

According to the party statute, the highest decision-making body is the Congreso Nacional Ordinario (Regular National Congress, CON). The CON invites delegates of MAS-affiliated movements and organizations to participate and elect members to the party's National Directorate. It also invites allied movements and popular organizations to approve, reform, and/or modify the party's Declaración de Principios (Declaration of Principles), the Programa de Gobierno (Program of Government), and the Estatuto Orgánico (Statute) (Article 18, c). In addition, it reviews disciplinary sanctions imposed by the Comisión de Ética (Ethics Commision) and resolves disputes over statutory provisions. Another important party convention includes the Congreso Orgánico (Congress), which meets to decide matters of party organization and fundamental questions about the party's future (Article 19). These party conferences meet regularly and ensure a great deal of internal grassroots participation. Yet, although they help to coordinate campaign activities and resolve conflicts during and between election cycles, they lack real independent power.

Party structures also play a marginal role in coordinating the relationships between the MAS and its representatives in Congress. In fact, there is nothing in the party's statute that specifies the terms of those relationships. The expectation, however, is that representatives work closely with their social constituencies; that they contribute financially to the party organization; and that they regularly attend party conventions to inform authorities and the rank and file about their work in Congress.

Elected representatives for the MAS are only related to the party structure indirectly, as they are agents of many principals. Many have been nominated by civil society organizations with which they retain strong connections; others have been nominated "from above" due to their individual contribution to the overall party list; and finally, they all have been elected by voters, most of whom are neither party nor social movement members. The lack of a strong party structure coordinating legislative activity means that representatives typically lack common socialization inside the party. And because they come from multiple sectors of society, they have no common socialization outside the party either. This creates incentives for the executive branch to centralize power and discipline the behavior of MAS representatives. Most of the legislators I interviewed commented that they have limited capacity to initiate

became a governing party, revealing an increasing weakness of the formal party structures vis-à-vis power holders.

important legislation as independent agents. And, in fact, most legislative proposals are brought to the floor by the executive branch. The party's loose bureaucratic structures, again, create strong incentives for the executive branch to develop its own instances of coordination "from above," in order for the party's top leadership to centralize power and discipline the legislative behavior of MAS representatives.[11] Their behavior in office follows an executive-enforced party discipline that, at times, is at odds with the logic of constituency representation, with positions imposed by the executive often prevailing.[12]

In sum, though formal party structures do exist and operate on a regular basis, they lack independent power and their role is fairly limited. Coordination between the party leadership, party representatives in Congress, and the party's social movement bases happen mostly through nonbureaucratic and informal channels. I discuss how these channels operate in practice by examining a key process of horizontal coordination – the nomination of party candidates for electoral office – and a central process of political interest aggregation – national policymaking.

HORIZONTAL COORDINATION AND VERTICAL INTEREST AGGREGATION

Candidate Selection

As the editors of this volume rightly note, a central process of horizontal coordination is the nomination of party candidates for electoral office. It shapes who rises to leadership positions and who actually gets into public office using the party label. A critical question is then: how broad or

[11] My observations indicate that such efforts occurred in the vice presidency, where representatives met weekly to decide on legislative strategy. The presence of the president or the vice president and of key ministers was not uncommon in these meetings. The idea behind the meetings was to generate an internal space for debate before legislative proposals were sent to Congress, and to avoid open discussion on the legislative floor by projecting an image of unity. While some representatives conceived of this as a collective agenda-setting exercise designed to ensure a balance between territorial and sectoral demands, others saw it as an imposition from above.

[12] Rebeca Delgado, a former president of the Chamber of Deputies, commented: "If an individual legislator brings in a legislative proposal for a specific project, the executive branch generally does not send any financing for it. This leads me to say that, in a context where the executive gives you the agenda, constituency representation is undervalued and not fully exercised" (interview with Rebeca Delgado).

narrow is grassroots participation in the process? Both in opposition and after the MAS assumed national power, the party's grassroots social bases retained significant influence over the selection of party candidates for elective office, even though party leaders have sought to concentrate power in their own hands. The capacity of the grassroots social bases to wield at least some degree of control is key to ensuring vertical accountability and facilitating democratic representation.

No clear rules guide selection processes within the MAS. According to its statute, the MAS is "the political and ideological branch of the social organizations that represent Bolivia's cultural diversity in rural and urban areas" (Article 5).[13] The statute further stipulates that "members and activists participate in the different levels of the political structure [of the MAS] through their natural social organizations, which guide the work of these leaders and extend their own loyalty, work, and honesty to the structure of the MAS" (Article 9).

According to the party statute, moreover, the organizational structure of the MAS is decentralized along territorial and functional lines. The statute recognizes directorates at no fewer than eight levels: national, departmental, regional, provincial, municipal, indigenous territories, districts, and sectors (Article 12). For example, it recognizes the organizational structures of the social organizations and unions at the rural level, the districts and social sectors in urban areas, as well as the autonomous territories of indigenous peoples.

Although the party statute clearly defines the internal mechanisms for selecting leaders for internal leadership bodies such as the National Directorate, as noted previously, it is less clear on the procedures that regulate the selection of candidates for elective public office. Article 37 says that it is a responsibility of the National Directorate of the MAS to

> coordinate and respect the modes of selection, as well as the norms and procedures used by social organizations for the creation of the candidate lists – for national assemblies, departmental assemblies, regional or provincial assemblies, municipal governments, districts and sectors – that the MAS will present in electoral contests.

In short, there is no unified candidate selection method within the party, and the MAS employs several selection methods across the country. Generally, however, the MAS delegates responsibilities and control to the movements and civic networks that are present in a given electoral district. Generally, once candidates are prescreened and nominated by those

[13] All direct quotes that appear in the chapter were translated from Spanish by the author.

organizations, they then become candidates for the MAS – they use the same campaign logo, the party emblems and colors, and the party platform.[14]

It bears noting, however, that the degree of grassroots influence within the party varies widely across different localities, indicating striking levels of internal heterogeneity. Some of those methods, or how they unfold, help to diffuse power territorially and among many grassroots actors; they often act as countervailing bottom-up correctives to hierarchy and concentrated authority. Other methods help to concentrate power at the top (Anria 2018).

It also bears noting that party structures are unevenly developed across the country, and that, indeed, party builders have invested differently in creating formal party structures across social constituencies. For the most part, even where those structures exist, as in Santa Cruz and Cochabamba, those structures are strikingly irrelevant in shaping candidate selection outcomes. What really matters, however, is the configuration of civil society, or the nature of party–society relations. In electoral districts where civil society actors are strong, united, and aligned with the MAS, they can most effectively defy the tendencies toward top-down control by the leadership. Where civil society actors are strongly organized but lack unity, top-down elite choices are more likely to prevail. A similar pattern occurs where civil society is weak.

The MAS is one single party but it looks and operates strikingly differently in different environments based on the configuration of civil society and the nature of party-movement connections. These patterns can be seen as both the result of a deliberate mode of party development that privileges fluidity versus party institutionalization and as a reflection of existing de facto power distributions within the MAS and its social allies – and also among these actors themselves.

The influence of densely organized grassroots actors over candidate selection – over who represents them in high electoral office using the MAS label – has been highly consequential in the Bolivian political arena: it served as a crucial mechanism of political inclusion that led to the increased representation of previously underrepresented groups in both national and subnational political arenas. Table 4.1 illustrates the major trend lines. While the percentage of middle-class professionals has decreased from 48.7 percent in the 1993–97 legislative period to 17.7 in

[14] Failures of coordination among grassroots actors usually create an organizational space for the leadership to centralize power and dominate candidate selection from the top.

TABLE 4.1 *Representatives' occupations prior to being elected to Congress*

	1993–97	1997–2002	2002–06	2006–10	2010–14
Public Administration	14.2	16.3	21.9	16.5	18.6
Middle-Class Professions	48.7	37.8	28.1	25.0	17.7
Politician	4.3	4.1	7.6	7.3	11.1
Workers, Artisans, and Primary Sector	3.9	11.2	11.2	18.6	26.3
Transportation	–	2.0	1.2	4.2	5.2
Business and Private Sector	24.0	26.5	27.3	27.4	19.0
Retirees, Students, Other	7.7	2.0	2.8	1.0	2.1
Sample Size	74	98	80	96	97

Source: Zegada and Komadina (2014, 57).

the 2010–14 period, the percentage of peasants, artisans, and both formal and informal sector workers – groups strongly linked with the MAS – grew from 3.9 percent to 26.3 percent in the same period.

Groups that gained increased representation through their links with the MAS include peasant unions, cooperative miners, transport unions, and urban workers in Bolivia's large informal sector, among others. Partially as a result of this political inclusion, the sociodemographic composition of elected representatives has changed dramatically in the country, such that there is an increasing number of women, as well as members of indigenous, peasant, and urban-popular groups.[15] Today, representative institutions at the national and subnational levels more closely mirror Bolivia's social and cultural diversity – an exceptional change in a society characterized by deep ethnic divisions and social exclusion.[16]

[15] Bolivia's 2009 Constitution established seven special seats for indigenous peoples and Afro-Bolivians. Although these "special" seats are a key component in the construction of Bolivia's Plurinational State, it would be historically inaccurate to attribute them to the MAS; rather, they were put on the agenda by lowland and highland indigenous movements during the Constituent Assembly. By the same token, although there was a shift to greater representation of women after the 2006 Constituent Assembly, this increase cannot be attributable only to the MAS; it is, rather, a by-product of the mobilization of Bolivia's women's movement. Bolivia introduced a gender parity law with the 2009 constitution.

[16] Zegada and Komadina (2014) reached similar conclusions. To be sure, as Wolff (2018b) notes, greater political inclusiveness in Bolivia is "far from egalitarian or universal" and has brought about new exclusions. For one thing, the national peasant organizations that

The impact of inclusion on representation is also felt strongly at the subnational level, where greater representation of previously marginalized groups consolidated since the MAS came to power (Zegada and Komadina 2014). These representatives enjoy comparatively higher levels of autonomy from the executive than do representatives in the Asamblea Nacional Plurinacional (Plurinational National Assembly) (Zegada and Komadina 2014).

Policymaking

As the editors of this volume note, policymaking is a critical process of interest aggregation. The way in which parties set agenda items, priorities, and policy choices once in office is of crucial importance because it reveals who actually wields power within the party. In the case of the MAS, the party's grassroots social bases wielded significant influence over the crafting of public policies, even though the party's top leadership concentrated a great deal of power during its tenure in office. However, formal leadership bodies never played an important decision-making role and they lacked authority vis-à-vis MAS office holders. In more general terms, party organs do not generate policies or shape party strategy. Political interest aggregation does occur within the party, but it happens mostly though informal channels. As key advisor to the National Directorate Ximena Centellas commented in a personal interview: "The formal party organs at the local, departmental, and national levels are 'political' bodies, and, for the most part, they do not have the strength or the experience to propose anything, really" (interview with Ximena Centellas; also with Concepción Ortiz).

As discussed, the lack of a strong party structure providing policy guidance also means that representatives lack common socialization inside the party. The result is that, when in power, the executive branch played the upper hand in shaping the legislative behavior of MAS representatives – mostly through informal channels. In fact, many of the MAS representatives I interviewed expressed high levels of discontent with this decision-making pattern, conceiving of themselves as relatively powerless

founded the MAS have enjoyed privileged access to and direct participation in policymaking, whereas identity-oriented indigenous movements (e.g., Confederación de Pueblos Indígenas del Oriente Boliviano/Bolivian Confederation of Eastern Indigenous Peoples, CIDOB and Consejo Nacional de Ayllus y Markas del Qullasuyu/National Council of Ayllus and Markas of the Qullasuyu, CONAMAQ) have been comparatively sidelined from the policy process (Silva 2017; Silva and Rossi 2018).

to generate independent decisions. It is telling that most of them could not identify important or controversial legislative proposals that they had introduced to Congress.

While MAS representatives lacked independent influence while the party was in power, there were elements in the organization of the MAS that worked against the top-down control of the party leadership and that functioned as effective channels of political interest aggregation. Most prominently, the party's loose bureaucratic structure provided – and continues to provide – opportunities and incentives for the social bases to act autonomously, with few bureaucratic constraints. While the party was in power, this allowed MAS-affiliated groups to place issues and priorities on the agenda or block and veto executive proposals. Examples of this can be observed in the behavior of representatives of the transportation sector or cooperative miners, two of the most powerful groups that gained representation through the MAS. Both became pressure groups from within and made it difficult for the MAS to pass legislation that threatened their group interests. And they also became pressure groups from without, leading to resistance to legislation in the streets. In general, the capacity of the party's social bases to mount and sustain autonomous collective action often helped to promote responsiveness and leadership accountability to organized constituencies in a more or less continuous way.

While the MAS wielded power, mobilized pressure from below generally served as a mechanism to aggregate political interests. It helped to bring issues to the public agenda and forced the party leadership to negotiate and reach compromises with social allies, which contributed to maintaining the party's responsiveness to (at least parts of) its grassroots social bases. This happened at two levels. On the one hand, sponsoring and allied groups generated decisions by putting issues and priorities on the public agenda. In fact, the policy influence of the party's social bases should not be overlooked because decision-making was an interactive, negotiated, and contentious process (Anria 2018). This means that the party leadership in power could not impose its agenda without facing challenges, and setting the agenda requires consultation and negotiation.

Consultations over policy happened mostly through informal channels, however. Not only did Morales consult about strategic decisions with the leadership of major popular movements, but he also included their demands, claims, and priorities on the agenda. The overwhelming majority of these consultation channels, however, were and still are nonbureaucratic and noninstitutionalized. An example would be the Encuentro Plurinacional de Cochabamba (Cochabamba Plurinational Summit) of December 2011, which was an ad hoc meeting convened by Morales and the MAS to aggregate collective interests and receive input on public policies from below.[17]

On the other hand, sponsoring and allied groups generally had constraining capacities. This refers to the veto and countermobilization power of the party's social bases. Social mobilization erupted several times during Morales' governments – in 2010, forcing Morales to reverse his decree ending gasoline subsidies, and again in 2011 when the government stated its intention to build a highway through an autonomous indigenous territory – the Territorio Indígena y Parque Nacional Isiboro Sécure (Isiboro Sécure Indigenous Territory and National Park, TIPNIS). Here, too, Morales was forced to back down. In both cases, Morales' capacity to govern unhindered by the demands of his organized social bases was at play. Each time, Morales failed.[18]

The vertical interest aggregation capacity that the MAS initially achieved on its road to power became much more complicated once the MAS took power, and interest aggregation became especially difficult after the aforementioned TIPNIS crisis. In its aftermath, the MAS proceeded with a form of state-led developmentalism that alienated some of the indigenous movements that had come together behind the MAS when the party was in opposition, leading to harsh conflicts between the MAS and its social movement bases over aspects of policy.

Despite co-optation attempts, groups linked to the MAS maintained a strong capacity for autonomous collective action, particularly when seen in comparative perspective. Their capacity to mobilize autonomously helped to reproduce the party's "genetic imprint" over time and also provided a social accountability mechanism by which social allies could steer policy in their preferred direction – thereby enhancing vertical accountability (Conaghan 2018; Wolff 2018b). By responding to mobilized pressure from below, the party remained relatively open and vibrant between election cycles, which helps to explain its political longevity (Anria and Huber 2018). In Bolivia's MAS, moreover, mobilization

[17] By the end of the summit, which ensured the participation of a wide array of allied and nonallied groups, seventy legislative proposals were made and sent to Congress. Critics argue that the MAS uses these types of meetings instrumentally to boost its image and its alleged participatory ethos when its relationships with social movements are contested in the streets.

[18] These dynamics have been observed in additional instances (Mayorga 2019; Silva 2017).

turned interest aggregation into a contentious bargaining game between the MAS and its social allies, where in the absence of strong national and local party structures serving as transmission belts, such groups regularly forced the party to respond to (or at least try to reconcile) mobilized pressure from below in a continuous way.[19]

CONCLUSIONS

Best described as a movement-based party, the MAS is not the creation of strategic legislators devoid of social bases (*à la* Aldrich 1995); it is, rather, the creation of densely organized social actors, which still form the party's core constituency – its anchor. The party's deep roots in autonomous social movements set the case apart from other electoral vehicles discussed in this volume.

More than twenty years since the party's founding, with thirteen of those years spent in national-level power, the MAS still does not have an elaborate bureaucratic structure. Yet, it meets the two criteria established in this book's theoretical framework at fairly high levels: The MAS does coordinate the behavior of ambitious politicians both in and between election cycles, and it does aggregate collective political preferences in office. The bulk of this horizontal coordination and political interest aggregation, however, occurs through nonbureaucratic, informal, and often-contentious channels – and among the very same organized mass constituencies that spawned and shaped the party. The MAS not only represents those constituencies in the electoral arena, but also coordinates party strategy and government action with them. Critical internal processes, including the selection of candidates for elective office, provide good examples of how the party functions. They also show how, in the absence of a strong bureaucratic party apparatus, the party operates differently depending on how the political space is structured across the country's territory. Party builders did not invest evenly in developing formal party structures across social constituencies, and as a result the party experienced strikingly diverse development trajectories in differing local contexts. It is when these nuances are examined that the party's organizational complexity and heterogeneity becomes visible.

Other authors have made the similar argument that Latin American parties are not always uniformly bureaucratic. Levitsky (2003) focused on

[19] This is a difficult game: while, in a democracy, mobilization enables groups to make their weight felt between elections, it can also make democracy ungovernable and undermine it.

party organizational characteristics, such as informal and weakly institutionalized party structures, to explain the politics of labor-based parties. In the case of Peronism, Levitsky's core case, informal party organization allowed the party leadership to act autonomously, with few bureaucratic constraints. As I have shown in this chapter, the obverse is true in the case of the MAS, where similar organizational attributes generally provide incentives and opportunities for the social bases to act autonomously – with few bureaucratic constraints – and wield influence over some of the party's most important decisions. Informal, loose channels thus provide a means for the party's social bases to shape the party's agenda and also constrain the behavior of the party leadership.

The MAS also helps to illustrate a path whereby fluid party organizational attributes can facilitate responsiveness and help to keep parties open and leadership accountable to organized mass constituencies. In the case of the MAS, open candidate selection procedures have boosted the representation of previously underrepresented groups and contributed to the inclusion of their interests in the political power game. Weak bureaucratic development also enabled the party's movement bases to operate autonomously and influence, constrain, and hold the leaders accountable in the realm of national policymaking, not only shaping strategic decisions but also serving as a "social veto" over the policy objectives of party leaders. These mechanisms of accountability, however, are far from perfect. As the chapter has described, they are reliant on social mobilization, which is hard to sustain and can also make democracy ungovernable.

At the moment of this writing, in January 2021, the MAS is undergoing a sea change and internal restructuring after it experienced a massive political crisis in 2019 that forced Evo Morales from power. The party's impressive electoral comeback in October 2020 so soon after losing power marked a partial solution to a tense political impasse in the country and demonstrated that the MAS cannot be viewed merely as the personalistic tool of a charismatic leader or understood simply as a co-optative machine. It performs classic representative functions for major segments of Bolivia's population and remains Bolivia's only national-level force that is anchored in and connected to Bolivia's popular sectors and movement constituencies.

Social movements played an important role in maintaining vertical aggregation and horizontal aggregation when Morales was in exile and MAS leaders and supporters faced violent persecution; indeed, in the absence of major bureaucratization, movements made the return of the MAS to power possible in a changing context. In recent months, moreover, social movements have pushed hard to reclaim ownership of the "political instrument" and have challenged what used to be a fairly unified leadership. The result has been what might be considered a process of "returning to the origins" while the party appears to be outliving its dominant leader – a process in which social movements are reclaiming ownership of the party and pushing, with some successes and setbacks, for leadership and programmatic renewal. It remains to be seen how this process will unfold, and what kinds of relationships and lines of tension will develop along the way, in light of the many governing challenges that the party faces today in the context of the COVID-19 pandemic. Only time will tell.

5

The Complex Interaction between Vertical Interest Aggregation and Horizontal Coordination

The PRD and MORENA in Mexico

Hélène Combes

INTRODUCTION

During the last thirty years, two left-of-center political parties, the Partido de la Revolución Democrática (Party of the Democratic Revolution, PRD) and Movimiento de Regeneración Nacional (National Regeneration Movement, MORENA), were successfully built in Mexico. In 1989, the PRD was launched; it grew throughout the 1990s, becoming the second or third largest political force in the country. In 1997, the party won Mexico City's mayoral post, which it retained until 2018. MORENA was officially born in 2014, in the midst of an internal PRD crisis, and quickly achieved electoral success, winning the presidency in 2018. The PRD and MORENA satisfy the definition of political party presented in the introduction to this volume, that is, a political organization that establishes coordination mechanisms among its leaders and vertically aggregates social interests. According to this conception, these parties are not merely personalistic vehicles. However, during the 1990s, the media and the academic world often alleged that the PRD was the party of Cuauhtémoc Cárdenas, who ran twice for president under its banner (1994 and 2000). When it was founded, MORENA was seen as a vehicle to serve the political ambitions of Andrés Manuel López Obrador (AMLO), who broke with the PRD leadership after also running twice for the presidency (2006 and 2012).

It is important to note the uniqueness of the Mexican regime that held power throughout the twentieth century. At the end of the 1920s, the organization that would later be called the Partido Revolucionario Institucional (Institutional Revolutionary Party, PRI) was formed to bring together the "revolutionary family." The PRI, which had hegemonic pretensions and was described by analysts (and its detractors) as a "party state," was institutionalized as a semi-corporatist regime in the early 1940s. The hegemony of the PRI lasted until 2000. Its endurance can be explained by a mixture of (local) repression, co-optation of potential rivals, and strong politicization of the popular sectors in certain bastions. As Bruhn (1997) stated, building a new party in this context is tantamount to confronting Goliath.

Moreover, Mexico's electoral law supported the development of strong parties in a country characterized by a weak, fragmented the party system (Coppedge 2001). Thus, since the end of the 1920s, the rather maximalist electoral law limited election competition by setting very strict requirements for an organization to register as a political party, and only registered parties could participate in elections. These rules, which underwent certain adjustments over the years, both limited party competition and favored strong parties. Only those parties that developed a strong structure, such as the Partido Acción Nacional (National Action Party, PAN) and, later, the PRD, were able to enter the electoral arena. Thus, in Mexico, certain aspects of horizontal coordination – for example, monopolization of candidates and electoral strategy, use of common electoral labels – are stipulated by law.

As highlighted in the introduction of this volume, the mainstream literature on political parties has focused more on the dimensions of political life vis-à-vis elections, which the conceptual framework of this volume terms horizontal coordination. This chapter shows how in Mexico, as in Bolivia (Anria this volume), the cultivation of leadership and, more generally, candidate selection cannot be understood without considering vertical interest aggregation. In the two cases studied in this chapter, the selection of leaders and candidates is strongly connected to the party's complex interaction with civil society and social movements. This link is especially important when new electoral vehicles are under construction. Thus, the PRD relied on numerous social movements both to build its party apparatus at the territorial level and to recruit regional and national cadres. The vast majority of cadres maintained dual-party membership throughout the 1990s in both PRD and social organizations. In this volume, dual membership is seen as an indicator of vertical interest aggregation. The PRD also exhibited all the indicators of horizontal coordination. For example, the PRD monopolized candidate selection by controlling candidate nominations at all levels despite strong internal electoral disputes. The party had a motto and an emblem, a standardized brand (Offerlé 2011) that it used for all positions, both internal and those obtained through the popular vote. In addition, throughout the 1990s, the strong party discipline that had existed within its parliamentary group weakened due to internal conflicts, eventually leading to the creation of a new vehicle, MORENA. The PRD clearly satisfied all the criteria set out in this volume for an electoral vehicle to be considered a political party in the fullest sense of the concept. While MORENA also met the criteria for horizontal coordination, including exhibiting certain institutional innovations, such as the use of a raffle to select some of its candidates, the question of whether MORENA satisfies the criteria of vertical interest aggregation is more complex. Although informal ties between the party and organizations continued to exist, MORENA's sudden success at gaining power at multiple levels (local, regional, national) put vertical aggregation to the test.

I argue that, since their formation, these two vehicles on the political left have clearly merited the label of political party, in accordance with the typology proposed in this volume. In this chapter, I show how horizontal coordination and vertical interest aggregation have evolved within the PRD and MORENA in order to gain insights about the development of these two parties and, especially, their leadership. I use a historical-sequential analysis, combined with an analysis of the two dimensions of the model outlined in the introduction of this book. I argue that observed differences between these two parties can be explained by the way the interaction of horizontal coordination and vertical aggregation of interests affects party organization.

This chapter is based on ongoing research I have been conducting on Mexican parties that began in 1998. Since the inception of this research project, different methods and approaches have been used: surveys, interviews with leaders and party activists, archival work, and ethnographic observations. I assert that a method focusing on the everyday life of organizations – going beyond consideration of the role of prominent leaders in the media spotlight – including attendance at party congresses, local and national meetings, rallies, gatherings of political currents, and the careful and systematic analysis of internal sources, is crucial for clarifying or even countering the personalistic reputation of these parties and for understanding the types of links that exist between horizontal coordination and vertical aggregation of interests.

In the first part of this chapter, I analyze how these vehicles became political parties. In the second section, I discuss how vertical aggregation affects horizontal coordination. And in the final section, I scrutinize how these political parties influence Mexican democracy.

NEW PARTIES IN A PARTIAL DEMOCRACY

The PRD

The PRD was founded in 1989 after the controversial 1988 presidential election (López Leyva, 2007). In 1997, it became the second-largest political party in Mexico's national Congress and won the first democratic election held in Mexico City, claiming the mayor's office and an absolute majority in the Asamblea Legislativa del Distrito Federal (Legislative Assembly of the Federal District, ALDF). Despite this success, its leaders encountered numerous difficulties while building the party. The two main problems were: (1) bringing together groups of political activists with very different political perspectives; and (2) competing with a hegemonic party in a context of violence at the local level.

As Agustín Guerrero said, "we paid the price of merging with different sectors. Just imagine. In a blender, a mix of peppers, garlic, onions ... in the same party, Trotskyists, Maoists, Stalinists, and former [PRI] members."[1] Indeed, the PRD founders included members of the democratic current of the PRI (which thrust figures such as Cuauhtémoc Cárdenas and Porfirio Muñoz Ledo into leading roles[2]), with members of several small leftist parties that were strong in several districts and already had cadres with legislative experience, and with social organizations and social movements that made up the majority of the new party's membership. Throughout the 1990s, there was a general consensus in Mexico regarding Cárdenas's leadership (Prud'homme 1996; Sánchez 1999) and unifying role among groups of diverse origin, groups that would later cluster into different political factions.[3] At the local level, however, building the party was even more complex. Panebianco (1988)

[1] Personal interview with Agustín Guerrero (General Secretary of the PRD-Mexico City), May 2000. All direct quotes that appear in the chapter were translated from Spanish by the author.

[2] This faction broke away in 1987 when the PRI chose its presidential candidate because its members concluded that the principle of ideological rotation within the PRI was not respected in the run-up to the 1988 election (Bruhn 1997).

[3] In my research I have shown that the key concern behind how different groups in this faction regrouped was the nature of the political transition and the acceptance or rejection of mobilizations (i.e., collective protest) as a way of eliminating what these groups called the PRI-State.

outlines two types of party building: territorial penetration by which the center stimulates, guides, or restricts the periphery, and territorial diffusion, whereby local elites form groups that later connect to the national structure. Taking into account the history of political activist groups and their presence in different areas of the country, in Combes (2011) I apply Panebianco's typology to the cases of the PRD and MORENA and discuss the territorial integration that was implemented with greater or lesser success. The PRD had many organizational problems in its foundational stage.[4] In addition, building the party through territorial integration led to tense dealings between national and state leaderships in 37 percent of the cases (Combes 2011, 150). This type of party building also tended to favor interpersonal links between local activists and national-level cadres, who, in many cases, were linked by previous political loyalties. In addition, the way the party was assembled led to its very unequal territorial presence in the country as a whole (i.e., two strongholds in the center and south of the country and an extremely weak electoral presence in the north).[5]

The second difficulty, highlighted in initial research on the PRD (Bruhn 1997), was the establishment of a new vehicle (PRD) in the context of a hegemonic party (PRI) (Magaloni 2006). The PRD was built with very little access to the media, without resources, and without access to public financing (until the 1994 electoral reform, implemented nationally for the first time in 1997). In addition, political violence was an important factor (Schatz 2001), even though other studies paid little attention to this phenomenon (Bruhn 1997; Vivero-Ávila 2006). Between 1989 and 1996, more than 600 PRD members were murdered. Cross referencing several data sources shows that violence was concentrated in the states of Guerrero and Michoacán, where the PRD had obtained its best electoral results.[6] Some 64 percent of the deaths occurred during post-electoral conflicts and 55 percent occurred during a party activity; 20 percent of the victims were party cadres and the rest were local party members. This

[4] The PRD's organizational problems arose in 50 percent of Mexico's thirty-two states: in 20 percent of them, the difficulties were moderate, in 10 percent the problems were severe, and in 20 percent of the states the party failed entirely to establish a local presence. Based on reports from the organizational secretary in the early 1990s (Combes 2011, 146–149). These problems ranged from verbal clashes in meetings to physical confrontations that, for example, prevented state-level foundational congresses from taking place.

[5] Vommaro's chapter in this volume studies similar challenges faced by the PRO in Argentina in its efforts to build a national organization starting from the country's federal district, faced by a right-wing party in Argentina.

[6] I created a database of 400 murdered PRD members, based on official reports, newspapers, and internal party files.

context of government's campaign of violent repression alienated the population and increased PRD support from social movements that opposed the government. Despite this political violence, in 1997 the PRD became Mexico's second-strongest political force and consolidated its party apparatus, partly through the public financing that it obtained as a result of its electoral successes.[7]

MORENA

MORENA was born as a political party in 2014. However, to understand the rapid success of this party, which won the presidency in 2018, we need to go back to 2006. In that year, AMLO, the candidate of a coalition headed by the PRD, after a very close election result that raised suspicions of fraud, refused to recognize the victory of Felipe Calderón, the candidate of the PAN. In November 2006, AMLO's followers proclaimed him the legitimate president. A series of mobilizations followed: the post-election sit-down protest in 2006, the Adelitas movement against the privatization of PEMEX (Sánchez Garrido 2011), and the movement for the defense of the popular economy. These actions set the stage for AMLO's departure from the PRD, as well as that of numerous cadres and party members. We found in our studies that these mobilizations galvanized activist networks linked mainly to the popular urban movement in Mexico City (see Table 5.1).[8]

AMLO embarked on a tour that took him, before 2012, to every municipality in the country. He disseminated his planned governmental projects at rallies, through the sale of his books, and through a database of supporters. Stands were set up at every rally where supporters could register. By 2008, this database, which the PRD could not access, was used to record phone messages from AMLO calling on supporters to undertake particular activities or to participate in elections; and to let territorial leaders – known as representatives of true change – maintain contact with supporters. Beginning in 2010, this territorial work was complemented with a unique tool: five million copies of the Regeneración (Regeneration)

[7] Cyr's chapter in this volume on opposition parties in Venezuela studies a negative case: new parties that, in nondemocratic contexts, have difficulties in establishing stable relations with social movements.

[8] With a team from the Autonomous Metropolitan University (UAM) led by Sergio Tamayo and the author, a questionnaire was administered to participants in a march headed by López Obrador ($N = 306$) (Combes, Tamayo, and Voegtli 2015).

TABLE 5.1 *Profile of López Obrador's supporters*

Category	Percentage
Age	
Under 30	28
Between 31 and 40	16
Between 41 and 50	16
Over 50	40
Education	
None	7.5
Primary	12.2
Secondary	20.3
Preparatory (or equivalent)	29.5
Bachelor's degree and more	30.5
Occupation	
Blue-collar workers	22
Work in the traditional professions (doctors, lawyers, etc.)	16
Public employees	14
Merchants (many from the informal sector)	14
Work in creative or intellectual professions (academics, artist, etc.)	12.5
Cadre professionals (in the PRD, social organizations, or NGOs)	10.4
Other	11.1
Level of Political Engagement	
Participation in more than ten marches	54
Vote in elections	80.5
Self-identify as leftists	46

Source: Palapa project survey.[9]

newspaper were distributed.[10] Representatives had to meet a goal of contacts – controlled at an electoral-district level by AMLO himself – using the database, but the goal also increased according to the number of voters in

[9] This survey, coordinated by Hélène Combes and Sergio Tamayo, was administered by a team from the Universidad Autónoma Metropolitana Unidad – Azcapotzalco (Autonomous Metropolitan University, Azcapotzalco) campus in November 2008 during a march of the Movimiento para la Economía Popular (Movement for a Popular Economy).

[10] Interview with the newspaper's director, November 2011.

favor of AMLO in each district. The objective was both to build a structure and to disseminate the movement's ideas: MORENA emerged in 2010 as a parallel structure within the PRD and then became publicly known in 2011. In 2012, when the electoral law still prohibited independent candidates, AMLO was picked as the presidential nominee to lead a coalition headed by the PRD. Yet the campaign was carried out in a context of competition between MORENA and the PRD, which prevented successful territorial deployment. A few weeks later, AMLO left the PRD, but lost the 2012 presidential election to Peña Nieto, the PRI candidate strongly supported by Mexico's private hegemonic television networks.

Although the construction of MORENA had a strong movement component, the party was built in a way that differed radically from the PRD. Its construction can clearly be attributed to territorial penetration (Panebianco 1988), predominantly planned from the center. This territorial work went unnoticed in the analysis of commentators or political scientists, who generally eschewed fieldwork. They emphasized AMLO's charisma, following a fairly well-established trope, hardly new in Mexican politics. However, the victory of AMLO cannot be understood without noting this extensive territorial work and the building of a broad AMLOist movement, which began in 2006 (Bolívar Meza 2014; Combes 2018).

When MORENA became a civil association on October 2, 2011:

> it had 2,217 municipal committees and 37,453 sectional committees, composed of 179,000 leaders and four million people registered in the movement as 'protagonists of true change,' a term that MORENA, from its inception, applied to its affiliates in its main party documents ... an advisory council made up of 84 outstanding citizens, writers, intellectuals, scientists, academics, businessmen, social leaders, journalists, political scientists, economists, and artists. (Bolívar Meza 2014, 76)

In 2012, MORENA developed a thematic dimension or brand (MORENA Culture, MORENA Labor, MORENA International) that helped support the work of former ministers of what the party's supporters viewed as the legitimate government as well as the organization's work with intellectuals and artists (Combes Forthcoming). It also broadened the alliance though outreach to different sectors, such as businesspeople or young people involved in various student mobilizations. In July 2014, the National Electoral Institute approved MORENA's registration as a political party after verifying that it complied with legal requirements by having held thirty state assemblies (a minimum of twenty were required) and registering 496,729 members.

Following this overview of how the two parties were established, I discuss in the next section how changes over time in the PRD help explain the birth of MORENA and I analyze this development in terms of the relationship between horizontal coordination and vertical aggregation.

IMPACT OF VERTICAL AGGREGATION ON HORIZONTAL COORDINATION

From Construction to Institutionalization (1989–1997)

In the PRD, activists with dual roles – in urban social movements and, to a lesser extent, in peasant/indigenous movements[11] – were very important, in that such activists existed both among party leaders and among the party's first grassroots representatives (at local and national congresses). The survey I conducted at the 2001 Zacatecas congress revealed that 27 percent of the cadres entered the party from a movement or a social organization (Combes 2013, 157). The figure among women rises to 33 percent, given that they found greater participation opportunities in the movements than in classical left-wing parties (Combes 2013, 180).[12] I observed in the late 1990s in Mexico City that recruitment of party activists occurred mostly at mobilizations or meetings of social organizations. Informal links prevailed because the PRI's corporate model was rejected. This combination of dual membership in, and informal ties between, the party and unions or movements is also observed in the Frente Amplio (Broad Front, FA) in Uruguay (Pérez Bentancur, Piñeiro Rodríguez, and Rosenblatt 2020 and Pérez Bentancur, Piñeiro Rodríguez, and Rosenblatt this volume).

What are the consequences of this of type vertical aggregation based on dual membership? First, the party had a presence only in those parts of the country where social movements had a presence, and where social movement leaders had dual roles. The PRI's hegemonic dominance limited PRD's access to the media and restricted PRD's campaigns to

[11] I note that Mexico is a country characterized by contention politics and activists' dual political roles occur within this context (Cadena-Roa 2003). For specific information regarding the relationship between the Movimiento Urbano Popular (Popular Urban Movement, MUP) and the PRD in Mexico City, see Tavera Fenollosa (2013) and Bruhn (2013).

[12] Greater numbers of women are found within grassroots activism.

door-to-door efforts and promotion through mutual-acquaintance networks. Thus, as previously stated, its presence was territorially uneven. Second, this type of vertical aggregation also had an impact on the nature of the party's repertoire of actions: Party activities occurred mainly through mobilization. The party's first years, in particular, were characterized by very important post-electoral movements, including seizure of municipal offices and the implementation of parallel municipal governments (Calderón 1994). More generally, the PRD returned systematically to demonstrations, especially in Mexico City (Combes 2011, 160). The analytical model proposed in this volume does not address the issue of political parties' repertoires of action (Tilly 2006). We see, however, that in the Mexican case this repertoire is important for determining how parties function.

Vertical aggregation affected horizontal coordination. Social movements leaders, who brought the political culture of internal democracy from the movements to the party (Kitschelt 1989) encouraged primary elections to be held for all electoral posts. Primary elections began in 1991 for those affiliated with the party and, since1996, have been open for any citizen. Internal and primary elections were organized in public spaces (parks, markets, etc.) and, in the 1990s, they involved as many as 650,000 voters. An analysis of the PRD candidates showed that nominating grassroots and/or female candidates yielded favorable results:[13] With its territorial presence in neighborhoods, the PRD was better positioned to convene followers.

Candidate selection for the 200 legislative seats elected by single-district, closed-list, proportional representation remained in the hands of the party council.[14] One out of every three seats was reserved for civil society leaders, such as members of NGOs (e.g., feminist organizations, human rights organizations, etc.); leaders of ongoing protest movements who were not yet affiliated with the party, such as El Barzón, a movement advocating for debt forgiveness; and the Congreso Nacional Indígena (National Indigenous Congress, CNI).

In a hostile context (e.g., violence, boycotts by the media, difficulty in establishing a national presence, and, more generally, the question of how to challenge a hegemonic party), all efforts were centered on organizational

[13] Source: PRD leaders' database.

[14] The influence of social movements in the candidate selection process, as a channel of vertical interest aggregation, is also observable in the case of the Movimiento al Socialismo (Movement toward Socialism, MAS) in Bolivia (Anria this volume).

matters and programmatic aspects received little discussion.[15] Party platforms were prepared by a small group of intellectuals close to the party and were voted on without discussion in party congresses. At the state and national levels, the party sent candidates party propaganda and campaign materials that were all prepared at the national office.[16] From the party's inception, its brand was crafted at the national office, including the PRD's Aztec sun emblem, while campaigns were standardized in terms of themes and visual presentation (e.g., yellow posters with the Aztec sun, party symbol, type of photo of the candidate alone or with the presidential candidate for general elections).[17] The party brand was not open to debate, partly due to Mexico's legal framework: Candidates at that time could not run as independents and the name of the party had to appear on campaign literature.

Party discipline in state-level congresses was also quite systematic but of little importance. This is because, until 1997, the PRD's presence in local and national legislatures was quite marginal. PRD legislators systematically voted against PRI policy without this leading to a problem of party discipline. Local and national congresses were mostly used by PRD representatives and senators (who generally came from social movements) to respond to civil society groups, channel demands to the national level, and help meet the needs of local organizations in their districts. The so-called Modules for Citizen Attention became an important site for horizontal coordination and vertical interest aggregation.[18]

In 1997, the PRD gained access to public financing for the first time. AMLO, then party president, promoted a far-reaching, door-to-door campaign by recruiting members as Brigadiers of the Sun, achieving a massive presence in Mexico City and in key states for the party, including Michoacán, Guerrero, and the State of Mexico. In that year, in Mexico City's first democratic election since the 1920s, the PRD won the mayor's office with Cuauhtémoc Cárdenas as its candidate, as well as winning a majority of the vote in all local races to elect representatives to Congress. The PRD became the second-largest political force in the

[15] Analysis of the archives of all PRD congresses from 1989 to 1999 and face-to-face observation of three congresses between 1999 and 2001, as well as observation of numerous meetings of the 2000 presidential campaign team.

[16] PRD Archives, Casa del Sol Foundation.

[17] Observations in several states and Mexico City between 1997 and 2015, as well as consultation of the PRD's campaign-poster database for 1989–2000.

[18] Analysis of federal representatives and ALDF representatives' annual reports; ethnography of the Modules for Citizen Attention.

Congress and began winning mayoralties in major cities, as well as governorships.

CONSOLIDATION THAT WEAKENED THE PRD AND PROMOTED DIVISIONS

The PRD's initial electoral victories in Mexico City's metropolitan area and particularly in Mexico City itself in 1997 had mixed effects. On the one hand, the electoral successes helped institutionalize the party apparatus but, on the other, they unleashed a struggle between factions for control of party posts and monetary resources within a spoils-system administration. In this section, I examine the consequences of electoral success on vertical interest aggregation and horizontal coordination.

With a landslide victory in Mexico City in 1997, numerous social movement leaders took up posts as state and federal representatives and many Mexico City leaders joined the ranks of the capital's government or the government of its delegations (similar to boroughs). This led to the uncoupling of the PRD from social movements, both because of PRD leaders' social ascent and because of the heavy demands placed on party members by the very absorbing nature of life within a national party.[19] Winning state governments also gave professional cadres a certain degree of mobility. Consequently, the party no longer needed to curry favor with "civil society actors." Also, the territorial weakness of certain factions (such as Nueva Izquierda – New Left) led the party to expand the selectorate (Rahat and Hazan 2001) and seek alliances with local figures who were quite far from the party, such as businessmen and PRI politicians who were not picked as candidates to run for office.

Heightened competition within the party had several consequences throughout this period. Two are particularly relevant. First, competition between leaders and factions also played out on a territorial level, leading to greater complaints of clientelism (Hilgers 2008). By studying the social and political characteristics of all the actors in these controversies, I found that complaints arose from political staff lacking activist credentials and experience in working-class neighborhoods (Vommaro and Combes 2016). In addition, because of the history in these neighborhoods and the struggle among factions, the same political practices were labeled by

[19] Social ascent resulted from the extremely high salaries – 40–60 times the country's minimum wage – paid to grassroots representatives. Sources: Observation, financial statements, and interviews.

some as clientelism and by others as political mobilization (Combes Forthcoming). Second, competition between factions meant internal elections became more conflictive and internal disputes frequently occurred. Nominations were increasingly challenged, leading to candidate selection by surveys (in 2000 for Mexico City) or by the National Council (as of 2003) for key positions (Palma 2011). Yet, over the years, these rules often fluctuated depending on internal battles, elections, and where they took place. News of internal struggles was picked up by the mass media, contributing to an image of a highly divided party. AMLO's position within the party after 2006 exacerbated this situation. Despite having been president of the PRD and its presidential candidate, AMLO did not have a faction of his own within the party. Beginning in 2007, the "legitimate government" and, later, MORENA played this role. Internal confrontations came to a head with the "Juanito scandal." In 2009, the New Left candidate, Silvia Oliva Fragoso, running in the local election of the Iztapalapa delegation in Mexico City, lodged a formal complaint before the Electoral Tribunal (and not within the party), challenging the result of the internal election she lost to the candidate supported by AMLO. The Electoral Tribunal ruled in her favor. AMLO then called on his supporters to vote for the Labor Party (PT) candidate, nicknamed Juanito, who promised, if elected, to step down in favor of AMLO's candidate (Cadena-Roa and López Leyva 2013, 34). Armed with their voter database, the representatives of the "legitimate government" organized a short and intensive door-to-door campaign to convince supporters to vote for Juanito (Combes Forthcoming).

Throughout the period, PRD candidates continued to run virtually identical campaigns, given the centralization of all electoral propaganda and a very visible presence of the party brand. At the local level, however, the incorporation of new members created some confusion. This confusion also occurred among the voting public and among supporters of diverse electoral coalitions, which varied quite a bit from state to state.[20] The result was that, in spite of its strength, the party brand became blurred; this phenomenon was reinforced by a certain degree of party hopping by both local representatives and mayors.[21]

In the local and national congresses, strong party discipline required adhering to a simple position: the rejection of the PRI's legislative projects

[20] See, for example, the case of Chiapas (Sonnleitner 2012).

[21] This was also a problem with local coalitions made up of many different parties. For example, Chiapas.

(until 2000) and those of the PAN until 2006. However, in 2001, PRD senators from the New Left faction helped pass the Indigenous Law by voting in favor of it, notwithstanding opposition by the Zapatistas and the PRD's national leadership. This episode then deepened internal tensions. Yet the PRD's work within the national legislature had had little relevance internally until 2006, when infighting became severe. At that point, there were two de facto PRD parliamentary groups: the official group and the group of the Frente Amplio Progresista (Broad Progressive Front, FAP) that bound together the representatives backing the "legitimate government" (even donating a portion of their salary to the FAP). The FAP consisted of PRD representatives and others from the Partido del Trabajo (Party of Work, PdelT) and Convergencia (Convergence). The ministers of the "legitimate government" issued a statement regarding legislative policy that conflicted with the traditional role of the caucus leader. In 2007, representative Ruth Zavaleta, from New Left, was elected President of Congress, a result interpreted by FAP representatives as a form of collaboration with a government that AMLO did not yet recognize. Then, in December 2012, the PRD's future in the legislature was abruptly decided: the New Left faction joined forces with the PRI and the PAN to sign the Pact for Mexico.[22] Cadres from the other factions expressed their disagreement. Yet, these actions did not lead to a massive resignation of these representatives despite AMLO's leaving in October of 2012.

The massive departure of PRD members to join MORENA occurred in late 2014 and early 2015. The phenomenon had multiple causes. First, the party was experiencing a degree of lethargy after governing its main stronghold, Mexico City, for almost twenty years (Cadena-Roa and López Leyva 2013, 33; Tejera and Castañeda 2017). Furthermore, the party encountered difficulties in certain states, particularly Guerrero (Cadena-Roa and López Leyva 2013, 35) and Michoacán (Le Cour 2017), which had a very strong presence of assorted drug cartels embedded in local society. In fact, the massive wave of resignations from the PRD occurred at the end of September 2014, after the disappearance of forty-three students of the Ayotzinapa Normal School in Guerrero. This tragedy occurred in the city of Iguala, governed by a PRD mayor, a businessman aligned with the New Left faction. New Left was a political group that, in the face of its territorial weakness, formed

[22] This agreement between the main parties supported legislative reforms in governance, security and justice, economy, etc.

alliances with questionable local figures from other factions, even in cities, such as Iguala, with a strong, long-standing presence of the party. After the disappearance of the students, it became public that the mayor, who had no previous activist role, was the father-in-law of local drug bosses. The historical and moral leader of the PRD, Cuauhtémoc Cárdenas, resigned from the party a few weeks after the tragedy, followed by other leading figures. In Mexico City, however, mass defections occurred, beginning in February 2015, when the polls showed MORENA to be the frontrunner in the city, an important factor in seasoned politicians' decision to change parties. By jumping ship, they virtually secured their political future after almost a decade of uncertain support for AMLO. Thus, the exodus of former PRD cadres and activists to join MORENA, which obtained its legal registration in July 2014, was continued throughout 2015.

Between 2016 and 2018, the main task of MORENA's national organizational secretariat was establishing sectional committees with at least eight "protagonists of true change" in each of Mexico's 68,436 electoral districts. This meant recruiting a minimum of 547,488 people who would be tasked with representing MORENA in all of the 156,857 polling stations where voting would take place on Election Day. The Left's historical distrust of electoral processes made monitoring the elections a key task for PRD activists and subsequently for MORENA activists.[23] A 2017 report of the Plan Nacional de Organización (National Organization Plan) before the III Congreso Nacional Extraordinario (III Extraordinary National Congress) indicated that there were already "61,362 Protagonists of True Change Committees,"[24] each having at least eight members, representing 91.56 percent of Mexico's 68,436 electoral districts. Organizational work then focused on the recruitment of activists both to monitor the elections and to build the party at a territorial level.

Following the tradition established in the PRD, certain slots in representatives' lists were reserved for external civil society candidates, which is a pervasive feature of vertical interest aggregation among the left in Mexico. This did not prevent MORENA from being challenged. The list of activists – the "protagonists of true change" – was at the center of internal disputes that surfaced shortly after MORENA came to power. In October 2019, the electoral court canceled MORENA's congress for not

[23] In the 1990s, the party even had a secretary in charge of defending the vote.
[24] Translation from Spanish by the author.

having a reliable membership register,[25] which led to an internal crisis in the party over its national leadership (i.e., a crisis over the party's horizontal coordination capacity).

MEXICO'S PARTIES AND DEMOCRATIC REPRESENTATION

The PRD played a key role in promoting pluralism at the local and national level.[26] Many PRD activists or local cadres paid for their affiliation with their lives. The PRD, along with multiple social movements (Cadena-Roa 2003) and leaders who wore multiple hats (Combes 2013; Bruhn 2013), struggled to achieve greater democracy. The arrival of the PRD on the national political landscape coincided with a political opening – called transition at the time – and several party rotations at the presidential level that confirmed, at least in a formal sense, the democratic nature of the Mexican state. Certain authors (e.g. Tejera and Castañeda 2017) argue that what has occurred is simply a reproduction of political hegemony. However, the party rotation within Mexico City's delegations throughout the period and in the mayor's office in 2018 confirms that political pluralism is occurring.

As previously mentioned, the construction of the PRD coincided with the assimilation of new sectors into politics. Historically, the PRI guaranteed the access of grassroots sectors to positions of popular representation. Yet, since the 1980s, this avenue of access had been closed and it had also been criticized for its corporatist selection of political membership. Thus, the PRD, as a new national party, was a novel structure that created political opportunities. It was the first party to offer women significant participation in Congress and in local legislatures. In Mexico City, most of the first PRD women legislators came from the popular urban movement, as did the vast majority of representatives in 1997 who also had grassroots origins. Thus, the arrival of the PRD allowed these social sectors to be included, a development that was significant for having occurred in an unequal society. Although some of its cadres came from the PRD, MORENA helped renew political operatives, opening new spaces and integrating people who had no previous activist experience or who came

[25] In August 2019, MORENA submitted a register of its 3,072,673 members to the Instituto Nacional Electoral (National Electoral Institute, INE), as required by law. However, only 670,000 affiliations were accompanied with supporting documents (e.g., voter IDs).

[26] The PRD's fight for pluralism in Mexico co-occurred with the longer-term struggle of the PAN, founded in 1938 (Loaeza 1999; Mizrahi 2003).

from other political sectors. The founding of MORENA coincided with several student mobilizations, which led young people to join its ranks. In 2018, following AMLO's election as president, long-standing figures became government ministers, but so did younger activists. It also introduced a raffle system to select candidates for Congress. During the 2015 midterm elections, 3,000 applicants participated. The names of those who participated in the raffle were chosen in assemblies held in the country's 300 electoral districts. Five representatives were elected in this manner. In 2018, thirty-seven candidates were selected this way, of which ten were elected to Congress – that is, fewer than 4 percent. The use of a raffle should be understood within the context of the Mexican left (especially given the difficulties of the PRD's internal elections). The raffle also constitutes a symbolic search for a more democratic and egalitarian method of nominating candidates. It continues to be of only marginal use in recruiting candidates and has its challenges, especially in terms of maintaining party discipline in the legislature. In 2015, several of the twenty-six candidates for local legislators selected by raffle became independent candidates after conflicts with various state committees (Serafin Castro 2018). Leaving aside the cases of the raffle legislators, the arrival of a large number of new political personnel created some difficulty in terms of parliamentary discipline due to a lack of experience or a lack of ideological guidelines.[27]

Quite notably, Mexico achieved the status of having the world's fourth-highest percentage of women in the national legislature, having almost achieved parity with men in the House and the Senate, explained by the large number of female MORENA legislators.[28] In conclusion, the PRD and MORENA promoted political pluralism in Mexico and contributed to the renewal of political leadership and activism by incorporating women and new sectors, including a new generation of activists.

[27] For example, in December 2019, without her party's consent, a senator from MORENA proposed a bill that sought to review the separation of church and state, notwithstanding the fact that secularity is an important principle for the party and for the Mexican left in general.

[28] With regard to representative democracy, a more in-depth analysis is pending regarding the extent to which the indigenous population can access political posts through elections. In the 1990s, against the backdrop of a complex relationship with Zapatismo, the PRD accepted nominations from the CNI for electoral posts. It is remarkable that in spite of its significant indigenous population, no indigenous party has emerged in Mexico.

CONCLUSIONS

On July 1, 2018, AMLO was elected President of Mexico with 53 percent of the vote. MORENA attained an absolute majority in both congressional chambers, also winning five governorships, the majority in seventeen state congresses, and more than 400 municipalities. Given this result, MORENA's main task was to meet the challenge posed by the governmental executive's agenda, the legislative agenda, filling vacancies in various governmental and representational institutions, and implementing what AMLO called the Fourth Transformation of the Republic.[29] Many cadres and activists were incorporated into the government, thus leaving behind the grassroots locales where they had worked so hard. Even the party's strategic post of Secretary of Organization went unfilled from July 2018 to August 2019. According to different interviewees, in November 2019, the party no longer had a presence at the territorial level, an indirect effect of its sudden tremendous electoral success. Recall also that both the PRD and MORENA mobilized their activists through protest actions and, to a certain extent, this was how MORENA built its membership. After the elections, taking the reins of power posed a real challenge in terms of MORENA's ties with its activist base. More generally, MORENA's survival will depend on its ability to renew its vertical interest aggregation capacity while in government.

The analytical model proposed by Luna et al. in the introduction to this volume provides useful guidelines for studying the evolution of parties of the Mexican left. In particular, this chapter highlights the heuristic value of analyzing the impact of the interaction between horizontal coordination and vertical interest aggregation. In contrast to the classical approach in the literature that disregards the parties' social environment in order to focus on their institutional rules, internal organization, and the disengagement of civil society (Mair 1997), the case of Mexico as presented here demonstrates that it is precisely by taking into account how parties connect with their environment that we can understand the stability (or instability) of the party. Further, the classical approach obscured how, in Mexico, the vehicles of the left exhibit the characteristics Luna et al. deem necessary for an electoral vehicle to merit the designation political party.

[29] According to AMLO, Mexico has already experienced three key transformations: Independence (1810–21); the Reform, under the mandate of Benito Juárez (1858–61), which among other changes enacted the separation of church and state; and the Revolution (1910–17), which ended with the adoption of the current constitution (1917). AMLO has committed his presidency to implementing the "Fourth Transformation."

6

PLN and PAC

Two Costa Rican Parties with Constituencies Evolving in Opposite Directions

Ronald Alfaro-Redondo and Steffan Gómez-Campos

INTRODUCTION

Under circumstances of decay, political parties become incapable of performing their basic functions, thus providing some grounds to remain "pessimistic about the effects this would have on parties, representation and democratic governance [feedback loop]" (Hale 2009, 594). According to Luna et al. (this volume), there remains a significant lack of theorized mechanisms and attributes of the political party concept that connect to democratic representation.

Traditional theories generally have mis-conceptualized the great diversity of political parties that have existed in Latin America's history. Scholars have also noted that many parties, in democratic contexts, fail in various ways to fulfill the function of democratic representation. In response to this, Luna et al. (this volume) challenged the canonical view by devising a new conceptualization and typology of electoral vehicles based on two attributes: horizontal coordination and vertical interest aggregation. They restrict the label *political party* to those electoral vehicles that exhibit both attributes. The practical implication of this is that not all electoral vehicles that compete in elections fulfill the two basic functions that, for Luna et al., define a political party. According to these authors, a political party is, then, an electoral vehicle subtype that coordinates ambitious politicians (during campaigns and between elections) and vertically aggregates collective interests. Many electoral vehicles perform either one or the other of these functions but not both. Under these circumstances, vehicles that win electoral contests are not necessarily functional for democratic representation.

In this chapter, we apply this conceptualization and typology to describe the Partido Liberación Nacional (National Liberation Party, PLN) and Partido Acción Ciudadana (Citizen Action Party, PAC). In the Costa Rican case, there exist organizations that fit the familiar, classic definition of political party as well as those that fit Luna et al.'s notion of a diminished subtype. Briefly, the PLN, the oldest and best-organized party, accomplishes both horizontal coordination and vertical interest aggregation. However, data reveal that its constituency has diminished significantly over time, such that the number of its supporters is now insufficient to guarantee an electoral victory, as evidenced in 2018. The PLN is the best example of a party with a solid constituency that has eroded over time. In sum, the PLN is a traditional political party type with an electoral base that has shrunk in recent elections (since 2002). On the other hand, the PAC is a good example of a relatively new electoral vehicle whose constituency is not yet fully developed. The PAC supporters are mostly young and reside in urban areas. In that sense, PAC is a young electoral vehicle with an evolving constituency undergoing transformation.

The remainder of this chapter is structured as follows. In the following section we present a brief background regarding the PLN and the PAC. Then we describe the main features of horizontal coordination and vertical integration for both parties. Finally, concluding remarks are presented.

BRIEF HISTORICAL BACKGROUND OF THE PLN AND THE PAC

In 1948, Costa Rica begun a new political era. After an extremely contentious electoral process plagued by irregularities and violence in February 1948, the Electoral Tribunal declared that the opposition candidate Otilio Ulate, of the National Union Party, had been elected president. The incumbent coalition, commanded by Rafael Angel Calderón Guardia, alleged that the opposition committed fraud and petitioned Congress to invalidate the results and to call for a new election. The vote of the National Assembly, dominated by pro-government forces, to annul the results precipitated a civil war with tremendous political implications. A rebel army commanded by José "Pepe" Figueres rose up against the government and defeated it. A provisional government, a civil junta led by Figueres, was in charge for a year and a half following the war. The junta abolished the army and a constitutional assembly prepared a new constitution in 1949.

The events of the 1940s not only created the conditions for the emergence of two political forces (winners vs. losers) but also destroyed what had been until then the country's dominant party, the Republican Party. This opened the political competition to many parties and political figures. One faction, the emergent and victorious PLN, organized and structured themselves more quickly than others. Thus, the civil war winners rapidly created a party identity. At the other end of the political spectrum were an amalgam of forces (*Ulatismo*, *Calderonismo*, Communists) with only one thing in common: to be anti-*liberacionistas*. This party system structure remained in place until the late 1990s.

The PAC, the most prominent party of the early twenty first century, emerged in 2002 as a strong contender appealing to urban, middle-class, more educated, and younger voters. Its ideology is center-left with a strong emphasis on ethics, a larger government role, LGBT rights and anti-corruption in public service. A vast majority of the party elite and leadership came from the PLN. First, in 2002 and later to a greater extent from 2006 to 2018, the PAC electorally relegated the PLN to the peripheral provinces, reconfiguring the traditional two-party system. After a poor electoral performance in 2010, the party won the Executive in 2014 and won reelection in 2018.

HORIZONTAL COORDINATION IN THE PLN AND THE PAC

In Costa Rica, both political parties are quite similar due to national legislation regarding many aspects related to horizontal coordination. For example, the Electoral Code stipulates that candidates run exclusively through political parties. Running as an independent is not allowed. In spite of the existence of generic norms, parties have their own rules and mechanisms for nominating candidates. In fact, there are party mechanisms based on a territorial hierarchy designed and implemented for this purpose. Parties organize constituency meetings called assemblies, in municipalities, provinces, and at the national level. In each assembly, party members choose candidates and their delegates to the assembly at the next level of the organization using a local-national pyramid. Candidates must win the nomination process at each level in order to finally secure the nomination at the Party National Assembly. Potential candidates compete against each other in local towns. If they win, they run at their provincial level and, if they succeed, they compete at the national assembly.

The differences between the PLN and the PAC regarding horizontal coordination are marginal in elections and more significant between elections. As opposed to other Costa Rican parties, the PLN and the PAC have a formal internal life determined by party statutes. Statutes of both parties define their structure and their functioning in the territory. This supports the claim that both vehicles have institutionalized bodies, at different levels, that produce horizontal coordination.

In Elections

The PLN statute (articles 87–90) stipulates that all nominations must follow the party's method in any election process regardless of the level. First, candidates must pay a fee to compete that varies across nomination type. Also, individuals must be free from judicial processes at the time of being nominated. Moreover, in terms of membership, the candidate should demonstrate at least two years of activism in the party. Candidates of the PLN are selected in primaries, where there are groups of constituents conventionally named *tendencias* (tendencies) defined as "organized groups of individuals that promote the nomination of candidates" (Partido Liberación Nacional 2017, 49).[1] These groups must be registered in the party's electoral tribunal and show that an aspiring candidate has a significant number of supporters.

Candidate selection processes in the PAC are quite similar to those in the PLN in aspects such as the levels at which nominations are made (municipal, provincial, and national) and requirements. The most important requirements in the PAC case are: party contenders must contribute economically, they should not have any judicial issue at election time, and must be a regular party member. A salient difference is that PAC rules set higher barriers to entry such as requiring four years of party membership. Another remarkable difference is that people who are not regular members, are allowed to be nominated after embracing the party's principles (Partido Acción Ciudadana 2019, 9).

In terms of accepting nomination processes and results, the PLN has an explicit procedure that dictates that candidates must respect the outcome of the election. It is established in the party's statute, article 120, that contenders must show: "c) … absolute respect for the decisions of the Electoral Tribunal and, especially, for its final verdict regarding the results of the [National Party's] Convention" (Partido Liberación Nacional 2017, 50). The PAC's process for accepting candidate nominations requires candidates to submit information to the

[1] All direct quotes that appear in the chapter were translated from Spanish by the authors.

Electoral Tribunal, such as their regular fee contributions to the party, their proposals for addressing national issues, a signed copy of the party's Code of Ethics as a "signal of acceptance and of their promise to comply with what is stated in it" (Partido Acción Ciudadana 2019, 47), and at least 3,000 endorsement signatures of party members (Partido Acción Ciudadana 2019, 2).

As seen, the PLN restricts, in a certain way, candidates' probability of joining the competition by imposing minimal requirements, excluding the possibility that newcomers win an election without strong support from their electoral base. Also, these mechanisms decrease the probability of there being numerous contenders. As a result, party primary winners look for support from other tendencies or factions once the election is over. In the PLN's history, there have been no cases of candidates refusing to concede. Another difference between the two parties is that, in the PAC case, there is no explicit obligation for contenders to endorse the nominated candidate in national elections. Thus, prospective candidates recognize that their probability of winning office may be compromised if one or more contenders decide not to endorse the party's nominee (or the results, overall) and instead help others to win the national election, because there is no restrictive mechanism in this matter.

Both the PLN and the PAC require candidates and campaign staff to use party logos, emblems, colors, and propaganda. There are explicit mechanisms to force them to use the official version of these elements during the campaigns. In the PLN case, article 4 of the party's statute defines official party symbols and colors. Most of the time, candidates adapt all their propaganda, particularly colors and logo, to the style predefined by party leaders and authorities.

Between Elections

There is a long tradition of analyzing how legislators vote in Congress. In one of the most canonical studies in this area, Poole and Rosenthal (2000) point out that the decisions of legislators not only reflect their preferences but also the interference of other political actors, advisors and their representatives. In addition, they conclude that chaotic behaviors are expected instead of disciplined behaviors. In the particular case of Costa Rica, the conditions of political fragmentation and the manner of electing lawmakers, in combination with the prohibition on consecutive reelection, favor chaotic voting patterns, in the terminology of Poole and Rosenthal.

In order to determine whether the legislators align with their party leaders or vote chaotically, the voting pattern of each of legislator is analyzed and compared with that of the party leader in the National Assembly.[2] This analysis shows the degree of discipline within the party. The main finding of this section is that, paradoxically, there is a strong association between the way the party leader and congressmen vote, regardless of the political party they belong to. That is, the voting patterns of Costa Rican lawmakers are counterintuitive, because, despite occurring in a context of high political fragmentation, a majority of the votes are decided by broad consensus. This pattern is repeated even among representatives who are perceived, by the media or citizens, as dissidents within their parties or strong opponents of the Executive. In fact, the majority of the votes of the legislators do not depart from that of their party leaders.

A possible explanation for this behavior is that the votes under study constitute the final link in a long chain of decisions and preliminary negotiations, whose results and outcomes are not faithfully captured in the analysis data. In this sense, it is worth keeping in mind that in this section of the chapter the votes made in the Plenary are considered, not those of the legislative commissions; by their nature, the latter are more likely to manifest the dissent of legislators. In spite of this clear analytical limitation, it is remarkable that in a divided congress the representatives vote so similarly.

An analysis of legislators' votes in the Assembly in two recent legislatures (2016–17 and 2017–18) reveals three patterns.[3] First, legislators

[2] Data for tracking how each legislator votes in Costa Rica is available but only for very recent years. The reform for making roll-call votes public was approved in 2015 and implemented for the first time in mid-2016. Before that period, Congress only reported the aggregate outcome during legislative sessions.

[3] In August 2016, the Legislative Assembly implemented the electronic system for voting that takes place in the Plenary. As a result, it is now possible to register track individual representatives' votes. For the 2016–17 legislature, 6,669 records are included, corresponding to 117 votes on bills. For the 2017–18 legislature, the number of votes is 13,380, which includes 223 votes of each of sixty legislators. It should be noted that in this last year there were four substitutions: Maureen Fallas and Ronald Calvo, of the (PLN), Steven Núñez (PAC), and Alexandra Loría (PRN), who replaced Antonio Álvarez, Juan Marín, Henry Mora, and Fabricio Alvarado, respectively. The analysis takes into account only the bills passed in after the second debate on them, because in the 2016–17 period three bills were voted on after the first debate but were archived due to expiration of the four-year legislative term. In the 2017–18 legislature, seven laws bills were voted on only after a first debate and then filed (i.e., they received no further action). In the database, the cases votes of the leaders of each of the parties and the president of the Congress are codified, to compare the way in which they vote with how the rest of the legislators do (PEN 2019).

vote similarly to their leaders; that is, there is a high level of party discipline. According to roll-call votes available (2016–18), both parties are cohesive and disciplined political organizations. Over time, the PLN has fully enforced strict obedience among its legislators (they voted as a unified parliamentary bloc on 98 percent and 99.7 percent of the votes in the 2016–17 and 2017–18 sessions, respectively). In a small number of cases, a few party representatives have voted differently than their fellows. In contrast, PAC has mutated from a not-very-disciplined organization, given the fact that PAC first groups of legislators in Congress experienced severe fractures and divisions, into a much more disciplined fraction in the last two legislative terms (in the PAC case, during the 2016–17 and 2017–18 legislative terms they voted 98 percent and 99 percent of the cases as a unified political organization).

With regard to party organization, political parties in Costa Rica are organized based on what is specified in the Electoral Code. It establishes the minimal structure that they must comply with. Party organizations have a ladder form, from the smallest territorial level (municipalities) to the national level. The structures of the party are organized in assemblies, made up of activists from all over the country responsible for making the decisions of the party at each of the territorial levels they represent (Figure 6.1).

Parties may establish district assemblies to organize the party at the level closest to the community. The Electoral Code establishes the cantonal assemblies as the first level, which must have a Cantonal Executive Committee and one Prosecutor's Office (Costa Rica has eighty-one cantons). At the next level, provincial assemblies must have an Executive Committee, and also a Prosecutor's Office (Costa Rica has seven provinces). These assemblies, in turn, form the National Party Assembly, which has a Superior Executive Committee and an Attorney General. The National Assembly must also have an internal Election Court, an Appeals Court and a Court of Ethics and Discipline to oversee internal processes and resolve possible conflicts between party structures throughout the country. In their statutes and in practice, the parties add new bodies according to their needs. Therefore, party organization in the country varies around this basic structure.

The PLN and the PAC have the most complex organizations. Along with the structure required by law, they have also created multiple organs of political leadership, internal party life (for example, training and education) or representation of sectors (such as youth, women, and entrepreneurs, among others). These variations show the greater strength of these

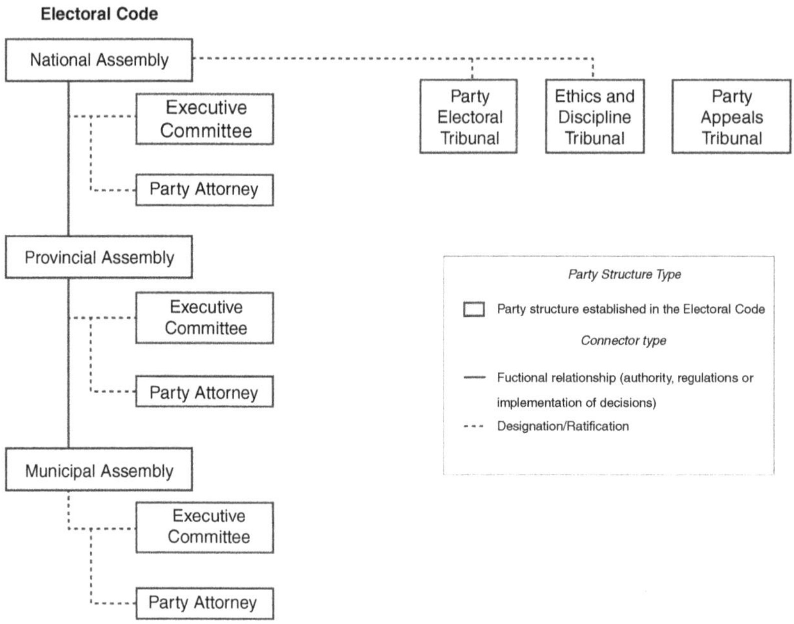

FIGURE 6.1 Basic party structure specified by electoral law
Source: PEN 2017.

two partisan vehicles, in terms of horizontal coordination, compared to the rest.

Partisan consistency across levels is facilitated by partisan control of local governments. If a party controls the majority in the municipal council it can promote policies at the local level that are much more consistent with its national policies. The 2016 municipal elections reveal two trends. On one hand, the PLN maintained its hegemony in the localities, although with a slight reduction compared to 2010. On the other, no party achieved a clear control of the municipal councils, due to the high volatility and party fragmentation. In fact, these elections consolidated the multiparty composition without majorities that has prevailed since 2002 (Alfaro-Redondo 2006). This high level of political fragmentation at the local level poses a serious challenge to policy consistency.[4]

[4] The PLN won fifty of the eighty-one mayoralties in dispute – 62 percent of the total – which is nine fewer than it won in 2010. The PAC, the party in control of the Executive, won only six. The number of municipalities controlled by this party has not changed significantly over time despite its maintaining control of the Executive for the last two terms.

A way to assess parties' strengths in the municipalities is to determine whether there is a hegemonic party in the local councils, measured by the control of the mayor's office during four elections between 2002 and 2016 and the distribution of seats in the local government. With respect to mayoralties, only in fifteen of the country's eighty-one municipalities has one party maintained strong control. In eleven of them, the PLN, which continues to have the highest representation at the municipal level throughout the country, has predominated.

The party composition of the municipal councils in the period 2002–16 shows increasing fragmentation in the distribution of seats across local governments. Municipalities can be classified based on two criteria: the distribution of seats in the councils and the party that controls the mayor's office. These indicators allow one to distinguish five patterns of governance and the places where there may be higher costs for decision-making. First, united government: the same party won the mayor's office and the majority of seats in the municipal council (50 + 1). Second, divided government with plurality: no party obtained the majority of seats in the council. However, the same party won the mayor's office and a plurality of seats. Third, moderate divided government: the mayor belongs to one party and a different party has a plurality of seats in the municipal council. Fourth, divided government with strong opposition: the mayor belongs to one party and a different party holds a majority of seats in the municipal council. Fifth, fragmented government: the mayor belongs to one party and all parties have the same number of seats on the municipal council.

Applying these categories to local governments elected in the 2016 municipal election illustrates the challenge for governability at this level. For instance, only fourteen municipalities (17 percent) have united governments. In this scenario, the main party is, at least in theory, in a favorable political position, as the mayor has the support of the council, a majority of whose members are of his own party. In these types of municipalities, nine are controlled by the PLN (out of fifty won by the party) and just one by the PAC (out of six won by the party). The other municipalities have different levels of fragmentation: sixty-one are divided governments with plurality, forty-one out of the fifty controlled by the PLN and four out of the six controlled by the PAC; four are moderate divided governments (none are from the PLN and one from the PAC) and, two are fragmented governments (PLN and the PAC are not controlling any municipality in this category). The steady increase of fragmentation at the local level poses big challenges for the two parties studied in this chapter in terms of policy consistency at the local and national levels. In the PLN case, the party needs to reestablish links with its constituency at a time when it is losing control of the municipalities. The PAC's challenges are different. The party does not have defined a broad electoral base yet. Therefore, PAC support in local governments is limited, concentrated in urban communities and scarce. Under these circumstances, both parties are able to coordinate their actions and decisions at the local level, but with increasing difficulties associated with fragmentation and electoral volatility.

VERTICAL INTEGRATION IN THE PLN AND THE PAC

In this volume, the vertical interest aggregation is conceptualized as comprising two central dimensions: the intermediation and channeling of collective demands and the electoral mobilization of collective interests. Most of the literature on Costa Rican political parties focuses at the party-system level to study and explain political gridlock, weak representation, and citizen de-alignment that prevails in the country (Hernández Naranjo 2001, 2007; Lehoucq 2012; Vargas Cullell 2007, 2008). Instead of focusing on the interaction between political parties, this volume develops a different approach: the study of party organizations and their vertical integration. The analysis of party structures, links with local leaders and affiliates, party life between election cycles, and political socialization mechanisms in Costa Rica, reveals generally weak organizations not prepared to fulfill a political party's core functions, although some organizations are better prepared than others (Gómez-Campos 2015). In this regard, the PLN and the PAC are the country's best-organized parties, although both face strong challenges that need to be overcome in order for them to function effectively into the future.

Based on the size of their organizational structures, the PLN and the PAC have ample party structures for vertical interest aggregation although some differences persist. Both are organized internally, according to their statutes, around two structures. One is related to party leadership and the renewal of internal organs, which includes the assemblies (national, provincial, and cantonal) and the internal courts (elections, ethics). The other structure is one of political action that articulates a sectorial and territorial network for the coordination of political-electoral guidelines, including organizing the party ideological congresses (Gómez-Campos 2015). This second level of political action is stronger in the PLN than in the PAC, due to the latter's lack of a sizeable national assembly that is linked to an independent political action body and territorial action committees. There are also differences in party organization linkages. The PLN historically had strong relationships with sectoral organizations – labor unions, cooperatives, etc. – and with grassroots movements, though these relationships weakened considerably during the last two decades. This weakening may, in part, explain the erosion of the PLN's political base. The PAC, on the other hand, still lacks durable connections to community-based groups and sectorial organizations. Building these connections is one of the party's main current challenges.

These party configurations explain to some extent the parties' electoral performance. In the last two decades, the center of the country has been mobilized electorally by the PAC and the geographical periphery, with a more traditional base, exhibits greater support for the PLN. However, from a historical perspective, it should be noted that the PLN – founded in 1951 – has a long tradition of electoral mobilization of various sectors throughout the country. By contrast, the PAC was established only recently, in the year 2000, in the Central Valley. Its growth as a party is concentrated in that region, which is the most densely populated and the one with the highest level of development in the country.

Intermediation and Channeling of Collective Demands

The PLN and PAC statutes clearly establish institutional channels to process vertical interest aggregation among party members. This is partially explained by the requirements set forth in the Electoral Law. Both parties have party leadership and political action structures, although the institutional development within the PLN is more robust than that in the PAC. The PLN's longer experience in Costa Rican politics plays a central role in this regard. Despite these differences, when compared to other national political parties, the PLN and the PAC belong to the group with the greatest organizational development for vertical integration (Gómez-Campos 2015).

The PLN always had defined constituencies (Gómez-Campos 2015). The structure of political direction and action highlights the importance given to union and worker sectors according to the statute. These groups are identified in the party statutes as priority sources of party activism. The PLN also traditionally had strong ties with cooperative organizations and business chambers of diverse productive areas. The party has a broad sectoral organizational structure (teachers, businessmen, and professionals) and movements (youth, women, workers, and cooperatives).

With these types of groups, the party seeks to create the internal organization to attract specialized sectors and other groups with a more local profile (youth or women at the cantonal level, for example). Consequently, the party used to offer its electoral bases functional and territorial representation. Notwithstanding the formal existence of these channels, over the years these instances of interest aggregation have lost significance within the party. This phenomenon has created internal conflicts related to the consistency of its electoral base and the subsequent reduction of such groups' participation within the party structure. A further point: long-standing parties such as the PLN experience multiple transformations of their ideology over time. Such changes may also be associated with changes to the party's programatic agenda, its connections with social groups and constituencies and, therefore, its electoral support. The PAC has focused its efforts on building ties with middle-class sectors in conjunction with grassroots citizens and youth organizations, but there is still no evidence of a specific set of social organizations that fully identify with the party. However, the PAC gives a significant role to the youth within the party's structure and activities. Within the formal structure there is a Comisión Nacional de Juventudes (National Youth Commission) with full autonomy and independence. This autonomy is expressed in the existence of the Comité Ejecutivo Nacional de Juventudes (National Executive Committee of Youth), which is the governing body and official representative of the PAC Youth to any other internal or external body. This has brought members of the younger generations into the main bodies of party leadership and political action. The election of thirty-eight-year-old Carlos Alvarado as president of the Republic in 2018 is an example of the influence that the youth movement has within the PAC.

Electoral Mobilizing of Collective Interests

The second dimension of vertical interest aggregation is the mobilization of voters (Luna et al. this volume). If a party manages to obtain support from different regions and groups with different socioeconomic profiles, it is understood that it has greater capacity for vertical integration and articulation of demands from the society. By contrast, if votes are concentrated in homogeneous regions and among those with similar living conditions, it reflects a weaker capacity for vertical integration. To accurately analyze this dimension, the evaluation of electoral data for the PLN and the PAC over time is required.

Data show that the PLN and the PAC have electoral support networks identifiable in the territory, although with some variations across time. The main difference is that, between 2002 and 2018, the PLN was stronger at mobilizing those in rural areas who live outside the Central Valley (the urban and metropolitan center of the country), and the PAC, by contrast, has had more support in the regions within the Central Valley. The distribution of electoral support for the PLN changed since the 2000s. In the period 1953–90 the PLN dominated in most of the country and particularly in the Central Valley. The political opposition, disorganized during much of the second half of the twentieth century, received some support in the peripheral provinces and, during times of PLN weakness (e.g., 1966, 1978 and 1990), successfully expanded to the center of the country and won the electoral contests. But the electoral predominance of the PLN in the territory was a constant for four decades (1953–90).

Territorial voting patterns changed substantially in the 1990s. During the bipartisanship period (1990–2002), articulation of the opposition forces around the Partido Unidad Social Cristiana (United Social Christian Party, PUSC) limited the territorial scope of the PLN in most of the constituencies. Afterwards, with the increase in party-system fragmentation between 2002 and 2018, a center-periphery cleavage became evident in the country. In 2002 and, to a greater extent, in 2006, the PAC electorally relegated the PLN to the peripheral provinces and took over the urban, middle-class, and more highly educated voters. The PLN remained strong on the coasts and border regions of the country until the electoral process of 2018, when the Partido Restauración Nacional (National Restoration Party, PRN) recieved the majority of support from those regions (Figure 6.2).

The geographical location of the electoral support for each party also reflects citizen support clusters according to socioeconomic profiles. When considering the level of economic and social development of the country's eighty-one municipalities, it is clear that the PAC receives more support from the areas with a higher level of development while the PLN, in contrast, receives its greatest support in the least developed areas. In the 2014 election, the PAC obtained strong support from the most urban municipalities and from those with the greatest level of economic development, while it received far less electoral support in the regions with the greatest levels of poverty. The PLN came in second in the election and the majority of its votes came from regions with lower levels of development. Unlike the PAC, however, it received a similar level of support across different socioeconomic groups.

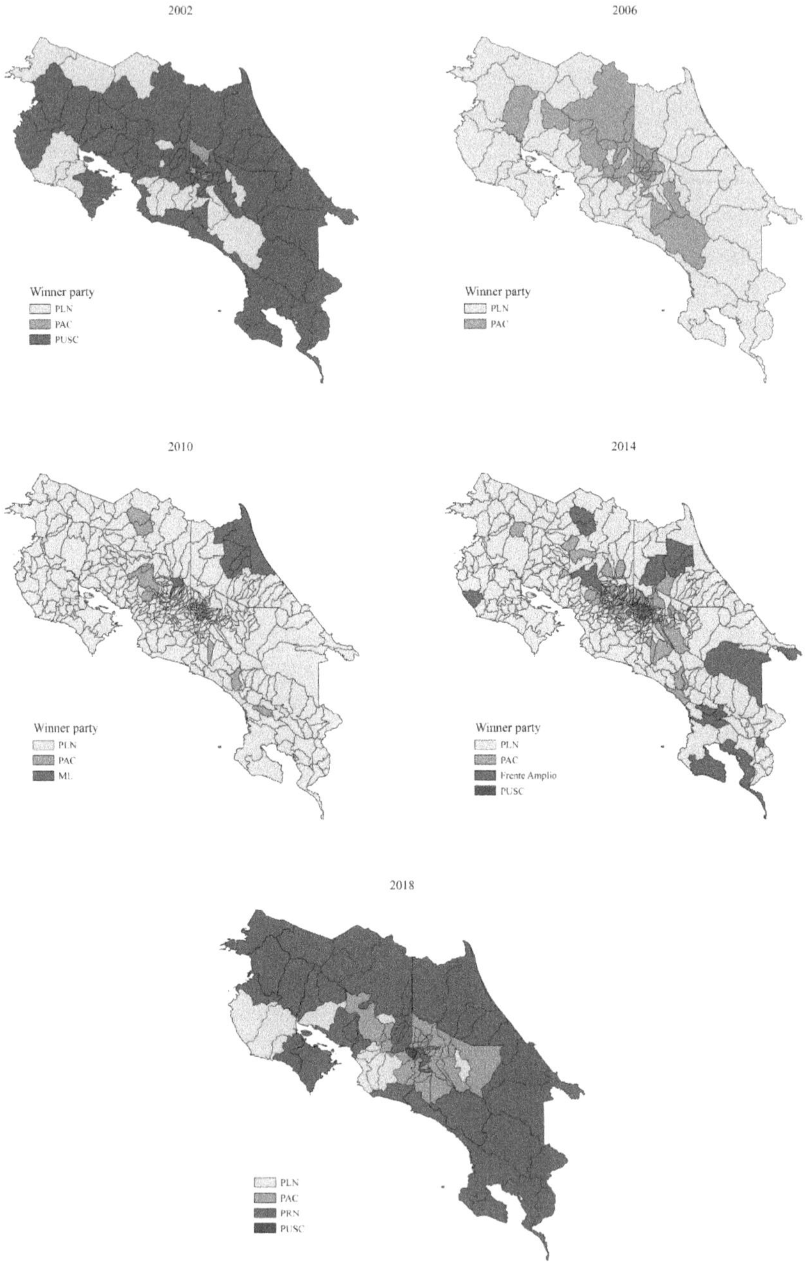

FIGURE 6.2 Winning Political Party by Constituency, 2002–2018
Source: Based on Supreme Electoral Tribunal data.

This electoral pattern occurred again in the 2018 election. In this case, as mentioned previously, the plurality of the votes in the first round of the election were obtained by the PRN party. The PAC came in second and retained the support of the most affluent zones, although the level of support was lower than in the previous election. The PLN, which came in third, confirmed that its level of support is similar across different socioeconomic groups, although it is slightly higher among the poorest and most vulnerable groups of society.

Cultural value cleavages strongly influenced the 2018 electoral process. Issues such as family traditions, same sex marriage, abortion, sexual rights, and religion, polarized the electorate and evidenced the existence of two Costa Ricas: one that professes traditional or conservative views and another that adopts more progressive positions on these matters. Based on *Votómetro* data, it is possible to describe the differences between voters with respect to the classic economic-ideological division between the left and the right and, cultural values between traditional and progressive (Norris and Inglehart 2019).[5]

The data show that the PLN enjoys greater support from social groups that espouse traditional cultural values. In particular, its supporters are people who mostly oppose abortion, oppose abolishing the Catholic Church as the official state religion, oppose same-sex marriage, and support the elimination of sex education classes in schools and colleges. These positions of PLN supporters are aligned with those of conservative parties such as PRN and the PUSC. PAC supporters are more aligned with progressive cultural values. That is to say, they support access to abortion, eliminating Catholicism as the official state religion, same-sex marriage, and the existence of sex education classes in schools and colleges (Gómez-Campos 2020).

In both political parties, individuals and groups differ in the strength of their ideological commitments and thus their location within the space defined by the two dimensions. Social groups that support the PLN hold traditional views but less so than those who support the PRN and the PUSC, for example. In that sense, PLN supporters are closer to the center. Regarding the PAC, the progressive values its supporters claim to espouse

[5] *Votómetro* is a web application developed by the Programa Estado de la Nación (State of the Nation Program) for the presidential elections of 2018. *Votómetro* administers an online questionnaire and shows respondents how their views compare to those of the candidates. The question items of the *Votómetro* were conceptualized and designed based on the theoretical framework proposed by Norris and Inglehart (2019), but adapted to the Costa Rican context.

occupy a more extreme position (Figure 6.3). The *Votómetro* data is consistent with the electoral results: the PAC won in regions where people are more aligned with progressive values.

In general, although PLN and the PAC are, like other cases, singular party organizations, older versions of them and their current incarnations share some features with their counterparts in the region. For instance, the original version of the PLN used to be connected to popular movements and associations (such as unions, farmers, youth) in a manner similar to the Movimiento al Socialismo (Movement toward Socialism, MAS). However, PLN has lost its ability to vertically aggregate collective interests, in the same manner as have the Partido Liberal (Liberal Party, PL) and the Partido Conservador (Conservative Party, PC) in Colombia. The PAC, for its part, behaves like Propuesta Republicana, (Republican Proposal, PRO) in Argentina, that is, as a fully functional political party in some districts and as an unrooted or poorly organized electoral vehicle in others.

CONCLUSIONS

Parties are quintessential actors in democratic regimes. The canonical view in most of the literature says that any political organization that competes in elections is considered a political party. The party politics literature has paid more attention to the roles parties play in society than to analyzing whether a specific political group satisfies the criteria for being considered a party.

The PLN and the PAC, two of Costa Rica's most prominent parties, are quite different from one another. The latter is a newer party that represents a younger constituency and it has controlled the Executive twice in its short history, whereas the former has been in office eight times and it is the oldest of the Costa Rican party system parties. Regardless of their significant differences, both parties have evolving constituencies that are moving in opposite directions: the PLN base has experienced long-term erosion while the PAC base is at the early stages of development. The PLN fits the classic definition of a party with a well-organized and fully developed constituency suffering from declining membership in recent decades. The PAC, on the other hand, while it has activists, is still in the process of growing its membership.

The analysis of horizontal coordination and vertical interest aggregation in the PLN and the PAC reveals similar organizational structures and processes. Both parties face challenges for policy consistency between the

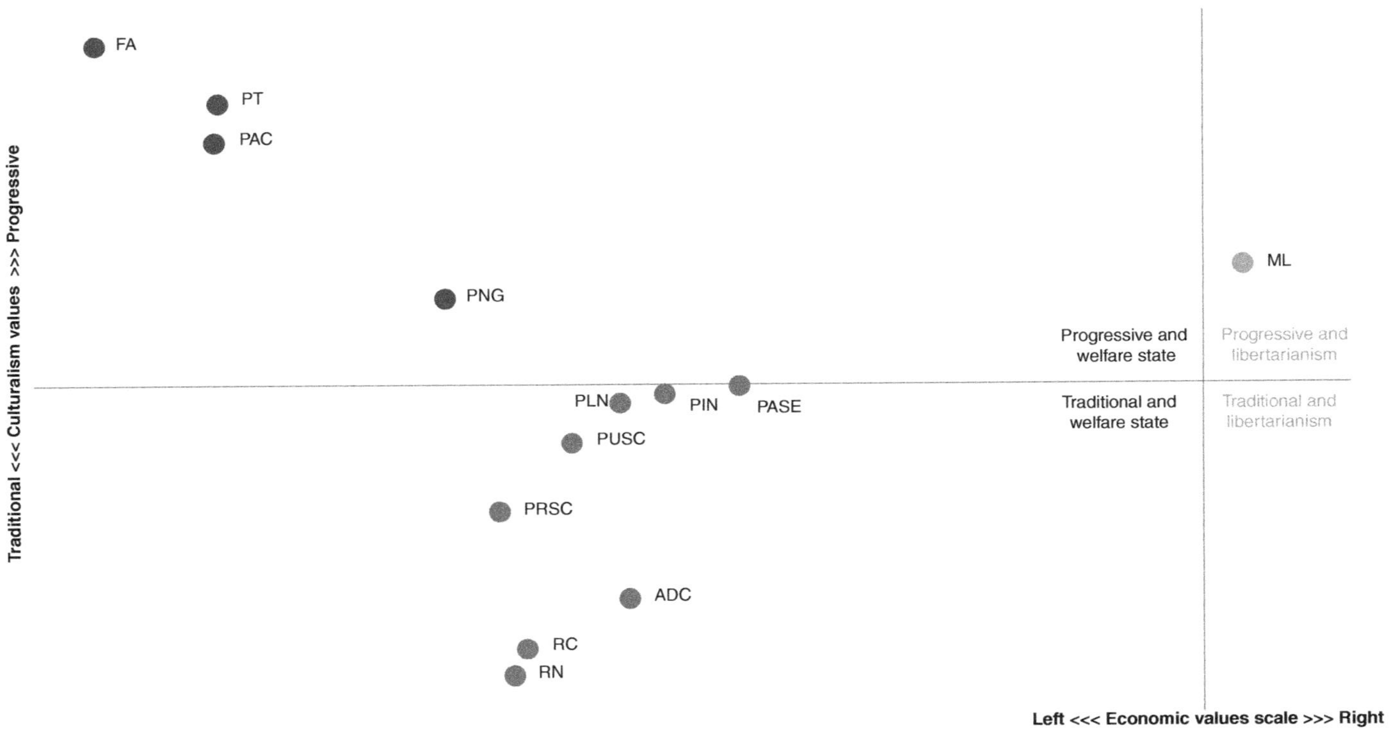

FIGURE 6.3 Classification of *Votómetro* responses by party affiliation and in terms of economic and cultural values, 2018 election
Source: Gómez-Campos (2020)

local and national level, while they differ in their capacities to aggregate collective demands. Most Costa Rican parties are weak organizations that lack the capacity to fulfill a political party's core functions. The analysis of their party structures, their links with local leaders and members, their functioning between election cycles, and their political socialization mechanisms show organizational fragility. However, the PLN and the PAC are the two most capable organizations in the Costa Rican party system. For instance, both the PLN and the PAC have party leadership and political action structures, although institutional development within the PLN is more robust than within the PAC. In addition, the PLN and the PAC have clearly identifiable electoral support clusters in the territory and population segments with some variation over time. In the last five elections, the densely populated geographic center of the country has been mobilized electorally by the PAC while the geographical periphery, with a more traditional base, shows greater support for the PLN. Finally, an analysis of individuals' cultural values and preferences during the 2018 campaign shows that the PLN has greater support among social groups with traditional cultural values and PAC supporters are more aligned with progressive cultural values.

7

The Case of the Traditional Parties in Paraguay

Diego Abente Brun

INTRODUCTION

The Paraguayan political party system, which hinges on two 132-year-old parties seemingly poised to remain alive and well for years to come, constitutes an anomaly in Latin America. Even though traditional nineteenth-century parties remain relevant in Uruguay, Honduras, and, to a lesser extent, Colombia, in none of these countries do they retain the same centrality they have in Paraguay. In Paraguay there is no politically viable way to access power except through one of these two electoral vehicles. The Paraguayan case, thus, offers a good testing ground to address the provocative theoretical questions raised by the organizers of this volume. Is this atypical case, this outlier, amenable to being understood in terms of their conceptual framework? If not, does its idiosyncratic nature render it of little value in terms of its explanatory model? Conversely, along the lines of Przeworski and Teune (1970), does this "most different case" make it even more relevant?

The key question asked by the editors, Luna, Piñeiro, Rosenblatt, and Vommaro, is, "What distinguishes full-blown parties from diminished subtypes?" This key question is highly relevant because even though the term *political party* is widely used, the label may encompass different structural organizations – some looser and some tighter – that vary significantly but are lumped together.

The two key variables identified by the organizers as distinguishing parties from diminished subtypes are the extent to which they exhibit horizontal coordination and vertical interest aggregation. By focusing on the Paraguayan "traditional" parties, the Asociación Nacional

Republicana (National Republican Association, ANR), or Partido Colorado (Colorado Party), founded on September 11, 1887, and the Partido Liberal Radical Auténtico (Authentic Liberal Radical Party, PLRA) or Partido Liberal (Liberal Party), founded on July 10, 1887, this chapter seeks to shed light on the questions raised by the organizers.[1]

The first section of this chapter will discuss the evolution of the Paraguayan parties in historical perspective. It will highlight the changes and continuities experienced by the parties in two different historical settings: the nondemocratic period, which includes a semi-competitive (1870–1940) and a dictatorial subperiod (1954–89), on the one hand, and in the post-1989 democratic period on the other.

The next two sections will examine the dimensions of vertical interest aggregation and horizontal coordination and how they changed over the course of these three eras. The gap in this discussion, the 1940–47 period, corresponds to the first and only purely military dictatorship in the history of Paraguay, led by Gen. Higinio Morínigo, that brought party life to an abrupt stop. The brief 1948–54 interlude marked a return to the pre-1940 semi-competitive period but under Colorado hegemony. In the midst of rampant instability, which saw the election of seven different presidents in eight years, General Alfredo Stroessner executed his May 4, 1954, coup d'etat. The conclusion will elaborate on some possible trends for the future.

FROM POLITICAL TO ELECTORAL MACHINES

The Paraguayan traditional parties were born in the aftermath of the War of the Triple Alliance (1864–70) that Paraguay fought against the allied forces of Argentina, Brazil, and Uruguay. The country was left in ruins, the population decimated, the society elite-less, the State nonexistent; this was the structural context of the parties' emergence. The parties, thus,

[1] The Colorado Party's legal name is ANR, although it is popularly known as the Colorado Party and, for the sake of simplicity, we call it Colorado Party. During the Stroessner regime political parties needed *"personería jurídica"* granted by the Colorado-controlled Junta Electoral Central. As a result, the Liberal Party was forced to change names twice because the name was awarded to small splinter groups. To distinguish itself from the regime-created and sanctioned splinter "parties," it adopted the name Radical Liberal Party (PLR) in 1967 and in the late 1970s, when the Stroessner regime again allowed another splinter group to keep the PLR name, it became the Authentic Liberal Radical Party (PLRA). For the sake of simplicity, we use the original name, Liberal Party, which is now widely accepted even though legally it is called Partido Liberal Radical Auténtico (PLRA).

were constructed on a *tabula rasa* with no clearly discernible links to prewar developments, cleavages, or political alignments.

In spite of having emerged from such fragile conditions they managed to survive, develop deep roots in society, and thrive. This raises at least four important questions. Why and how did the traditional parties establish such deep social roots? Why they have been so resilient? What were their organizational characteristics? What made them distinct enough to trigger the "us versus them" effect?

The Constitution of 1870 opened the door to a formally democratic political system and, by adopting universal suffrage, encouraged political organizations to recruit followers from throughout the country and weave a strong and extensive network of followers (Abente Brun 1995). This led to the early incorporation of the population into the political system and benefitted the first two parties that swiftly monopolized the market of political allegiances.

The parties gradually evolved from being loosely structured followers of a caudillo held together by primary affinities to becoming political machines and full-blown political parties in the modern sense of the word. Their success in doing so and the very slow rate of transformation of Paraguay's socioeconomic structure to a large extent explain the parties' endurance and resilience. By 1950, only 20 percent of the population lived in Asunción, the only urban center that could be considered a city. Some 66 percent of the population was rural, yet only seven districts had a population exceeding 20,000 people and each of these districts contained just a small urban center with the rest of the inhabitants living scattered in the so-called *compañías*, or rural surroundings. Furthermore, Paraguayan urban migration exhibited the particular characteristic of having Buenos Aires, not Asunción, as the primary destination (Abente Brun 1989).

Both parties were born and organized around the leadership of notables, distinguished military or civilian caudillos, and, like oligarchic parties elsewhere, were run in top-down fashion. Yet, because electoral politics was not consolidated and elections were marred by countless irregularities or outright fraud, the parties became political, rather than electoral, machines. Elections were a possible – but not a guaranteed – path to power. The political game evolved in manifold arenas, including not only elections but also civil military uprisings. Parties had to be ready to compete on these multiple, different fronts and to develop the appropriate repertoire of power resources to ensure success.

The task of explaining the distinctiveness of each party is more challenging than explaining their deep rootedness, resilience, and structure. In fact, the perennial quest to identify the distinctive traits characterizing each party has yielded much debate (Abente Brun 1989; Bourscheid 2018; Brezzo 2010; Caballero Aquino and Livieres Banks 1993; Chartrain 1973; Gómez Florentín 2013; Morínigo 2005; Warren 1985). Ideologically, both parties were liberal, in the laisser-faire, laisser-passer mold of nineteen-century liberalism.

The demographics of the parties were similar. Their social base of support followed a similar pattern including sectors of the elite, the small middle class, and the peasantry. Leaders would rightly define their parties as multi-class, which evokes the idea of a catch-all party so well developed by Otto Kirchheimer (1966). No discernible difference could be found in the parties' regional bases of support. The parties represented neither a regional nor an urban-rural divide.

The parties did not differ much with regard to the role of religion. Classical disputes over issues such as separation of church and state, the status of religious marriage, and divorce did not emerge until much later and both parties had a small minority faction opposing them. The most evident difference between them was one of cultural orientation, rather than ideology, with the liberal elites being more outward-looking, cosmopolitan, and urban-oriented, while, conversely, the Colorado leadership was more rural, traditional, and inward-looking. This distinction is consistent with the preambles of the founding charters of the Colorado Party and the Liberal Party, originally denominated Centro Democrático (Democratic Center). The foundational document of the Colorado Party states: "Our program can be synthesized in two words: peace and respect for our institutions. Maintaining social order and public tranquility can only be achieved by respecting the principle of authority" (Centurión 1947).[2]

In contrast, the foundational document of the Liberal Party begins by stating:

> Since the Constitution has given citizens, among other rights such as freedom of the press, expression, organization and the full respect of the electoral law ... we, the citizens here assembled ... have met to set up an organization that will allow us to fully exercise the rights accorded by the Constitution.

[2] All direct quotes that appear in the chapter were translated from Spanish by the author.

Thus far, it remains a puzzle how, from such a homogenous matrix, there emerged two nationally organized political rivals that not only competed politically but also clashed militarily. If all the variables generally considered significant explanatory factors, such as ideology, class, and demographics, were common to both parties, can the differences between the parties be reduced only to cultural outlooks or personalistic differences or competing leaderships?

One alternative explanation (Lewis 1993) observes that a key cleavage separating one party from the other was generational. The Colorado Party had adherents among the older generation of survivors of the Triple Alliance War, including the leading figures of Generals Bernardino Caballero and Patricio Escobar, both of whom played an important military role in the Paraguayan Army. The Liberal Party, in contrast, drew support from the younger generation and, among the veterans of the War, from lower-ranking officers such as Colonel Florentín Oviedo and Major Eduardo Vera. The difference in the rank of the veterans associated with each party does not seem coincidental.

Other theories note that parties can best be identified, in reality, as communities, and not parties in the modern sense of the word. Therefore, if, as some authors contend, both parties were communities, not associations – that is, "gemeinschaft" rather than "gesellschaft" (Morínigo 2008; Nichols 1968; Tönnies 1957 (1887)) – the very question of what distinguished the parties would lose relevance.

Undoubtedly the dimension of belonging to a community of "co-religionists" has been a strong element that has held the parties together. Upon the adoption of universal suffrage, the two emerging parties developed a strong set of symbolic elements of identity and adherence to charismatic leaders, and built a network of socioeconomic support. The Colorado Party adopted the color red, its own hymn, the polka Colorado, and its pantheon of heroes, chiefly Generals Bernardino Caballero and Patricio Escobar as the main leaders and José Segundo Decoud as its key ideologue (Caballero Carrizosa 1993, 2003) On the other hand, the Liberal Party seized the color blue as its flag, the polka "18 de Octubre" as its hymn, and a more diverse pantheon of heroes with a heavier presence of civilian leaders, such as Facundo Machaín and José de la Cruz Ayala (Alón), and Cecilio Báez as its leading ideologue. One key indicator of how successful this dimension of belonging became is the fact that, by and large, party affiliation was transmitted within families from one generation to the next.

However, the community thesis describes more than it explains. Why did the parties not emerge from preexisting communities, if the latter existed, and how did they manage to outlive the conditions that characterized their emergence? Communities did not evolve into parties; rather, parties created communities in order to survive and thrive. They were communities of a sort, but they were primarily political instruments. Were they only communities, they would have been narrow, closed, and self-sufficient social groups, isolated from the national political scene. Moreover, an analysis of the proto-parties, or "clubs," that preceded the founding of the traditional parties and from which they developed, are a further indication that the structuring cleavage was intra-elite competition (Lewis 1988, 1993; Warren 1985). The defining and founding cleavage was a congressional by-election. In fact, the Liberal Party was founded by the followers of a popular candidate, Antonio Taboada, who lost that election due to fraud and intimidation. Founded only two months later, the Colorado Party was organized to support the members of the faction in government. Every important event in the life of both parties was related to their power-seeking or power-retaining activities and strategies. This includes the massive mobilization of civilians in the many armed conflicts waged to gain or retain power.

This relentless will to power, deeply interwoven with a strong sense of belonging and community, explains why the Colorado Party survived as a major political force for forty-two years, from 1904 until 1946, without access, or even the chance of access, to control of the state except during the election of 1928. Likewise, it explains why the Liberal Party survived its dissolution in 1942 by the dictatorship of General Higinio Morínigo, who outlawed the party, and forty-seven years of brutal persecution until the fall of the dictatorship of General Alfredo Stroessner in 1989. The persistence of both traditional parties in the face of these challenges is testament to how remarkably successful they have been as political entities.

The coup d'état of February 3, 1989, opened the doors to the transition to democracy and with it the doors to electoral politics. For the first time, both traditional parties became fully fledged electoral machines, and only electoral machines. No longer would elections be sporadic, irregularly held, occasionally uncontested events. With the advent of democracy, the parties had to reinvent themselves (Arditi 1993; Filártiga Callizo 2016; Martínez-Escobar 2015; Pérez Talia 2017; Sánchez, González-Bozzolasco, and Martínez-Escobar 2015). The transition to democracy also opened the doors to the consolidation of the hegemonic role the two traditional parties played.

The dominance exercised by the traditional parties prior to 1989 continued thereafter. Paraguay has one of the highest levels of party membership of any country. By 2017, the combined membership of the two parties accounted for 80.82 percent of the country's registered voters (see Table 7.1).

This very high level of partisanship is directly linked to the dominant position both parties retained throughout the previous period. In the case of the Colorado Party, its quasi-monopoly was the result of sixty-one years of uninterrupted control of the state (1947–2008) and the strategies implemented by the Stroessner dictatorship. Yet, with the advent of democracy and the gradual weakening of the Colorado Party's hold on power and the state apparatus, these Colorado strategies had to be modified to employ less outright coercion and more patronage. It is worth mentioning that in 1991 the Colorado Party slogan for the election of members to the Constitutional Convention was as simple as it was powerful: "*No patées tu olla*" (Do not kick out your cooking pot).

The case of the Liberal Party is quite different. Persecuted for forty-seven years, with its leadership imprisoned, tortured, or exiled and its membership intimidated, it made a strong comeback in the general election of 1993, garnering almost 35 percent of the popular vote, in spite of multiple voting irregularities and, in some cases, outright electoral fraud. The explanation for the party's durability lies in the enduring nature of the communal bonds among its members, as discussed previously, but also in its members' shared values (PNUD-Congreso de la República 2009, 27). The social ties among members of the Liberal Party were particularly strong in the countryside and among Guaraní speakers. Fully 60 percent of the liberals speak Guaraní as their first language, as opposed to 48 percent of the Colorados who do so. Fewer than 15 percent of the liberals lived in Spanish-speaking homes as opposed to 25 percent of the Colorados. Its

TABLE 7.1 *Level of partisanship, 2017*

Party	Membership	% of Registered voters
Colorado	2,309,061	48.47
Liberal	1,258,719	35.29
Total	3,428,339	80.82

Source: Tribunal Superior de Justicia Electoral. The membership data comes from the data of the primary elections of December 2017. The data on the number of registered voters are from the voters' roll for the April 2018 election: www.tsje.gov.py (last accessed January 19, 2021).

strong adherence to the idea of liberty played a significant role. In the 1930s, Justo Pastor Benítez, a leading liberal intellectual and leader, wrote:

It would be a mistake to believe that liberalism [the Liberal Party] has been the result of a doctrine. No. It has, instead, been a social reality in search of a doctrine that affiliated itself with the universal and human tendency toward freedom ... Liberalism chose a banner – electoral freedom – and a program, the enforcement of the Constitution. (Benítez 1988 (1932), 10)

The most recent poll indicates that 37 percent of the liberals have a democratic profile and 33 percent an authoritarian profile. By comparison, 30 percent of the Colorados have a democratic profile and 42 percent have an authoritarian profile (PNUD-Congreso de la República 2009: 36).

VERTICAL INTEREST AGGREGATION

The 1870–1940 period, although nondemocratic, exhibited a varying degree of competitiveness and allowed parties to contend for power in several alternative arenas: always in the public forum of civic contestation, occasionally in semi-competitive elections, and sometimes in civil-military insurrections. Neither the period of Colorado hegemony (1870–1904) nor the period of Liberal hegemony (1904–1940) can be characterized as dictatorial. Throughout this period, elections, even if not competitive, were held regularly both for the Executive as well as for both chambers of Congress, a situation tantamount, in certain ways, to "elections without choice" (Hermet, Rouquié, and Linz 1978). The opposition party would split between *participacionistas* and *abstencionistas*. Hence, this period can be considered semi-competitive.

Parties exhibited very early a clear and significant level of vertical interest aggregation, even if these interests were weakly linked to a class or group demand. When not in power, parties resorted to what can be considered private clientelism, that is, using private, as opposed to state, resources. Saturnino Ferreira Pérez, a Colorado leader from the Department of Misiones, describes it thus:

[In the countryside] cattle raisers would rent oxen to farmers. In the majority of cases, cattle raisers helped their co-religionists: Liberals helped Liberals and Colorados helped Colorados. [Peasants paid a tithe and after three years returned the oxen to the owner, who would then sell it to the meat-packing plant.] The same applied to cart owners who rented steers ... Liberal and Colorado caudillos were great men because of their behavior, honesty, and generosity. They acted as guarantors of their co-religionists vis-á-vis the merchants who supplied the seeds, insecticides, other goods, and some cash ... With this organization, it is understandable why traditional political alignments remained so deeply entrenched in the Paraguayan population. (Ferreira Pérez 1986, 137–138)

In a groundbreaking 1968 study, Nichols (1968) carried out the first quantitative study on the expectations of political parties' followers. Although the sample was small and the study was conducted under very precarious conditions and thus must be treated with caution, one of the most important findings has to do with the reason for party affiliation. Only 5.7 percent of the Colorados and 13.6 percent of the liberals saw their party solely as an instrument to gain power. Rather, 69 percent of the Colorados and 58 percent of the liberals responded that parties combine the aspects of a family, a network to protect mutual interests, a custodian of traditions, and an instrument to gain power.

When asked whether the parties were expected to provide social and economic assistance in times of need, 39 percent of the Colorados and 41 percent of the liberals responded "yes." Among those with primary education, 76 percent of the Colorados and 54 percent of the liberals said "yes." Most party members – 67 percent of the members of both traditional parties – also expect their organizations to provide them with medical assistance.

Finally, an unsurprising but still telling finding concerns the extent to which the family plays a role in party identification. Some 47 percent of the Colorados and 48 percent of the liberals indicated that both their parents belonged to the same party. If only the affiliation of the father is taken into account – and in Paraguay politics has traditionally been regarded as the realm of men – 66 percent of Colorados and 60 percent of liberals had fathers of the same party as themselves; 79 percent of the Colorados and 84 percent of the liberals mentioned that some family dimension played a role in their affiliation. These findings show that parties were strongly influenced by family ties and were perceived as networks of support but that there was a reciprocal relationship between gaining power and providing support: gaining power was a means to provide support and providing support was a means to gain power.

Another important implication of these findings is that parties always performed vertical interest aggregation. Members expect parties to meet their needs. That aggregation has a distinctive clientelist nature that can also be observed in other contexts (Fox 1994; Kitschelt and Wilkinson 2007; Luna 2014; Roberts 2002), but whose pervasiveness and endurance is peculiar to the Paraguayan case.

The fact that vertical aggregation has been clientelistic demonstrates as well that strong vertical aggregation may take place in the absence of a strong civil society. In fact, the Paraguayan case shows that, after the advent of democracy in the 1990s, civil society afforded an alternative channel of interest aggregation that bypassed political parties. The peculiarity of the process of vertical aggregation is the result of what I have called the invertebrate nature of the social matrix (i.e. the lack of collective actors bound together by social-class links). I borrow the expression, if not the concept, from the famous work of José Ortega y Gasset (1921).

Paraguay lacked the hacienda-like structure of other Latin American countries. The rural area exhibited a stark contrast between vast cattle-raising estates, or *latifundios*, and a multitude of smallholdings, or *minifundios*. For about a century, from 1870 until 1970, the peasantry comprised a very large number of individual small farmers or simple tenants lacking any formal relations of labor dependence. As late as 2017, 20.5 percent of the labor force was still employed in the agricultural sector and only 11 percent were employed in the manufacturing sector (Dirección General de Estadística, Encuestas y Censos 2018: 10). On the other hand, at least 66 percent of the urban labor force worked in the informal sector. A World Bank study put that figure at between 55 and 77 percent, depending on the criteria used (Mauricio Vargas 2015, 12).

The consequences of this rather traditional, pre-industrial structure are far-reaching for they hinder the emergence of collective actors capable of developing a collective identity and thus of having a universalistic impact on the political process. This lack of social articulation in a large part of the population favored even more the emergence of clientelistic politics, that is, of politics based on dyadic and asymmetrical relations that prevent the emergence of horizontal ties and encourage instead vertical, hierarchical, and essentially exploitative relationships. The consequence of this type of incorporation of members of the popular sector is their inclusion as clients, but their exclusion as citizens.

What other kind of politics, civil society, collective actors, interest articulation and aggregation – and, hence, political parties – could emerge from this fragmented, "invertebrate" social matrix? The answer is that parties did perform the function of vertical interest aggregation but in the context of the Paraguayan socioeconomic structure. Actors, in this case, clients, behaved in a rational way and sought the representation of their interests through particularistic channels. Political parties responded by ensuring that these needs were met, even if in a most suboptimal manner.

The long persistence of the parties is a testimony to the fact that they met their client's needs successfully.

During the Stroessner dictatorship, the Colorado Party experienced a transformation that converted it, too, into an apparatus of political control. Party affiliation was required for access to the public sector and to the police and the armed forces. This led to a massive wave of people affiliating with the party to gain a position in the public sector and subsequent development of ties to the party in order to retain these positions. During the Stroessner regime, all public employees had to contribute a percentage of their salaries to finance the party and to buy *Patria*, the party's official newspaper. The contributions were compulsory and were simply deducted from their paychecks.

Under the Stroessner dictatorship, the Colorado Party became the best-organized party in the country and provided a staunch and well-structured base of political support to the government. It greatly strengthened the local branches (*seccionales*), who numbered 240 at their peak. The *seccionales* – not the Congress or the state agencies – controlled the process of vertical interest aggregation. Patronage was dispensed though them. Government agencies would not hire an employee unless he had a party identity card and, in most cases, the recommendation of a *seccional* president. Members of their governing boards were also employed by government agencies, which constituted an integral part of the reward associated with their political position.

The military-like structure of the *seccionales* was implemented by General César Gagliardone, at the time the party's Secretary of Organization, who, in 1955, adopted such a model to ensure loyalty, discipline, order, and efficiency. The operation of the *seccionales* was modelled after the counterinsurgency philosophy of "civic action," except that in this case it was executed not by the military but by a civilian structure. The *seccionales*, thus, were not limited to administering patronage but also worked to co-opt the opposition and repress any attempt at resistance. The wide array of social and political functions the *seccionales* performed is well illustrated in the job description provided by the president of one of them:

> Look, we have just received a prescription; when there is a need for medicine, people come here. We have a G 8,000 [US$10 at the time] prescription, if the *seccional* has the money it will pay for it, if not the president will have to pay for it (...) A President of a *seccional* is a little bit of a judge, a midwife, a doctor, a lawyer, a father, a grandfather, he is the support and the one who protects the humble ones in his jurisdiction. (Abente Brun 1995, 305)

Its police function is described in the second part of the interview: "I have a permanent secretariat. In *Seccional* No. 3, we control fifty people, and we keep close tabs on them in our files. We include in our files all the inhabitants of this jurisdiction, the foreigners, etc. In summary, we have everything under control" (Abente Brun 1995, 306).

The *seccionales* were also instrumental in mobilizing support for the regime. The "neither intensive nor extensive" (Linz 1964, 297) demonstrations of public support organized generally once a year were the work of the *seccionales* that were assigned a given number of people to bring and the necessary number of buses, food, and alcoholic drinks to do so. The *seccionales*, in sum, were the quintessential expression of vertical interest aggregation during the Stroessner dictatorship.

In the case of the Liberal Party, there was genuine competition, but the national leadership of the different factions drew the list. This was the case for the elections conducted by the Stroessner regime in which the Liberal Party participated: the municipal election of 1965, the constituent convention of 1967, and the general elections of 1968, 1973, 1978, 1983, and 1988. These elections were marred not only by widespread fraud and that they were organized for the purpose of pretending that the regime was a democratic one (Hermet, Rouquié, and Linz 1978) but also by the system of "*mayoría con prima*" which ensured most of the contested seats to the majority party. Deprived of any significant possibility of overturning the Stroessner regime, the Liberal Party participated in this charade for the purpose of retaining some degree of organizational resources both for the leadership and their followers and a limited space for political activism.

At the beginning of the transition to democracy, the Liberal Party appealed to the same strategies utilized by the Colorado Party to strengthen its electoral muscle. The adoption of this strategy was, by and large, a function of its ability to win elections at the municipal and gubernatorial level. In the case of the municipalities, it went from winning 21 percent of the mayoral elections in 1991 to 34 percent in 2015 (see Table 7.2).

Likewise, the Liberal Party won, over time, an average of four to five of the nineteen governorships, including those of the two largest departments (Central and Caaguazu) where 37 percent of the population lives. Meanwhile, the Colorado Party retained its firm hold on the other two departments, Alto Paraná and Itapua, which are home to 20 percent of the country's population.

TABLE 7.2 *Number of municipalities won by party*

Parties	1991	1996	2001	2006	2010	2015
Colorado	155	162	146	152	135	148
Liberal	41	48	66	68	86	75

Source: Došek, Duarte Recalde, and Pérez Talia (2016, *143*).

Once in control of the governorships and municipalities, the liberals resorted to the same patronage and clientelist practices once considered the trademark of the Colorado Party. The difference was that, having inherited an already large number of employees, they had a more limited opportunity to satisfy their clientele. The extent to which these trends evolved is well captured in the expression *aparato* (political machine). The Colorado Party had an electoral advantage because of its stronger political machine. Likewise, no opposition candidate can win without the support of the Liberal Party because it would lack a political machine. That was the case in 2008 when Fernando Lugo was elected president. Even the emerging parties of the Left use their limited access to municipal governments to build a political machine.

From time to time, the Colorado Party failed to perform the functions of vertical aggregation swiftly enough. During the early years of the transition to democracy, *seccionaleros* complained that they no longer had the power enjoyed under Stroessner. The emergence of a more competitive arena and the reallocation of party power to both the government and the parliamentary party weakened them. Yet they remained key actors, albeit through intermediaries, namely, the elected leaders who depended on them to win the primary elections and then the national elections. Two recent cases vividly illustrate this reality. The president of the Senate, Silvio Ovelar, complained repeatedly that the Minister of Education was not "receiving" their coreligionists. It was obvious that the meetings were sought to ask for appointments, promotions, relocations, and a whole array of requests that should not have been granted if legal procedures were followed. Another well-known case was the decision of the Governor of Alto Paraná, Roberto González Vaesken, to abandon the internal faction of the president, Colorado Añeteté. The alleged reason was that his coreligionists were not being "heard." The underlying reality was again the ability of his followers to access well-paid positions at the Itaipú Binacional, the hydroelectric dam shared with

Brazil, and gain lucrative contacts. Once his coreligionists were "heard," González Vaesken returned to the Colorado Añeteté faction arguing that all was due to a misunderstanding. As this example shows, the Colorado Party continues to perform its vertical aggregation function.

The advent of democracy brought about a change in the way the parties fulfilled their vertical interest aggregation function, but not in its intrinsic clientelist nature. It is common to criticize the parties for resorting to these practices. While this criticism may be justified, these practices are necessary for a party to win elections and remain in power. On the other hand, as I have argued elsewhere, clients respond rationally when they resign themselves to this state of affairs because of the absence of the provision of public goods on the part of the state (Abente Brun 2014).

Clientelistic relations are the most "efficient" tool of vertical aggregation in the absence of strong collective actors making collective demands for public goods. It is, thus, a vicious circle. Consider that fully 84.4 percent of the respondents in a recent survey somewhat or completely agreed with the statement that parties were expected to provide help to their members as part of their mission. Another 78 percent agreed that a party that won an election should always – or at least in cases of need – help its members. The three most frequently cited types of expected help were: provide jobs, 74.6 percent; secure health services, 67.8 percent; and give scholarships, 42.7 percent. Fully 83 percent of the members of the traditional parties showed a predisposition to engage in clientelistic relations (Lachi and Rojas Scheffer 2018, 149, 152, 159).

The exception to this rule is the collective demands of corporations: state employees, retirees, teachers, university professors, and doctors and nurses. This is the area where parties play a different aggregation role. The demands – chiefly salary and pension increases – are made directly to Congress, not to the executive power, because the most likely response of the Finance Ministry would be negative or insufficient to meet their expectations. The leaders of these corporations therefore would meet with Congressional party leaders to solicit their support. In Congress, all parties would agree because all of them are equally interested in gaining the support of the interest groups. Thus, parties – in this case "parliamentary parties" – are again efficient tools of vertical aggregation.

On occasion, however, the pressure is directed to the party in power, that is, the Colorado Party. For example, during the month of March 2019, public employee unions, in addition to reaching out to Congress, organized demonstrations to protest an attempt by the government to reduce their numerous perks and benefits. While threatening a general strike, they carried a huge placard depicting a big Ferris wheel and this text: "Marito [Abdo Benítez, the President], watch out: the wheel turns. HC waits." "HC" refers to Horacio Cartes, the main rival of the president. As expected, the government backed down.

While this analysis shows that parties perform vertical interest aggregation functions, an interesting question is why levels of electoral support for the Colorado Party vary depending on whether the contests are for the presidency, the Senate, or the Chamber of Deputies. The Colorado Party has consistently obtained more votes for the presidency than for Congress, especially for the Senate in spite of the fact that in all cases all three lists were the lists of the Colorado Party, *Lista 1*. Just as the color identifies the party, since 1989 the party has also been strongly identified in elections with the expression *Lista 1*. On average, in the last five elections, the presidential ticket garnered 42.7 percent of the votes while the Senate list obtained 35 percent, a difference of 7.7 points. This was particularly acute in the elections of 2003, 2013, and 2018 when the average difference was 10.3 points. Electoral support for Colorado Party presidential candidates has also been consistently higher than the votes for Colorado Party representative candidates (see Table 7.3).

This disparity is likely due to voters' perception of how effective each candidate can be in terms of aggregating their interests. First, the presidency controls the government and the whole public sector and thus has greater power to respond to its followers' demands. Secondly, the representatives, who are elected by departments, are closer to the voters and can be more easily influenced. Finally, the Senate is elected from a national list and is the most distant from the voters and the least responsive to voters' concerns. According to this perspective, voters view the parties as instruments of vertical aggregation of interests and behave accordingly.

The level of consistency between presidential and senatorial votes in the Liberal Party, identified with *Lista 2*, is also significant, although more difficult to quantify because the party's presidential ticket was in a coalition list in the 1998, 2008, 2013, and 2018 elections. However, this pattern is clearly seen in the 1993 and 2003 elections, which can be considered test cases because the Liberal Party competed alone.[3] In 1993, the PLRA garnered 32.21 percent for the presidential ticket and 34.85 percent for the senatorial list while in 2003 it received

[3] The election of 1993 is not included in previous tables because it was held under the Stroessner regime's electoral authority and system. The results are from Political Database of the Americas (1999).

TABLE 7.3 *Party share votes in national elections (presidential, senate, and representatives)*

	Colorado Party (ANR)			Liberal Party (PLRA)		
Year	President	Senate	Representatives	President	Senate	Representatives
1998	53.6[a]	49.3	52.0	42.6[f]	40.1	41.3
2003	37.1[b]	32.9	33.8	23.9[g]	24.3	24.6
2008	30.6[c]	27.2	31.1	40.9[h]	27.0	26.7
2013	45.8[d]	35.9	38.3	36.9[i]	24.4	27.3
2018	46.4[e]	29.6	35.9	42.7[j]	22.0	16.3

Source: Tribunal Superior de Justicia Electoral (Superior Tribunal of Electoral Justice).
[a] Colorado Party united with the Oviedo faction.
[b] Colorado Party without Oviedo and without his candidacy.
[c] Colorado Party without Oviedo. Oviedo candidate.
[d] Colorado Party. Oviedo died before election.
[e] Colorado Party with *oviedista* support.
[f] Liberal Party + rest of the opposition.
[g] Liberal Party alone.
[h] Lugo as candidate of the Liberal Party.
[i] Liberal Party and one small party support.
[j] Liberal Party + leftist parties.

23.95 percent for the presidential ticket and 24.27 percent for the senatorial candidates. The level of support for the party's senatorial list has remained relatively steady in the last four elections: 27.01 percent in 2008, 24.43 percent in 2013, and 22.01 in 2018. This could be interpreted as an indication that the liberal vote enjoys greater loyalty and that the degree to which voters see the party as an efficient instrument of interest aggregation has been stable across the presidency and the Congress.

HORIZONTAL COORDINATION

The degree and type of horizontal coordination performed by the parties has varied over time. Horizontal coordination may take place in three different settings: electoral, insurrectional (civic-military uprisings) and mobilizational (strikes, mass demonstrations, lockouts). In the case of Paraguay, horizontal coordination should be analyzed in the context of the first two scenarios, those that characterized the political system for much of the post-1870 period.

During the periods of semi-competitive politics between 1870 and 1940, and especially from 1912 to 1936, parties mobilized their followers for the elections. The candidacies were decided by the party's central authorities but the mobilization of voters had to be done by regional and local leaders, especially in an era when the only means of communication was the printed media that reached a very small readership. The best example of this horizontal coordination during elections was the presidential election of 1928. While in the other elections the numbers may have been manipulated and therefore might not reflect the true extent of horizontal coordination, in the 1928 election, the only truly competitive election, José P. Guggiari, of the Liberal Party, obtained 57 percent of the popular vote and the candidate of the Colorado Party, Eduardo Fleytas, obtained almost 27 percent. These numbers would not have been possible had the parties lacked a national structure and a degree of horizontal coordination. Moreover, the level of participation was unusually high, with 11 percent of the population voting. In three other national elections held in the same year in Latin America the rates of participation were: Mexico, 10.4 percent; Argentina, 12.9 percent; and Uruguay, 16.7 percent (Abente Brun 1989). Although there is no historical data available to ascertain the degree of horizontal coordination between elections, it is clear that the clientelist structures could not have endured without it.

A distinctive characteristic of the Paraguayan case that sets it apart from the general rule – with the possible exception of Colombia – is that, during nonelectoral periods, the degree of horizontal coordination was evidenced by the civilian population's massive participation in the many uprisings that characterized the 1900–40 period and that, in a more sporadic manner, lasted until the middle of the twentieth century. While horizontal coordination, in the theoretical framework posited by the editors of this volume, denotes the role of parties in facilitating the coordination of ambitious politicians during campaigns and between electoral cycles, in the case of Paraguay coordination is also visible when the contest for power shifted away from the electoral arena. Just as parties mobilized their followers for the electoral contests, they recruited them for the uprisings. This coordination, which included leadership selection and strategic planning, was even more powerful, as party members were recruited for warfare, not for elections. Coreligionists were incorporated not just as voters, but as combatants.

The number of political armed conflicts in Paraguay has few parallels in Latin America. Paraguay ranks perhaps second only to Colombia. The

Liberal Party attempted the first insurrection on 18 October 1891. In 1904, the Liberal Party mobilized thousands of civilians to topple the Colorado Party from power after more than four months of confrontations.[4] Between 1908 and 1912, there were several civil-military uprisings. These lasted many months at a time and involved legions of armed civilians.

The last and largest uprising of the period of liberal hegemony was the 1922 uprising, which lasted over a year. In this uprising, the radical faction of the Liberal Party, with the support of thousands of armed civilians, defeated their rivals, who had the support of the bulk of the armed forces but also included legions of civilian recruits (De los Santos 1984; Velásquez and Angulo Aponte 2019).

All these uprisings were staged with the decisive participation of armed civilians because, for all practical purposes, a professional military only came into being in the early part of the 1920s. The last major conflict was the civil war of 1947, which witnessed the massive incorporation of civilians into the conflict, including the civilian Colorados known as *pynandi*, or "barefooted combatants."

Subsequent attempts to overthrow the Stroessner regime took place in November 1956 when armed civilians and some retired military officers attempted to capture the First Cavalry Division in the outskirts of Asunción, the country's main military garrison, as well as in the late 1950s and early 1960s, when the Liberal Party supported several attempts at mounting a guerrilla resistance (Arellano 2004; Montero 2019). In short, throughout the period that preceded the advent of democracy, the traditional parties maintained a significant degree of horizontal coordination, albeit sui generis, be it for electoral purposes or for the many uprisings, none of which would have been possible without the massive participation of civilian recruits from both parties.

Until the beginning of the democratic transition, both parties developed a strong centralized system that linked the national with the local leadership. In the case of the Colorado Party it was the Junta de Gobierno (Government Junta) and, in the case of the Liberal Party, the Directorio (Directorate). Candidates for the congressional elections were selected in party conventions by delegates elected by the membership. In the case of

[4] The 1904 "revolution" that toppled the Colorado Party and put the Liberal Party in power resulted from the mutiny of one warship sailing from Buenos Aires to Asunción and the recruitment of thousands of armed civilians in the port of Villeta and other areas around Asunción.

the Colorado Party, the list was drawn up by General Stroessner and "elected" by unanimity.

The first electoral law approved during the transition introduced two major changes that were to have long-lasting consequences. First, the law adopted a proportional representation system utilizing the D'Hondt formula for the allocation of seats in Congress and municipal councils, with parties presenting a closed list. Second, it established the direct election of candidates by the party membership using the same electoral formula. As a result, the national leaderships were weakened, the party conventions lost relevance, and the fragmentation of the parties increased exponentially. This, combined with the creation of "governorships" and departmental councils in the framework of the decentralizing Constitution of 1992, further exacerbated the fragmentation of the traditional parties.

The strengthening of competing party factions also hindered the ability of parties to exercise a strong degree of coordination with Congress and local governments between elections. Rarely do all factions follow the party line dictated by the central party authority. More often than not, they are ignored, as factions derive their power from their own electoral clienteles and the central authority has no way to impose discipline. The recent adoption of a system of open lists will exacerbate this fragmentation further. According to the change adopted in late 2019, electors will have to vote for one, and only one, candidate in any list. This candidate will of course owe his/her seat to nobody but him/herself.

Horizontal coordination during elections, however, remained possible because of the need to use the party label and because the state electoral subsidies created in the electoral law and the state apparatus are controlled by the national authorities. This power of the purse is not absolute, though, and, thus, the control of the central leadership, especially between elections, has been weakened, as noted. The high degree of horizontal coordination during elections is evidenced by the electoral turnout level. The most recent survey shows that 79 percent of the Liberals and 80 percent of the Colorados voted in the election of 2008 whereas the national rate of participation was 66 percent. Among respondents not affiliated with either of the two major parties, only 34 percent voted. Furthermore, 30 percent the Liberals and 26 percent of the Colorados indicated that they were transported to the polling places by their parties, but the real number may be higher due to a sort of shame factor. These figures reflect a dense organizational capacity geared to voter mobilization. On Election Day, parties provide buses, trucks, taxis, and cars with party signs around the polling places (PNUD-Congreso de la República 2009, 29–33).

Since the adoption of the primary, parties have faced the challenge of replicating at the national level the degree of mobilization occurring for the internal elections, that is, bringing together winners and losers. An example of successful coordination of electoral strategies can be seen by comparing the votes in the primaries and the votes in the national elections. As we have noted, the rules governing the primaries are a recipe for fragmentation – anyone can compete and set up a list – while, conversely, the national elections provide a test of party discipline. In December 2017, some 1,119,278 Colorados voted in the primary election while 460,000 Liberals voted. In the April national election of 2018, the candidate of the Colorado Party, Mario Abdo Benítez, obtained 1,204,067 votes, only some 86,000 – or 7 percent – more than in the party primary. This is a clear indication of how effectively the multiple factions have coordinated with regional and local leaders to translate the votes of the primaries to the national elections. In the same election, the Liberal Party obtained 558,509 votes for the Senate, some 98,000 – or 21 percent – more votes than in the primaries, another indication of strong coordination. In this case, the Senate election provides the most comparable data because the presidential candidate Efraín Alegre ran as the candidate of a broad alliance (data from the TSJE and the Electoral Tribunals of the Colorado and Liberal Party). Parties succeeded in coordinating their electoral strategy not only because of the resources at the disposal of the national leadership, but also because of the system of closed lists. The fragmentation that characterized the primaries ended with the creation of a single party list for the national elections and the various rival groups had to work to achieve it.

CONCLUSIONS

What makes the Paraguayan case unique is that, for more than 130 years, the two traditional parties have remained the backbone of the Paraguayan political system, during both democratic and nondemocratic periods. During the nondemocratic period, and when a degree of semi-competitive politics flourished, parties in government remained strong vehicles of horizontal coordination and vertical interest aggregation. This coordination was necessary to compete in elections but also to mobilize armed combatants during the periods of civil unrest. The party that was in the opposition played the same role but had a more difficult task of vertical interest aggregation because of its lack of access to state resources. In such cases, it resorted to symbolic rewards and to a degree of support provided by party leaders who occupied positions of economic power in the countryside. Thus, parties complemented purely strategic political functions with a number of other activities of social support and a strong cult of devotion to the party founders and leaders, the "guiding ideas" presented as ideology, and an elaborate ritual to celebrate the sense of belonging.

Once the transition to democracy began, the parties underwent a transformation. Without losing their original characteristics, they increasingly became electoral machines perfecting a system of horizontal coordination during elections and vertical interest aggregation that allowed them to retain the loyalty of between 60 and 70 percent of the electorate, election after election. While this system provides a great deal of stability and predictability, it also freezes in place a democracy of low quality. The question is whether at some point a rebellion against this *partidocracia* will emerge and thus bring down the country's democratic system as we know it.

On the one hand, the high level of party identification and affiliation indicates that such an outcome is unlikely. On the other hand, the level of support for political parties hovers around 21 percent, the lowest level of support for any institution in the country. How, then, does one explain that while 80 percent of the population is affiliated with the parties, only 21 percent of the population rate the parties favorably? It seems clear that the population acts in a rational and cynical way. Support for the parties may well be a function of the recognition that, given the traditional parties' monopoly of political influence, only through them can individuals' interests be aggregated efficiently.

The issue is akin to what Hirschman (1970) described as the dilemma of exit, voice, or loyalty. Voters are profoundly disappointed with the parties but do not see exit as a practical option (i.e. they do not see a viable electoral alternative). Second, voters continue to revere their parties, their colors, their music, and the galleries of heroes on the altar, while they consider the present leadership to be people not up to the task who pale in comparison with the glorious standards of their predecessors. For voters this is an effective way to reconcile their love/hate relationship. Finally, because voters are rational and pragmatic, they vote for the traditional parties, which are the only available vehicles for vertical interest aggregation. Limited as they are, they provide a degree of voice.

A final brief consideration comparing the Paraguayan case with that of other Latin American cases is in order. In the case of Uruguay, as the legitimacy of the Partido Colorado (Colorado Party) and Partido

Nacional (National Party, PN) parties eroded, the Frente Amplio (Broad Front, FA) offered an exit option to the urban-based working class and the middle classes (Pérez Bentancur, Piñeiro Rodríguez, and Rosenblatt this volume). In the case of Chile, neither the Liberal nor the Conservative Party were able to retain the loyalty of their constituents and strong challengers – the Christian Democrats and the Socialists – led to their demise. In Colombia, parties managed to survive and adapt but have experienced continuous weakening since the 1990s (Wills-Otero, Ortega, and Sarmiento this volume). In Honduras, both traditional parties remain strong, even though the Liberal Party is experiencing a profound schism. Once again, the Paraguayan traditional parties have been remarkably successful at horizontal and vertical coordination over time.

Social and economic factors played an important role in the longevity of Paraguay's traditional parties. The slow process of socio-economic modernization and urbanization prevented and or delayed the emergence of new social actors who may have deemed the repertoire of power resources at the disposal of traditional parties insufficient and who could have become a potential source of supporters for alternative parties.

Institutional changes may weaken or even bring about the demise of traditional parties. The diminishing level of horizontal coordination between elections that resulted in the adoption of the direct election of candidates; the decentralization of the administrative structure adopted by the 1992 Constitution; the increasing decentralization of fiscal resources via direct transfer of resources from the central to the departmental and local governments; and, the adoption of the open list system may portend, in the medium term, the weakening or perhaps even the demise of the traditional parties. Given the lack of organized constituents demanding programmatic commitments, Paraguay is unlikely to follow the path to more programmatic competition observed in Chile or Uruguay (Kitschelt et al. 2010). Rather, Peru may offer a model of what lies in store for Paraguay (Vergara and Augusto this volume). Peruvianization will further degrade the quality of democracy and will put the political system at the mercy of a powerful groups of financiers, either from the growing criminal organizations engaged in drug- and arms-trafficking and money laundering and/or from the all-powerful syndicates of the agricultural, livestock, and financial oligarchy. As a result, Paraguay may end up stuck between a rock and a hard place.

8

The Colombian Liberal Party and Conservative Party

From Political Parties to Diminished Subtypes

Laura Wills-Otero, Bibiana Ortega, and Viviana Sarmiento

INTRODUCTION

Colombia's Partido Liberal (Liberal Party, PL) and Partido Conservador (Conservative Party, PC) are two of the oldest party organizations in Latin America. They both arose in the middle of the nineteenth century (in 1848 and 1849, respectively), and have participated in almost all national and subnational elections that have taken place since then. Over 170 years of history, they have managed to adapt and to survive changing conditions, both structural and circumstantial, and to maintain a substantial degree of electoral political power. While the Paraguayan traditional parties, the Liberal and Colorado parties, remain to this day the main electoral vehicles for accessing power (see Abente Brun this volume), the electoral powers of Colombia's PL and PC have declined since the 1990s. Even though both organizations are still able to win votes and elect candidates in popular elections, they do not always do so in a coordinated way. Their internal fragmentation has prevented them from accumulating a greater number of votes and from integrating programmatic agendas within the representative organizations in a coherent manner throughout the different levels of power (e.g., national, regional, and local). Between elections, and thanks to legal incentives – the Law on Blocs of 2005[1] – these parties achieve a minimum degree of coordination when promoting or blocking certain policies in Congress. Nevertheless, party leaders usually leave their legislators free to vote as they please most of the time. While this parliamentary freedom in decision-making enables the traditional parties to

[1] See "Horizontal Coordination between Elections" section.

survive despite their extreme factionalism, the confluence of contrary interests and positions erodes programmatic coherence and thus undermines the parties' connection with their voters.

The PL and the PC have lost much of their ability to aggregate collective interests vertically. Their electorate has declined substantially since the early 1990s, and there are no substantial sociodemographic or ideological differences between the voters of the two parties at this time. Furthermore, the linkages to formal and informal organizations of the PL and the PC have not always been stable, so there have been no real incentives to promote programmatic agendas that respond to the interests of a clearly defined electorate. In other words, the vertical interest aggregation that is characteristic of political parties falls short in these organizations. Therefore, taking into account their lack of vertical interest aggregation as well as their minimal degree of horizontal coordination, both the PL and the PC exhibit characteristics of the Independents and Uncoordinated types (Luna et al. Introduction this volume). Both electoral vehicles still manage to compete in elections with relative success, but without representing a clearly defined electorate.

This chapter describes the behavior of Colombia's traditional PL and PC, and argues that these organizations classify as diminished subtypes. In this chapter, we concentrate on the period that began with the promulgation of the new constitutional charter of 1991 and lasted until 2018. The Constitution of 1991 promoted the political opening that transformed the traditional two-party system into a multiparty one. Since then, both the PL and the PC have suffered a systematic decline in electoral results.

The next section synthesizes the history and trajectory of the PL and the PC from the time of their birth in the middle of the nineteenth century to the 2018 presidential and legislative elections. The section following describes and illustrates some of the characteristics of the two organizations in terms of horizontal coordination and vertical interest aggregation. In the last part, we present our conclusions. We used official and secondary sources and we reviewed laws regarding parties and party by-laws, election results, opinion-poll results, interviews with officials and activists from both parties, as well as academic and press articles.

ORIGINS AND TRAJECTORY

Colombia's traditional parties, the PL and the PC, arose in the late 1840s. The first to promulgate a political program was the PL in 1848, while the PC did the same in 1849. Each party presented a presidential candidate for the election of 1849, and the ideas they defended were clear in each case. The programs of the two parties contrasted clearly with each other. On the one hand, the PL promoted the decentralization of political power and the weakening of executive power, with federalism as the conceptual basis for institutional design. It also fostered separation of the state and the Catholic Church, defended civil liberties such as universal suffrage along with freedom of speech and press, and advocated for the abolition of the death penalty. For its part, the PC promoted centralization and strong power at the head of the executive branch, union between the state and the Catholic Church to promote anti-liberal moral values, the defense of private property, and limitations on voting rights and individual liberties for the population (Bushnell 2016; Dix 1987; Melo 2018). With some variations and innovations, these were the central and general principles that defined the programmatic agendas of the traditional parties from the time of their birth to the middle of the twentieth century.

Throughout that period, there were moments in which the PL dominated over the PC, and others in which the PC won electoral power and went on the offensive against liberal ideas. For that reason, there were various civil wars during the second half of the nineteenth century in which the winner imposed a new constitution and a new type of structure for the state. Although elections were held without interruption over almost the entire period, at times the losing party – or one that abstained from taking part in the elections – was entirely or almost completely excluded from political participation afterwards. This is why historians have classified successive periods as the Hegemony or Republic of one party or the other (Bushnell 2016; Melo 2018).[2]

During the first century of PL and PC existence, political society was sharply divided between liberals and conservatives: one group excluded the other entirely and instilled hatred for the counter-party among their supporters. This inherited hatred nourished a sectarianism that divided the country into two separate and almost always antagonistic political subcultures (González 1997; Sánchez and Meertens 1983) that shaped a two-party system which lasted for almost a century and a half even though the parties themselves suffered constant internal ruptures that sometimes generated attempts to create new groupings of dissident

[2] The historical periods in which one or the other party predominated electorally and/or politically, have been defined in the following way: (1) the Liberal Revolution of the nineteenth century (1849–85); (2) the Regeneration (1885–1904); (3) the Conservative Hegemony (1904–30); and (4) the Liberal Republic (1930–46).

factions. At different times, the elites managed to bring an end to periods of liberal-versus-conservative violence by reaching political or programmatic agreements (e.g., 1905–29 and 1957), thus ensuring the survival of their parties and maintaining the exclusionary two-party system.

Both the PL and the PC were originally parties of elites that defended the interests of clearly identified sectors of society: large landowners, merchants, large and small coffee-growers, and industrialists. Their constituencies, therefore, mainly comprised members of the country's political and economic elites. Neither party responded to the interests of the lower classes or marginalized sectors of society, although there were artisans in the ranks of the PL and peasants in the PC in rural areas (Bushnell 2016).

After twenty-five years of relatively peaceful and prosperous PC governments between 1905 and 1930, the PL regained the power of the presidency in 1930 and managed to remain in power until 1946. The PL incorporated the interests of the working class into its political agenda at that time and thus broadened its electorate and changed the nature of the political competition (Albarracín, Gamboa, and Mainwaring 2018, 229). Between 1948 and 1953, the PL and the PC faced each other once again in a conflict known as *La Violencia* (the violence) that was waged throughout much of the national territory, with greatest intensity in remote zones far away from the center of political power. The main goal of the parties to this conflict was to achieve control of state power through violent elimination, co-optation of political institutions, and exclusion of the opposition party (Guzmán Campos 1962).

As a result of the interparty conflict, a coup d'état carried out by General Gustavo Rojas Pinilla in 1953 imposed a military government that lasted until 1958, when the period known as Frente Nacional (National Front, FN) began as a result of negotiations between leaders of the traditional parties. For sixteen years (1958–74), the PL and the PC would alternate in the presidency every four years and divide up the political and bureaucratic power of the state on a parity basis. While there was a return to electoral democracy and the period of *La Violencia* was left behind, the FN agreement eventually led to the de-ideologization and the clientelization of the PL and the PC. The confrontations between the parties were no longer about the type of state that each promoted but were instead transformed into bureaucratic conflicts over the distribution of government resources (Chernick 1989, 288). Competition took place not between parties but within them, among different lists. This competition led to their fragmentation, and both parties became divided into two or more major factions.[3] In some cases, these internal conflicts led to the formation of dissident factions that would eventually dare to challenge the traditional parties in the predetermined elections – for example, the Movimiento Revolucionario Liberal (Liberal Revolutionary Movement, MRL) in 1960 and 1962, and the Alianza Nacional Popular (National Popular Alliance, ANAPO) in 1970.

The de-ideologization of both the PL and the PC and the absence of programmatic differences between them led to their decline and voter disenchantment with and detachment from them. The candidates from both parties, and even candidates who dared to challenge the pact between the elites, promised the same things: "health, education, land and work, agrarian and urban reform. … In this way, voters ceased to receive a message that motivated them" (Melo 2018, 239).[4] Abstention increased during the period, along with a "gradual deterioration in the numbers of those voting in favor of the FN candidates, and continuous growth of the flow of candidates of the ANAPO" (Gutiérrez Sanín 2006, 148).

To remedy the decline in electoral participation, those running for popularly elected office who needed to obtain votes resorted to clientelistic strategies: they did favors for their clientele in exchange for votes (Melo 2018, 239). Thus, popular mobilization was concentrated on very concrete and particularist requests. Projects of national scope were reduced to reliable solutions, many of them short-term and regional in scope (e.g., a country road, an electrical grid, a local school). Regional party bosses or caciques of both the PL and the PC occupied bureaucratic posts in state institutions and awarded contracts and government jobs strategically, so that "the relations of intermediation increasingly became the most important link between the leaders and the followers of the parties" (Hartlyn 1988, 238). Patronage relationships, particularly in terms of parliamentary aides and provision of jobs, grew much deeper during the FN period (Dargent and Muñoz 2013; Dávila Ladrón de Guevara and Delgado 2002; Hartlyn 1988; Leal Buitrago and Dávila Ladrón de Guevara 1990; Wills-Otero 2015, 2016). At the subnational level, parties dedicated themselves to seeking quotas for their factions so they could

[3] In the PC, each faction revolved around one of their leaders: the *ospinistas* (Ospina Pérez) vs. the *laureanistas* (Laureano Gómez). In the PL, the initial division arose between the establishment, known as *oficialismo,* and the MRL, which was led by the more liberal López Michelsen.

[4] All direct quotes that appear in the chapter were translated from Spanish by the authors.

have bureaucratic power. In other words, "the factions at the regional level became guardians of patronage resources" (Dargent and Muñoz 2013, 58). In this process, regional leaders acquired a power that diminished the traditional power of the party center, and that generated problems of collective action (Gutiérrez Sanín 2007).

In cities that had become urbanized at an accelerated pace due, among other things, to the displacement of peasants from rural areas, the traditional parties proved unable to channel the new social forces that arose. During the years of the FN there were strikes and civic work stoppages by means of which citizens expressed their discontent in the face of inaction on the part of their elected representatives. Given the lack of attention to their demands, some opposition movements persisted in their objective of becoming recognized as political parties despite the politics of exclusion (Chernick 1989, 289). The relative inaction of the PL and the PC during this period was due to the centralization of political power at the head of the executive branch, the parity pact between the parties, and the two-thirds majority requirement for decision-making in the collegial bodies, among other things (Hartlyn 1988).

Although the coalition regime was originally conceived to last sixteen years (1958–74), a constitutional reform adopted in 1968 determined that "the losing party in the presidential election [that would be held with unrestricted competition as of 1974] should receive an adequate and equitable quota of power" (Art. 41, Legislative Act 1, 1968). The coalition mandate was prolonged until 1986 (Bushnell 2016, 319). In the meantime, the perception of political crisis was extended as a result of "the high levels of political immobility and the corruption scandals associated with this clientelistic political system" (Dargent and Muñoz 2013, 58). This led to a set of political reforms at the end of the 1980s. However, in addition to the political crisis, the social demands associated with the violence produced by drug-trafficking and the guerrilla and self-defense movements also promoted a desire for constitutional change that would create a window of political opportunity for the traditional parties.

The latest stage in the trajectories of the PL and PC began with the promulgation of the Political Constitution of 1991. The new constitution sought to reduce the power of regional bosses, as well as to increase the representation of national interests (Dargent and Muñoz 2013, 59). This is reflected in the changes introduced in the composition of electoral districts for the Senate and the House of Representatives, to the effect that senators would be elected based on a single national district and would no longer represent regional and particularistic interests.

Moreover, the new constitution eliminated what had been known as parliamentary subsidies in order to decrease the resources available for clientelistic exchanges. A series of political and electoral reforms were also proposed to allow the party system to evolve from a two-party system into a multiparty system. Some of the reforms aggravated certain problems within the traditional parties and party system. On the one hand, the fractioning of the political parties and the dispersion and atomization of electoral lists increased in the first few years after the Constitution of 1991 went into effect. The opening up of the political system did not lead to a greater organization, nor did it necessarily lead to better political representation (Vélez, Ossa, and Montes 2006). In 2003, a political reform, aimed to strengthen the parties and to reverse their fragmentation, was approved in Congress.[5] Although the institutional design created incentives for ambitious politicians to coordinate and modify intraparty competition, the reform did not produce strong parties. The winner of the 2002 presidential election was Álvaro Uribe Vélez, a former PL politician who ran as the candidate of an independent movement. Neither of the two traditional parties has been able to win the power of the presidency since then. The triumph of Uribe Vélez generated new dilemmas of collective action for the parties. In the case of the PL, there was an exodus of politicians to the new Uribista movement, while in the PC the members remained within the party but constantly disputed the scope of the coalition with Uribe. This dynamic increased with the legalization of presidential reelection in the constitutional reform of 2004.

In this scenario, and given a para-political scandal,[6] enthusiasm grew for the idea of a new political reform that would punish the illegal funding of electoral campaigns and promote mechanisms of internal democracy within the parties. The political reform of 2009, regulated by Law 1475 of 2011, was another attempt to strengthen the political parties. Nevertheless, phenomena such as *transfuguismo* (switching of party affiliation), interparty coalitions, and scandals concerning illegal campaign

[5] Some of the reforms were the following: elimination of multiple lists for parties, and the approval of a single list in each electoral district; allowing parties to choose the type of list they want (closed or with preferential voting) as a mechanism for coordinating ambitious politicians; the establishment of an electoral threshold for a party to win seats in the legislature; a change from the Hare quota to the d'Hondt method; and finally, a system of blocs regulated through Law 974 of 2005.

[6] This scandal broke out in 2006 when legislators from the opposition alleged that government officials and around 35 percent of congressmen had links with paramilitary groups from the country's northern regions. A group of politicians were convicted and imprisoned after it was proved that they did, in fact, have these links.

financing indicate the weakness of traditional party organizations with respect to the ability to unite ambitious politicians in a cohesive group and maintain a programmatic coherence that favors the identification and representation of political preferences.

In observing the electoral trajectories of the PL and the PC (see Figures 8.1 and 8.2), it is clear that the voting numbers obtained by these organizations have fallen sharply since 2002 with Álvaro Uribe's accession to power as president of the country and the rise of the Uribismo phenomenon that attracted politicians from both parties, especially from the PL. It is in presidential elections that both parties have suffered the greatest voting losses. In congressional elections, on the other hand, while the number of votes received by the traditional parties has declined for both chambers, the Senate has suffered a greater decrease than the House of Representatives. This may be related to the profile of each chamber. New parties with national demands have arisen in the Senate, which is organized based on a single national district. The powers rooted in certain local PC and PL caciques can be more easily maintained in the House of Representatives, which is based on the representation of departmental electoral districts. In local elections, the

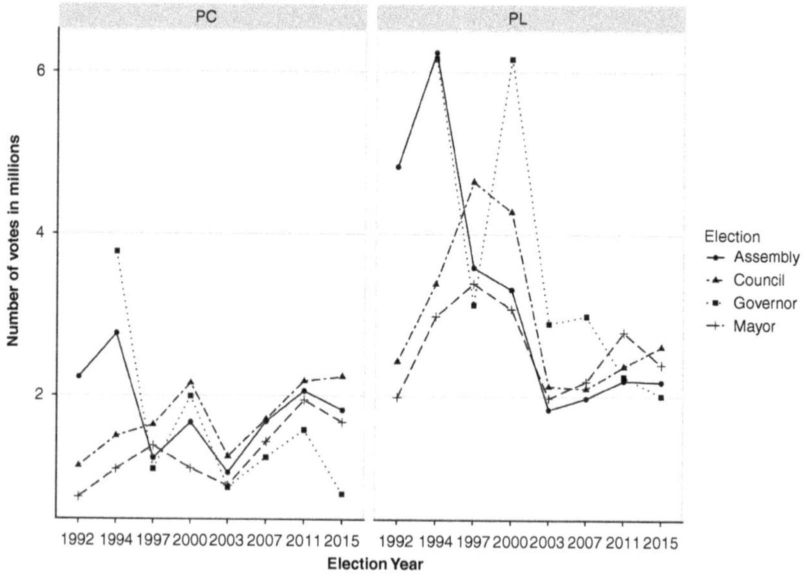

FIGURE 8.1 Local elections
Source: Registraduría Nacional del Estado Civil.
* Governor elections were not held in 1992

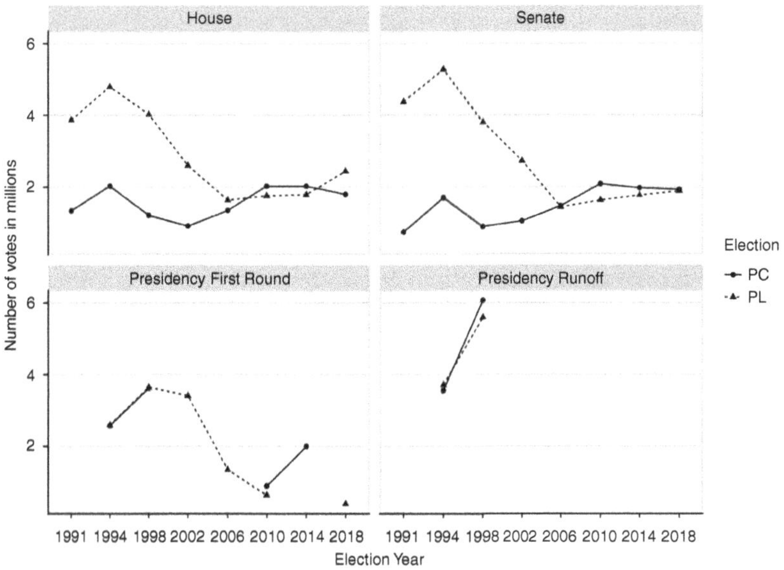

FIGURE 8.2 National elections
Source: Registraduría Nacional del Estado Civil.
* The PC did not run for the 2002, 2006, and 2018 presidential elections. The party did not qualify for the second round of the presidential elections in 2010 and 2014. For the PL, the party did not run in 2014, taking part in the coalition for the reelection of Juan Manuel Santos. The party did not qualify for the second round of the presidential elections in 2010 and 2018, in 2002 and 2006 no second round was held.

reduced number of votes for governors may be related to the increased number of coalition candidates. Despite their historic rivalry, PL and PC candidates have united in trying to win office through popular election. In elections for mayors' offices, municipal councils, and departmental assemblies, after the reduction in the number of votes due to the rise of Uribismo, the voting levels for both parties have remained constant in recent years Although the two traditional parties have declined in electoral power and face greater coordination problems during elections, they are still able to coordinate ambitious politicians during electoral processes and to win offices.

HORIZONTAL COORDINATION

During the 1991–2018 period, the PL and the PC successfully coordinated ambitious politicians and thus gained power in all the legislative elections that took place. In this sense, these organizations have been relatively successful as electoral vehicles. Despite this, the amount of electoral power that they have won has notably diminished due to their inability to monopolize the candidate selection process efficiently and to coordinate the electoral strategy of all members of the respective parties, among other things. All of this is in addition to the rise of Uribismo, which has absorbed members from both parties.

In both organizations, the coordination of politicians for coherent action in representative institutions between elections has varied widely. While the PL and the PC have acted with discipline and have managed to advance programmatic proposals at certain times and on specific topics, their internal fragmentation has manifested itself in their inability to promote public policies on which all the members agree. The historical regionalization of politics in Colombia makes it difficult for the parties to propose, coordinate, and manage policies that traverse the different levels of government (local, departmental, regional, and national).

Horizontal Coordination during Elections

The PL and PC statutes define the way their candidates are selected. Formal rules, however, do not always define the parties' behavior. Candidate selection often involves debates and internal negotiations that do not follow the formal rules (Batlle 2011; Montilla 2011). Over time, the two organizations have made various adjustments to these procedures. The mechanisms the PL uses most frequently to select candidates for executive posts include popular consultations (on either an open or an inter-party basis), opinion polls, and designations by the party's National Convention, its most important organizational body (Batlle 2011; Gehring 2016). In principle, those who vote in internal consultations should be the members of the respective organizations. Nonetheless, any citizen can participate in them because there is no strict control over the members. On many occasions, consultations have been held because the leaders have been unable to reach consensus on a single candidate. These processes usually produce internal fractures and lead unsuccessful aspirants to withdraw from the party (Barrero and Acuña 2015). In 1998, for example, when Serpa was designated in a closed and anti-pluralistic convention as the PL presidential candidate, PL leaders and activists decided to support Pastrana, the conservative candidate who won the election (Hoskin 1998). Another example occurred in 2018, when Gaviria – the PL leader – decided in the second round of voting to support presidential candidate Iván Duque from the Centro Democrático (Democratic Center) party, which, unlike the PL, had opposed the peace process during the administration of Juan Manuel Santos.[7] In these processes, particularly when internal fights occur, former presidents wield considerable influence in the selection of candidates. From the level of the national committee of each party, they act as national leaders who mediate these fights, and, in some cases, they decide who the candidates will be.[8] There have been occasions where not all aspiring candidates accepted the results of popular consultations.[9]

In the PC, national and decentralized conventions have been common. Through party conventions, the National Committee seeks the consensus that gives the party its internal cohesion and facilitates coordination of the politicians' electoral strategy. However, as in the PL, these processes have produced internal fractures. Dissident candidates form alternative political movements, support candidates in other parties, or look for other parties' endorsements (Batlle 2011; Hoskin 1998). There have been presidential campaigns (2006 and 2010), in which the PC decided not to present candidates, and instead supported those whom it viewed as having a greater probability of success (Uribe in 2006 and Santos in 2010). In 2014, a strong division occurred when a sector within the party agreed to support the reelection of President Santos, and another sector preferred to present its own candidate. This division affected the candidacy of Marta Lucía Ramírez, who finished third with 15.5 percent of the votes (Barrero and Acuña 2015). In 2018, the party did not present candidates and

[7] Between 2012 and 2016, a peace process between the government of Juan Manuel Santos and the Fuerzas Armadas Revolucionarias de Colombia (Revolutionary Armed Forces of Colombia, FARC) took place in La Havana, Cuba. They signed the final agreement in November 2016. The process was supported by the parties that belonged to the government's coalition. The PL, led by former President César Gaviria, was part of that coalition.

[8] "Impugnan sanción a congresistas" (*El Tiempo*, April 18, 2005, pp. 1–7); "4 sancionados por votar reelección irán al congreso liberal" (*El Tiempo*, May 21, 2005, pp. 1–3); "Propuesta de Unidad Liberal hacen ex presidente Julio Cesar Turbay Ayala y ex ministros del Partido" (*El Tiempo*, May 26, 2005, pp. 1–17); "Liberales declaran oposición al gobierno" (*El Tiempo*, June 11, 2005, pp. 1–5); "Senadores Uribistas critican congreso liberal" (*El Tiempo*, June 15, 2005, pp. 1–10); "Peñalosa se va del Partido Liberal" (*El Tiempo*, August 9, 2005, pp. 1–6); "CNE levanta sanción a congresistas liberales" (*El Tiempo*, August 26, 2005, pp. 1–5).

[9] An example of this was Noemí Sanín, from the PC, who decided to leave the party and run as an independent in 1998. For other examples see: "La encrucijada conservadora: dos puntas tiene el cambio" (*El Espectador*, November 12, 1995, p. 5A) and "Reglas de juego para el candidato conservador" (*El Espectador*, December 5, 1997, p. 14A).

decided to instead support the winning Uribista candidate, Iván Duque, from Centro Democrático.

Although the influence of national political leaders is significant in these processes – more so in the PL than in the PC – the regional political bosses in the departmental and municipal directories – many of whom are members of Congress – also influence the decisions and independently grant their endorsements. The power of subnational political bosses is partly explained by the political decentralization processes that have been occurring in the country since the late 1980s. Since that time, the parties have suffered an accelerated process of organizational decomposition, especially in terms of their ability to control the processes of nominating candidates (Albarracín, Gamboa, and Mainwaring 2018, 235). This decentralization eroded the national elites' control over regional and local forces that have gained considerable power. Given the lack of control on the part of the central elites, the granting of endorsements is very often indiscriminate, and those who aspire to become candidates look for the organization that is willing to grant an endorsement without requiring programmatic commitments. Receiving the endorsement of the PL or the PC provides candidates with resources that would be more difficult to obtain in smaller parties that are less prominent. Resources are very often obtained only in exchange for electoral effort.

The electoral strategy of the PL and the PC has been mediated by the rules of the electoral system. The possibility of registering an unlimited number of lists before 2003, and the preferential vote after that year, produced incentives for the internal fragmentation of the parties (Pachón and Shugart 2010). With the reform of 2003, the parties exhibited an increased tendency to become confederations of politicians, instead of centralized and hierarchical organizations (Albarracín, Gamboa, and Mainwaring 2018, 251). Preferential voting lists have promoted intraparty competition, even though the votes of all candidates are added up at the party level. These rules have negatively affected the horizontal coordination that they were intended to achieve through consultations and other selection mechanisms. Tables 8.1 and 8.2 show the number of lists registered by the PL and the PC between 1986 and 1998 for the election of the Senate, and from 2003 and 2018 for election to both the Senate and the House of Representatives. Table 8.1 also shows the effective number of parties and the effective number of lists. Table 8.2 shows the electoral strategy that these parties have chosen (i.e., either closed lists or preferential votes). As can be seen, ever since the first legislative election following the adoption of the reform of 2003, the

TABLE 8.1 *Number of lists registered for the senate election, 1986–1998*

	1986	1990	1991	1994	1998
Lists	201	213	143	251	309
NEP	2.14	2.16	2.70	2.56	2.57
NEL	103.3	102.3	37.6	153.7	164.4

Source: Gómez Albarello and Rodríguez-Raga (2007, 49–83).

TABLE 8.2 *Number and type of lists registered by the PL and the PC in legislative elections, 2006–2018*

		PL		PC	
Election	Chamber	Open list	Closed list	Open list	Closed list
2006	Senate	1	0	1	0
	House	30	1	29	0
2010	Senate	1	0	1	0
	House	30	1	28	0
2014	Senate	1	0	1	0
	House	33	0	26	0
2018	Senate	1	0	1	0
	House	32	1	25	0

Source: Registraduría Nacional del Estado Civil, 2006–18.

two parties have preferred the open list. This has also been the case in subnational elections for departmental assemblies and municipal councils. Open lists produce competition between candidates from the same party. This hinders coherent performance by the organization.

Before the reform of 2003, the multiple lists of the parties in multi-candidate elections, as well as the difficulty of nominating single candidates for presidential elections, favored personalism in political campaigns. Each list represented a certain faction of the party. Therefore, until the 2002 elections, the electoral ballots for legislative bodies at the national and local level included photos of the candidates without party-associated logos. For single-candidate elections, by contrast, both the PL and the PC have made use of their respective logos on the ballots and campaign materials at least since 1990 when the electoral ballot was created. Although the political parties in Colombia have defined logos and labels, they are not associated with clearly defined programmatic agendas, so the labels do not have much meaning. Therefore, the incentives for protecting the party trademark and remaining in one party or the other are very weak, and there is little pressure for members who exhibit the label to render accounts (Albarracín, Gamboa, and Mainwaring 2018, 252; Pizarro Leongómez 2006).

Horizontal Coordination between Elections

Since 2005, Colombia has had a system of rules governing political blocs (Law 974 of 2005) to maintain political-party discipline within the collegial bodies.[10] By this legislation, the members of the parties elected by popular vote have the legal obligation to act as a group in a coordinated manner. National and local directorates should orient the blocs and the spokespersons regarding the positions within the corporate bodies. The blocs may establish mandatory voting for all of their members on specific issues, and sanctions were established to be applied in case of disobedience. The law determined that, on some occasions, the members of the bloc may deviate from the position of the bloc (e.g., as conscientious objectors), and the parties decide when one of their members may invoke this right. Although disciplinary codes establish sanctions for those who disobey the voting decisions of the blocs, some disciplinary processes are carried out through informal channels, such as calls from regional directorates for national observers to intervene in cases of possible disobedience by verbally urging attention before the voting. This shows that the party prefers to informally dissuade its members in advance from infringing the decisions of the bloc to avoid having to establish formal disciplinary processes.

Before and after the enactment of the law regarding congressional blocs, the PL has had various experiences in which its members in the Congress have been notoriously divided. For example, in 1998, when the conservative Andrés Pastrana was president, the PL was divided between those who collaborated with and those who opposed the government. The former believed that it was inappropriate to oppose the government at a critical juncture for the country's economy. For that reason, they called

[10] Colombia is the only country that has a specific law regulating parliamentary blocs and party discipline. No other country includes such regulation in its legislation governing political parties and, where disciplinary processes have existed, they are promulgated under the statutes of the parties.

for "patriotic collaborationism."[11] For its part, the *oficialista* faction led by the party leadership held that the PL was obliged to present democratic opposition to the conservative government.[12] The rupture within the PL led to a situation in 2002 in which the collaborationists created an alternate national liberal directorate that caused their expulsion by the official party bloc.[13]

Another situation that divided the party was the election of Álvaro Uribe Vélez to the presidency in 2002. Uribe Vélez, who had been a member of the PL, was elected president as an independent candidate. Some members of Congress who were elected from the liberal lists wanted to form part of the government coalition to support the new president. This divided the party between *uribistas* and *no uribistas*. In 2005, nineteen liberal members of Congress voted in favor of a constitutional reform to permit presidential reelection and to allow Uribe to participate in the race. This led the party leadership to expel those members of Congress.[14] After the second Uribe administration (2006–10), the PL managed to unite around the presidency of Juan Manuel Santos (2010–18) and formed part of the National Unity coalition that obtained representation at different levels of the government. In some cases, the PL has managed to discipline its members or to sanction them through informal mechanisms. One example of this was the case of liberal senator Viviane Morales, who gave up her seat after twenty years of activism in the organization, upon receiving pressure from PL members of Congress who believed that her initiatives to prohibit the adoption of children by same-sex couples were contrary to the programmatic agenda of the party. Morales was unable to seek the PL presidential nomination for that same reason.[15]

[11] "Caicedo plantea colaboracionismo patriótico" (*El Espectador*, June 25, 1998, p. 6A); "¿Oposición o colaboración patriótica?" (*El Espectador*, June 30, 1998, p. 3A).

[12] "Serpa declara oposición patriótica" (*El Espectador*, June 24, 1998, p. 6A).

[13] "Surge una nueva dirección liberal" (*El Tiempo*, November 10, 1999, p. 6A); "El neoliberalismo ha sido sepultado: López" (*El Tiempo*, November 11, 1999, p. 8A); "Estalló la división liberal" (*El Tiempo*, November 11, 1999, p. 6A); "Liberalismo socialdemócrata Jaime Castro" (*El Tiempo*, January 3, 2000, p. 5A); "'Agarrón' en el liberalismo" (El Tiempo, January 22, 2000, p. 9B).

[14] "Impugnan sanción a congresistas" (*El Tiempo*, April 18, 2005, pp. 1–7); "4 sancionados por votar reelección irán al congreso liberal" (*El Tiempo*, May 21, 2005, pp. 1–3); "Propuesta de Unidad Liberal hacen ex presidente Julio Cesar Turbay Ayala y ex ministros del Partido" (*El Tiempo*, May 26, 2005, pp. 1–17); "Liberales declaran oposición al gobierno" (*El Tiempo*, June 11, 2005, pp. 1–5); "Senadores Uribistas critican congreso liberal" (*El Tiempo*, June 15, 2005, pp. 1–10).

[15] "Liberales ¿se liberan de Viviane Morales?" (*Semana*, September 19, 2017, www.semana.com/nacion/articulo/partido-liberal-manifiesto-contra-viviane-morales/541067, last accessed

The PC, for its part, has since the early 1990s established various channels to articulate the legislative activity of its members of Congress and the position of the National Directorate. For example, the main function of the Parliamentary Board, which is composed of the party's senators and representatives, is "to harmonize the parliamentary action of the party and to determine the policy, rules, and conduct of members of Congress concerning the projects for their study and decision" (By-law 1996, Art. 1). The Secretary-General shall have the function of "communicating to the members of congress the political ideas, plans and programs that the party decides to present for consideration and study by the legislative chambers" (By-law 1996, Art. 1). This function was extended to all territorial levels in 2005. The statutes establish guidelines for determining the position of the bloc on different topics, to harmonize policies through all party levels, and to sanction those who fail to follow the rules defined therein. However, some examples show the autonomy of PC members of Congress concerning the National Directorate. For instance, Omar Yepes resigned from the presidency of the Directorate in 1999 given the refusal of PC members of Congress to "deny the extension of the terms of the current governors and mayors"[16] as enshrined in the political reform the government was negotiating with Congress at that time.

There are moments in which PL and PC legislators act as a bloc and others in which every legislator votes individually. The members of congress are generally disciplined when they discuss and vote on laws of great national significance. For example, during the first administration of President Santos (2014–18), there were laws – some of them regarding the peace agreement between the government and FARC – for which the coalition parties, which included the PL and the PC, voted in a very disciplined way, especially in the Senate. Similarly, during the inaugural year of Duque's, government (2018–19), the PL decided not to support Democratic Center's objections to the transitional justice procedures established in the 2016 peace agreement. Another party decision that showed discipline was the opposition to the main executive project, the Plan Nacional de Desarrollo (National Development Plan, PND). In the House of Representatives, given the diverse constituencies and

May 21, 2020); "#YoMeVoy: Así se da la desbandada del Partido Liberal" (*Semana*, September 19, 2018, www.semana.com/nacion/articulo/dirigentes-del-partido-liberal-renuncian-por-postura-frente-al-gobierno-de-duque/583381, last accessed May 21, 2020).

[16] "Cayó jefe conservador" (*El Espectador*, May 14, 1999, p. 5A).

internal factions, the levels of discipline are generally lower, although the PL scored higher than the PC on this measure (Congreso Visible 2014). Despite this, it is also evident that many legislative initiatives are drafted by individual members of these parties, and they do not always act as a bloc in decision-making when it comes time to vote. This prevents party cohesiveness, and hinders parties from either translating their programmatic agendas into consistent policies or from acting as a group in the opposition when they do not belong to the government coalition. The existence of different ideological tendencies within the parties – particularly within the PL – explains why some of their members do not vote according to their principles. An example of this behavior occurred during Duque's presidency among the right-wing Democratic Center. The PL declared itself in the opposition. However, not all legislators have concurred with this decision. Some of them preferred to be aligned with the official coalition. This has fragmented the party internally.

As far as coherence between government programs at both the departmental and regional level, where PL policies at the national level are concerned, the party's disciplinary codes of 2002 and 2013 establish the duty to comply with the programs adopted by the organs of the party. Despite this, in practice, no coherence exists across programmatic agendas between national and subnational levels (interviews with activists). The party at the national level participates only marginally in the party's regional decisions. As in other parties, legislators in their departments are the leaders who determine how politicians at the local level should act. A rupture between national and departmental leaders explains the difficulty of coordinating actions and agendas across the party. Personal interests prevail over shared interests. Coordination among the different levels of the PL and the PC has been affected by the great degree of autonomy that regional and local politicians have won with respect to national leaders through the processes of political, administrative, and fiscal decentralization (Muñoz and Dargent 2016).

The territorial presence of both the PL and the PC has diminished over the years. Before the Constitution of 1991, these two organizations put forth candidates for all congressional seats and collectively obtained the majority of the votes. After that date, they began to reduce their presence and became significantly denationalized (Batlle and Puyana 2011). This reflects their loss of electoral power. Thus, "the institutional changes of 1991 and 2003 had important effects, not only on the number of parties and their permanence in the political scene but also in terms of their arrival in the territory" (Batlle and Puyana 2011, 40). In this sense, the reforms and the rise of new political options influenced the denationalization of the PC, which gradually ceased to run candidates in different regions of the country. For its part, the PL has been able to maintain higher levels of nationalization than the PC, but lower than the levels it had before the institutional reforms of the 1990s and 2000s were introduced (Batlle and Puyana 2011).

VERTICAL INTEREST AGGREGATION

Electoral Mobilization of Collective Interests

In their programmatic platforms, the PL and the PC include general topics. The two organizations have a thematic agenda that is broad, and the predominance of departmental directorates has prevented the establishment of programmatic consensus. In addition, clientelistic linkages and the regionalization of politics has impeded the formation of ideological structures. Individual and, on occasion, regional or local interests, prevail over parties' programmatic agendas (Montilla 2011).

Toward the end of the 1980s, the PL defined itself as an organization that promoted social change, institutional security, protection of private property, and progressive values. Two decades later, in 2002, it included topics related to the promotion of human and union rights, protection of the environment, and rejection of neoliberalism. At that time, it called itself a social-democratic organization after having joined the Socialist International in 1992. Despite this, the party has been inconsistent in its economic orientation with junctures when neoliberal principles have prevailed over a more social-democratic approach. In 2011, the party declared itself a coalition of leftist groups and added its commitment to solving armed conflicts through dialogue and negotiation. The party has consistently advocated a negotiated solution to the country's armed conflict and favorable treatment of the war's victims. It has also shown consistency over time in its position on environmental protection policies (interviews with activists).

The PC appeals (still) to doctrinal bases linked to its foundational myth of 1849: the humanistic and Christian perspective continues to inspire many of the organization's principles (Roll 2002). It defends the rule of law and its legitimate authority, respect for life, the unitarian concept of the state, and the defense of values such as liberty, private property, and human dignity. In this sense, the PC led the presentation of legislative bills against abortion,[17] euthanasia,[18] and same-sex marriage.[19] In recent statutes, the goals of participation, pluralism, equity, gender equality, transparency, and morality were established as its guiding principles. Despite defending these interests, the party's policies usually respond to the electoral context instead of a particular ideology.

The social groups to which these organizations are addressed are also very broad, and no significant differences appear when analyzing sociodemographic characteristics. In its programs, the PL mentions "professionals, students, women, *campesinos*, artisans, small business owners, pensioners and workers" (Partido Liberal 1987, Art. 12). More recently, they have included victims of the armed conflict. The party also decidedly addresses liberal youth groups in its statutes. By including them – as well as women and ethnic minorities – it receives economic incentives established by law. Despite this, members of the PL admit that their activists have been growing old, fewer youths participate in and vote for the party, and the majority of its voters no longer live in big urban centers. Youth organizations are useful for their members to acquire status, while women are only important during elections. In general, base organizations have weak structures, and many of them represent individual rather than party interests (Roll 2002).

Existence of Formal and Informal Links with Civil Society Organizations

Historically, Colombian political parties have had weak connections with formal civil society organizations (Londoño 2009). The relationship of the PC and the PL with think tanks is mixed, since they do have contact with different local and international organizations, but these relationships are not exclusive, since the think tanks and NGOs try to promote their agenda among all actors in the party system and not just the PL and the PC (Garcé 2007). The strongest relationships the PL and the PC have with these organizations are with those who work in the areas of democracy and transparency. The relationship is centered around the strengthening of Colombian democracy and political parties in general and, particularly, in the promotion of electoral reforms and accountability. To achieve these goals, the think tanks and NGOs organize events and activities with the parties and have been successful

[17] "Hoy radican proyecto antiaborto" (*El Espectador*, August 3, 2011, p. 4).
[18] "El 'articulito' de los azules" (*El Espectador*, October 10, 2010, p. 4).
[19] "Unidos contra el matrimonio gay" (*El Espectador*, October 10, 2010, p. 7).

at creating an environment for electoral reforms in 2003 and 2009 (Leal and Roll 2013). Traditionally, the PL had formal linkages with trade unions, women and human rights organizations, and the Socialist International, among others. However, over time, it has lost the majority of these linkages, as well as the financial support of big entrepreneurs and productive sectors. Today, individual leaders (not organizations) support the party, but not consistently (interviews with activists).

The party statutes mention an "open sector" in which social groups that are not among the party's sectorial organizations participate. This open sector accounts for 20 percent of the delegates of the national, departmental, and municipal directorates and has representation in the party assemblies. Another type of link is the participation of local and regional mass-media directors affiliated with the party in municipal and departmental assemblies. Regarding the party's relationship with its donors, it is not clear what type of link exists because the private donations the party receives are directed to specific candidates rather than to the organization as a whole. According to the party directives, it is not clear how the candidates respond to the interests of those who donate to their campaigns.

The PC also has members who hold public office in the name of the party or belong to grassroots groups recognized by the party. There have been organizations attached to the national and regional directing committees ever since the statute of 1993 was introduced. For example, mention was made (art. II, Cap. IX, 1993) of the existence of the Comando de Trabajadores (Workers' Command), the Comando Femenino (Feminine Command), the Comando de Estudiantes (Students' Command) and the Comando de Defensa del Medio Ambiente (Command for the Defense of the Environment). With the changes introduced in the statutes of 2005, these groups were transformed into grassroots and local-organization groups. The PC paid special attention to party youth groups and encouraged the formation of such groups at the local level. More recently, the Secretaría Ténica de la Mujer (Women's Technical Secretariat) was established in 2012 to coordinate and encourage the participation of PC women, and the Secretaría Técnica de Minorías e Inclusión Social (Technical Secretariat for Minorities and Social Inclusion) was constituted in 2015. The current statute establishes rules for the formation of internal party organizations based on specific population groups. These organizations must have a national sphere of action and be present at all territorial levels.

The PC has relations with economic groups, with national labor unions, and with certain mass media. The party maintains important linkages with institutions for the promotion and formation of its bases such as, for example, the Konrad Adenauer Foundation, Hans Seidel, International Republican Institute (IRI), Universidad Sergio Arboleda, Universidad Católica, Universidad la Gran Colombia and Universidad del Rosario, Centro Pensamiento Siglo XXI, mass media such as El Nuevo Siglo, and entrepreneurial groups such as Grupo Éxito and Arturo Calle (Montilla 2011).

This section has shown that both the PL and the PC have lost much of their ability to aggregate collective interests vertically. At least until the mid-twentieth century, both parties were able not only to win elections, but also to represent the interests of their electorates. It was feasible to distinguish one party from the other in ideological terms, and therefore their programmatic agendas and constituencies were clearly defined. Today, however, these characteristics are no longer recognizable. Both political parties have transformed themselves into electoral organizations that seek to elect candidates, without paying attention to the representation interests of their voters.

CONCLUSIONS

In this chapter, we have concentrated on the two oldest electoral vehicles in Colombia – the PL and the PC – and have shown how, throughout their history, they have transformed themselves to adapt to the new political circumstances that have arisen at different moments. After a long formational process in the second half of the nineteenth century, these two organizations became consolidated as political parties capable of coordinating ambitious politicians both during and between elections, and of representing social interests. In the second half of the twentieth century, the two parties began to turn into diminished subtypes, that is, organizations that are able (partially) to coordinate their politicians horizontally to win popularly elected positions, and lack clear programmatic agendas, stable electorates, and a reduced the ability to effectively represent the collective demands of social interests. The PL is an electoral vehicle that is a borderline case between the Independents and unrooted party types, while the PC performs slightly better in terms of vertical interest aggregation and is a borderline case between the uncoordinated party and Independents types (see Table 1.1 and Figure 1.5 in Luna et al. Introduction this volume).

Currently, the PL and the PC participate in national and regional elections and are capable of maintaining a portion of electoral political power. In this sense, they survive despite predictions of their disappearance by analysts and the mass media. However, the differences between the electoral strategies they use and the representation functions they perform are blurred. To gain electoral power, these parties form coalitions among themselves and with other political organizations with whom they seem to have nothing in common in programmatic terms. By winning seats in this way, the representation function of these coalitions is confusing: To which voters do they respond? How do the interests of such diverse, and sometimes contradictory, electorates add up? What are the incentives for politicians at different levels to coordinate their programmatic agendas and act coherently?

The PL and the PC have more than 150 years of history behind them. They have been able to survive the challenges arising in a society that is constantly being transformed. They have been able to adapt their organizational structures and political strategies to the new institutional structures that have developed at different moments. They continue to be two of more than ten parties that obtain political power in national legislative elections and regional elections. Despite this, neither of them has been able to renovate its electorate or to reformulate its government programs successfully. The two parties fail in their representation function, that is to say, in their ability to vertically aggregate interests and they also have difficulty achieving horizontal coordination. Thus, the present challenge for these organizations is to recover their political identity and to construct agendas that are consistent with that identity and with the interests of their voters. Strengthening bonds with the electorate and responding to its demands will inevitably be a requirement for these organizations to increase their electoral power and to ensure their continued existence.

9

"Normal" Parties in Extraordinary Times

The Case of Primero Justicia and Voluntad Popular in Venezuela

Jennifer Cyr

INTRODUCTION

Venezuela has undergone significant regime change. At the turn of the twenty-first century, the country had one of the longest-standing democracies in the region. In the years following the election of Hugo Chávez (1999–2013), however, the country's democracy entered into decay. Its transition to authoritarianism has had serious implications for the new political parties that oppose the *chavista* regime.

The following chapter undertakes two tasks. First, it classifies two new opposition parties in Venezuela using the typology established by the editors of this volume. I examine Primero Justicia (Justice First, PJ) and Voluntad Popular (Popular Will, VP), two of the most influential parties within the Venezuelan opposition founded after the 1998 collapse of the party system (Morgan 2011; Seawright 2012).[1] I find that the PJ has evolved into an unrooted party. The VP, by contrast, sits somewhere between qualifying as a political party and an unrooted party.

The conceptual imprecision is driven, in great part, by the regime context in which the VP operates. The VP was founded in a moment

[1] The other two most influential parties are Acción Democrática (Democratic Action, AD) and Un Nuevo Tiempo (A New Time, UNT). AD was founded early in the twentieth century and is therefore one of the oldest existing parties in Venezuela today. The party's organizational prowess and history have been well addressed elsewhere (see, e.g. Cyr 2017; Martz 1966). The UNT, by contrast, is, like the PJ and the VP, a relatively new Venezuelan party, founded after party-system collapse. It has been far less successful electorally than the other three parties – a fact that merits examination in future work – and so I exclude it here.

when social movements for and against *chavismo* gained momentum and became a social source of pressure and clearly caters to these opposition groups. Yet, the increasing irrelevance of elections, together with the persistent persecution of competitive opposition candidates, has made it difficult for opposition parties to govern. Until the VP assumes a de jure position of power, we cannot assess the extent to which the social movements to which the VP appeals actually work with and constrain the party.

Indeed, regime effects must be considered when assessing the overall evolution of the PJ and the VP as new(er) parties in the Venezuelan context. The last part of the chapter, therefore, tackles the theoretical weight of regime type head on. In some ways, then, this chapter reverses the causal arrow that the broader project on diminished party subtypes considers. To be sure, as the editors have noted (Luna et al. Introduction this volume), the form of the electoral vehicles that dominate politics will affect the quality of the (democratic) regime. This chapter, however, takes a step back in the causal sequence to assess the extent to which regime type may, in itself, shape the electoral vehicles that emerge and evolve.

I begin by applying the editors' indicators of horizontal coordination and vertical aggregation of interest to the PJ and the VP. Then I look at the broader dynamics of the increasingly authoritarian context in which the parties were founded. I pay attention to the growing repression from the *chavista* regime and also the heightened polarization between *chavismo* and anti-*chavismo*. Government repression limited the opposition's capacity to gain positions of power; polarization, I suggest, truncated the organizational evolution of participating parties. Overall, I find that nondemocracies represent contexts of adversity (Levitsky et al. 2016; Van Dyck 2016) that can stimulate successful party emergence. Yet, the cases of VP and PJ suggest that nondemocracies provoke trade-offs in terms of how, specifically, parties develop organizationally.

CLASSIFYING PRIMERO JUSTICIA

The PJ began as a nongovernmental organization. Founded in 1992, the Asociación Civil Primero Justicia (Justice First Civil Association) was notable because it emerged independently from the formal party system. Successful, autonomous NGOs were rare in the 1990s. The PJ was one of the few to become visible, thanks in part to its television program, Justicia para Todos (Justice for All), which was hosted by one of its own: Julio

Borges. The NGO's name recognition and the popularity of the show helped the PJ when it transitioned to a formal political party in 2000 (Pérez Baralt 2004, 267–268).

Although the party aspired to compete in elections across the country (personal interview Briquet, May 28, 2014), the PJ began as a highly regionalized party (Cyr and Sagarzazu 2014). Its participation in the so-called mega elections of 2000 was restricted to the state of Miranda and especially Caracas, the country's capital (personal interview Ferrer, May 29, 2014). Even there, however, its early electoral campaigns were highly personalized (personal interview Briquet, May 28, 2014). As a party, then, the PJ's electoral origins were both geographically restrained and atomized, or tailored to the individual candidacy (personal interview Briquet, May 28, 2014). On March 1, 2002, after a campaign to grow the party's presence outside of Miranda, the PJ officially registered with the Consejo Nacional Electoral (National Electoral Council, CNE) as a national party (Núñez Muñoz and Pineda Morán 2003, 49).

Despite its regionalized origins, by 2014, the PJ was one of the most important parties within the national opposition movement, the Mesa de la Unidad Democrática (Democratic Unity Roundtable, MUD). It was a member of the G4, the central decision-making bloc of the MUD, alongside the VP, the AD, and the UNT. The party's success and notoriety led Venezuelans to see the PJ as potentially spearheading the renovation of the country's party system.[2] Indeed, its leader, Henrique Capriles Radonski, served as the opposition's chosen presidential candidate in two successive elections (2012 and 2013). In the latter election, Capriles lost by just under two percentage points.

The PJ began as an electoral party (Núñez Muñoz and Pineda Morán 2003; Pérez Baralt 2004). Yet, participation in the MUD pushed it to consolidate its horizontal coordination capacity. By the early 2010s, the party had evolved into an unrooted party – it had mechanisms for horizontal coordination in place, but its vertical aggregation was weak. Indeed, the party seems to have struggled to build enduring ties with Venezuelans, despite its popular NGO origins.

[2] Alonso Moleiro, "Quién es Quién en la Oposición Venezolana" (Las Historias de El País, Blog, Episode 28, 2019). https://poddtoppen.se/podcast/1440051890/las-historias-de-el-pas/ep-28-quin-es-quin-en-la-oposicin-venezolana (last accessed May 16, 2019).

HORIZONTAL COORDINATION

Horizontal Coordination during Elections

The party's electoral strategy early on was highly personalized. Each candidate built their campaign *a su estilo* and reflecting their strengths (personal interview Briquet, May 28, 2014). Still, certain elements were shared across candidacies, including the party's black and yellow logo and basic programmatic points about freedom, justice, and participation (Pérez Baralt 2004, 267). Moreover, candidacies were chosen during the party's Convención Nacional (National Convention), an annual meeting of Comité Político Nacional (National Political Committee) members (Pérez Baralt 2004, 271). Overall, some horizontal coordination existed from early on, even as the campaigns themselves were candidate driven.

Deference to individual candidate preferences changed, however, as electoral circumstances evolved. The increasingly authoritarian regime began to postpone and, over time, cancel elections. Moreover, broader opposition dynamics began to supersede the wishes of individual parties. For example, the PJ opted to participate in the 2005 legislative elections (personal interview Briquet, May 28, 2014). When, however, the AD, a more territorially widespread and organizationally developed party, decided not to participate, the PJ, alongside most opposition parties, joined the boycott (Cyr 2017).

These broader political dynamics forced the party to reevaluate how it organized its electoral campaigns and its overall territorial structure (personal interview Briquet, May 28, 2014 and Ferrer, May 29, 2014). Faced with challenges within the opposition and from the government, the party sought greater coherence across campaigns and in its larger organizational structure (personal interview Briquet, May 28, 2014). For example, in 2011, the MUD inaugurated internal primaries to, among other things, avoid multiple opposition candidacies. The move also fostered intraparty coordination. The PJ leadership worked to grow the party territorially and in terms of its internal structure, so that it could successfully compete against other primary candidates (personal interview Ferrer, May 29, 2014).

In all, the party's election-time coordination has evolved. Earlier campaigns focused more on the candidates. As pressures to compete within the MUD mounted, PJ leaders became more calculating. Alliances with other regional parties – a strategy used during the 2000 mega elections to multiply candidacies – were eschewed to preserve party autonomy (Núñez

Muñoz and Pineda Morán 2003, 60). A growth in electoral coordination corresponded with a major push to make the party national in scope. The tasks, it seems, were mutually reinforcing. According to Julio Borges – the mastermind behind the party's rapid organizational growth – the party committed to *trabajar como burros* (to work hard) to become, with time, the party with the most votes in the most remote regions of the country (personal interview Borges, May 29, 2014).

Horizontal Coordination between Elections

Formally, the party consists of a National Political Committee, which chooses a Junta de Dirección Nacional (National Board of Directors), from which an executive committee is self-selected and includes a Coordinador Nacional (National Coordinator) and a Secretario General (General Secretary) – the two most important figures in the party. This committee/board/National Coordinator and General Secretary structure is replicated at the regional and municipal levels (Núñez Muñoz and Pineda Morán 2003).

The PJ has come to impose a rather strict hierarchy with respect to decision-making on the party and its policies. Regional and municipal party committees, for example, have little autonomy; the national political committee manages most organizational and political matters (Immigration and Refugee Board of Canada 2016). In 2014, a party leader compared the party organization to that of a baseball team. The coordinators within the party manage the team. Everybody else is a player and acts in conjunction with those coordinators (personal interview Ferrer, May 29, 2014). Even day-to-day party activities, Ferrer suggested, were carried out with longer-term party goals in mind.

This top-down, more controlled approach to party structure, as with the party's approach to electoral strategy, has evolved. In its earliest stages, the party was much more decentralized. For example, each state branch of the party was self-funded. Support came mainly from PJ members and sympathetic civil society organizations (Núñez Muñoz and Pineda Morán 2003, 58). Moreover, each party branch operated as it saw fit: "The different regional coordinators ha[d] the autonomy to manage regional policies and develop their own strategies" (Núñez Muñoz and Pineda Morán 2003, 61).[3]

[3] All direct quotes that appear in the chapter were translated from Spanish by the author.

The PJ leaders with whom I spoke did not mention the motivations for centralizing decision-making over time – a move that heightened horizontal coordination even as it robbed subnational party leaders of their independence. One analyst suggested that the party has always been "very focused on national politics" (Immigration and Refugee Board of Canada, 2016). It may be that Borges and others focused on growing the party territorially and organizationally so that the PJ would become the party with the most national votes. At any rate, local level party leaders meet regularly with regional party directors to discuss strategy. Organizational and political matters are decided by the National Political Committee and passed down the party structure, through these regular meetings. As a consequence, there is "strict discipline within the ranks of PJ" (Immigration and Refugee Board of Canada, 2016).

In all, the PJ has attained a fairly high level of coordination both during and between elections. This has changed over time, thanks in part to a political context that led the upper echelons of the party to assert more top-down control and strengthen the party's horizontal coordination. Yet, as we will see now, vertical interest aggregation is much weaker in the PJ than we might expect given its strong impulse to establish an organizational presence in every municipality in the country.[4]

Vertical Interest Aggregation

The PJ party leaders insist that they want to be "a real party – not an electoral group" (personal interview Borges, May 29, 2014). Yet, a preponderance of evidence suggests that the party has spent more time growing its electoral prowess than cultivating strong, lasting ties with constituents. The PJ leaders confirm that they sought to become "the image of [electoral] unity" in the country (personal interview Briquet, May 28, 2014). Coordination, both within the party and among MUD membership, became the party's first priority. This choice may have come at the expense of the cultivation of stronger vertical ties. At the very least, none of the leaders I interviewed stressed the importance of social bases for the party. (This, as we will see, is quite different in the case of the VP.)

[4] On this point, in May 2014, Edilson Ferrer, the PJ's National Secretary of Organization, noted that the party has permanent communication with party members in 298 of 335 municipalities (personal interview). Those 298 municipalities include 1,141 parishes. The party, at that time, had militants (*justicieros*) in 905 parishes, and a permanent organization in 400, where 85 percent of the electorate resides (personal interview Ferrer, May 29, 2014).

For this reason, indicators of the party's vertical interest aggregation capacity are scarce.

According to Pérez Baralt (2004), the professional working class is the PJ's primary constituency (p. 267). The author also notes that many party leaders come from this constituency. It is therefore unclear if the party identifies this group as their core constituency, or if it has been ascribed to it due to the sociodemographic make-up of its leaders.

The party's NGO predecessor, Asociación Primero Justicia (Justice First Association), was, however, very active early on. The NGO helped write the Ley Orgánica de la Justicia de Paz (Law of Justice and Peace) and, upon its approval, helped train Jueces de Paz (Justices of the Peace) throughout the country (Borges 2012). These Justices of the Peace deliberated over local conflicts and worked to resolve them using the principles of reconciliation and arbitration. Eventually, Borges – an NGO and party founder – acquired a prime-time television show, entitled Justice for All, where he projected the ideals of the NGO and gained additional recognition.

The PJ's rather unique NGO origins meant that the party had substantive ties to a particular demand within Venezuelan society – that of making justice accessible to all. Indeed, some scholars suggest that the PJ's early successes with the *Jueces por la Paz* (Justices for Peace) program gave the party an initial advantage vis-à-vis other electoral alternatives (Pérez Baralt 2004, 268). The NGO's brand, associated with justice and the pursuit of human rights (personal interview González, May 30, 2014), should have given the party some currency with which to cultivate citizen ties.

Party brands, alongside other resources (Cyr 2017; LeBas 2013; Levitsky et al. 2016; Lupu 2016; Tavits 2013) have proven vital for parties founded in inauspicious moments. LeBas (2013), for example, demonstrates that nascent parties that can tap into pre-existing mobilizing structures – such as unions – acquire a resource they can use to challenge incumbents. Levitsky et al. (2016) contend that parties with a party brand and/or a territorial infrastructure are more likely to become successful, enduring parties. Cyr (2017) formalizes these insights and argues that different party resources, including organizational, ideational, elite, and material resources, acquire different values when it comes to party emergence, over-time electoral success, and survival.

To what extent did Justice First Association, the NGO, provide resources that helped the PJ, the party, foster ties with citizens? The answer to this is mixed. For one, the transition from NGO to political party was hugely controversial. Many individuals associated with the NGO chose not to join Borges, Leopoldo López, and others who sought to formally enter into politics. The two groups formally split. The soon-to-be political party kept the name, PJ. The NGO became known, instead, as Consorcio Justicia (Justice Consortium) (Cadenas Sangronis 2005, 51).

The split meant that those ties with citizens associated with the civil society group became indirect. Territorial resources that the NGO had cultivated also would have been lost.[5] Still, the decision to take the NGO's name, PJ, was a strategic one. López – who initially proposed to keep the name while adding Movimiento to it – did so precisely because it had recognition and an established media presence (Cadenas Sangronis 2005, 55). The NGO, therefore, served as a resource for the party. It was largely, however, an ideational one (Cyr 2017) and relegated to its reputation and brand. The PJ was a known quantity in the country. While this recognition undoubtedly helped the party early on – the PJ quickly became one of the most competitive parties among the opposition – it does not seem to have helped the party establish particular ties with any one group or constituency.

Another resource that would have helped with the cultivation of direct channels to social groups on the ground is ideology (Cyr 2017; Mainwaring and Torcal 2006). This, too, however, seems unlikely. For one, the party's ideology has been historically difficult to pinpoint.[6] Pamphlets identify *centro humanismo* (centrist humanism) as the party's worldview – a perspective that privileges the agency and values of human beings and seeks to protect their natural freedoms. This might be considered a centrist perspective, although party leaders have on multiple occasions located the party on the center-left.[7] Others have suggested that the party chose – again, strategically – to eschew any ideological definition at all, precisely because it espoused largely center-right positions at a time when those views were broadly rejected by Venezuelan society (Cadenas Sangronis 2005, 71–72).

[5] It is unclear how widespread the NGO's territorial resources would have been, as the NGO's infrastructure seems to have been limited to the "peace justices" set-up in different places throughout the country.

[6] Venezuelan politics in the twenty-first century do not revolve around ideas (or ideology) so much as they turn on the *chavista*/anti-*chavista* dimension. Few parties are known for their ideological position and, indeed, the opposition includes parties from both the left and the right (Cyr and Sagarzazu 2014).

[7] And, in fact, there is faction of self-denominated, more left-wing leaders within the PJ – a group that includes the party's former presidential candidate, Henrique Capriles Radonski.

Indeed, Venezuelans identify the party as rather elitist – specifically, that the party "appears to put forth an image of Spanish aristocracy and one that is far from the problems of the lower classes" (Pérez Baralt 2004, 270).[8] Overall, from an ideological perspective, it is unclear what the PJ's brand is. As one analyst commented, the PJ "is a bit of a strange party" on this front.[9] Its ideological ambiguity likely hinders the development of strong ties with specific social sectors (Lupu 2016; Mainwaring and Torcal 2006).

Overall, the establishment of clear, vertical ties with citizens seems to have been hampered by at least two factors. For one, the PJ struggled to define a coherent party brand. As demonstrated, there has been considerable disagreement about the party's ideological leanings in the country. Moreover, its ties to a justice-first movement were weakened when the party formally split from the NGO. Unlike, therefore, the Propuesta Republicana, (Republican Proposal, PRO) in Argentina (see Vommaro this volume), it was unclear which constituency would compose the party's core. This lack of clarity regarding the party's core would also hamper the pursuit of a more segmented linkage strategy (Luna 2010).

We must also take context into account here. The PJ became increasingly influential in national politics as the country's regime evolved away from democracy. Under successive *chavista* governments, led first by Hugo Chávez and then, upon his death, by Nicolás Maduro, politics became increasingly authoritarian (Corrales 2015). Citizen support, as a consequence, bifurcated. Venezuelans either fervently supported *chavismo* and its policies or fervently opposed it (Cyr and Meléndez 2016). In this increasingly polarized context, appealing to any one wing of the anti-*chavista* constituency would have weakened PJ's appeal to the group as a whole. This is especially the case given how diverse and divided the *chavista* opposition was early on (Cyr 2013). For the PJ to become the party of electoral unity, as its organizers espoused, it would need to bridge ideological differences across the anti-*chavista* camp, not underscore them.

[8] This point is highly speculative, of course, but it coheres with my own observations of the party in my multiple trips to Venezuela between 2010 and 2014.

[9] Alonso Moleiro, "Quién es Quién en la Oposición Venezolana" (Las Historias de El País, Blog, Episode 28, 2019). https://poddtoppen.se/podcast/1440051890/las-historias-de-el-pas/ep-28-quin-es-quin-en-la-oposicin-venezolana (last accessed May 16, 2019).

Primero Justicia, by Way of Conclusion

The PJ appears to have privileged horizontal coordination over vertical interest aggregation. To date, it is difficult to really isolate who the so-called *Justicieros* (party activists) are, beyond their commitment to elections and their shared opposition to *chavismo*. Indeed, in my interviews with PJ leaders, as well as in my analysis of primary and secondary documents, there has been very little mention of *el pueblo* (the people), *las bases* (the grassroots), or *Justicieros* at all. Overall, the party has evolved into an unrooted party. Early on, the party exhibited horizontal coordination during campaigns but less so between elections. Later it became much more coordinated across both time periods. Its capacity for vertical aggregation is, as of yet, undeveloped.

This classification disagrees somewhat with earlier interpretations, which labeled it an electoral party (Núñez Muñoz and Pineda Morán 2003; Pérez Baralt 2004). The difference seems to be an emphasis here on horizontal coordination and also vertical interest aggregation. Earlier works focused on the former. I take both dimensions into account. My conclusion is that the PJ's capacity for vertical interest aggregation remains underdeveloped and weak. An electoral party, by contrast, has ties with society, even if they are only activated during election time.

CLASSIFYING VOLUNTAD POPULAR

The VP was founded by Leopoldo López, former PJ leader and one of its earliest elected officials (as mayor of Chacao). His stated reason for leaving the PJ was that he had a different vision for democracy. Analysts note that he was largely responsible for creating and even curating the VP's party leadership early on. López sought out individuals to join him, one by one. He created a vision for the party and forged its programmatic platform, entitled *La Mejor Venezuela* (The Best Venezuela).[10]

Despite López's role in the party's creation, party leaders emphasize the social origins of the party. Juan Guaidó called it a "movement of movements whose goal is to be a party … that brings together those movements" (personal interview Guaidó, May 27, 2014). Omar España noted that the only prerequisite for VP candidates was that they be, first, social

[10] Alonso Moleiro, "Quién es Quién en la Oposición Venezolana" (Las Historias de El País, Blog, Episode 28, 2019). https://poddtoppen.se/podcast/1440051890/las-historias-de-el-pas/ep-28-quin-es-quin-en-la-oposicin-venezolana (last accessed May 16, 2019).

leaders (personal interview España, May 27, 2014). Samuel Olarte echoed this idea, insisting that VP leaders "should first be social leaders" (personal interview Olarte, May 27, 2014). It is, of course, possible for an individual, like López, to create a party with strong ties to social movements. And the VP, especially vis-à-vis the PJ, places great emphasis on its ties to movements and activists (more on this in the following section). Still, tensions exist between the desire to have a more bottom-up orientation with respect to party structure – wherein the party's social bases are privileged – and a tendency to take decisions in a hierarchical way.

Since its creation in 2011, the VP has become one of the most intransigent parties to oppose the *chavista* regime.[11] At various times, the party's leadership – and Leopoldo López in particular – has advocated for nonelectoral routes to change. In 2014, for example, the VP supported *La Salida* (The Exit) – a series of protests denouncing growing violence and scarcity in the country but aimed, ultimately, at pushing Nicolás Maduro from office. On April 30, 2019, the acting president, Juan Guaidó, called for Venezuelans to take to the streets to pressure Maduro to leave. Generally speaking, when the MUD takes actions that the VP opposes, the party has made its disagreement known. Still, party leaders emphasize that they have always remained committed to opposition unity (personal interview Iglesias, February 24, 2019).

Overall, the VP has developed strategies of horizontal coordination during and between elections. It has also established vertical ties with society, although it is unclear that its stated goal of privileging its popular bases is actually met in practice to the extent that its rhetoric suggests. Part of the problem is that the party has not had the opportunity to govern, and so its mechanisms for vertical interest aggregation remain untested. Nevertheless, they exist, as per the party's statutes and according to party leaders. All told, I classify the party as sitting somewhere between a political party and an unrooted party.

HORIZONTAL COORDINATION

Horizontal Coordination during Elections

As per party statutes, the VP has a governing body at each level of government. Like the PJ, it has an organization at the national, regional (state), and municipal levels. It also has a fourth governing body at the

[11] Ibid.

parish level.[12] At each level, the party has a team of activists. Membership into each team is by election and includes representatives that are chosen by social movements. Each level is accountable to the governing body at the higher level. An Equipo Federal de Activistas (Federal Team of Activists, EFA) brings together the national and state activist teams. It is mandated to meet every six months, and, as per party leaders, party mandates are fulfilled and the organizational structure is intact.[13]

Candidate selection occurs via elections. The elected candidate is then approved by the next-highest governing body. Municipal candidates, for example, are chosen by the municipal team of activists and then confirmed by the relevant regional team. Gubernatorial candidates are elected by the regional team of activists and must then be approved by the national team. Often, candidates emerge before the election takes place. One political figure typically has better name recognition or an established structure of support in place. The election itself, therefore, is often symbolic. When conflict over the elected candidate occurs, it is decided either via secret elections or by the superior governing body. Conflicts over candidate selection, however, are rare (personal interview Iglesias, February 24, 2019).

The extent to which campaigns are nationalized (that is, organized from above) or local is debated regularly within the party. Either way, a coordinating body, the Oficina Técnica de Atención al Candidato (Technical Office of Candidate Support, OTAC), exists to maintain communication among the different candidates in a given campaign. Even when campaigns are local, certain symbols (a logo, a slogan) are shared. The most nationalized campaigns, according to VP leaders, were those organized at the level of the MUD (personal interview Iglesias, February 24, 2019).

Overall, the VP has developed a system for coordinating across levels of government during election cycles. Informal selection processes take place, to be sure. Nevertheless, coordination occurs across elections. The

[12] These are called the Equipo Nacional de Activistas (National Team of Activists, ENA); Equipos Regionales de Activistas (Regional Teams of Activists, ERA), Equipos Municipales de Activistas (Municipal Teams of Activists, EMA); and Equipos Parroquiales de Activistas (Parrish Teams of Activists, EPA).

[13] I interviewed several VP leaders in 2014 for a different research project. While their comments are pertinent to certain areas of concern in this chapter, the great majority of my information on many specific questions related to coordination and aggregation comes from one source (personal interview Iglesias, February 24, 2019), with whom I spoke specifically for this project.

presence of the OTAC is evidence of this. Consequently, we may conclude that the VP meets the requirements of achieving horizontal coordination during elections.

Horizontal Coordination between Elections

Coordination also seems to be well-developed between elections, both in terms of discipline and with respect to policy and party matters. For example, when addressing sensitive or delicate party or policy questions, the party surveys multiple governing bodies before taking a decision. Specifically, it will convoke a meeting of the EFA and ask that, prior to that meeting, each regional team of activists meet with municipal teams to form an opinion on the matter. Consequently, the party undertakes a "cascade of discussions that flow up to the federal team" (personal interview Iglesias, February 24, 2019).

The party's federalized structure allows for a certain amount of autonomy with respect to party development across states (personal interview España, May 27, 2014). Still, for policy questions that are of particular importance to party leaders, the party makes decisions at the federal level that are then transmitted down through the party structure (personal interview Iglesias, February 24, 2019). Overall, the party has put into place mechanisms for coordination that make communication about policy and party across different governing bodies possible.

Finally, the party has achieved discipline within the National Assembly. According to Iglesias, VP congresspeople have always voted the same way. They have also devised a system for working within the MUD. The chair of the VP faction coordinates with the larger group. Where they disagree with MUD positions, the VP makes their disagreement known (personal interview Hasler, February 24, 2019). This dissent has meant that VP acts, at times, independently of the MUD, as with *La Salida*. Still, the VP has never formally split from the MUD, even as other parties from the G4 (e.g., the AD) have. Hasler emphasized the VP's commitment to opposition unity even when the party disagreed with MUD decisions:

> There were things that we did not agree with and thus did not support the MUD, but that did not mean we had broken the alliance. Because we thought that unity was much more important than those differences. … even today, when the MUD no longer exists and everyone is operating from the National Assembly, we think that the unity of all sectors is really important. (personal interview Iglesias, February 24, 2019)

This point is salient given the rather rebellious nature of the VP leader, Leopoldo López. He broke away from the PJ to eventually form the VP. He chose to pursue *La Salida* even when the MUD was against it. Finally, Lopez and acting president Juan Guaidó chose to initiate the May 1 call to protests, *Operación Libertad* (Operation Freedom), one day early, on April 30 – surprising both the government and other opposition leaders. The ostensible tension that manifests between the VP and the MUD does not impact the party's internal horizontal coordination across party branches and governing bodies. These moments of tension could have been opportunities for the VP members to express dissent with the party.

Overall, like the PJ, the party has attained a high level of coordination, both during and between elections. At least in terms of this dimension of the party typology, the VP has achieved the status of a full political party. And, as we will see next, it also has also worked to achieve vertical interest aggregation.

Vertical Interest Aggregation

With respect to the aggregation of citizen interests, the VP appears to be more successful than the PJ. Several leaders commented on the importance of social movements for the party. The VP website affirms this point. Of the four primary links on the party's website, one is dedicated to social movements and another to activism.[14] A click on a third link (*Quiénes Somos* – Who we are), takes the reader to a page that includes references to the popular networks (*Redes Populares* – Popular Networks) around which the party is organized. Further down on the same page, the party affirms that "the basic nucleus of our organization are the Popular Networks at the community level."[15]

Guaidó confirmed this sentiment almost word for word: "The basic nucleus lies in the popular networks" (personal interview Guaidó, May 27, 2014). Even organizationally, social movement language has permeated the party. Members are called "activists," not militants or members. Each governing body is called a team of activists. Rhetorically speaking, the VP takes great care to signal the importance of the social networks that officially underpin the party's formal structure.

[14] See www.voluntadpopular.com/ (last accessed June 12, 2020).

[15] See www.voluntadpopular.com/index.php/quienes-somos?view=featured (last accessed June 12, 2020).

Social movements also have a role to play in the party organization. Party statutes dictate that social movements help elect representatives to different activist teams. Social movement leaders are included on the EFA; they have a decision-making role on issues of particular importance. Indeed, as per the party's website, social movements helped create the VP. Between 2007 and 2009, aspiring party leaders met in a series of meetings alongside youth activists, workers, and political, social, and community leaders to consider what the VP should look like (personal interview España, May 27, 2014).[16]

The importance of activism to the party, and its formal ties with movement leaders, suggest that the VP is constrained by its social base. According to party leaders, the party's evolution to a party was laborious precisely because of the horizontal nature of decision-making (personal interview España, May 27, 2014). In interviews, party leaders assign an important role to social movements and activists in the party structure and operations.

We should nonetheless be wary of the de facto (versus the de jure or even stated) importance of social movements for the VP. It is not clear who these actors are. When asked about which social movements served as the party's base, Iglesias responded by listing nearly all identities around which movements have historically formed, including youth movements, unions, cultural movements, neighborhood groups, women's groups, advocacy groups for former convicts, and farmers' co-ops (personal interview Iglesias, February 24, 2019). A movement-based party, by contrast, must have a specific constituency (Anria 2018 and Anria this volume). The VP, by contrast, appears to want to appeal to all marginalized constituencies. It is unclear that any one group can shape what the party does.

Additionally, Leopoldo López does not come from a social movement. Although many VP leaders have ties to, for example, student movements, López has a much more elitist pedigree. He was educated in the United States and pursued a career at PDVSA. López is, for many, "very much a strongman; the boss; not one of many."[17] He is also very popular. VP leaders insist that López's, and the party's, role in more radical events, such as *La Salida*, were debated before acted upon (personal interview España, May 27, 2014). López has nonetheless become a highly visible

[16] Ibid.

[17] Alonso Moleiro, "Quién es Quién en la Oposición Venezolana" (Las Historias de El País, Blog, Episode 28, 2019). https://poddtoppen.se/podcast/1440051890/las-historias-de-el-pas/ep-28-quin-es-quin-en-la-oposicin-venezolana (last accessed May 16, 2019).

protagonist in his own right in Venezuela. Even with Guaidó as acting president, his ties to López are regularly visible, as when the latter stood beside him on the April 30 call to push Maduro from power.

I consider López at length because, as with Evo Morales and the MAS (see Anria this volume), the line is blurred with respect to what is more important for the VP: the party or the person. Unlike Morales, however, López's political experience and history have weak ties to a social movement or organization.[18] It is, therefore, unclear that he would be constrained, as Morales has been (see, e.g., Anria 2018; Anria and Cyr 2017; and Anria this volume), by the "popular bases" that VP insists are at the heart of the party. There could be, in other words, a latent personalism that might have affected (or may in the future affect) the VP's development, if not for the broader authoritarian context in which the VP had to operate for almost a decade.

Voluntad Popular, by Way of Conclusion

In all, the VP appears, on paper, to be a full political party, as per the editors' typology. The party has created mechanisms of horizontal coordination both during election season and between elections. Additionally, the party declares its ties with Popular Networks on the ground. In particular, party statutes delineate a set of formal channels through which social movements can express their opinions and make their demands. Social movement leaders have a spot in the EFA. They also have a vote in terms of constituting the activist teams at the national, state, municipal, and parish levels.

We cannot know if these ties to groups on the ground are merely formal or whether they actually constrain party leaders when they make decisions. This point merits fuller discussion. The evolution of the VP, like other opposition parties, has undoubtedly been shaped by the authoritarian context in which it operates. The VP has had few governing experiences at the national level, and so it is difficult to know how it might act in power. I consider this point in much greater detail in the next section. For now, however, I classify the VP as occupying a space somewhere between a full and unrooted party.

[18] Although he was a part of the group that worked in the PJ when it was an NGO.

THE CHALLENGES OF PARTY-BUILDING IN NONDEMOCRACIES

PJ and VP were founded after the collapse of the party system and at a time when political parties were reviled, both by the newly installed government and by citizens. The country became increasingly authoritarian as first the PJ and then the VP formed. It also became increasingly polarized around Hugo Chávez and his movement, *chavismo*. Undoubtedly, both parties emerged during a period of "conflict" (Levitsky et al. 2016, 14), or "adversity" (Van Dyck 2016).

A wealth of research has found that political parties are more likely to successfully emerge during difficult or "extraordinary" times (Greene 2007; Levitsky et al. 2016, 3; Panebianco 1988; Van Dyck 2016). Specifically, conflict tends to bring party leaders together so they can forge "partisan attachments, grassroots organizations, and internal cohesion" – all of which help create "robust" parties (Levitsky et al. 2016, 3).

The existing literature acknowledges the role that adversity plays in party-building. It is more speculative about those specific aspects of party-building that are helped (or hampered) by a nondemocratic context. Yet, the editors for this volume remind us that many successful, stable parties exist that accrue high levels of horizontal coordination or vertical aggregation, but not both. In this last section, I leverage the joint party-building experiences of the PJ and the VP to think through the systematic trade-offs that nondemocratic contexts may provoke for new parties. I focus in particular on two aspects of nondemocracies.

First, nondemocratic contexts can utilize repressive measures that make it difficult for opposing candidates to attain power. Second, they can provoke polarization between those for and against the regime. Each of these tendencies, in the Venezuelan case, affected how the VP and the PJ evolved as new parties.

The Struggle to Exercise Power

By the mid-2000s, Chávez's party – Movimiento Quinta República (Fifth Republic Movement, MVR), then Partido Socialista Unido de Venezuela (United Socialist Party of Venezuela, PSUV) – was clearly predominant. In 2005, it held a super-majority in the National Assembly, a plurality of seats in Municipal councils, and a near majority in terms of governorships and seats in state legislatures (Cyr 2017, 161). The opposition, which boycotted the 2005 parliamentary election, was essentially nonexistent. Competing in elections after 2005 became very difficult for the opposition – especially at the national level.

Greene (2007) spells out nicely the resource, or hyper-incumbent, advantage of a predominant party in such circumstances. *Chavismo* had more money, people, and access to patronage than the opposition. They had greater access to the media and, as the years went on, passed laws that disproportionately benefitted them with respect to when, where, and how the media was used. They utilized government buildings, vehicles, and personnel to undertake covert campaigning. Candidates acquired visible positions in public works' inaugurations.[19] The litany of resource and campaign advantages to which incumbents in nondemocratic regimes are privy is extensive (see also Levitsky and Way 2010).

Additionally, as the opposition became more coordinated, the government relied on *chavista*-friendly institutions, including the courts and the national electoral council, to keep competitive opponents from running for office (Corrales 2015). After Nicolás Maduro barely won the presidential election in 2013, persecution turned particularly repressive, ending in the exile or incarceration of politicians. Anti-government supporters were intermittently subject to torture, forced exile, and, in some cases, disappearance and/or death. The courts, which were stacked with judges friendly to the government, ruled over and over again in its favor (Corrales 2015).

This kind of autocratic legalism – or "the *use, abuse,* and *non-use* . . . of the law in the service of the executive branch" (Corrales 2015, 38) makes it difficult for opposition candidates to run for office. Those who can run often face insurmountable hurdles that keep them from campaigning competitively against the *chavista* candidate. Overall, opposition candidates are much less likely to be elected.

A consequence of hyper-incumbent advantage (Greene 2007) in nondemocracies is that new parties are hard-pressed to acquire governing experience. If they are prevented from assuming positions of power, then their campaign promises remain untested. They will struggle to channel demands from below. Ties with constituents – beyond a shared opposition to government – cannot easily be tested. The extent to which new parties are actually, therefore, constrained by their social bases is unknown.

[19] Phil Gunson "Elections 2015: A Tilted Playing Field" (International Crisis Group. November 26, 2015). www.crisisgroup.org/latin-america-caribbean/andes/venezuela/venezuela-parliamentary-elections-2015-tilted-playing-field (last accessed June 14, 2020).

A lack of governing experience can make it more difficult to foster mechanisms of vertical interest aggregation. Let us return to the example of the VP, which I tentatively classified as something between an unrooted and full political party. Its ties to social movements – which, at least rhetorically and with respect to party statutes, are strong – are unclear in practice. One reason for this could be that the VP, like many opposition parties, experienced persecution by the government. Most notably, Leopoldo López was arrested for inciting violence in 2014. Others in the party have also been targeted. For example, the government created an "auto-coup commando" unit in 2017 and began arresting VP activists, accusing them of terrorism and violence (Cawthorne 2017).

Additionally, although it successfully seated fourteen *diputades* (representatives) in the 2015 legislative elections, their ability to legislate has been severely delimited. Individual electoral results have been challenged. More importantly, the National Assembly as an institution was defanged when Maduro called for a constituent assembly and endowed it with de facto legislative powers.

Overall, the increasingly authoritarian context in which the VP (and other parties) operates has made it difficult to exercise power. We know, therefore, that the VP seeks to appeal to social movements on the ground. We do not know if these appeals are successful and if the VP is beholden to the interests of all (or any) of them. Nondemocratic contexts can yield natural alliances between opposition parties and groups on the ground. It can also, however, make it difficult to consolidate those ties or assess their strength.

Repression, Polarization, and Opposition Coordination

A longer-term consequence of repression has to do with how the opposition behaves. Specifically, as repression grows from a few, targeted instances to something that is more widespread, opponents may decide to set aside their differences and coordinate their campaigns (Chang 2008; Gandhi and Reuter 2013; Jiménez 2018). A single opposition candidate is better placed to compete against the incumbent than two or more. This is especially the case as society itself becomes polarized and bifurcates into groups who are for or against the incumbent.[20]

[20] The causal relationship here is not clear. Does polarization around an incumbent encourage opposition coordination, or does increased opposition coordination provoke greater polarization? The effect may be iterative. I do not seek to adjudicate this question one way

In Venezuela, citizens became increasingly divided between those who supported Chávez and his movement (*chavistas*) and those who did not (anti-*chavistas*) (Cyr and Meléndez 2016).[21] Early on, this polarization gave *chavismo* an advantage. Most open seats were fielded by one *chavista* candidate. A selection of opposition alternatives, by contrast, vied for the anti-*chavista* vote, diluting its impact. This electoral dynamic, alongside the growth of repression on the part of the government, led to the creation of the MUD, an umbrella group of opposition parties founded to coordinate an electoral strategy that would beat *chavismo* in the ballot box. By the 2010s, each individual race was fought between one anti-*chavista* (read: MUD) candidate and one *chavista* candidate.

The opposition's use of the *tarjeta única* – or a single ticket, opposition candidate – meant that parties had to compete against each other to acquire any one candidacy. The effect of this was twofold. First, parties were compelled to work together internally (i.e., within the party) so that their candidate selection process was coherent and consistent.

We saw this occur in the case of the PJ. The bifurcation of the vote between the *chavista* and the single opposition candidate affected the electoral strategy of the party. The PJ sought to be electorally strong within the opposition, which meant capturing as many unity candidacies as possible. This required much greater internal coordination than the party had previously promoted. In particular, for Henrique Capriles Radonski to be chosen as the MUD's 2012 presidential candidate, the party needed to make its territorial-wide campaign more "coherent" (personal interview Briquet, May 28, 2014). It bears noting that the VP also took broader MUD dynamics into account when organizing their campaigns (personal interview Iglesias, February 24, 2019). In both cases, the MUD's decision to coordinate candidacies compelled each party to consolidate or create mechanisms of horizontal coordination – fostering, as a result, one important dimension of a full political party (Luna et al. Introduction this volume).

Political polarization, and the resulting coordination around a single opposition candidate, can be a double-edged sword for party-building, however. Once the competition over each candidacy is decided,

or the other here. We do know that an increase in repression, from targeted to moderate levels, can compel individual opposition parties to work together and put forth a unity candidate (Jiménez 2018).

[21] A third group of so-called *ni-ni's* – those who were neither for Chávez nor for the opposition – also existed, but this group tended to be less politically active and outshadowed by the pro- and anti-*chavista* groups.

competition for the opposition vote essentially disappears. After all, the sole opposition candidate should naturally appeal to citizens who oppose the government. This leads to the second effect of intraparty coordination in nondemocratic contexts. There are fewer incentives to make appeals to specific constituencies on the ground. As a result, the vertical aggregation of interests – the second dimension underpinning a full political party – is weakened.

These dynamics unfolded within the MUD. Once the unity ticket was instituted, the internal primaries became the locus of competition. Achieving the candidacy became each party's primary goal. After the MUD candidate was chosen, the broader election converted into a contest between two candidates: a *chavista* and an anti-*chavista*. Within the broader context of social polarization, the natural, or obvious, constituency for the MUD candidate was the group of anti-*chavistas* in its entirety. An anti-*chavista*, by definition, would never vote for a *chavista* candidate (Cyr and Meléndez 2016). Therefore, once any one opposition party captured a particular MUD candidacy, there was less need to appeal to certain constituencies or engender ties with specific groups. Each candidate could seek, quite simply, the anti-*chavista* vote within their particular jurisdiction.

One counterintuitive consequence of this is that, broadly speaking, the ties between opposition parties and citizens need not be based on any specific appeal or demand beyond those associated with changing the regime and removing the incumbent for power. Especially for those parties that were founded after Hugo Chávez was first elected and the dynamics of polarization set in, the incentives to carve out a core constituency weaken, as does the impulse to diversify their appeal through a more segmented electoral strategy. It is perhaps for this reason that the PJ has struggled to establish stronger ties with citizens and that the VP's appeals to social movements have been fairly broad and overarching in nature.

Overall, party-building under the increasingly authoritarian regime in Venezuela has come with certain trade-offs. Increased repression, as well as growing polarization, compelled the opposition as a whole to organize electorally and promote single opposition candidates. The single ticket facilitated the electoral choice for anti-*chavista* citizens. The opposition's electoral victories increased. Capriles, the MUD candidate for the 2012 and 2013 presidential elections, narrowed the gap between the opposition and *chavismo* in his first contest[22] and lost by a razor-thin margin in

[22] Hugo Chávez won the presidency with roughly 55 percent of the vote. Capriles came in second with 44 percent. In the previous two electoral contests, however, Chávez's

the second.[23] Perhaps most importantly, the opposition – against serious institutional hurdles – won a majority in the National Assembly in 2015.

At the individual party level, repression, polarization, and the decision to institute a single ticket also had the positive effect of encouraging the VP and especially the PJ to increase their internal coordination. The PJ went from being decentralized and atomized organizationally to developing a more disciplined, hierarchical structure. In terms of horizontal mechanisms of coordination, an authoritarian regime can produce positive party-building outcomes.

It is also the case, however, that the adverse political context in which each party operated hampered other aspects of party-building. Specifically, it de-incentivized the development of concrete mechanisms of vertical interest aggregation. There are at least two reasons for this. First, the *chavista* government made it increasingly difficult for opposition parties to govern. As we have seen, the opposition made important electoral strides beginning in the 2010s. In response, the *chavista* regime pushed back against those victories through the use of electoral legalism. Opposition parties, including the PJ and the VP, therefore, had fewer opportunities to exercise de jure and also de facto power. Consequently, they had fewer opportunities to promote interests or demands from below.

Additionally, government repression and growing social polarization around the *chavista* regime compelled MUD members to coordinate their candidacies in an effort to maximize their vote share vis-à-vis the *chavistas*. Paradoxically, the success of the unity ticket had the unexpected consequence of weakening the cultivation of explicit connections with any specific group on the ground. There was little need to. Each opposition candidate had only to appeal to anti-*chavistas* more broadly as a way to maximize their vote share. Overall, the bifurcation of the electoral contest, along with the inability to govern, truncated the ties that the VP or the PJ might have wished to develop with society.[24]

victory was much more pronounced. In 2006, Chávez received 62.8 percent of the votes. Manuel Rosales, who came in second, only won 36.9 percent. Chávez won 59.8 percent of the vote in 2000, while the second place finisher (Francisco Arias Cárdenas) captured 37.5 percent.

[23] The 2013 election occurred after Chávez's death. His successor, Nicolás Maduro captured 50.6 percent of the vote, while Capriles won 49.1 percent.

[24] On this point, the fact that the PJ appears to place less emphasis on these ties also clearly matters. Still, the VP was very explicit in its desire to appeal to social movements, and, yet, the strength of the actual ties are unclear.

CONCLUSIONS

This chapter has undertaken two objectives. First, using the typology of diminished party subtypes developed by the editors, it classified two important parties from the Venezuelan opposition. The PJ and the VP both developed mechanisms of horizontal coordination during and between elections. The PJ's ability to vertically aggregate interests from below, however, has been limited. Party leaders do not seem to emphasize this objective, and the authoritarian, polarized context in which the party operates made such ties unnecessary.

The VP, by contrast, has established mechanisms for channeling voices from below. At least formally, it is constrained by the Popular Networks that sit at the party's base. Still, as with the PJ, the context in which it operates means that those ties remain largely untested. Without much governing experience, it is difficult to know how constrained the party is by those Popular Networks. Because of this, I classify the PJ as an unrooted party and the VP as a party that falls somewhere between an unrooted and full political party.

Second, the chapter sought to understand why the two parties developed as they did. It placed a lot of causal weight on the nondemocratic context in which both parties emerged. The *chavista* regime became increasingly repressive and used its hyper-incumbent advantage (Greene 2007) to make it difficult for the opposition to compete in elections and also to govern. The polemic regime sparked polarization – a tendency that bifurcated voter demand and further incentivized opposition electoral coordination (which itself was also stimulated by repression). All told, these dynamics encouraged the development of mechanisms of horizontal coordination while discouraging the development of vertical ties with society.

The mixed experience of the PJ and the VP suggests, at least tentatively, that authoritarian contexts present both opportunities and challenges when it comes to successful party-building. As per the findings of others (Levitsky et al. 2016; Van Dyck 2017), the "extraordinary" context of adversity in which both parties emerged helped to promote the growth of horizontal ties. It also, however, made the development of vertical ties more difficult. In the Venezuelan context, this trade-off – in which one dimension of party-building is promoted at the expense of the other – not only impacts individual party-building experiences. It will also impact the quality of representation by these parties, if and when the transition back to democracy occurs.

INTERVIEWS

Borges, Julio. *Fundador, Coordinador nacional, y Diputado nacional de* Primero Justicia. Caracas, Venezuela. May 29, 2014.

Briquet, Armando. Director of *Fundación Justicia y Democracia*; Member, *Junta de Dirección Nacional.* Primero Justicia. Caracas, Venezuela. May 28, 2014.

España, Omar. *Técnico,* Voluntad Popular. Caracas, Venezuela. May 27, 2014.

Ferrer, Edilson. *Secretario Nacional de Organización.* Primero Justicia. Caracas, Venezuela. May 29, 2014.

González, Gerardo. Venezuelan pollster and academic. Caracas, Venezuela. May 30, 2014.

Guaidó, Juan. *Coordinador Nacional de Organización; Diputado nacional,* Voluntad Popular. Caracas, Venezuela. May 27, 2014.

Iglesias, Hasler. Member, *Dirección Nacional del Partido.* Voluntad Popular. Caracas, Venezuela. February 24, 2019.

Olarte, Samuel. *Asistente al Secretario Nacional de Organización,* Voluntad Popular. Caracas, Venezuela. May 27, 2014.

10

Diminished by Design

Ecuador's Alianza PAIS

Catherine M. Conaghan

INTRODUCTION

Riding a wave of discontent with traditional parties, Rafael Correa campaigned as a quintessential outsider in Ecuador's 2006 presidential election. Correa touted his credentials as a leftist technocrat untainted by the corrupt party system. For voters fed up with politics-as-usual, Correa offered an attention-grabbing alternative. He was celebrated as the candidate of the newly minted electoral vehicle, the Movimiento Patria Altiva y Soberana (Proud Sovereign Country Movement, PAIS). Rapidly assembled for the election, PAIS began as a marriage of convenience – an amorphous collection of progressive political operatives and disgruntled groups rallying around a young, dynamic candidate.

In a crowded field of candidates, the formula worked. In the weeks just before the first-round election in September 2006, Correa rapidly ascended in the polls, edging out other left candidates. Correa went on to win a solid second-round victory against his right-wing populist opponent, billionaire Álvaro Noboa, and PAIS quickly became the gathering place for leftists, centrists, reformists, and opportunists jockeying for power and influence in the newly elected government.

Inaugurated in January 2007, Correa went on to become Ecuador's longest-serving chief executive: no small feat in a country where three chief executives had been forced to leave office early in the period from 1997 to 2005. Unprecedented stability in the executive went hand in hand with PAIS's march toward electoral hegemony and control over the legislative branch.

Correa used his power to shake up the political system, christening his policies as *La Revolución Ciudadana* (Citizens' Revolution). His controversial presidency was transformative; it produced an elaborate new constitution with expanded rights and restructured institutions. The new constitutional order heralded a return of the state; government was cast as the principal protagonist of social change and economic development. But at the same time, Correa steadily eroded liberal democratic norms and practices. Buoyed by high approval ratings and bolstered by new constitutional powers, Correa concentrated power in the presidency and in himself. Political scientists eventually categorized the regime as a hybrid type, another example of how unchecked executive power induced 'backsliding' toward authoritarianism (Bermeo 2016; Conaghan 2016).

Renamed as Alianza PAIS (PAIS Alliance, AP), PAIS became a formidable electoral vehicle. As shown in Table 10.1, the AP rallied support through serial elections and plebiscites: the 2007 referendum on

TABLE 10.1 *Vote percentage for the AP candidates in national-level elections and AP-endorsed positions in referendums*

Year	Election/referendum	AP national vote percentage	AP seats/total seats (percentage)
2006	First-round presidential	23	–
2006	Runoff presidential	57	–
2007	Referendum on Constituent Assembly	82	–
2007	Constituent Assembly deputies	–	73/130 (56)
2008	Referendum on Constitution	64	–
2009	Presidential election (no second round)	52	–
2009	National Assembly deputies	–	54/124 (43.5)
2011	9-Question referendum	53.5 (average)	–
2013	Presidential election (no second round)	57	–
2013	National Assembly deputies	–	100/137 (73)

(continued)

TABLE 10.1 *(continued)*

Year	Election/referendum	AP national vote percentage	AP seats/total seats (percentage)
2017	*First-round presidential election	39	–
2017	Second-round presidential election	51	–
2017	National Assembly deputies	–	74/137 (54)

Sources: Basabe-Serrano and Martínez (2014); Freidenberg (2012); Pachano (2010); Ortiz Crespo and Burbano de Lara (2017); Polga-Hecimovich (2013).
*This was the first presidential election in which Rafael Correa was not the AP candidate. The AP candidate was Lenín Moreno.

the constituent assembly and assembly elections, the 2008 referendum on the constitution, the 2009 national elections, the 2011 national referendum, and the 2013 national elections. The winning streak continued in 2017, even after Correa declined to push for a third term, though winning elections was not the sum total of the AP's achievements. By 2013, the AP had managed to do what few parties in Ecuadorian history had done: it turned itself into a national political machine that fielded candidates in every district and drew support from voters across the country's regional divides (Eichorst and Polga-Hecimovich 2014).

Electoral success, however, was not a prompt for turning the AP into a full-fledged political party. The AP's evolution as a diminished subtype in the spectrum of electoral vehicles was neither an accident nor a botched effort at party building: it was a development by design, an outcome that served Correa's one-man approach to governing and that no one inside the AP proved capable of challenging. Consolidating his control over the AP, Correa ensured that leaders personally loyal to him were entrenched in the upper echelons of the organization, with the most privileged sitting alongside him as members of an inner circle known as the political bureau, *el buró político*; dissent, along with any aspirations for organizational autonomy, was squashed.

Dependent on Correa's charismatic appeal and the financial resources wielded by the executive branch, the AP was relegated to the chores of electioneering and dutifully providing votes in the national assembly. Rather than reaching out to important sectors in society to broaden and deepen democratic representation, the AP selectively poached leaders from Ecuador's relatively weak civil society organizations and co-opted willing groups with government resources for electoral advantage. Overshadowed by the president, the AP was ruled through a top-down command structure and cast as an appendage of the government. Viewed through the typology of this volume (Luna et al. Introduction this volume), once in power, the AP evolved as an unrooted party: an organization that achieved a distinctive form of horizontal coordination under Correa's leadership, yet one that fell short in the tasks of vertically aggregating and representing Ecuadorian society.

The AP began as convenient scaffolding for winning votes that many leftists hoped could develop into a genuine instrument of democratic representation. Nonetheless, the AP progressively shed its diverse founding coalition in favor of government-sponsored interest groups and government-dependent constituencies. Horizontal coordination (during and between elections) was in evidence, albeit in a markedly nondemocratic form. The AP's impressive level of horizontal coordination as a national-level political machine was not the product of a programmatic or ideological consensus struck among political equals. Rather, coordination was imposed from above; compliance with political bureau directives was the "cost of the ticket" for access to the AP and government positions. During election cycles, AP candidates united around common symbols, talking points, and Correa. Between elections, party discipline reigned inside the ranks of the AP's national assembly caucus, with only occasional breaches that ended in resignations or expulsions. With such high-level horizontal coordination, voters could not be confused about what a vote for the AP signified. It was an unambiguous stamp of approval for Correa and the decidedly mixed bag of policies that was the Citizens' Revolution.

Examining the AP's origins is an essential point of departure for understanding its paradoxical fate: how it functioned as an electoral juggernaut for ten years yet remained stymied from becoming a fully realized political party capable of both vertical aggregation and horizontal coordination. This analysis begins with an overview of the AP's development as an instrument for Correa's 2006 presidential bid and how the rapid sequencing of elections and referenda from 2007 to 2013 secured the power of a new president and his partisan vehicle. From there, the attention turns to the principal categories in the volume's analytical framework by examining: (1) how the AP's potential to act as vehicle for vertical aggregation and democratic representation was undermined by Correa's leadership and governing strategy, and (2) how horizontal coordination inside the AP was achieved in a distinctive "top-down" management style. By 2017, the presidential transition from Rafael Correa to Lenín Moreno laid bare the weaknesses inside the AP. Correa's leadership and presidency, so pivotal to the AP's story of electoral success, were also the drivers that diminished the AP, effectively turning it into an unrooted party whose viability is increasingly uncertain.

FROM MOVEMENT TO GOVERNMENT

Rafael Correa's rise as a national political figure was meteoric. He was plucked from the relative obscurity of his work as an economics professor at Quito's San Francisco University to serve as finance minister. His hastily arranged appointment came when Vice President Alfredo Palacio succeeded to the presidency after anti-corruption street protesters (dubbed *los forajidos* or outlaws) forced President Lucio Gutiérrez from office in April 2005. Gutiérrez's fall laid the foundation for Correa's rise: not only did it catapult Correa into a high-profile cabinet position but many of the dissident groups that emerged in the protests ended up among the early supporters of his presidential candidacy (Herrera Llive 2017, 97).

Correa attracted media attention and quickly established his credentials as a fierce critic of neoliberal economic policies and the international financial order. It was a popular message. Ecuadorians were still recovering from the catastrophic financial meltdown of 2000, a collapse attributed to ill-conceived bank deregulation that wiped out family savings and sent around a half million people out of the country to seek work.

Correa's tenure as economic minister was brief but his media-attracting magnetism and unbridled ambition did not go unnoticed. Through friendships and professional interactions, Correa formed an informal network of political operatives, intellectuals, and activists who became interested in promoting his presidential candidacy. The circle included figures with previous ties to parties and those with backgrounds in organizing; these were important assets because Correa had no previous experience in electoral politics.

By early 2006, a handful of political, labor, and civil society groups announced their support of Correa. These included ethnically identified groups such as the Federación de Indios (Indigenous Federation, FEI) and Confederación Nacional de Organizaciones Campesinas, Indígenas y Negras (National Confederation of Peasants, Indigenous, and Black Organizations, FENACLE). Yet efforts to strike agreements with larger, more powerful organizations and political entities failed. Correa was rebuffed by the national indigenous organization, Confederación de Nacionalidades Indígenas del Ecuador (Confederation of Indigenous Nationalities of Ecuador, CONAIE), which ran its own candidate on the ticket of the indigenous-based Pachacutik Party. Similarly, the national teachers' union, Unión Nacional de Educadores (National Teachers' Union) stood by its traditional political vehicle, the Movimiento Popular Democrático (Popular Democratic Movement, MPD), which also ran its own candidate in the first round. The only established parties opting to support Correa in the first round were the Partido Socialista-Frente Amplio (Socialist Party-Broad Front, PSFA) and the tiny Partido Comunista (Communist Party). Indeed, the PAIS-PSFA alliance proved crucial since PAIS had not yet attained the legal status required to register a presidential candidate. In a move that reflected the AP's skeletal organization and Correa's desire to avoid a messy conflict inside his heterogenous coalition, the AP did not run a list of candidates for the unicameral national assembly. By doing so, Correa sent the message that he was prepared to use presidential power to ignore the incoming legislature altogether and convoke a constituent assembly to write a new constitution.

The AP did not aspire to act as agent of vertical aggregation in any formal sense in the lead-up to the 2006 election. Rather, groups latched onto the AP's skeletal structure in support of Correa's presidential bid. The aura that AP leaders exuded was that the AP was something entirely new – a movement set apart from traditional partisan clientelism and corruption. Despite this rhetorical distancing, Correa and the AP captured and synthesized many of the demands that social movements, civil society groups, and the left had been making for years. The interest aggregation that the AP initially achieved in 2006 was symbolic, informal, rhetorical, and electoral. For a good portion of the original supporting groups, this aggregation was relatively short-lived.

The AP's first platform staked out clear positions on hot-button political issues: ending US Air Force access to the coastal air base in Manta, demanding renegotiation of Ecuador's international debt, blocking a US free-trade agreement, and installing a constituent assembly to write a new constitution. The AP served up the wish list of policies and reforms that appealed broadly to currents in Ecuadorian society, insisting that it was enlisting support from people as "citizens" rather than interest groups. Campaign officials structured their get-out-the-vote efforts around creating neighborhood-based *comités familiares* (family committees), using family and friendship networks to distribute information, including a biographical video about Correa (Almeida and López 2017, 176–177). Meanwhile, Correa emerged as a charismatic leader on the campaign trail. In the lead-up to the first-round election in September 2006, Correa barnstormed the country, wielding a belt and promising a smackdown (*¡Dale correa!* – Go Correa!) of corrupt politicians. The message was reinforced by clever broadcast advertising. Rivals were portrayed as everything from clowns to menacing animals of prey.

Winning 22 percent of the vote in the first round, Correa advanced to the November run-off election. With the race polarized between two candidates, groups and parties that had not previously endorsed Correa got on board: Pachacutik, CONAIE, National Teachers' Union, and MPD. Other emergent citizen groups associated with the uprising against Gutiérrez working under the umbrella of Alternativa Democrática (Democratic Alternative) did the same – among them Ruptura de los 25 (Rupture of the 25), Foro Urbano (Urban Forum), and Mujeres por la Vida (Women for Life) (Cordero Cordero 2016, 43). Correa scored a - comfortable second-round victory, earning 57 percent of the vote to Noboa's 43 percent of the vote.

After taking office in January 2007, Correa quickly scored another victory. The April referendum on convoking a constituent assembly to write a new constitution passed with 82 percent of the vote. The September 2007 assembly election was the first real test of the AP's reach into the electorate. The AP still lacked a national organization, so the business of selecting candidates was done directly by Correa and the political bureau. As one bureau member recalled, candidate selection was based largely on personal relationships and limited information from polls (Harnecker 2011, 145). The results were impressive. The AP won seventy-three seats on its own and another seven at the provincial level by sharing the ticket with other left-leaning and regional vehicles. With eighty seats, the AP took control of the 130-member constituent assembly and elected Alberto Acosta as its president.

The constituent assembly offered the first glimpse of the internal tensions accruing inside the AP and between the AP and allied groups. Built as a loose umbrella for winning the 2006 elections, many individuals and groups on the left embraced the AP as the vehicle for environmentalism, indigenous rights, and women's and LGBT rights. Correa, in turn, regarded the AP as the vehicle that he conjured up and therefore it was his to control. Sympathetic to demands of social movements and interested in broadening public participation, Acosta pushed back against Correa on various planks of the constitution as well as the time frame for completing it. Correa responded by forcing Acosta out of his job as assembly president. When the AP majority finished the constitution, Correa congratulated the assembly while noting that the biggest obstacle in the process had come from "our own contradictions" – namely, "leftism," "infantile environmentalism," and "infantile indigenism."[1]

The 2008 constitutional referendum provided a respite from the AP's internecine conflicts. Despite disappointment about many of the provisions in the constitution, the AP retained support from the constituencies on the left that brought it to power (Hernández and Buendía 2011, 135). The long list of groups supporting the "Yes" vote included CONAIE, Pachacutik, MPD, National Teachers' Union; the "No" vote was endorsed mostly by a smaller collection of moderates and conservative parties. In September 2008, the constitution was approved by 64 percent of voters.

A fresh round of national elections was held in April 2009. The contest provided Correa with the opportunity to entrench the AP as the country's major electoral force. Facing no direct challenge from the left, Correa coasted to a first-round victory with 52 percent of the vote, easily defeating former president Lucio Gutiérrez and his 2006 rival Álvaro Noboa. Correa won a majority of the vote in seventeen of twenty-four provinces, including the three most populated provinces: Guayas on the coast, Pichincha in the interior highlands, and Azuay in the southern highlands (Bowen 2010, 187). The national legislative elections generated an AP majority of fifty-four seats in the 124-member assembly, with seven of those seats won in the balloting for the fifteen nationally elected assembly deputies. Five additional seats came by way of joint alliances between the AP and local movements in the southern provinces of Azuay and Tungurahua. Concurrent local elections produced respectable yet more modest results. the AP won nine of the twenty-three races for prefectures and seventy-one of the 221 mayoral contests including the country's capital city of Quito and Azuay's capital, Cuenca. The coastal city of Guayaquil, Ecuador's commercial hub, remained under the control of incumbent Jaime Nebot and the conservative Partido Social Cristiano (Social Christian Party, PSC).

[1] Presidencia de la República del Ecuador "Intervención del Presidente de la República, Rafael Correa en la Ceremonia de Clausura de la Asamblea Nacional Constituyente." July 25, 2008. www.presidencia.gob.ec/wp-content/uploads/downloads/2012/10/25-07-08IntervencionPresidencialClausuraAsambleaConstituyente.pdf (last accessed June 3, 2020). All direct quotes that appear in this chapter were translated from Spanish by the author.

By mid-2009, the leaders and groups that had united around Correa and the AP had what they wanted from the man and the vehicle: a new constitution and a relatively strong government to implement it. However, unity gave way to the contradictions that Correa railed against. Correa regarded the AP legislative caucus as a tool for delivering his version of legislation, not as a sounding board for stakeholders. By 2010, conflicts over new laws on water, mining, and education reform mobilized indigenous groups like CONAIE and the teachers' National Teachers' Union and led to their outright break with Correa and the AP. In 2011, Correa pushed forward with yet another referendum; the most controversial item on the ballot was one that would rearrange the procedure for judicial appointments, overriding the 2008 constitution. More leaders and groups peeled away from the AP, including founding figures. The "No" coalition opposing the referendum brought together many of the organizations that once had supported Correa: CONAIE, National Teachers' Union, MPD, Pachakutik, Ruptura de los 25, along with student associations and labor unions. Nonetheless, Correa and the AP weathered the storm and won the referendum.

As one AP founder observed, the AP was born as a "network of networks" (Cordero Cordero 2016, 54). But the networks around the AP frayed considerably as Correa charged ahead without the input of grassroots groups that brought him to power. The dissolution of the original networks around the AP was displayed vividly in the 2013 national elections. Alberto Acosta, one of the founding figures of the AP who had turned into a virulent critic of Correa's economic policies and authoritarianism, ran as the presidential candidate of the Unidad Plurinacional – a leftist vehicle supported by Pachacutik, MPD, National Teachers' Union, and CONAIE. Norman Wray, who led Ruptura 25 in its original alliance with the AP, ran as Ruptura's presidential candidate. Both Acosta and Wray performed poorly in the February 2013 presidential race, polling just 3 percent and 1 percent, respectively. Correa's principal challenge came from the center-right Guayaquil banker Guillermo Lasso and his newly created Movimiento Creando Oportunidades (Creating Opportunities Movement, CREO). Yet Lasso proved no match for Correa who dispatched his rival in a single-round election. Winning a plurality of votes in twenty-three of twenty-four provinces, Correa took 57 percent of the nationwide vote to Lasso's 23 percent.

Correa's decisive victory in the 2013 presidential race was matched by a sweeping AP win in the national assembly elections. Gaining 100 of the

137 assembly seats, the AP claimed a supermajority in the legislature, a feat achieved by no other political organization since the 1979 transition to civilian rule. The AP registered wins with 50 percent or more of the vote for provincial assembly seats in districts across coastal provinces (Santo Domingo, Manabí, Los Rios, Guayas, El Oro), the metropolitan Quito area of Pichincha in the interior, and the three external districts covering Ecuadorians voting abroad (Eichorst and Polga-Hecimovich 2014, 99). Notably, the AP drew on alliances with other partisan vehicles to carve out its wins in the coastal provinces of El Oro and Manabí and in the interior provinces of Bolivar, Chimborazo, and Loja (Eichorst and Polga-Hecimovich 2014, 100). As in 2009, the AP's otherwise impressive geographical reach was only blunted by its weaker performance in the sparsely populated Amazonian provinces. As the 2013 results showed, though the AP lost many of its original leaders and organizational allies, its ability to win national elections was not undermined. A closer look at the state–society–AP nexus shows why.

STATE OVER PARTY

That parties should act as channels for mobilizing and representing citizens is engrained in our contemporary understanding of how democracies should function: an expectation shared by political scientists and citizens. As the volume's editors underscore (Luna et al. Introduction this volume), however, electoral vehicles vary dramatically when it comes to whether, how, and with what frequency they do the work of representing societal interests.

Before examining how the state and the AP managed relations with societal actors in ways that ultimately proved detrimental to democratic representation, it is worth noting that Ecuador's party system has a long history of dysfunctionality (Conaghan 1995; Pachano 2006). As Santiago Basabe-Serrano (2016) astutely analyzed, the relative weakness of civic associations contributed greatly to the disconnect between partisan actors and society. In the absence of sustained ties to robust civil society actors, electoral vehicles were organized mostly around caudillos and maintained through clientelism and the AP's lapse in performing the tasks of vertical aggregation is hardly surprising. Basabe-Serrano (2016, 955) underscores the continuity: "Although the Ecuadorian political system underwent superficial change, the trajectory of AP is not different from that of other *caudillista* parties that were previously present in Ecuadorian political life."

The AP's relations with civil society were vexed in a distinctive way for reasons having to do with how Correa and his government conceptualized and managed issues of representation. As a candidate, Correa rolled out an anti-corruption platform that promised to entrench technocratic rationality in policymaking, putting an end to the intrusions of special interests. As president, Correa used litigation and rule changes to remove interest group representation (business, unions, and social movements) from government policymaking boards. That was followed by the creation of sweeping new rules aimed at monitoring and regulating civil society organizations (CSOs) (Conaghan 2017). These policies folded neatly into the notion that the government was undertaking a "revolution" to privilege new forms of citizen-based participation rather than by organized interest groups (Burbano de Lara 2017). In addition to ideological and programmatic angles, Correa's hostility toward organized civil society was also rooted in practical political considerations. Coming to power in the wake of the *forajidos* mobilization that unseated President Gutiérrez, Correa understood that civil society could pose an existential threat to his presidency. That view was reinforced by a dramatic daylong standoff that pitted Correa against striking police officers in September 2010. Controlling, rather than empowering civil society, became a top priority.

During Correa's presidency, the government executed a strategy to recast state–society relations. Rather than being beholden to groups in civil society, the executive branch wielded the government's considerable resources to weave its own networks of support. In addition to the measures that directly penalized and marginalized CSOs resistant to Correa, the government-led initiatives involved: (1) creating wholly new organizational allies; (2) striking deals directly between the executive branch entities and individual organizations; and (3) selectively poaching leaders from existing organizations and parties. Government dealt with civil society through a patchwork of clientelism, co-optation, and selective concessions.

To undercut the leftist trade unions, government ministries organized forums leading to the creation of new pro-government labor organizations, including sectorial and national confederations (Trujillo and Spronk 2018, 182). In 2014, the labor minister opened talks that gave birth to a new labor confederation, the Confederación Unitaria de Trabajadores (Unitary Workers' Confederation, CUT). In the same vein, the Ministry of Education upended the militant National Teachers' Union by sponsoring a new teachers' union, Asociación Red de Maestros y Maestras (Teachers' Network Association, RED) in 2015.

A new executive-branch entity, the Secretaría de Pueblos, Movimientos Sociales and Participación Ciudadana (Secretariat of Peoples, Social Movements, and Civic Participation) served as a conduit for establishing direct links and channeling resources, especially to indigenous communities. It engaged in everything from training community leaders to negotiating land titles. The efforts at managing organizations included the president. Correa personally intervened in policy negotiations with strategically important groups such as the Federación Nacional de Taxistas (National Federation of Taxi Drivers) (Cordero Cordero 2016). At the same time, government ministries dived directly into community politics, striking deals with local organizations to oversee development projects. Adding to the executive's reach into local governments were measures that recentralized fiscal revenues and heightened the president's powers for discretionary spending (Mejia Acosta and Meneses 2019, 226).

Correa's fixation on directly linking the executive branch with communities and local notables was on display nearly every weekend in the *gabinetes itinerantes* (traveling cabinets). Cabinet members were dispatched to a selected site to meet with local and provincial leaders in advance of the president's arrival for his Saturday-morning radio and television broadcast, *Enlace Ciudadano* (Pluá Cedeño 2014). Correa used the program to celebrate his accomplishments, laud local supporters, and lash out at his critics. Social events and working sessions surrounding the visit provided Correa with on-the-ground intelligence about what was happening in villages and towns across the country. In Quito, Correa established the ritual of holding long, festive Monday lunches in the presidential palace – a practice which also served to reward individuals and groups deemed to be supportive. On at least one day a week, Correa conducted business in his office in Guayaquil, another practice that kept him closely in synch with local notables.

The government's reach into society left the AP as a secondary player. The government's public relations operations, managed by the same personnel who masterminded Correa's first campaign, borrowed the imagery and symbols originally developed for 2006. The signature fluorescent green color used in campaign materials, along with the graphics, slogans and fonts, were used in official government communications, erasing any distinctions between the government and the AP in the minds of voters.[2] The collapse of any distinction between the government

[2] Gabriel Vommaro's chapter on the Argentine PRO (Vommaro this volume) party analyzes a similar process of symbiosis between party brand and government brand, although in the case of a right-wing party.

and the AP was not just stylistic. At the AP's first national convention, high-ranking government officials were designated by acclamation to hold all the positions in the AP's National Board, the Dirección Nacional (Benavides Vásquez 2012, 30).

In contrast to the government, the AP lagged notably behind in its outreach to society and organizational development. While founded in late 2006, the AP did not hold its first national convention until 2010. That was followed by a 2011 effort to formally affiliate the AP's membership (*carnetización*) (Cordero Cordero 2016, 62). The ballyhooed plan to turn the family committees into the organizational base of the AP as Comités de la Revolución Ciudadana (Citizens' Revolution Committees, CRCs) was never coherently executed; patchwork organizing took place under the auspices of provincial officials. Even Correa complained about the lackadaisical approach to the CRCs and the lack of reliable information about how many committees were operative (Herrera Llive 2017, 106).

The overwhelming emphasis on linking government directly to citizens through executive branch action and saturation media coverage sidelined the AP from acting as an important intermediary between state and society. The disconnect reached down into the day-to-day practices of politics, disrupting the traditional practices of clientelism. In one of the few recent ethnographic studies of partisan life in Ecuador, José Antonio Villarreal Vásquez (2015, 170) documented how neighborhood the AP bosses in Guayaquil grew frustrated by their inability to act as effective intermediaries for procuring resources as ministry bureaucrats hived them off from access.

Two intersecting factors diminished the prospects that the AP could evolve into an effective instrument for democratic representation. First, the governing philosophy underlying the Citizens' Revolution was hostile to such an outcome given the disregard for extant interest groups and parties. The Citizens' Revolution celebrated the return of the state under the purview of technocrats as the pathway for establishing new linkages between citizens and the state, thus eliminating the corruption associated with the old ways of doing politics. Technocrats, and Correa in particular, were deemed as the best interpreters of what society needed (De la Torre 2013). Second, Correa almost immediately embarked on a mission to ensure his personal control over the electoral vehicle that made him president. The notion of empowering constituent groups within the organizational umbrella of the AP or strengthening the AP as an autonomous entity was never on his agenda. Thus, the aspirational project of the government-controlled Citizens' Revolution, in tandem with Correa's considerable ambitions, confined the AP's role to electioneering.

LEADER-CONTROLLED COORDINATION

In this volume, horizontal coordination – the extent to which politicians affiliated with a partisan organization act as cohesive collective during and between elections – constitutes another key dimension for categorizing and distinguishing among electoral vehicles. As the editors argue, when a partisan organization operates with significant horizontal coordination, it provides citizens with vital information about what they can expect, thus allowing voters to hold politicians accountable at election time (Luna et al. Introduction this volume). When horizontal coordination is operative, voters can make reasoned judgments about what politicians stand for and whether they can be counted on to make public policy in alignment with the promises made in a party platform.

During the Correa presidency, the AP's electoral history was marked by a significant degree of coordination, achieved by the top-down governance of the organization. Correa appointed and dismissed members of the political bureau at will. Members of the larger executive board, National Board, were appointed, not elected. Similarly, the AP's top bureaucratic post of executive secretary was at Correa's discretion. At the first national convention in 2010, Correa handed the post to his own private secretary, Galo Mora, bypassing other candidates as well as the expectation that the post might rotate through an election.

For the most part, "down ballot" candidates (for the national assembly, provincial and local offices) were either directly selected or subject to final vetting by Correa and the political bureau. In the absence of any real party structure, Correa and his advisors chose their first ticket of candidates for the 2007 constituent assembly on the basis of personal contacts and public opinion polling. In 2009, the original plan to use primaries for the national elections went awry in the wake of chaotic infighting and allegations of corruption, with last-minute fixes of the provincial and district assembly candidate lists engineered from above. In 2013, the AP opted for lower-level candidate selection using the cover of provincial conventions – a format more easily managed by regional bosses and subject to behind-the-scene intervention by Correa and his closest advisor and minister, Ricardo Patiño. In both 2009 and 2013, national-level assembly candidates were poll-tested and approved by Correa in consultation with the political bureau. The same approach to candidate selection prevailed in 2017. The 2017 ticket was another demonstration of the unyielding control exerted by Correa and the political bureau. Informed by polling data, they made decisions on which candidates were placed at the topmost part of ticket (presidency, nationwide candidates for the assembly) behind closed doors and rubberstamped at the national convention.[3] Other candidates proposed by provincial AP offices were also subject to final approval by the bureau.[4]

Once chosen, candidates were enveloped in a uniform branding strategy that connected them to the AP (and its designated #35 on the ballot) and to Correa. The successful 2006 election campaign became the template for how the AP framed all its subsequent electoral propaganda, enshrining Correa as the centerpiece and the sloganeering associated with him. In 2006, Correa struck a chord by invoking emotional images of national renewal in his slogan, "*La Patria Vuelve*" (the homeland returns). Subsequent AP campaigns re-invoked the *patria* theme in its advertising, overlapping with government advertising in the same vein. In 2009, voters were reassured that "*La patria ya es de todos*" (the homeland already belongs to all). In the 2013 election, the AP continued to celebrate the government's accomplishments in the slogan "*ya tenemos patria*" (now we have a homeland), linking it to Correa's reelection, "*ya tenemos presidente ... tenemos a Rafael*" (now we have a president, we have Rafael). In campaign advertising, voting for the AP was rendered the equivalent of voting for Correa as captured in the 2013 slogan "*Votar por la asamblea es votar por Rafael*" (An assembly vote is a vote for Rafael) (Kattán Hervas 2018, 49). One 2013 poster showed Correa's profile, with the admonition to vote for the AP across the board, urging "*todo, toditos*" (all, every single one) alongside its #35 number. The logos, slogans, and signature green color were de rigueur in the campaigns of AP candidates across the country.

As judicial and journalistic investigations revealed, the power that Correa and the political bureau wielded over AP candidates extended to their control over party finances: a system supported through an elaborate system of illegal campaign donations. Preliminary estimates put the

[3] Carvajal, Ana María. "Buró de AP delinea plan para ganar Asamblea." (El Comercio, September 4, 2016). www.elcomercio.com/actualidad/buro-ap-delinea-plan-ganar.html (last accessed June 8, 2020).

[4] González, Mario Alexis. "Alianza Pais intenta consolidar sus listas definitivas." (El Comercio, November 15, 2016). www.elcomercio.com/actualidad/alianzapais-consolidar-listas-elecciones.html (last accessed June 8, 2020).

amount of illegal money flowing into AP coffers from 2012 through 2016 at more than eleven million dollars.[5] Domestic and foreign businesses, including the notorious Brazilian construction firm Odebrecht, were in on the schemes.[6] Donors transferred cash directly to the AP or paid campaign expense bills indirectly through intermediaries with the expectation of repayment through lucrative government contracts. The money went to candidates, underwrote campaign events and security, and paid for the party's elaborate election advertising.

In conjunction with his considerable presidential powers, Correa's vice-like grip over the party machinery kept the AP's legislative majority cowed and under control. All of the government's major legislation was submitted to the assembly by the executive branch. Of the sixty-two pieces of legislation proposed directly by the executive in the period 2009–13, sixty were approved (Observatorio Legislativo 2013, 2). More than half of all legislation in the same period originated in the executive branch. Executive dominance in the legislative process continued in the 2013–17 assembly (Observatorio Legislativo 2015). Executive-led legislation involved sweeping new laws spanning communication, the penal code, the tax system, and labor regulations. Neither the AP's caucus nor opposing parties proved adept in moving their own legislation through the assembly; projects were introduced, then floundered (Pachano 2010; Polga-Hecimovich 2013). Discrepancies between the executive and legislative branches on legislation were resolved in favor of the executive, thanks to the constitutionally prescribed partial veto power that the president enjoyed. Correa was able to rewrite legislation with little risk that the assembly could muster a two-thirds majority to override his version. Both legislatures were moribund in relation to investigations and oversight as the executive stymied requests for pertinent information (Observatorio Legislativo 2013, 6; Observatorio Legislativo 2015, 7).

In short, party discipline – manifested in the AP majority's obsequious adherence to their leader – prevailed in the national assembly throughout Correa's presidency. With no power to shape decisions, a few notable leaders peeled away from the AP caucus in protest. Such was the case of high-profile legislators Betty Amores and Maria Paula Romo. Amores was

[5] "Caso Sobornos: las 130 evidencias de la Fiscalía." (Plan V, August 12, 2019). www.planv.com.ec/historias/politica/caso-sobornos-130-evidencias-la-fiscalia (last accessed June 3, 2020).

[6] Fundación Mil Hojas. "Odebrecht y otras multinacionales pusieron presidente en Ecuador." (April 30, 2019). https://milhojas.is/612540-odebrecht-y-otras-multinacionales-pusieron-presidente-en-ecuador.html (last accessed June 8, 2020).

among the original founders of the AP and Romo headed Ruptura de los 25. In other cases, the upper echelon of the AP took steps to quash dissidents. In 2013, three female AP legislators took a thirty-day suspension from their seats when they spoke out against Correa's position that a criminal penalty remain on the books for rape victims seeking abortions (Basabe-Serrano and Martínez 2014, 163). In 2016, assemblyman Fernando Bustamante complained of being bullied and renounced his partisan affiliation after being sanctioned by the AP executive for abstaining from a vote on a package of controversial constitutional amendments.[7] Correa's message to the AP caucus was loud and clear: deviations from the official line would not be tolerated.

The blurred lines between the government and the AP also facilitated substantial coordination between the national and subnational units of the AP. In accordance with the constitution, the president appoints seventeen provincial governors who act as representatives of the executive branch. Correa used this power to elevate regional AP loyalists to the positions. Many governors simultaneously held positions in the AP's National Board or in the regional directorates.

FROM CORREISMO TO MORENISMO

Under Correa, the AP enjoyed unprecedented electoral success. By 2013, the AP had established its dominance as a national political force, setting itself apart from older regionally based vehicles. Correa rode the AP to three successive presidential elections, with no runoffs required in 2009 and 2013, making him the only president to win in a single round since the return to democracy in 1978 and Ecuador's longest continually serving president. On the legislative side, the AP scored majorities in the constituent assembly, the 2009 national assembly, and a super-majority in the 2013 assembly. The string of electoral successes was no accident; important rule changes made them possible. The 2008 constitution overturned the previous ban on immediate presidential reelection, opening the way for Correa to stay in place until 2017. Election reforms in 2012, which mandated re-districting and the application of the D'Hondt formula for distributing provincial assembly seats, further tipped the scales in favor of the AP (Polga-Hecimovich 2013, 146).

[7] "Fernando Bustamante es el tercer asambleísta en dejar Alianza País." (El Universo, January 28, 2016) https://www.eluniverso.com/noticias/2016/01/28/nota/5373631/fernando-bustamante-es-tercer-asambleista-dejar-alianza-pais (last accessed June 3, 2020).

AP's electoral appeal was rooted in a combination of popular policies and a popular leader wielding presidential power. In 2006, the AP served as platform for the policy demands of constituencies on the political left, social movements, and a disgruntled middle class. Once in power, however, Correa parted ways with many of his original allies and deployed state resources to weave a patchwork of support across the social spectrum. Aggressive public spending, subsidies, and other reforms solidified the AP's appeal among selected constituencies privileged by the government. As Verdesoto Custode (2014, 402) pointed out, the AP benefited electorally from a public policy agenda targeting welfare and social security recipients, small farmers, municipalities, and businesses with government contracts.

Building an electoral base on a bedrock of state power, the AP had the good fortune to act as the vehicle of an exceptionally popular leader who governed mostly in a period of economic expansion. Enjoying windfall revenues from oil exports and enhanced tax collection, the government pushed growth through aggressive public-sector spending (Sánchez and Polga-Hecimovich 2019; World Bank 2018). The buoyant economy made for high presidential approval ratings. The AP became subsumed in the aggressive political marketing of Correa and his Citizens' Revolution; it was a successful formula for all partners. For the targeted beneficiaries of government subsidies, the AP served as the mechanism for collecting their votes but never provided a working venue for active representation inside the organization. Designated groups reaped material benefits but none of them significantly shaped policy inside the AP.

Paradoxically, the fortuitous circumstances that contributed to the AP's growth were also the sources of organizational weaknesses. The AP burst onto the political scene alongside Correa with no developed organization. The AP's precipitous rise to power stands in stark contrast to the experiences of other leftist parties that spent many years cultivating grassroots support under challenging conditions before coming to power.[8] As Brandon Van Dyck (2016) has shown, grappling with adversity and working at the local level before winning national office can work in favor of party development; such a process enhances activist commitment and is more likely to result in strongly rooted territorially based

[8] For discussion of a left-wing party with strong grassroots activism, see Pérez Bentancur, Piñeiro Rodríguez and Rosenblatt (2020) and Pérez Bentancur, Piñeiro Rodríguez, and Rosenblatt (this volume) about the Uruguayan FA. The authors show how the influence of this grassroots activism reinforces partisan vertical accountability.

organizations. The quintessential example of such party building was the experience of Brazil's PT. Founded during the military dictatorship, the early PT lacked access to media and state resources; its growth emerged from developing a strong identity, linking with social movements and unions and accruing experience in municipal politics. Bolivia's MAS provides another example. Strongly rooted in social movement politics, MAS cut its teeth on running candidates for a range of offices years before it installed Evo Morales as president (Anria 2018).[9]

Before coming to power with Correa, the AP was nonexistent and so it had no experience in building from the "bottom up" in local politics. While the AP performed respectably in subnational contests, its performance in local and provincial elections never matched its masterful numbers in national races. In the face of its territorial unevenness, the AP turned to running some provincial assembly candidates on joint tickets with other parties or local movements in 2009 and 2013.

The AP's vulnerability to competition by local notables became even more evident in the 2014 municipal races. Rather than improving on its 2009 municipal results and building on its 2013 national win, the AP suffered some high-profile defeats in 2014. The AP's incumbent mayors in Quito and Cuenca were bested by candidates from local independent movements; other major urban centers along the coast including Manta, Portoviejo, and Guayaquil also rejected AP candidates. In Guayaquil, Correa's decision to impose his personal favorite, Viviana Bonilla, as the party's mayoral candidate was derided by the AP's own base. The 2014 provincial elections previewed what would become glaringly evident in 2017: without Correa on the top of the ticket, the AP was a far less formidable electoral contender.

Under Correa's control, the AP had little chance to develop an organizational identity or mission of its own; leaders who remained inside the ranks of the AP succumbed to Correa's personality cult. Using the government communications apparatus in a manner unlike any previous president, Correa became a ubiquitous master of self-promotion as he traveled, Tweeted, and televised every move. Correa, the government proper, the Citizens' Revolution agenda, and the AP were virtually indistinguishable in their public projection: all part of the same package of a seemingly undefeatable regime. As long as the president remained popular and in power, the mash-up worked.[10] That was the case for nearly eight years;

[9] See also Anria's chapter (this volume).

[10] For another example of the importance of a leader's popularity for the ability to achieve horizontal coordination, see Vergara and Augusto (this volume).

from 2007 through 2015, Correa's presidential approval rating never dipped below 50 percent and the AP dominated national elections (Conaghan 2016).

By mid-2015, however, the fundamentals began to change. Public finances were rocked by a dramatic downturn in the international price of petroleum, calling into question how much longer the government could continue to subsidize the groups in the AP's base. Many of the groups that had previously deserted the AP in fights over policy began to mobilize in concerted opposition to Correa's prospective third reelection in 2017. By 2016, the economic malaise and revitalized opposition had taken in its toll. Rather than risk a highly contentious reelection bid, Correa and the political bureau advanced a formula offering voters a fresh face yet ensuring sufficient *continuismo* to keep a possible return to the presidency open to Correa in 2021. Designated as the presidential candidate, Lenín Moreno was a popular disability rights advocate who served as Correa's vice president from 2007 to 2013. Jorge Glas, the incumbent vice president and Correa's Boy Scout chum, was slotted again for the vice-presidency.

The 2017 election results confirmed that the AP weakened in the absence of a Correa-led ticket. In a hard-fought race that included accusations of fraud, Moreno failed to win in the February first round, falling just short of the 40 percent cut-off needed to clinch it. The April second round was another close and controversial contest; Moreno emerged victorious with 51.16 percent of the vote, defeating Guillermo Lasso, a noted Guayaquil banker, with 48.84 percent of the vote. The AP hung on to its majority in the national assembly but saw it whittled down to 74 seats from the 100 seats it had claimed in 2013. While the results did not overturn the AP's domination as a national political force, they displayed its vulnerabilities. In comparison to 2013, A the P hemorrhaged support in the highlands and Amazonian provinces while retaining its base in coastal provinces. The outcome prompted speculation that the unprecedented nationalization that the AP had established as an organization might give way to a more traditional pattern of regionally based support, a "coastal-ization" (Ortiz Crespo and Burbano de Lara 2017).

Expectations that Moreno would act as a loyal caretaker of *Correismo* were dashed as he quickly distanced his administration from his predecessor. The scope of Ecuador's economic downturn and the magnitude of public corruption under the previous government became evident and Moreno used his bully pulpit to denounce it (Wolff 2018a). Moreno's rapid break with Correa had widespread repercussions. Top officials and assembly deputies, as well as AP rank and file, were forced to take sides in the fight over who would control the AP's future. As the struggle played out in the last half of 2017 and early 2018, it confirmed what many scholars had already concluded regarding the personalistic and opportunistic nature of the AP. With state resources under the control of President Moreno and public opinion firmly aligned with him, many AP members shed their previous loyalties to Correa and jumped on the Moreno bandwagon to retain influence and access to jobs. The AP's rapid flip from *Correismo* to *Morenismo* provided further evidence of how ideologically and programmatically pliable the organization had become. As León Trujillo (2012) argued, Correa succeeded in leading the AP away from a clearly defined leftist agenda in favor of an ill-defined and shifting *proyecto* which he defined and claimed to embody. In the absence of any binding ideology, Moreno effectively upended the *proyecto* as he laid bare the massive corruption, economic mismanagement, and authoritarianism of the Correa administration. With little left to hold on to, many AP activists swung their support to Moreno and his more pragmatic approach to governing.

By January 2018, the battle for control was over. The National Electoral Council ruled in favor of Moreno, awarding him control over the AP's legal registration. Correa and a core of loyalists announced their official exit from the electoral vehicle that had dominated the political scene for a decade. Moreno consolidated his control in a 2018 referendum that squarely took aim at Correa: undoing the constitutional reform allowing for unlimited reelection. Correa retreated to a home in Belgium, as prosecutions of his former ministers and AP cronies proceeded. In 2020, Correa was found guilty *in absentia* of bribery in the illegal campaign finance scheme. Along with an eight-year prison sentence, the conviction rendered Correa ineligible to run as a presidential candidate in 2021.

LOST DECADE: REPRESENTATION RELEGATED

As the editors of this volume rightly maintain, a robust democracy is one that does a good job in turning citizens' preferences into public policy and providing the tools that citizens need to make reasoned political judgments in elections. To make this happen, democracies need partisan organizations capable of collecting and synthesizing popular demands into coherent policy agendas and coordinating the behavior of their leaders such that voters know where they stand and what they plan to accomplish in office.

While this volume's framework provides a roadmap for assessing how the structure of partisan organizations impacts representation and the quality of democracy, Ecuador's recent experience suggests the need for a deeper dive into how horizontal coordination is achieved and its implications for vertical aggregation and representation. In particular, we need to closely examine whether (and to what degree) mechanisms of internal democracy are used in bringing about horizontal coordination. As the AP case underscores, coordination that takes place in the absence of any internal democracy has ramifications for democratic representation. Without clear mechanisms allowing for influence and negotiating outcomes, the AP progressively lost any capacity for representation as disaffected leaders and groups dropped away from the fold.

In 2006, the AP held out the prospect that it might become a permanent home for Ecuador's fragmented political left and social movements. In its original platform, the AP aggregated many of the demands already articulated by these groups. Winning the 2006 presidential election put Correa and the AP on a trajectory to satisfy these demands, especially by laying the groundwork for a constituent assembly in 2007 and a new constitution in 2008. But Correa's unrelenting ambitions to retain control over the AP and dictate policy from the presidency eroded the original alliance and undercut the prospects that the AP would evolve into something other than a personality-driven vehicle. Instead of approaching representation as a process of organizing and channeling interest from the bottom up, top-down modes of organizing politics prevailed in the government and the AP. Inside the AP, influence was reserved for leaders and groups prepared to offer up demonstrations of fealty to Correa. With no internal democracy, the AP was rendered unresponsive to important segments of Ecuadorian society. In their place, the AP targeted groups beholden to the government bureaucracies that administered subsidies and the like. When Correa lost power, what remained of the AP's networks reassembled for the spoils around the winner, Lenín Moreno.

The AP story is a tale of lost opportunities for democratic representation. Bursting onto the scene at a time when Ecuadorians were eager for change, the AP seemingly offered a new option with a youthful leader and ambitious promises of a Citizens' Revolution. But democratic aspirations took a backseat to other impulses as the AP consolidated state power. By failing to develop internal mechanisms for power sharing and accountability, the AP devolved into a traditional *caudillista*-style vehicle (Basabe-Serrano 2016, 955).

Such an outcome was not inevitable. While the weight of Ecuador's history – the weakness of civil society, the personality-centric tradition in politics, the pervasiveness of clientelism and regionalism – had long been obstacles in developing the party system, the AP came to life at a moment as traditional vehicles collapsed. Nothing precluded the AP from taking advantage of that historical moment by opting for audacity, innovation, and democratization. Instead, Correa and the leaders who remained at his side choose strategies and policies that effectively diminished the AP's potential to act as a vehicle for democratic representation. Rather than imagining the Citizens' Revolution as a genuinely democratic experiment, Correa opted for an autocratic, technocratic project (León Trujillo 2012). Instead of constraining Correa and pushing back against his top-down approach to politics and government, the AP leaders who remained ceded power. In the course of doing so, they ceded more than just their own movement. By diminishing the AP, they became participants in a decade-long process of democratic backsliding.

11

The Chilean PPD

A Loose Confederation of Leaders

Rafael Piñeiro Rodríguez, Fernando Rosenblatt, and Sergio Toro Maureira

INTRODUCTION

The Partido por la Democracia (Party for Democracy, PPD) was born on December 15, 1987, as an electoral label in the context of the difficult Chilean transition to democracy. It was the solution some former socialist leaders found to overcome the ban Pinochet's dictatorship imposed on the Partido Socialista de Chile (Chilean Socialist Party, PSCh). It was founded by former socialist leaders but also by a new generation of progressive leaders without a prior affiliation to the PSCh. Some of the founding leaders of the PPD aimed to make the PPD a party that could be joined by the entire opposition to Pinochet. This never occurred and thus the PPD essentially remained as an electoral tool for former PSCh leaders. After the ban was lifted, most of the PSCh leaders returned to their party and the PPD thus comprised a mixture of progressive and liberal leaders. Throughout the twenty years that the center-left coalition, the Concertación (Concertation) governed Chile (1990–2010), the PPD was one of the main partners – with the DC and the PSCh.

In Levitsky et al.'s (2016) edited volume, the PPD is described as a case of successful party building. The authors emphasize that successful party building is rare in Latin America and the PPD is one of the eleven cases they identify in their study. The authors define party building as:

> The process by which new parties develop into electorally significant and enduring political actors. We seek to explain not party formation, which is widespread across Latin America, but instead cases in which new parties actually take root. Thus, our operationalization of successful party building includes both electoral and temporal dimensions. To be considered a success, a new party must achieve

a minimum share of the vote and maintain it for a significant period of time. It need not win the presidency, but it must, at a minimum, consistently receive a sizable share of the national vote ... Based on this operationalization, we count eleven cases of successful party building in Latin America since the onset of the third wave. (Levitsky et al. 2016, 29–30)

Thus, according to the editors of Levitsky's volume, the PPD is one of the few cases of successful party building in Latin America. However, as we will show throughout the chapter, even though the PPD has successfully garnered meaningful levels of electoral support, it is an electoral vehicle that has neither a basic organizational structure, a defined party platform, nor a solid partisan base. Instead, the party's leaders created a structure of personalistic linkages in some regions of the country enhanced by strong coordination in Congress. As we will show in the following pages, it is a party that took advantage of the role of important leaders from the party during the transition to democracy and during its twenty years in government. By the end of those years, the PPD had to operate in a context where parties were increasingly and deeply distrusted (Luna 2004, 2007a; Luna and Altman 2011; Luna and Mardones 2010). Also, political competition favored territorial caudillos vis-à-vis party organizational structures (in the case of the PPD, these caudillos were a few senators and some representatives and mayors). Electoral competition became increasingly personalistic and financial resources were directly channeled to these caudillos (Luna 2014; Luna and Mardones 2017; Luna and Rosenblatt 2012).

The PPD is a perfect case to illustrate the different processes that gradually evolved in the Chilean party system and that were also observed throughout every party organization: the disconnect with organized civil society, social movements, or unions and the gradual deterioration of ideological debates. The PPD is a typical case (George and Bennett 2005) for describing the breaking of the spine that Chilean parties had been, with deep roots in society and as the most important channel between state and society (Garretón 1989; Luna and Rosenblatt 2017; Valenzuela 1977). In this process, parties lost their ability to reproduce strong partisan identities (Luna 2014; Luna and Mardones 2017; Rosenblatt 2018). Finally, the case of the PPD calls into question the minimalist definition of political party and suggests instead that an adequate definition of political party must include a clear theoretical connection to the concept of democratic representation.

THE CONTEXT OF THE BIRTH AND THE EVOLUTION OF THE PPD

On December 14, 1989, after sixteen years of authoritarian regime, national elections took place in Chile. The presidential election was won by the center-left coalition, the Concertation, and its presidential candidate, Patricio Aylwin, became the first president of the restored Chilean democracy in 1990. This coalition comprised several center and left-of-center parties, most notably the Partido Demócrata Cristiano (Christian Democratic Party, DC), the PSCh, the Partido Radical (Radical Party), and the PPD. These four became the main partners of this coalition that would govern Chile for the next twenty years. The PPD played a very significant role throughout the Concertation years. Several PPD ministers were part of these governments. The PPD had thirty-seven ministers in the cabinets of the Concertation's governments[1] and eleven during Michelle Bachelet's second government (2014–18) with the New Majority coalition (Olivares 2017).[2]

Ricardo Lagos was the most influential leader of the party and one of the most important leaders of the Concertation.[3] He was president of Chile between 2000 and 2006. Even though his coalition did not hold a majority in the Senate – explained by the binominal electoral system that favored the Right – the Lagos presidency was a milestone of the process of the Concertation years (Funk 2006). During his presidency, major structural reforms were implemented, most notably a Constitutional reform in 2005 and the health reform, known as the Plan AUGE (Pribble 2013). Sergio Bitar, Carolina Tohá, and Guido Girardi were also three of the main leaders of the party during the Concertation years. More recently, Ricardo Lagos-Weber (Ricardo Lagos's son), gained notoriety as the Minister of Government during Michelle Bachelet's first term (2006–10).

Carolina Tohá was the young face of the Concertation in the transition to democracy. She was with Ricardo Lagos when he famously pointed the finger to Pinochet on TV.[4] She was a prominent member of a new generation of emerging young leaders. She was the daughter of José Tohá, a Socialist

[1] Patricio Aylwin (1990–94), Eduardo Frei Ruiz-Tagle (1994–2000), Ricardo Lagos Escobar (2000–6), Michelle Bachelet (2006–10).

[2] The New Majority coalition, in contrast to the Concertation, included the Communist Party.

[3] He was the only leader that retained a dual affiliation (PPD and PSCh).

[4] See "El dedo de Lagos"; various videos are available on Youtube, e.g., https://youtu.be/BBeBEXzG1vI (last accessed October 29, 2019).

Party leader who was vice president and Minister of Interior under Salvador Allende (1970–3) and who was assassinated during the Chilean dictatorship in 1974. Carolina Tohá was a Representative, Senator, Minister of Government, and Mayor of Santiago during the Concertation years. She was also president of the PPD. Guido Girardi has been a Representative, Senator and president of the PPD. Sergio Bitar, an older leader who was a minister under Allende, was also a major leader of the party and a prominent politician during the Concertation years. For example, he was Minister of Transportation during the Lagos government.

The PPD has been an important political party of the Chilean party system. It has held a significant number of seats in the House of Representatives (see Figure 11.1), averaging 16 representatives (out of a total of 120) in the seven legislatures between 1993 and 2017 and receiving an average 11.76 percent of the vote. The dramatic reduction in the number of seats it won in the 2017 election is partially explained by the change in the electoral rules, which fostered an increase in the effective number of parties, a measure of the degree of fragmentation of the party system. However, electoral support for the PPD had already begun to wane. The PPD has also had a significant presence in municipal elections (Figure 11.2).

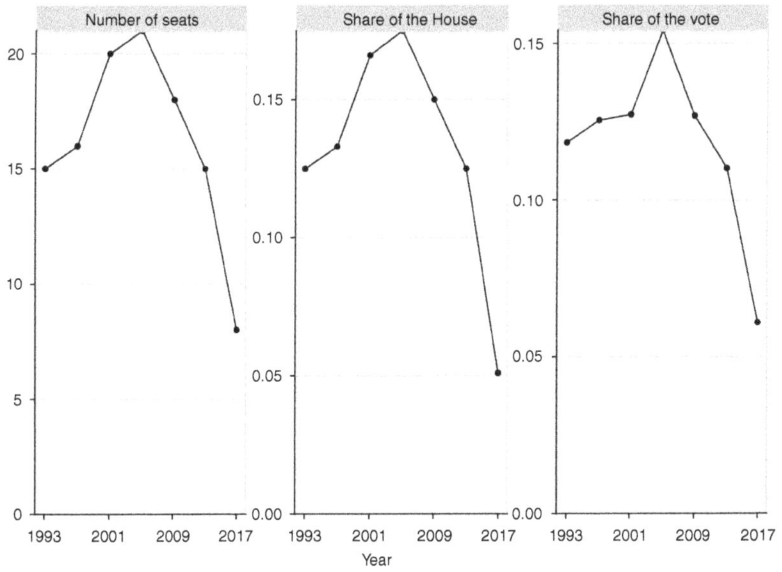

FIGURE 11.1 Seats and votes, 1993–2017
Source: SERVEL.

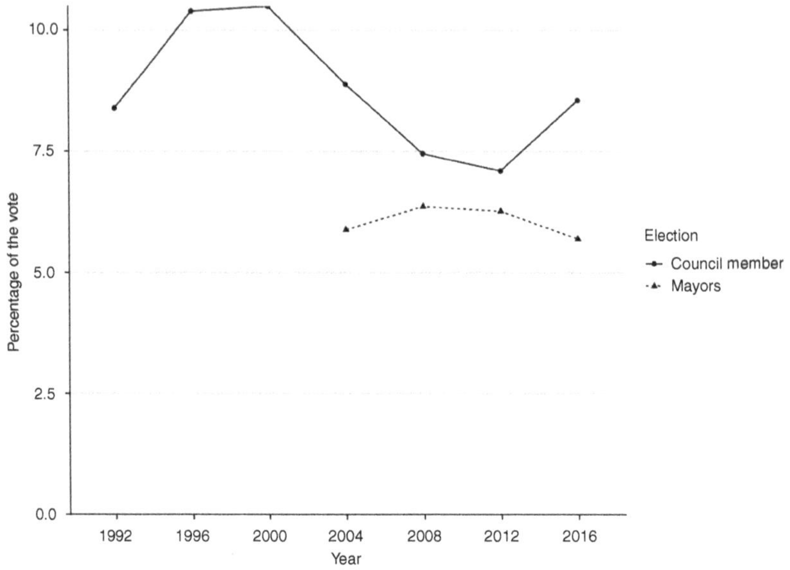

FIGURE 11.2 PPD's percentage of the vote in municipal elections, 1992–2016
Source: SERVEL.
Note: Between 1992 and 2000, the council member who received the most votes was chosen as mayor.

The Ley 20,900 para el Fortalecimiento y Transparencia de la Democracia (Strengthening and Transparency of Democracy Law, SDL) required all existing parties to formally register their adherents during the twelve-month period, from April 2016 to April 2017, in order to retain their legal status (i.e., reinscription) as a political party. According to the new law, the minimum required number of members per region to qualify for reinscription is 500 citizens or 0.25 percent of the turnout in the last congressional election, whichever is greater. Table 11.1 presents the number of reregistered members in this period, by party. The PPD, as had the rest of the Chilean parties, encountered several difficulties gathering the required number of signatures to formalize its existence as a political party in the context of the new law. The total number of registered PPD members represented 0.21 percent of the total electorate.[5] The two parties that fared better were the Partido Comunista (Communist Party, PCCh) and

[5] We calculated this number using the 2017 electoral registry. The total number of registered voters for 2017 was 14,308,151.

TABLE 11.1 *Adherents by party*

Party	PPD	PCCh	PSCh	DC	RN	UDI	Total
Number	30,691	52,356	37,600	29,719	31,214	40,990	222,570
% of registered voters	0.21	0.37	0.26	0.21	0.22	0.29	1.56

Source: SERVEL 2019.

the Unión Demócrata Independiente (Independent Democratic Union, UDI). The other three parties (the PSCh, the DC, and the Renovación Nacional – National Renewal, RN) were able to gather signatures equivalent to 0.2 percent of the total electorate. This is well below the membership density observed in European democracies (Scarrow 2015). The difference between the number of new and old members who confirmed their membership in the PPD (25,776 new adherents and 4,915 ratified adherents) illustrates a problem that was common among Chilean parties: their records of adherents were completely outdated. The last time Chilean parties made an effort to register adherents was during the transition to democracy in 1988.

THE PPD AS A GROUP OF INDEPENDENTS

The introduction of this volume identifies two main attributes – horizontal coordination and vertical interest aggregation – that characterize an electoral vehicle; when both attributes are present, the vehicle can be classified as a political party. Categorizing different types of electoral vehicles based on the existence (or lack) of horizontal coordination and vertical interest aggregation elucidates the actual operation of party organizations. For example, what does a group of independents look like? A group of independents achieves neither horizontal coordination nor vertical interest aggregation. However, this does not imply a complete absence of either trait. In the case of the PPD, the party can achieve coordination among its cadre (in Congress) and some degree of electoral coordination. Also, it does not aggregate societal demands and interests, qua an organization. As we will detail, some leaders are able to channel demands, yet they do so as individual leaders and the party brand is not necessarily associated with the aggregation of demands. The PPD is a perfect case to illustrate the importance of looking beyond an organization's electoral performance and level of discipline in Congress to describe the nature of a political party. As the authors of the theoretical framework suggest, electoral stability does not suffice to explain the role of political parties in terms of democratic representation. The example of the PPD nicely supports that claim.

In the case of the PPD, vertical interest aggregation is not observed. Even though there remains a generation of PPD leaders and voters whose loyalty to the party was forged in a period of intense engagement during the late-1980s transition to democracy, the mobilizing power of that long-ago struggle is fading with time (Bargsted and Maldonado 2018). Public opinion polls did not show significant levels of support for the PPD in the context of generalized low levels of party identification (Luna 2007a; Luna and Altman 2011; Segovia 2009). Thus, low levels of party identification with the PPD have occurred in the context of a generalized decline of citizens' attachment to parties.

"The PPD is an abstraction" (Chile 45 in Rosenblatt 2018). "[The PPD] is almost a non-organization. The PPD is a virtual organization" (Chile 24 in Rosenblatt 2018). These two excerpts from interviews with PPD leaders, conducted by Rosenblatt (2018), highlight the fact that the PPD does not have a functioning organizational structure. These interviewees pointed out that only a few governance structures of the party actually operate and that the party's national board has little political influence. The PPD was a relevant political group, it had maintained stable electoral performance, and it was an important ally in the Concertation. However, since its foundation, it has exhibited very low levels of vertical interest aggregation of collective demands and has displayed very little organizational density.

The combination of the persistence of the party label and a weak organization can be attributed mainly to the electoral performance of its candidates and electoral rules that heavily punished defectors or independent candidates. The genetic imprint of the PPD (Panebianco 1988) is associated with pragmatism. It was born as a practical solution to a formal barrier, namely the ban of the PSCh. This pragmatism was clearly manifested by the quick return of leaders and adherents in general to the PSCh when the ban was lifted.

HORIZONTAL COORDINATION

Since the transition to democracy in 1990 and throughout the twenty years during which the Concertation held power, horizontal coordination operated at the coalition level (Carey 2002; Toro Maureira 2007). Relevant negotiations were conducted at the Concertation level, diminishing the significance of the party's caucus. The explanation for this arrangement was the ability of party leaders in Congress to organize and coordinate decisions with the coalition and government.

Coordination in Congress aids incumbents' accumulation of power but it did not translate into organizational strength. It reinforced incumbents' influence over the nominations of candidates in their district. It also enabled members of Congress to serve their constituencies throughout the bargaining within the PPD's caucus in Congress, based on a strongly hierarchical seniority system. As a result, the party developed an organizational structure in which internal party decisions were coordinated in Congress instead of in the party's central offices.

The strengthening of Congress members' territorial influence was the first step toward controlling partisan decision-making. Moreover, PPD leadership was essentially constructed by capturing a key Congressional district through personalistic linkages. Gradually, these incumbents began funding partisan activities in their districts and the regular operation of the party depended on the Congress members' funding. Thus, political clans emerged in the districts. Considering only the family networks, it is possible to illustrate the configuration of these clans. For example, in Santiago, the Girardi family obtained several positions at both the municipal level (mayors and councilors) and parliamentary level (representatives and senators). Furthermore, in southern Chile,[6] the Tuma family (in the Araucanía region)[7] and the Jaramillo family (in the province of Panguipulli)[8] also controlled party growth and nominations for popularly elected positions.

The clan-building logic curtailed the capacity to build a common party organization throughout the territories. The PPD's offices in several areas of the country were gradually subsumed by the congressmembers' offices.

[6] Guido Girardi Lavín was representative (1994–98, 1998–2002, and 2002–6), and Senator (terms 2006–14 and 2014–22), Cristina Girardi Lavín was mayor of Cerro Navia (a municipality in Santiago, 1997–2000, 2001–4, and 2005–8) and representative (2010–14, 2014–18, and 2018–22); Dino Girardi Lavin was councilmember for Lo Prado (a municipality in Santiago, 2009–12 and 2012–16); Guido Girardi Briere was representative (2006–10) and Paula Echeñique Pascal was councilor for Cerro Navia (2004–8). All were sponsored by the PPD label.

[7] Eugenio Tuma was representative (terms 1994–98, 1998–2002, 2002–6, and 2006–10) and senator (2010–18). Joaquín Tuma was representative (2010–14, 2014–18) and Romina Tuma was councilmember (2010–14). All were sponsored by the PPD label.

[8] Enrique Jaramillo was representative (1994–98, 1998–2002, 2002–6, 2006–10, 2010–14, and 2014–18). María Angélica Astudillo was mayor of La Unión (a municipality in Los Lagos region, 2004–8, 2008–12, and 2012–16), and Enrique Jaramillo Jr. was councilmember of La Unión (2000–4). All were sponsored by the PPD label.

Moreover, administrative and professional staff and political activists were funded by the representatives and senators themselves in a manner resembling a confederation of local political machines (Jones and Hwang 2005). One illustration of this phenomenon is the answer given by a member of congress's assistant who worked in a parliamentary office located in southern Chile. When we asked about the location of the PPD office in the city, the assistant responded, "The office of the representative is the office of the party" (personal communication).

The relatively high cost of maintaining clan-building in the districts made necessary the coordination of partisan decisions at the national level. Since 1990, in the PPD, coordination was not carried out at the party central office but at the offices of the party's congressmembers. Unlike other leftist parties in the Concertation (or New Majority) coalition, the PPD used Congress as the central venue for political coordination, as opposed to other arenas such as the Executive, think tanks, or party structure. Indeed, it was PPD members of Congress who determined the fate of the party and its members. For example, one PPD leader stated, "The PPD is a highly parliamentary party, much more so than other parties. Its most visible expression to the people is given through the action of PPD members of Congress" (Chile 13 in Rosenblatt 2018).

In addition to congressmembers' district offices serving as the locus of party activity at the local level, PPD members of Congress coordinated the party's national-level decisions. This coordination was a result of a seniority system that operated at the party level based on the territorial power of each congressmember. This coordination was the key factor that enabled the party to negotiate successfully with the rest of the coalition and the government, which, in turn, reinforced this Congress-based organization as opposed to any party organizational structure. Thus, it was the power of a few congressmembers that ensured the relevance of the PPD vis-à-vis the rest of the coalition partners. For the party, the most important person was the head of the caucus.[9]

[9] Since the return to democracy, thirteen PPD representatives have assumed this function. Of those thirteen, five individuals have controlled the party the longest and have influenced the maintenance of internal discipline: Aníbal Pérez, Enrique Accorsi, Eugenio Tuma, Adriana Muñoz, and Jaime Quintana. The latter three were senators in the two or three most recent legislatures. In the upper chamber, they met with Guido Girardi, one of the party's most influential politicians.

Figure 11.3 shows the internal discipline of the PPD in the period between 2002 and 2018, measured by the Rice index, a measure of degree of agreement within a voting body.[10] Here the indicator shows the unity of members of Congress within the party. An index value closer to 1 implies a highly disciplined party where members always vote similarly and a value closer to 0 implies that the party has no internal discipline. Figure 11.3 shows that the PPD exhibited high levels of party discipline. Even though the index is lower than the average observed for the rest of the parties in the coalition, these differences are not significant and show, in general terms, high intraparty unity in the center-left coalition.

The discipline of PPD's congressional caucus also expressed itself in a high level of coordination with the rest of the coalition. The success of the party's congressional leaders at maintaining unity among its members facilitated an efficient coordination with its coalition partners. Moreover, since 1990, the PPD has always been a reliable ally for the other

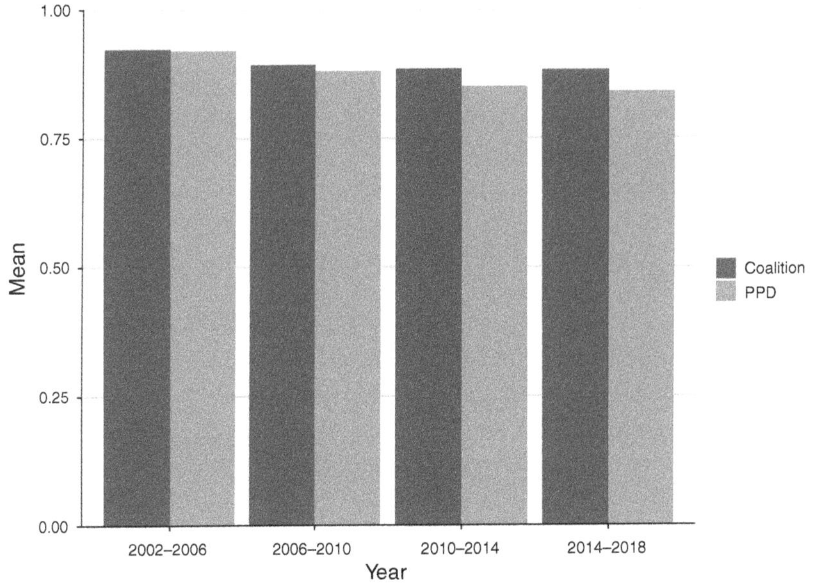

FIGURE 11.3 Rice index evolution
Source: Chamber of Deputies. Author's elaboration based on roll-call votes.

[10] The Rice index (Rice 1925) is one of the first attempts to measure levels of partisan unity. There have been other formulas to adjust the index (Carey 2007).

Concertation parties despite their personalistic dynamics. In this way, loyalty to the party (essentially, loyalty to the congressional leaders) translated into loyalty to the coalition.

Figure 11.4 shows the index of intraparty loyalty, as well as loyalty toward the coalition. The index ranges from 0 to 100, where 0 signifies zero loyalty to the party and /or coalition, and 100 signifies maximum loyalty.[11] Again, a high degree of uniformity is observed among the party's members of Congress, showing an effective party strategy. Moreover, despite the fact that the PPD does not have a strong activist structure, the pragmatic strategy of allowing for strong territorial personalism of its leaders and control of party decisions within Congress worked well. The PPD combines high levels of personalism and high levels of discipline in Congress. By contrast, similar organizations, such as the Brazilian Partido do Movimento Democrático Brasileiro (Party of the Brazilian Democratic Movement, PMDB) (Mainwaring and Perez Liñán 1997) and the Colombian Uribismo (Sanchez 2008), do not exhibit similar levels of discipline in Congress over such a long period.

Because the organization does not exist at the national level, and congressmembers hold power over their own territories, there is no coordination between the PPD's local politics and the party at the national level. Given that there is no referent at the national level, local-level political expressions – when in office or in the opposition at the local level – vary substantially from one territory to another. This is a difference in kind with the conventional differences observed between the national party and their various local-level expressions. While, in general, parties exhibit specificities associated with characteristics of the different local politics, they still exhibit general traits that resemble the national organization. In the case of the PPD, there is no national organization that local-level expressions can emulate. As a result, the local-level expressions of the party are diverse and their similarities are explained by the same logic of organizational building based on personalistic leadership.

Horizontal coordination in elections mimics the same pattern observed regarding horizontal coordination between elections (i.e., in Congress). Candidates run their campaigns without any type of constraint from the party. For example, they do not necessarily use the party logo or colors.

[11] The loyalty index was developed by Poole and Rosenthal (1985). The index seeks to measure congressmembers' behavior with respect to their party or coalition. Thus, it seeks to measure how well aligned a congressmember's voting record is with respect to his or her fellow partisans or coalition partners.

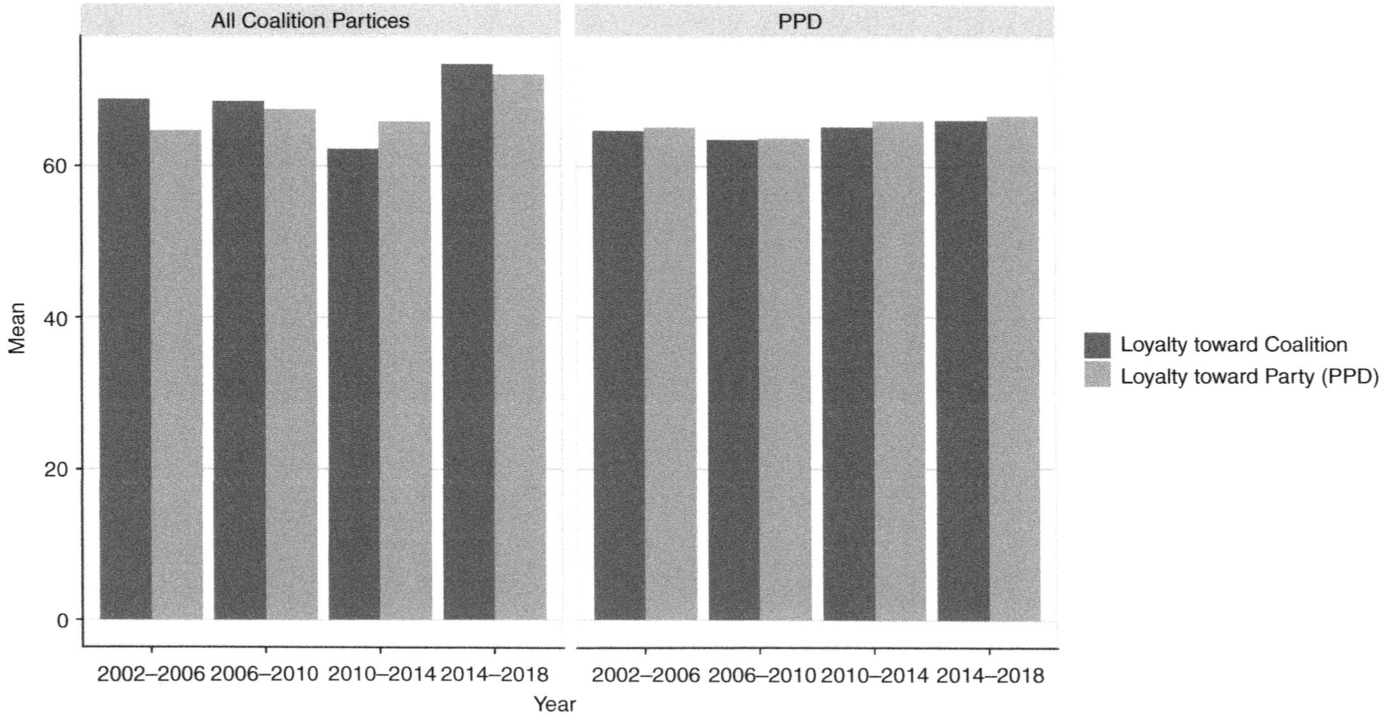

FIGURE 11.4 Loyalty index evolution
Source: Authors' construction based on roll-call votes in the House of Representatives.

Thus, there is no common campaign organization and the party does not distribute campaign resources. However, there is electoral coordination in the PPD. There is control over the number of candidates that enter the electoral competition in each district, to avoid the negative effects of uncoordinated strategies on the joint probability of accessing office.

VERTICAL INTEREST AGGREGATION

The PPD was born as an electoral vehicle for PSCh leaders. It was not the political organization of preexisting social currents, civil society organizations, social movements, or unions. It was not a political organization of a specific social class or a religion that would have provided the party with a defined programmatic identity. Even though it was essentially formed by former PSCh leaders, it simply emerged to facilitate their inclusion in the first democratic elections in Chile since 1973. Thus, the PPD did not emerge with a preexisting identity that could easily articulate a clear set of interests or demands.

Since it was born in the beginning of the transition from Augusto Pinochet's authoritarian regime (1973–90), a strong emphasis on democracy, and civil and political rights in general, were central issues in the programmatic and ideological definitions of the party. In its first platform, it stated, "a construction of democratic and participatory institutions; the blossoming of a culture of respect and the guarantee of human rights and the overcoming of economic and social injustices aggravated during the dictatorship" (Partido por la Democracia 1989, 10). Regarding the role of ideology and the representation of specific interests, one PPD leader said: "I believe what works best in the PPD is its analysis and its ability to capture societal changes, it's a much less rigid party, in its structure of thought, in its societal linkages, also because it is a new party" (Chile 13 in Rosenblatt 2018). While the interviewee acknowledges that the party has a weak ideological commitment and is more "flexible," he also emphasizes that this might be attributable to the PPD being a relatively new party organization.

A clearer and more specific programmatic imprint came from new leaders that joined the party. Since its beginnings, party leaders placed a certain emphasis on the protection of health rights, the environment, and consumer rights. Those were new issues for the Chilean political agenda (Chile 13, Chile 24, and Chile 45 in Rosenblatt 2018). The PPD played a major role in the first public campaigns in Chile, promoting the use of condoms, for example. Notwithstanding the inclusion of such issues on its declaration of principles, the promotion of this agenda was more clearly emphasized by some of its (well-known) leaders. These leaders had no prior affiliation to the PSCh or other leftist parties (e.g., Guido Girardi). They tried to give the PPD a modern liberal-left imprint. Girardi, for example, sought to develop a hybrid agenda that combined progressive and liberal goals. He put forth an agenda of health rights and environmental issues. However, these new issues were not channeled through the organization. The electoral platform of the PPD thus included clear liberal and progressive issues, yet they were not channeled through the party organization of any defined constituencies. Party leaders acknowledge a relationship with different "citizens' movements" but they were not incorporated in a party organizational structure (Chile 13 and Chile 24 in Rosenblatt 2018). In this vein, the party did not have a stable core constituency. While some leaders have always had a territorial stronghold, securing and maintaining it depended on the leaders' own effort, and was not an organizational strategy.

Individual leaders have a programmatic agenda though they also segment their strategy (sometimes within the same district, in other cases between districts) as explained by Luna (2014), describing the territorial work of Guido Girardi:

> While Guido Girardi profits from continuous TV appearances (usually while leading specific popular protests in the streets or raising controversial topics in the media), his family has had personal ties with the district for fifty years. Additionally, he manages to be permanently present in the district, even when that means he needs to have "a siren on the car, to go from [the National Congress in] Valparaíso to the district, whenever that's necessary." Besides, his "media protest" style (sometimes used to criticize the Concertacion's governmental decisions) leads people in the district to identify him as a "leftist." (Luna 2014, 160)

In an interview (in Rosenblatt 2018), a PPD leader (Chile 13) described the nature of the territorial linkage between the party and its constituencies:

Q: Is there an homogeneous distribution throughout the Chilean territory?
A: No, not at all, there are regions that work much better than others. It varies region by region.

Q: What explains why it works better in one place than in other areas?
A: Certain people are active and the presence of some congressmembers that are active in the party. Thus, in some places we have some

congressmembers that move the party a lot, in other places we have congressmembers that do not move the party at all, and in other places we do not have congressmembers.

Later in the same interview, Chile 13 also mentioned, "In general terms, the PPD is organically fragile, and thus that relationship is centered on specific leaders that hold public offices: congressmembers and mayors."

As discussed in the Introduction to this edited volume, the PPD, as a group of independents, fails to build effective channels for vertically aggregating collective interests. The PPD does not perform vertical interest aggregation through the mobilization of collective interests or through the intermediation and channeling of collective demands. Notwithstanding this organizational weakness, as mentioned previously, its leaders – especially its senators, representatives, and some mayors – have been able to distribute private goods to their constituency and/or have led the agenda in some issues. One of the most salient cases is Guido Girardi who has been promoting environmental and health rights and the "agenda of the future" (materialized in the Congress of the Future).

CONCLUSIONS

Given the description presented here, the reader might wonder how an electoral vehicle that performs only minimal horizontal coordination and does not vertically aggregate interests has nonetheless been able to survive for three decades. Even though it is beyond the scope of this chapter and the volume, part of the explanation for this puzzle lies in the peculiar electoral system Chile had until 2015. The binominal electoral system, the combination of mandatory voting and voluntary registration, and citizens' increasing alienation from institutional politics (e.g., the sustained decrease in electoral participation among the younger generations) reduced the level of electoral competitiveness. Chilean parties' electoral fortunes, until the national elections of 2017, essentially depended on negotiations among the elites within an electoral coalition to secure nominations to safe seats. This low level of competitiveness freed Chile's parties and political leaders from the need to ascertain and respond to citizens' changing demands and reinforced citizens' alienation from parties.

In October 2019, Chile experienced major social unrest. The cities were full of angry citizens. The unrest began as a protest against the increase in the metro fare. The increase in the price was thirty pesos (four US cents). The unrest, however, was not simply a protest against the thirty pesos fare increase. It was an uprising against Chile's social and political order. Many essays have been written about those days. What was the PPD's role in Chile's main critical event since democratic transition? Heraldo Muñoz, the party's president, former Chilean Ambassador to the United Nations, and former Minister of Foreign Affairs of Chile in Bachelet's government (2014–18), was invited to be interviewed on several different TV programs during those days. Guido Girardi also had some minutes on national TV. However, it was not the PPD that was consulted. It was Heraldo Muñoz and Guido Girardi, major national leaders, icons of the Concertation years. What was the role of the party's adherents? Not one PPD flag could be seen in the thousands of minutes of TV coverage. Nor do we recall seeing the party logo. The disconnection between the party system and Chilean society is very deep. While some leaders of the PPD do have loyal constituencies (in the context of voluntary voting and low intensity of electoral competition), the PPD does not gather adherents throughout the country, but, rather, there are some loyal electoral supporters who mainly identify with particular individual leaders, though not with the PPD per se (Luna and Rosenblatt 2017).

The social unrest that occurred in Chile during October 2019 challenges this type of organization, a type that functioned effectively in normal times despite the lack of strong ties with society. Whether the PPD will be part of the configuration of the party system after the social unrest of October 2019 is impossible to determine at this point. We must be cautious, as we are writing this chapter only a few weeks after the declaration of a state of emergency and a curfew. Certainly, the PPD is facing this juncture at perhaps its weakest point since its birth because Chilean citizens do not trust it – or any party – and have little confidence in their ability to legitimately aggregate social interests and lead the country to a peaceful resolution of this conflict.

12

Fujimorismo and the Limits of Democratic Representation in Peru, 2006–2020

Alberto Vergara and María Claudia Augusto

INTRODUCTION

Early in this century, academics observed that Peru's crisis of representation was no passing phenomenon (Conaghan 2000) but rather a peculiar "democracy without parties" (Levitsky and Cameron 2003). Almost two decades later, this characterization endures. Levitsky et al.'s (2016) study finds just eleven cases of successful party-building in Latin America, none of them Peruvian. In their place are precarious, opportunistic, and ephemeral arrangements aimed solely at winning elections: what Zavaleta (2014) calls "coalitions of independents." However, *Fujimorismo* may constitute a rare case of party formation, making Peru a possible one-party democracy. Carlos Meléndez has termed this "a case of rightwing party-building success" (Meléndez 2014, 173). Levitsky and Zavaleta (2016), and Loxton (2016) propose that *Fujimorismo* could consolidate itself as a party given the assets it inherited from Alberto Fujimori's authoritarian regime of the 1990s.

The electoral performance of Fuerza Popular (Popular Strength, FP) – the vehicle of *Fujimorismo* – over the past decade gives reason to consider it an emerging party. The FP reached the second round of the 2011 and 2016 presidential elections – though it lost them both – and in the latter case secured an absolute majority (56 percent) in Congress. In this chapter, we analyze the FP's strength using the categories employed by Luna et al. in the introduction to this volume. Our aim is not to present a history of *Fujimorismo* but an analysis of an upward trajectory subject to clear limits from 2016 onwards. We explore the FP's capacity to coordinate politicians horizontally and to vertically integrate social interests, during both election and nonelection periods. Our study centers on the intra-party, legislative and subnational spheres, observing the party's capacity to coordinate horizontally and aggregate vertically in each sphere. We find *Fujimorismo* to be a loose electoral coalition that, in vertical terms, lacks the stable social links required to aggregate interests; and, in horizontal terms, can only coordinate politicians to a limited degree. Finally, we explore the relationship between political parties and democracy. Are all parties assets for democratization? Luna et al. seem to propose that if a political vehicle aggregates interests vertically and coordinates politicians horizontally, it will have achieved the representation expected of a party in a democracy. What *Fujimorismo* shows, however, is that such a vehicle can achieve both functions while eroding democracy. That is, *Fujimorismo* may yet succeed in aggregating vertically and coordinating horizontally, but its recent performance in power demonstrates that these capacities can be exploited to weaken democracy and the rule of law.

This chapter is organized as follows. In the next section we provide a brief historical background of *Fujimorismo*. In the following section, we consider the FP's capacity for horizontal coordination. Then, we examine its ability to forge links with society. Finally, we ask how democratic the FP's representation really is.

BRIEF HISTORICAL BACKGROUND

In 1990, Peru was in critical condition. The economic mismanagement of prior administrations produced one of the highest rates of inflation in global history, GDP was steadily deteriorating, and poverty was rampant. Politically, the country was engulfed in a bloody conflict against a fundamentalist armed group, the Maoist Shining Path. In that desperate context, an unknown outsider candidate named Alberto Fujimori defeated the world-renowned writer Mario Vargas Llosa, who was the candidate of a broad right-wing coalition. President Fujimori lacked a political structure around him and soon found support from the army. This became an open alliance on April 5, 1992, when the army perpetrated an auto-coup that dismantled the Peruvian democracy. Although authoritarian, the administration succeeded in defeating the Shining Path and reconstructing the economy. Peruvians were exultant about a leader whose ambiguous legacy included these military and economic achievements but also rampant corruption and violation of human rights. In 2000, amid a huge scandal that involved the crooked advisor Vladimiro Montesinos and which exposed the regime's corruption, Fujimori fled to Japan and resigned the presidency from abroad. Years later, in 2009, he was convicted of several crimes by the Peruvian Supreme Court and was sentenced to twenty-five-years in jail.[1]

HORIZONTAL COORDINATION: FROM MYSTIQUE TO FRATRICIDAL CONFRONTATION

According to studies that view *Fujimorismo* as a party en route to consolidation, one of *Fujimorismo*'s primary assets is a communal mystique among party cadres and activists (Meléndez 2014; Navarro 2011; Urrutia 2011). The collapse of the Fujimori regime in 2000, and the hundreds of judicial proceedings brought against its officials, fostered solidarity borne of perceived political persecution and an inherent cohesion that no other Peruvian party possessed. If any experience came close, it would be the supposedly analogous mistreatment of the Alianza Popular Revolucionaria Americana (American Revolutionary Popular Alliance, APRA) in the early twentieth century. This cohesiveness served as a tool for horizontal coordination. The FP has succeeded in uniting its loyal core of activists and cadres, for whom abandoning the party would be difficult. Indeed, some academics argue that politicians outside the shared experience of persecution do not readily ascend to positions of control. However, over the last decade, *Fujimorismo* can just as easily be described in terms of divisive rancor as of cohesive mystique.

Days before the 2016 presidential runoff, Keiko Fujimori seemed assured of victory against Pedro Pablo Kuczynski. Anticipating victory, Fujimori attempted to quell fears about any revival of her father's authoritarianism, and about another Fujimori prolonging their spell in power, by declaring that no one from the dynasty would run for president in 2021. But her brother Kenji Fujimori – who ended up as the most-voted-for member of Congress – resented this announcement and its unstated implications. He insisted that if Keiko failed to win, he would have every right to be the *Fujimorista* candidate in 2021.[2] No one was left in any doubt that a sibling struggle for control of the FP had commenced. To make matters worse, Kenji did not vote in an election in which Keiko ultimately

[1] For a review of Alberto Fujimori's administration, see Conaghan (2005), Murakami (2007), and Godoy (2021).

[2] "Si Keiko no gana, yo postularé el 2021" (Radio Programas del Perú, April 25, 2016). https://rpp.pe/politica/elecciones/kenji-fujimori-si-keiko-no-gana-yo-postulare-el-2021-noticia-956683 (last accessed June 5, 2020).

lost. This fraternal rivalry compounded other rifts that had been simmering within the party since the 2000s, provoking an outright schism.

Classical *Fujimorismo* had always dismissed the idea of party formation. Alberto Fujimori – who, as the head of an authoritarian regime that controlled the media, enjoyed the backing of the armed forces during elections, and set up an infrastructure of clientelistic programs – had neither the interest nor the need to build a party (Roberts 2006). But in Peruvian democracy of the 2000s, *Fujimorismo* no longer had such advantages. If 1990s *Fujimorismo* was a collection of disparate cadres aligned to the president, the following decade it sought to transition to a more organic structure. This party-building drive was spearheaded by Keiko Fujimori. Of necessity, it marked a departure from Alberto Fujimori's noninstitutionalized personality cult, whereby everything was settled through proximity to or decisions by the founder and leader.

In 2013, Keiko Fujimori said that her father "does not believe in parties. Like a good *caudillo*, he does not like to cede power. And to build a political party one must cede power."[3] That is, Keiko always knew that party-building went against the interests of her father, who was serving a sentence for human rights violations and corruption while she was engaged in this endeavor. Moreover, for many analysts and actors, Keiko Fujimori did not want her father to leave prison lest he dispute her leadership. For Kenji Fujimori, his sister's two closest collaborators were complicit: "Figari and Ana Hertz de Vega have connived for years, systematically, against the freedom of Alberto Fujimori."[4] In sum, Keiko Fujimori's FP project was antithetical to Alberto Fujimori, and, quite plausibly, its viability depended on keeping him – the old *caudillo* reluctant to cede power – in jail. This went against the interests of Kenji Fujimori, who has claimed more than once to be in politics to secure his father's release.[5]

The growing autonomy of Keiko Fujimori bred disaffection among the cadres who had surrounded Alberto Fujimori in the 1990s, most notably Kenji Fujimori. Increasingly, the public came to divide the *Fujimoristas* into two camps, "*Albertistas*" and "*Keikistas*," especially following the 2011 runoff when Keiko disassociated herself from her father's legacy in

[3] Quoted in Levitsky and Zavaleta (2016), 433.

[4] Kenji Fujimori, Twitter Post, December 27, 2017, 5:22 pm. https://twitter.com/KenjiFujimoriH/status/946114017080365056. All direct quotes that appear in the chapter were translated from Spanish by the authors.

[5] Kenji Fujimori, Twitter Post, July 11, 2017, 12:10 pm. https://twitter.com/KenjiFujimoriH/status/884822320845553664.

a bid to expand her electoral appeal. And though in 2012 she defended her father's 1992 self-coup, in 2016 she promised "never again an April 5th."[6] Her other commitments included the defense of democratic order, freedom of press, non-reelection, separation of powers, and the continuation of the Truth and Reconciliation Commission. All of these pledges were at odds with classical *Fujimorismo*.[7] Keiko Furimori's gradual estrangement, and the emergence of the two factions, can be detected in several party spheres. Most important is the shifting composition of the *Fujimorista* leadership, cadres, and candidacies during the 2000s.

Regarding the leadership, Table 12.1 shows the *Fujimorista* presidential tickets for the last three Peruvian elections. The transformation has been notable. In 2006, all three candidates were veterans of 1990s *Fujimorismo*. In 2011, the first vice-presidential candidate, Jaime Yoshiyama, had been one of Alberto Fujimori's enforcers, but the other, Rafael Rey, was an invitee. In 2016, no one from classical *Fujimorismo* remained. This was the product of a decisive removal of those closest to Alberto Fujimori, a pattern also evident in other spheres of the organization.

Table 12.2 presents the composition of the FP's Comité Ejecutivo Nacional (National Executive Committee, CEN), showing that the party's upper echelons went from being predominantly *Albertista* to not at all. The congressional party was also purged: Alberto Fujimori pleaded from his cell that four of his closest former collaborators (Alejandro Aguinaga, Martha Chávez, Luisa María Cuculiza, and Luz Salgado) be allowed to run, but the FP only included Salgado. José Chlimper, ex-secretary general of the party, noted that "the turning point . . . is when Alberto says from prison 'these four are going to be Congress members' and Keiko says 'no, only Luz (Salgado).'"[8]

The gradual reshaping of the *Fujimorista* leadership gained impetus in the congressional elections of 2016, when the FP selected as its main spokespersons politicians who had only recently joined the party. One *Albertista* actor affected directly by the *Keikista* ascendancy noted: "For us it is hurtful that people who recently insulted *Fujimorismo*, or a guy with an *Aprista* background, are coming into the party. Do you think APRA would stand for

[6] Date of Alberto Fujimori's self-coup in 1992.

[7] "Los compromisos firmados por la candidata" (*El Comercio*, May 6, 2016). https://elcomercio.pe/politica/elecciones/keiko-fujimori-compromisos-firmados-candidata-395674-noticia/ (last accessed June 5, 2020).

[8] Interview with José Chlimper, January 2018.

TABLE 12.1 *Composition of presidential tickets*

	2006		2011		2016	
	Name	**Faction**	**Name**	**Faction**	**Name**	**Faction**
President	Martha Chávez Cossio	*Albertista*	Keiko Fujimori Higuchi	*Keikista*	Keiko Fujimori Higuchi	*Keikista*
First Vice President	Santiago Fujimori	*Albertista*	Rafael Rey	Invitee	José Chlimper Ackerman	*Keikista*
Second Vice President	Rolando Sousa Huanambal	*Albertista*	Jaime Yoshiyama Tanaka	*Keikista*	Vladimiro Huaroc Portocarrero	Invitee

Source: Infogob.

TABLE 12.2 *Composition of the FP's CEN*[9]

	2010–2014	2014–2018	2018–2022
Albertistas	9 (64.3%)	2 (11.8%)	–
Keikistas	3 (21.4%)	10 (58.8%)	15 (88.2%)
No data	1 (14.3%)	5 (29.4%)	2 (11.8%)
Total members	14	17	17

Sources: Jurado Nacional de Elecciones, actors' resumes, and media statements. The increase in CEN membership was due to the creation of three new secretarial positions in 2014.

Haya de la Torre being insulted? That is where they went wrong."[10] Thus, the construction of a more organic structure precipitated a replacement of the *Fujimorista* old guard with Keiko Fujimori and her inner circle. This renewal of leaders and cadres – and the weakening of those closest to Alberto Fujimori – constitutes the most important change within the party. Legislator Cecilia Chacón stated that "Alberto Fujimori still does not believe in political parties. The FP is not the party of Alberto Fujimori. The FP belongs to the activists, to everyone equally. He, if he wants, can join as well."[11] Another lawmaker, Héctor Becerril, remarked following the failed impeachment of President Kuczynski in December 2017, that "Alberto Fujimori breeds corruption."[12] Úrsula Letona, head of the FP's 2016 party platform, asserted: "I have nothing to do with the 1990s … It does nothing for me, I am here for Keiko and because I am convinced that I have to give back to the country what it gave me."[13]

The displaced sectors accuse this new wave in the FP of "defujimorizing" *Fujimorismo*, cleaving the movement from the party organization.

[9] Based on key dates, leaving aside minor changes between times. We classified the actors by reviewing their resumes and their links with *Fujimorismo*.

[10] Interview with Alejandro Aguinaga, February 2018.

[11] "Fuerza Popular no es el partido de Alberto Fujimori" (*El Comercio*, October 9, 2017). https://elcomercio.pe/politica/cecilia-chacon-fuerza-popular-partido-alberto-fujimori-noticia-464032-noticia/ (last accessed June 5, 2020).

[12] "Alberto Fujimori alienta la corrupción" (Radio Programas del Perú, December 22, 2017). https://rpp.pe/politica/congreso/hector-becerril-alberto-fujimori-alienta-la-corrupcion-noticia-1095821o (last accessed June 5, 2020).

[13] Interview with Úrsula Letona, January 2018.

For one ex-Congress member, the true *Fujimoristas* (those from the 1990s) "have been banished, excluded because they want to do away with *Fujimorismo*, but no one can do away with *Fujimorismo*."[14] In turn, for one grassroots activist, "Fuerza Popular does not represent *Fujimorismo*. They themselves have broken their party, they have taken it over, because it has cost them nothing. They want to keep Fuerza Popular? They can have it."[15] Thus, the party's main feature is hardly a mystique that binds it together. But all parties have their factions and their disagreements, and the FP was still able to maintain a capacity for horizontal coordination that prevented its politicians from defecting. However, this retentive ability waned from 2016 to 2019.

In December 2017, President Kuczynski survived a first FP-sponsored attempt to oust him thanks to the support of ten *Fujimoristas,* led by Kenji Fujimori, in defiance of the party. Days later, Alberto Fujimori received a so-called humanitarian pardon. This triggered a public confrontation in which Keiko Fujimori's spokespersons branded Kenji a traitor, presaging his expulsion from the party. As a result, Kenji Fujimori's renegade faction promised a new kind of *Fujimorismo* along with a new party.[16] However, the illusion was not to last. In March 2018, before a second impeachment, the FP disclosed that Kenji and his group had colluded with Kuczynski's government to bribe opposition legislators into voting in the president's favor. The revelations forced Kuczynski's resignation, while three of the rogue *Fujimoristas*, Kenji Fujimori among them, were suspended pending criminal proceedings. Thus, *Fujimorismo's* fratricidal struggle, with its far-reaching implications, is a far cry from normal party divides. If internal conflict split *Fujimorismo* into two blocs led by either sibling, what repercussions did this have in the legislative arena?

First, it is important to consider the FP's candidate selection process. Is this a party of cadres, or of special interests marshalled for elections? The structure has shifted gradually toward heterogeneous candidacies composed of newcomers, invitees, and figures with links to other political camps. This is a common approach among parties in Peru, which are essentially shells pursuing political free agents on the national electoral market (Levitsky and Zavaleta 2016). Prospective candidates are gauged

[14] Interview with Bienvenido Ramírez, February 2018.

[15] Interview with Patty Vásquez, March 2018.

[16] "Kenji Fujimori anunció que formará 'Cambio 21,'' su nuevo partido político" (Radio Programas del Perú, March 20, 2018). https://rpp.pe/politica/congreso/kenji-fujimori-anuncio-la-creacion-de-cambio-21-su-nuevo-partido-politico-noticia-1111513 (last accessed June 5, 2020).

less by programmatic proximity and more by the capital on offer, allowing parties to widen their recruitment drives and do without grassroots development. According to Chlimper, "one needs power to be a party; we have made agreements with regional leaders who are not, well, *Fujimoristas*."[17]

This approach is evident at all governmental levels. Seventy-three FP members (out of a possible 130) were elected to Congress in 2016, but they did not conform to strict partisan criteria. Zavaleta and Vilca (2017) calculate that over 80 percent of candidates across all parties were political novices, or had previously represented other parties. The FP candidate list was drafted by the CEN, representing a centralization of decision-making. In discourse, the FP claimed it had conducted a rigorous selection process,[18] but in practice, screening was somewhat flexible. Thus, while some candidates received more than one interview,[19] others were accepted following minimal vetting and no interviews; instead, they negotiated their candidacies behind closed doors, and many were selected at the last minute, on the promise of an elevated list position. For instance, FP legislator Bienvenido Ramírez was "invited ... just one or two days before the close of registration."[20] Thus, the majority of those elected to Congress do not share a common party experience.

This approach has been duplicated subnationally. In regional elections, the FP has opted for invitees, who have the freedom to call up candidates at the province or district level and to establish their own platform. This usually creates discord with local party bases, who are resentful of the difficulty they face accessing elected posts despite long-standing activism. In these circumstances, many exited the party for rival candidates. Our study concurs with Rejas (2015) in finding that provincial *Fujimorista* committees have little to no influence on candidate selection at the subnational level. Acting in their place are CEN-appointed coordinators, who orchestrate the electoral apparatus in top-down fashion. Coordinators are handpicked and survival in the post depends on the party leadership, as a coordinator from Lima East observed.[21]

[17] Interview with José Chlimper, January 2018.

[18] "Cuando Keiko aseguró que fueron "estrictos" para evaluar a sus congresistas" (*La República*, April 22, 2018). https://larepublica.pe/politica/1231690-cuando-keiko-asegurو-que-fueron-estrictos-para-evaluar-a-sus-congresistas-video/ (last accessed June 4, 2020).

[19] Interview with Milagros Salazar, May 2018.

[20] Interview with Bienvenido Ramírez, February 2018.

[21] Interview with Obed Bernuy, February 2019.

The lack of institutionalized procedures for selecting candidates, and the prioritization of those who can finance their own campaigns, has seen the FP dominated by cadres without a *Fujimorista* pedigree. Many have assumed important positions within the FP parliamentary grouping: roles such as committee chairs, spokespersons, and even the presidency of Congress have all been entrusted to individuals who just a few years ago were active elsewhere or completely unknown. The party has struggled to keep hold of its new politicians. The FP, acknowledging its failure to secure the presidency, and the short-term expediency motivating many of its legislators, promoted a law – later declared unconstitutional by the Constitutional Court – prohibiting the formation of new parliamentary groupings (*bancadas*).[22] But, in 2017, two lawmakers left the *Fujimorista* ranks nonetheless. The FP ended up losing twenty-three of its initial seventy-three legislators,[23] splitting the grouping between the rump FP and Kenji Fujimori's Cambio 21. Thus, if it was easy to represent the FP in the first place, the costs of leaving were low. The leadership admitted that commanding a majority[24] and coordinating a fractious group had been a burden. With the party flagging, there were few incentives to stay. Daniel Salaverry, the 2018–19 president of Congress, had been backed by Keiko Fujimori herself. In office, he quickly distanced himself from *Fujimorismo*. In adherence to the Constitutional Court's ruling, Salaverry accepted and encouraged the formation of new parliamentary groupings. This provoked a motion of censure by *Fujimorismo* – against someone they themselves had installed weeks earlier. Following this incident, Salaverry and other FP representatives resigned, citing irreconcilable differences.[25] In retaliation, the *Fujimorismo*-dominated Ethics Commission suspended Salaverry from Congress. The FP's comings and goings reached an extreme when legislator Yeni Vilcatoma resigned from the party two months after her election, only to return

[22] "Curules con candado: alistan ley para evitar cambios de bancada" (*El Comercio*, September 19, 2016). https://elcomercio.pe/politica/congreso/curules-candado-alistan-ley-evitar-cambios-bancada-260434-noticia/ (last accessed June 5, 2020).

[23] This total also includes the party's three dissident Congress members, Kenji Fujimori among them, who have been suspended and replaced by alternate members. It does not include Yeni Vilcatoma, who resigned from the group.

[24] Interview with José Chlimper, January 2018.

[25] "Daniel Salaverry presentó su carta de renuncia a Fuerza Popular" (Radio Programas del Peru, January 9, 2019). https://rpp.pe/politica/congreso/daniel-salaverry-presento-su-carta-de-renuncia-a-fuerza-popular-noticia-1174348 (last accessed June 5, 2020).

in exchange for membership in the 2017 Mesa directiva del congreso (Bureau of Congress).[26]

In 2019, the executive-legislature standoff was settled constitutionally. The *Fujimorista* majority, in conjunction with APRA, tried to appoint new Constitutional Court members arbitrarily, against public opinion, and with undue haste. In response, the executive lodged a motion of confidence aimed at forestalling the appointments. But when Congress rejected the motion, the executive dissolved parliament in accordance with established procedures and the Constitution. Although the FP initially disavowed this ruling, accusing the government of a "coup," *Fujimorismo* soon confirmed its participation in the 2020 election.

As of this writing, the FP was finalizing its candidate selection for the 2020 election. Martha Chávez, one of the most familiar faces from classical *Fujimorismo* who was excluded in 2016, returned to top the list. Another six officials sought reelection, while several of the new generation were cast aside. Carlos Tubino, ex-secretary general of the parliamentary group, resigned when the party blocked his candidacy,[27] and Rosa Bartra, chief spokesperson and two-time Constitution Committee president, ran for Solidaridad Nacional (National Solidarity) instead.[28] Finally, Daniel Salaverry declared his intention to run for the Peruvian presidency in 2021 under the banner of a new party.[29]

Fujimorismo's capacity for horizontal articulation on the subnational front is also weak. In 2014, the FP won three regional governorships (out of twenty-five), which some interpreted as a sign of strength. One might have expected to find horizontal cohesion in the regions where *Fujimorismo* achieved success, but it proved short-lived. Just like in Congress, the selection strategy entailed the offer of candidacies in

[26] "Yeni Vilcatoma: su antes y después con Fuerza Popular" (*El Comercio*, July 26, 2018). https://elcomercio.pe/politica/yeni-vilcatoma-despues-fuerza-popular-noticia-540111-noticia/ (last accessed June 5, 2020).

[27] "Había molestias con la actuación de legisladores de FP" (*La República*, November 10, 2019). https://larepublica.pe/politica/2019/11/10/fuerza-popular-habia-molestia-con-la-actuacion-de-congresistas-rosa-bartra-carlos-tubino-solidaridad-nacional/ (last accessed June 5, 2020).

[28] "Rosa Bartra: El poder, sobre todo cuando es absoluto, necesita control" (*El Comercio*, November 21, 2019). https://elcomercio.pe/elecciones-2020/elecciones-2020-rosa-bartra-el-poder-sobre-todo-cuando-es-absoluto-necesita-control-noticia/ (last accessed June 5, 2020).

[29] "Daniel Salaverry: Es una decisión tomada postular a la presidencia de la República" (*El Comercio*, September 8, 2019). https://elcomercio.pe/politica/daniel-salaverry-decision-tomada-postular-presidencia-republica-ecpm-noticia-672910-noticia/ (last accessed June 5, 2020).

exchange for political and financial capital. During the 2014 subnational campaign, the FP's main asset was Keiko Fujimori, then leading the polls for the 2016 presidential election and keen to boost her own prospects. Her visits – to raise the profile of little-known candidates and open party offices – reaped rewards in the form of the three governorships. For one winning governor, "Keiko was a rock star, she took me from last to first place."[30]

Party consolidation was quickly relegated. After the election, the disconnect between the FP and its new office-holders was evident. Without channels of communication between the governors and the CEN, the former had the freedom to set their own agenda and decide on the makeup of their teams. In two regions, there were open hostilities between the governors and local leaders, who wanted their say in government,[31] while in the third, the party kept its distance.[32] These local confrontations, combined with the FP's behavior nationally, contributed to a failure to win any regional governorships in 2018.

This assessment of horizontal coordination in the FP portrays a party exposed to departures in which the retention of politicians is contingent on the leader's presidential hopes. Candidates for both congressional and subnational posts advance in approximate proportion to the presidential candidate's prospects of victory. If politicians feel they have to abandon the FP to survive, they have no qualms about doing so – just like in all other Peruvian political vehicles. What defined *Fujimorismo* over the last decade, then, was not a cohesive mystique but a conflict that remained subdued so long as the polls favored Keiko Fujimori's chances of winning a presidential election, as they did in 2011 and 2016. But after both attempts failed, and with 2021 in sight, the low-intensity conflict escalated into open war between sibling-led factions – prompting nonaligned politicians to abandon the party at no great personal cost.

VERTICAL AGGREGATION: ORGANIZATION AND IDEAS

In a representative democracy, elections are the key moment in political life and are what legitimize representatives to act. However, unless one subscribes to the radical notion of the elected official as a trustee with total freedom to act on behalf of the citizen (Przeworski, Stokes, and Manin 1999), channels of communication between society and politics must

[30] Interview with Fernando Cilloniz, September 2018.
[31] Interview with Víctor Noriega, September 2018.
[32] Ibid.S

extend beyond election day. Political parties fulfill this intermediary role; they mobilize certain interests during elections, and representatives are elected because of their relation to these interests. In between election cycles, parties and their representatives serve as conveyor belts between society's demands and public institutions.

A party requires programmatic coherence to ensure candidacies are identifiable with its proposals (Roberts 2014a). As the literature has noted, ideological consistency enables the creation of a party label, helps stabilize public preferences, and facilitates institutionalization of a party system (Lupu 2014). On the other hand, if it is to fulfill its role of linking its representatives with society from one election to another, a party requires nationwide organizational robustness.

A Programmatic Vehicle?

Does *Fujimorismo* have an ideological core? And if so, does it differ from the other options on the Peruvian political market? To address these questions, we draw on two types of sources. First, we conducted twenty interviews with *Fujimorista* cadres and activists, asking what they consider the programmatic heart of the party. Second, we reviewed opinion polls to discern the programmatic characteristics that FP voters ascribe to its candidates. We find, first, that there is no common program. Second, we find that there is a disparity between the ideological confusion/dispersion of party cadres and how voters perceive *Fujimorismo*.

Across our interviews with *Fujimorista* cadres, we posed the same question: can you name the party's three programmatic priorities? The interviewees cited very different themes, highlighting a lack of programmatic unity within the party. Indeed, several respondents, including the party's general secretary, refer to *Fujimorismo* as a pragmatic more than a programmatic force. Table 12.3 outlines their responses. Despite this heterogeneity, one can glimpse a common belief in safeguarding the free market model introduced in 1993, skewed toward assisting small businesses. "Popular capitalism" also emerged in some responses.

While many analysts have referred to *mano dura* (firm hand) politics as something distinctively *Fujimorista* (Meléndez 2014), somewhat surprisingly, no cadres mentioned this approach, nor did they allude to drastic public security plans with such connotations. This reveals a gap between what voters look for and what the party offers, creating problems of representation. Indeed, during the last election, the public cited (lack of)

TABLE 12.3 *Perceived programmatic attributes of* Fujimorismo

Attribute	Percentage of mentions in interviews
Alberto Fujimori	55.6
Public services for the most vulnerable	55.6
Pragmatic governmental style	27.8
Economic policies for business and the vulnerable	27.8
Balance between state authority and individual liberty	5.6
Sense of urgency	5.6
Multi-class party	5.6
Others	22.2

Source: Personal interviews compiled by authors.

public safety (70 percent) and corruption (49 percent) as Peru's most serious problems.[33] And the capacity to tackle precisely these two problems were among the attributes voters valued most about Keiko Fujimori's candidacy (Figure 12.1). However, the interviews show that these are not programmatic priorities for the FP.

A concrete sign of programmatic weakness – and of a purely strategic motivation – is *Fujimorismo's* adoption of the conservative agenda pushed by evangelical churches. One year before the 2016 presidential election, Keiko Fujimori sought to cast herself as liberal on various "social issues." At a Harvard University event, the candidate expressed her approval of civil union ("as far as it refers to respecting the patrimonial rights of couples") and therapeutic abortion ("to save the life of women").[34] Moreover, the FP's 2016 party platform stated its commitment "to each and every one of the social programs and public entities … with a life-cycle approach [and] *a gender-based approach* [as well as] the Concerted Development Plans of the districts participating in the SDG clusters" (Fuerza Popular 2016, 25).[35] However, as the election campaign progressed and resources and activists became more important, the FP

[33] Ipsos Opinión Data, January 2016. www.ipsos.com/sites/default/files/publication/2016-01/Opinion%20Data%20Enero%202016.pdf (last accessed June 5, 2020).
[34] "Keiko en Harvard" (*La República*, October 1, 2015). https://larepublica.pe/politica/885593-keiko-en-harvard/ (last accessed June 5, 2020).
[35] Our emphasis.

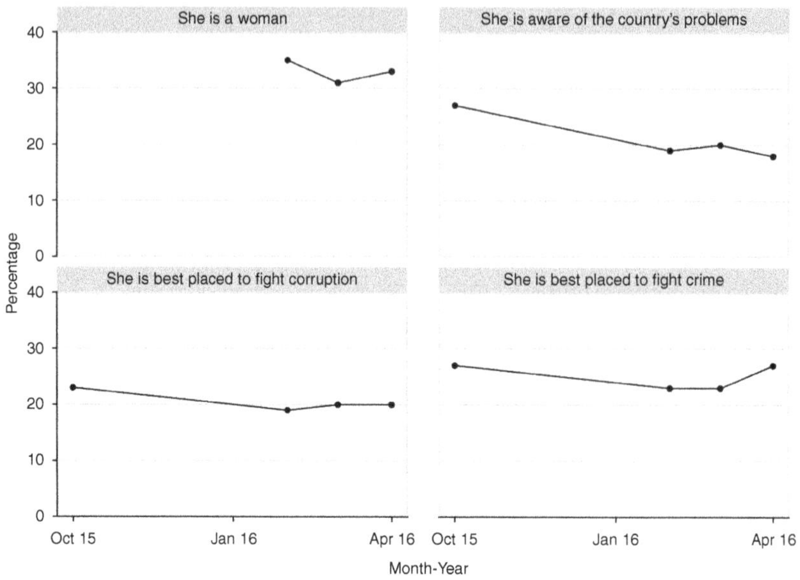

FIGURE 12.1 Perceived characteristics attributed to Keiko Fujimori
Source: Ipsos Opinión Data.

resurrected its alliance with the Catholic and several evangelical churches, reversing its liberal positions and avowing opposition to abortion and civil union for homosexuals – a stance it consolidated through an agreement with evangelical leaders.[36] After the FP won its majority, the sway of these religious interests grew increasingly powerful. Indeed, a group of evangelical legislators within the party became known among peers as *Agua Viva*, after a local evangelical church (De Belaunde 2019). One member said that they had been effective in blocking the government's gender-related initiatives, with party backing.[37] Thus, important public-policy measures from the *Fujimorista* benches stem not from the leader's convictions or programmatic guidelines, but from pragmatic short-term alliances forged in the heat of the campaign. The *Fujimorista* leadership is clearly aware of the diversity of interests within the party and the legislature. Thus, as José Chlimper has observed, the party cannot subscribe to a strict set of ideals lest this limit its flexibility and create a bottleneck.

[36] "Keiko y la polémica por el apoyo del pastor Alberto Santana" (*El Comercio*, May 6, 2016). https://elcomercio.pe/politica/elecciones/keiko-polemica-apoyo-pastor-alberto-santana-395652-noticia/ (last accessed June 5, 2020).

[37] Interview with congressman Juan Carlos Gonzáles, April 2018.

The FP's programmatic elasticity is also evident in the quantity and content of the bills presented by *Fujimorista* legislators and approved by Congress. Over the 2016–21 legislative period, the FP held a parliamentary majority, the presidency of Congress for three years running,[38] and the chairs of most congressional committees, so one might assume that the laws passed reflect their programmatic priorities. By September 2019, *Fujimorismo* had presented 1,819 bills, 405 of which were approved. However, less than thirty are directly related to measures included in the FP's platform. That is, reality overtook Keiko Fujimori's assertions that a commanding parliamentary presence would let her party implement its platform directly, bypassing the executive.[39] Indeed, the evidence suggests that FP legislators prioritized their own interests over those of the party. Similar initiatives presented by different Congress members from the *Fujimorista* grouping, as well as bills shaped by short-termism or personal interests, indicate a lack of coordination. Moreover, in some cases, implementing proposals from the party platform induced congressional resignations, suggesting contradictory and competing interests.[40]

This programmatic weakness extends to the subnational level. In the three regions where *Fujimorismo* governed between 2014 and 2018, the picture is similar to the national one; rather than imposing a programmatic agenda upon her candidates, Keiko Fujimori gave them freedom to prioritize their own ideas and discretion to hire whomever they felt appropriate. Indeed, one candidate openly distanced himself from the FP, leveraging his invitee status.[41] The candidates who triumphed did so because of their personal capital and, especially, the boost they received from the presence of Keiko Fujimori at some of their public appearances.

[38] In 2019, Pedro Olaechea was elected president of Congress. Although Olaechea was not an FP representative, his affinity for *Fujimorismo* has been notable; indeed it was votes from the party that secured his victory.

[39] "Keiko: "Convertiremos propuestas del plan de gobierno en leyes" (*El Comercio*, July 28, 2016). https://elcomercio.pe/politica/actualidad/keiko-convertiremos-propuestas-plan-gobierno-leyes-397999-noticia/ (last accessed June 5, 2020).

[40] In 2016, *Fujimorista* legislator Yeny Vilcatoma presented a bill for the creation of an independent Office of Attorney General, detached from the executive. As Caballero (2019) shows, this proposal was unveiled as a priority measure in the party platform, but was not supported by her colleagues. The ensuing clash led to a disciplinary process and, ultimately, Vilcatoma's resignation.

[41] "Entrevista exclusiva con el candidato al Gobierno Regional Teódulo Quispe H" (Radio Cumbre, October 22, 2014). www.radiocumbre.com.pe/nacional/10/2014/entrevista-exclusiva-con-el-candidato-al-gobierno-regional-teodulo-quispe-huertas (last accessed June 5, 2020).

Fujimorismo was not marked apart by any ideological elements in the regions where it was victorious.[42] Thus, in the case of the subnational candidates, we find no evidence of consistent programmatic alignment with the party; rather, there is a disconnect between their ideological self-perception and how voters perceive them. And, at this level, successful *Fujimorista* candidates do not follow common party lines. Under these conditions, it is no surprise that the dispute behind the party's split was wholly personal, between two *caudillo* heirs disputing the throne, and devoid of programmatic content.

The Party Organization

In this section, we study the "material" consistency of *Fujimorista* organization. According to Cyr (2017), stable organizational resources comprise party activists, staff, and offices throughout the country. To what extent has the FP developed an organization that penetrates Peruvian society and territory? How organized is the party?

In the 2016 legislative elections, the FP obtained at least one legislator in each of Peru's electoral constituencies. This success might point to an extensive party organization that allows for nationalization of the party. To assess whether this is the case, we base our analysis on three dimensions: the structure of party venues in the country, comparing those that the party has formally registered with those actually used; subnational election results; and activists.

As with all Peruvian parties, there is a gulf between the FP's territorial reach on paper, and in reality. The party has seventy-seven provincial committees registered with the National Elections Board, in twenty-one of the country's twenty-five regions. However, the vast majority of these are either inactive or engaged in activities unrelated to politics. After visiting FP committees in seven regions, we found that just three were operational. The party branch offices, in most cases, host activities related to anything but the party.

Second, party reach should be measured not only in terms of legislative elections but subnational elections as well (Vergara 2011). How has the FP performed at the subnational levels? And is this performance connected, or not, with that recorded at presidential or legislative levels? Table 12.4

[42] This section and its focus on the subnational level are based on Vergara and Augusto (2020).

TABLE 12.4 *Average intention to vote (percentage) for* Fujimorismo *by level of government, 2010–2018*

Elections	Presidential	Legislative	Regional	Provincial	District
2010	-	-	8.1	9.0	11.5
2011	23.6	23.0	-	-	-
2014	-	-	9.8	9.7	12.3
2016	39.9	36.3	-	-	-
2018	-	-	4.5	7.5	12.1

Source: Compiled by the author based on INFOGOB and ONPE data. Electoral alliances are not taken into account.

presents the average vote received by the FP in every election, showing the gap between the national and subnational levels. A good place to start is with the regions where the FP gained more than half of the vote during the 2011 and 2016 presidential elections. In 2011, it reached these heights in La Libertad, Piura, and Tumbes. Of the 185 available offices in these regions, the FP ran for seventy-four in 2010, securing three – one in each region. In 2016, the FP took more than 50 percent of the vote in Tumbes, Piura, and Madre de Dios, but in the 2014 subnational elections, it did not win any of the 106 elected posts available in these regions. Thus, there is no concordance between the high percentages the FP obtains in certain regions during national legislative and presidential elections, and what it achieves in these same regions in subnational contests. The difference in 2014 is particularly stark, suggesting that the electoral fortunes of the FP, as a personalistic party, owe more to the national campaign of a particular candidate than to territorial penetration.

This can be seen nationwide on an aggregate basis. In 2014, the FP took three of the twenty-five regional presidencies, four out of 195 provincial mayoralties, and seventy-five out of 1,647 district mayoralties. Of the 1,867 elected posts available, the FP only won eighty-two: 5 percent of the total, though the party did not run candidates everywhere. In the 2018 elections, the proportion dropped further. The party did not win any governorship, gained just three provincial mayoralties, and secured forty-six district mayoralties. Its share at the provincial level also fell (Figure 12.2).

Alberto Fujimori's administration deployed multiple social programs to establish clientelistic linkages with different sectors of society, with local organizers and beneficiaries forming the basis of an effective *Fujimorista* network. According to some studies of contemporary

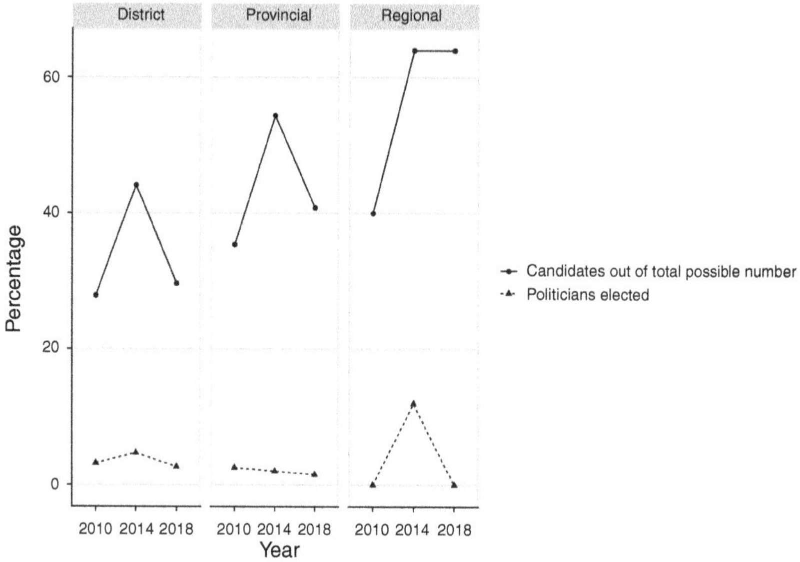

FIGURE 12.2 *Fujimorista* candidates and electoral success, 2010–2018
Source: Compiled by the author based on INFOGOB. Electoral alliances are not taken into account.

Fujimorismo, the survival of these networks has assured the FP of social penetration and an activist network that distinguish it from other Peruvian electoral vehicles. However, during our fieldwork in the regions of Ica, San Martín, and Lima, which included interviews and meetings with local *Fujimorista* groups, we found diffuse activists more than articulated networks. Indeed, all of our interviewees refute the suggestion that the FP is founded on networks from the 1990s. If they did exist, insists Úrsula Letona, head of the FP's 2016 party platform, they were displaced by groups set up by Keiko Fujimori. In addition, when we accompanied *Fujimorista* legislators to their constituencies, we found that they meet much more with civic organizations than with local *Fujimorista* groups.

During election campaigns, *Fujimorismo* does manage to mobilize its activists. However, they play a utilitarian role, performing logistical tasks such as distributing posters, painting murals, or kitting out properties to serve as campaign bases. This work is voluntary and is conditioned by support of Keiko Fujimori and affinity with local candidates. In the three regions where *Fujimorismo* won regional governorships in 2014, we detected some degree of party penetration during the campaign. Again, this is linked to the presence of Keiko Fujimori. In 2013, the presidential candidate traveled to Pasco and San Martín, opening party venues and announcing local candidates. This buoyed the local activists tasked with coordinating her visits.

By the time of the 2018 campaign, the FP's limited organization had vanished. Some candidates attribute this to the accusations surrounding the party, including the leader and her inner circle, limiting the FP's appeal. In early 2018, various cadres predicted that activists would support other parties. Indeed, one coordinator conceded that activists scattered after calculating that backing a different group would be more advantageous.[43] Thus, the few visits that Keiko Fujimori made went unnoticed and, in reality, were a liability for candidates.

If vertical interest aggregation is one of the key functions of a political party in a democracy, *Fujimorismo* has failed; the two prerequisite dimensions – programmatic coherence and nationwide party organization – are not sufficiently established. Thus, since the FP only fulfills the function of horizontal coordination to a limited degree and does not fulfill the function of vertical aggregation at all, it might be described as a loose coalition without territorial penetration.

Fujimorismo in Reality

Notwithstanding the weaknesses in the horizontal and vertical dimensions of representation, *Fujimorismo* has played an important role in Peruvian politics over the last decade. Considering its limited horizontal and vertical assets, to what extent does *Fujimorismo* actually exist? One must recall the current volatility of Peruvian politics, whose long-standing cast succumbed between 2017 and 2019 to the Odebrecht scandal. However, many of those implicated had been rejected decisively at the polls. In 2016, former presidents Alan García and Toledo obtained a mere 5 percent and 2 percent of the vote, respectively, and former president Humala's nationalist party did not even field a presidential candidate. Susana Villarán, who had been elected Lima's mayor in 2010, lost her reelection in 2014, finishing third. Kuczynski surrendered the presidency in the face of impeachment. Thus, consigned to irrelevance, the Odebrecht scandal only served to ratify the exclusion of these once-major players.

[43] Interview with Obed Bernuy, September 2018.

More than eliminating them from the running, Odebrecht showed that they deserved to be out of the race.

Keiko Fujimori's case is different. She was sentenced to three years of pretrial detention – her main advisors were likewise imprisoned – for her part in the scandal, leaving the FP headless, but she was not an electoral irrelevance. In November 2019, she was released by the Constitutional Court; proceedings were still ongoing at time of writing. The interviewees concur that Keiko Fujimori was contemporary *Fujimorismo*'s foremost asset. Young, dedicated, and industrious, she succeeded in organizing a weak coalition. In a partyless polity such as Peru's, this organization, however minimal, was an advantage. As we have seen, Keiko Fujimori as a passable presidential candidate was *Fujimorismo*'s primary means of horizontal collaboration.

The Odebrecht case marks an important shift for *Fujimorismo*. Today, just 10 percent of the population back Keiko Fujimori,[44] while 75 percent consider her investigation justified.[45] Meanwhile, 81 percent disapprove of the performance of the *Fujimorista* parliamentary group,[46] and 76 percent disapprove of the FP-dominated Congress.[47] Our exploration of *Fujimorismo* at the subnational level shows that Keiko Fujimori's unpopularity by late 2018 was such that candidates did not want her to campaign in their jurisdictions, lest she tarnish them by association.[48]

Between 2006 and 2016, *Fujimorismo* had the same major asset as any party in a system of personalistic vehicles: an effective leader. The great unknown is whether she will be able to reestablish these personalistic links despite her imprisonment and proximity to corruption. However, another key feature of the FP is its amenability to various special interests whose financial contributions during electoral periods bought them prominence within the party. Given that Keiko Fujimori was the favorite to win the presidency in 2011 and 2016, many actors seeking to advance their own interests gravitated toward the FP. These interests, which can be legal, informal, or even unlawful, have been crucial to financing the party and its

[44] Ipsos Opinión Data, August 20, 2019. www.ipsos.com/sites/default/files/ct/news/documents/2019-08/opinion_data_agosto_2019_0.pdf (last accessed June 5, 2020).

[45] Ipsos Opinión Data, July 23, 2019. www.ipsos.com/sites/default/files/ct/news/documents/2019-07/opinion_data_julio_2019_0.pdf (last accessed June 5, 2020).

[46] Ipsos Opinión Data, January 22, 2019. www.ipsos.com/sites/default/files/ct/news/documents/2019-01/opinion_data_enero_2019.pdf (last accessed June 5, 2020).

[47] Ipsos Opinión Data, August 20, 2019. www.ipsos.com/sites/default/files/ct/news/documents/2019-08/opinion_data_agosto_2019_0.pdf (last accessed June 5, 2020)

[48] Interview with campaign manager, October 2018.

presidential candidate at election time. The party is currently under investigation for money laundering through so-called "phantom donors,"[49] and the Attorney General has found that double accounting was practiced. Without party funds of its own, all contributions are welcome. In the words of one interviewee, "the only thing that parties do is take the money, cover their eyes and believe that those supporting you [*sic*] are first-rate."[50]

Among those financiers representing legal interests, the sectors most cited by the interviewees are private university education and transportation. In the former case, the aim is purportedly to block or stall the Ministry of Education from proceeding with the regulation of poor-quality private universities.[51] In the case of transportation, the FP's general secretary admitted that the party has a pair of legislators who only take part in the congressional transport committee, shunning other areas of national political life. As noted earlier, the evangelical churches have also contributed to the party, and in so doing have captured the anti-secular education policy that *Fujimorismo* has advanced in Congress.[52] Moreover, as part of the investigations into money laundering in FP's campaign funding, the general manager of Credicorp (a financial holding company) admitted that the company had given almost U$S 4 million in cash to Keiko Fujimori's candidacy. Coincidentally, the FP fiercely opposed the introduction of public information on food quality, measures with which Alicorp – a subsidiary of Credicorp that controls 30 percent of the Peruvian food industry – was also at odds.

As to informal interests, the interviewees single out proximity to informal mining. During the 2016 presidential campaign, Keiko Fujimori signed an agreement with sectorial actors in support of repealing legislation that distinguishes informal from unlawful mining, regulates prohibitions on the latter, and makes provisions for the formalization and registration of small-scale miners.[53] It is well known that informal interests seek to practice mining unencumbered

[49] Ernesto Cabral y Aramís Castro, "Fiscalía: Fuerza Popular lavó US$ 1,2 millones con "pitufeo," remesas pendientes y aportes falsos" (*Ojo Público*, October 10, 2018). https://ojo-publico.com/883/fuerza-popular-lavo-us12-millones-con-pitufeo-dinero-offshore-remesas-fantasmas-y-aportes-falsos (last accessed June 5, 2020).

[50] Interview with Guido Lucioni, April 2018.

[51] Interview with Marisa Glave, May 2018.

[52] Interviews with Alberto de Belaunde and Juan Carlos Gonzáles, April 2018.

[53] "Keiko Fujimori firma compromiso con mineros informales para captar votos" (*La República*, April 29, 2016). https://larepublica.pe/politica/763857-keiko-fujimori-firma-compromiso-con-mineros-informales-para-captar-votos-video/ (last accessed June 5, 2020).

by regulations designed to protect Amazonia. Along similar lines, some highlight the approval of "infrastructure development" projects that involve the construction of roads and highways to facilitate unlawful activities.[54] One case that illustrates these connections is that of Modesto Figueroa, subjected to money laundering allegations. Figueroa is a congressional representative of Madre de Dios, a scene of illegal mining whose firms have been linked to the unlawful sale and transportation of fuel. In addition, one of his advisors is a former prosecutor who was dismissed for benefiting interests under investigation in the region.[55]

A lack of institutionalization in the selection of candidates, coupled with the prioritization of those able to fund their own campaigns, has seen the FP embroiled in a series of scandals involving all manner of complaints against legislators, exposing the extent to which informal and illegal interests have infiltrated the party. Five lawmakers are linked to money-laundering allegations, which also entail party financing during election campaigns. The accusations extend across the entire parliamentary group, including spokespersons. For instance, Héctor Becerril, a former Congress member and the FP's national secretary of organization, is under investigation for links to organized criminal gangs. Reflecting a prevailing view among the interviewees, a cadre in charge of selection conceded that "some, a lot, may have escaped us,"[56] while one legislator asked of some of her fellow *Fujimorista* representatives: "Where did we get them from? What kind of casting has there been?"[57]

As to the illegal interests that have penetrated the FP and its congressional grouping, many judicial and journalistic investigations point to narco-trafficking. Joaquín Ramírez, a former general secretary, was investigated for money laundering by the DEA; according to media reports, he had connections with individuals and organizations

[54] Interview with Marisa Glave, May 2018.

[55] "Informe: Las transacciones sospechosas de Modesto Figueroa" (*El Comercio*, July 20, 2017). https://elcomercio.pe/politica/transacciones-sospechosas-modesto-figueroa-informe-443663-noticia/ (last accessed June 5, 2020); "Congresista fujimorista Modesto Figueroa contrató como asesor a exfiscal destituido" (Radio Programas del Perú, April 22, 2018). https://rpp.pe/politica/congreso/figueroa-contrato-como-asesor-a-exfiscal-destituido-por-irregularidades-en-caso-de-mineria-ilegal-noticia-1118225 (last accessed June 5, 2020).

[56] Interview with José Chlimper, January 2018.

[57] Interview with Úrsula Letona, January 2018.

involved in the illegal drug trade.[58] Despite the allegations, Ramírez's brother was elected to Congress to represent the region of Cajamarca. More recently, another congressman, Edwin Vergara, was found to be in a business partnership with a drug trafficker.[59] And even Kenji Fujimori is under investigation, after several kilograms of cocaine were found on a site owned by a company in which he is a partner. Another *Fujimorista*, a spokesperson, has also been implicated in this haul.[60]

Legal, informal, and unlawful interests "buy" places on *Fujimorismo*'s congressional lists, and then steer the party's behavior in the legislature.[61] The legislators put in place by these varied actors deploy strategies to frustrate government initiatives, or propose their own to further their special interests. Examples include deliberate absences to prevent a quorum, last-minute telephone calls before votes, shelving of initiatives and freezing of bills. In a context in which the decision-making bodies largely set the agenda, and the majority party also commands a majority on congressional commissions and the Bureau, it is relatively easy for the FP to thwart, shelve or hasten specific projects – sparking complaints from other parties.[62]

Over the decade during which the FP consolidated itself, its main assets were an effective presidential candidate, sizable congressional groupings for two consecutive terms (2011 and 2016), and linkages with special interests, oftentimes informal and unlawful, that financed and shaped the party's legislative agenda. However, the second and third of these assets is dependent on the first. Indeed, the party's prospects of survival hinge on restoring Keiko Fujimori's reputation in the eyes of the electorate. *Fujimorismo* is a loose coalition, bound by a popular candidate who has acted as a powerful magnet in a political system populated by free agents. As a result, the FP has offset its horizontal and vertical shortcomings.

[58] "Papeles de la DEA revelan que Joaquín Ramírez era investigado desde el 2012" (*Ojo Público*, June 3, 2016). https://ojo-publico.com/241/los-papeles-de-la-dea (last accessed June 5, 2020).

[59] "Edwin Vergara constituyó empresa con narcotráfico que cayó con 800 kilos de cocaína" (Radio Programas del Perú, April 7, 2018). https://rpp.pe/politica/congreso/edwin-vergara-constituyo-empresa-con-narcotraficante-que-cayo-con-800-kilos-de-cocaina-noticia-1115116 (last accessed June 5, 2020).

[60] Correo, April 2018.

[61] Paulo Vilca, "¿Quiénes (y por qué) llegan al Congreso?" (*El Comercio*, May 10, 2018). https://elcomercio.pe/opinion/colaboradores/quienes-llegan-congreso-paulo-vilca-noticia-518883-noticia/ (last accessed June 2, 2020).

[62] For instance, the Ethics Committee has shelved more than ten complaints against *Fujimorista* legislators. In September 2019, for the second time, five members resigned from the committee, criticizing its composition and its misuse by the majority party.

PARTIES AND DEMOCRACY: BEYOND HORIZONTAL AND VERTICAL CAPACITIES

Returning to the framework of Luna et al., could *Fujimorismo* give rise to democratic representation? That is, if, over time, the FP succeeded in coordinating ambitious politicians and preventing their abandonment (horizontal aggregation); and if it institutionalized its links with the special interests that finance its campaigns (vertical interest aggregation), would it be providing representation befitting of a democratic system?

Parties are considered fundamental to democracy because in modern and representative polities, they channel citizens' demands – expressed through elections – and apply the idea of self-governance through representatives (Aldrich 1995; Mainwaring, Bejarano, and Pizarro 2006; Schattschneider 1942; Stokes 1999). But this function is distorted when parties neglect electoral outcomes or voters' preferences in favor of their campaign financiers. The FP's legislative agenda has owed more to these special interests than to its party platform. The party has served as a federation of special interests seeking to curb state regulation of their activities and to sponsor initiatives that further them, and not as a guarantor of democratic representation or institutions.

This tendency is consistent with the FP's repeated contravention of Peru's democracy and rule of law. In the terms of Javier Corrales (2015), we argue that the FP's congressional activities conform to "autocratic legalism." From 2016 to 2019, the majority-*Fujimorista* Congress weakened the Contralor General's (Comptroller General) ability to investigate Congress;[63] threatened the free functioning of the Attorney General, which had been investigating alleged acts of corruption, through a constitutional complaint against the lead prosecutor;[64] attempted to take control of the Constitutional Court;[65] sought to alter electoral competition rules to prevent the admission of new political proposals; tried to make major constitutional changes by amending the Regulations of Congress; reduced the investigative powers of the unit that oversees financial crimes; and endangered the press through a bill aimed at

[63] "El Congreso es el único ente público que elige a su contralor" (*La República*, March 30, 2018). https://larepublica.pe/politica/1219511-el-congreso-es-el-unico-ente-publico-que-elige-a-su-contralor/ (last accessed June 5, 2020).

[64] "Fiscal Salas: Tendrán que destituir a todos para evitar pesquisas" (*La República*, November 15, 2017). https://larepublica.pe/politica/1146242-fiscal-salas-tendran-que-destituir-a-todos-para-evitar-pesquisas/ (last accessed June 5, 2020).

[65] "Caso TC: fujimorismo aprueba recomendar la destitución y suspensión de magistrados" (*La República*, December 14, 2017). https://larepublica.pe/politica/1157954-fujimorismo-aprueban-destituir-y-suspender-a-magistrados-del-tc/ (last accessed June 5, 2020).

regulating state publicity in the media, among many other acts. In sum, the FP has actively undermined Peruvian liberal democracy in both its republican dimensions (representation to assure the self-governance of the country) and its liberal dimensions (checks and balances to impede accumulation of power). One can imagine that if *Fujimorismo* had taken the executive as well as the legislature, the consequences for Peruvian democracy would have been grave indeed.

This compels us to qualify the near-automatic enthusiasm with which political scientists greet political parties. That is, our evaluations must question the extent to which they are performing their duties of democratic representation. Around the world, parties have often been agents of stability but not necessarily of democratization (Brownlee 2007; Huntington 1968). Elsewhere in Latin America, Mexico's Partido Revolucionario Institucional (Institutional Revolutionary Party, PRI) was for decades a perfect example of a party machine that represented and stabilized the country without strengthening democracy. More recently, the Movimiento al Socialismo (Movement Toward Socialism, MAS) in Bolivia, Partido Socialista Unido de Venezuela (United Socialist Party of Venezuela, PSUV) in Venezuela, Alianza PAIS (PAIS Alliance, AP) in Ecuador (Conaghan this volume) and the Colorado Party in Paraguay (Abente Brun this volume) offer proof that parties can be antidemocratic agents. *Fujimorismo* is but another case of a party that is, in fact, a threat to democracy.

CONCLUSIONS

In this chapter, we have studied the FP as a stable actor in Peruvian politics. Aided by the concepts of horizontal coordination and vertical interest aggregation, we have seen that the party has had moderate success in keeping politicians under its roof and in coordinating strategies with them; but that, on the other hand, it lacks programmatic and organizational linkages conducive to a stable relationship with the population. In sum, *Fujimorismo* is a weak electoral coalition composed of politics devoid of major societal connections. Rather than being representatives of the nation, *Fujimorista* legislators resemble facilitators of special interests.[66]

[66] Eduardo Dargent, "Fujimorismo y Crisis de la justicia" (*La República*, July 20, 2018). https://larepublica.pe/politica/1282413-fujimorismo-crisis-justicia/ (last accessed June 2, 2020).

This leads us to two general conclusions. First, the FP is, essentially, just another Peruvian personalistic electoral vehicle in which congressional and subnational candidacies are offered to the highest bidder, to the neglect of established organizational or ideological relationships. And in common with the other players, the capacity to recruit good candidates reflects the electoral prospects of the party leader. So long as Keiko Fujimori's prospects of winning a presidential election were robust, the FP was a prized destination for political candidates. But once the leader was weakened, politicians had less of an incentive to select the FP as their vehicle of choice. When Keiko Fujimori seemed unlikely to win the presidency, the FP looked even more like Peru's other political vehicles.

It is important, therefore, to highlight the fact that, beyond the FP itself, the Peruvian political system dos not seem conducive to party building. Several critical variables have been identified as explanations for why "Peru may be the most extreme case of party collapse in Latin America" (Levitsky and Zavaleta 2016, 412). One perspective points to society: the increase in the size of the informal sector since the 1990s diluted the linkages between workers and parties (Cameron 1994; Martuccelli 2015). A more historical explanation suggests that the authoritarian regimes of Velasco Alvarado (1968–75) and Alberto Fujimori (1990–2000) defeated regional elites who used to compose the leadership of the country's main political parties (Vergara 2014). Several researchers also have pointed to the damaging legacies resulting from the campaign against the Shining Path (1980–94) (Soifer and Vergara 2019). On the political side, the fact that neoliberal reforms were introduced by an outsider who campaigned against the political establishment helped to disorganize the party system (Roberts 2014a). Finally, Levitsky and Zavaleta (2016) offer a path-dependent argument that, since the 1990s, Peruvian politicians have learned to play by the informal rules of a "democracy without parties" and, thus, lack any incentive to modify a game they have now mastered.

The second conclusion concerns the ultimate aim of this chapter: to observe the potential disconnect between the implicitly positive connotation of the term "party" when it is affixed to an electoral vehicle, and the actual political activity of that vehicle, which does nothing to provide democratic representation. In the case of *Fujimorismo*, its most important linkages have not been with specific social classes, organizations, or unions, but with campaign contributors, many of whom represent informal and unlawful interests and all of whom wish to see direct representatives of their interests in power. This is not liberal democratic representation. If *Fujimorismo* succeeds as a party, it will be the latest to fulfill the two functions theorized by Luna et al. at the expense of democracy.

13

The Unidad Nacional de la Esperanza: Guatemala's Only True Political Party?

Omar Sanchez-Sibony and Jonatán Lemus

INTRODUCTION

The Unidad Nacional de la Esperanza (National Unity of Hope, UNE) party is worthy of detailed study for at least two reasons: first, because it is the only nominally left-of-center party to have won a national election and to have held the executive branch during Guatemala's post-1985 democracy, which was otherwise dominated by conservative electoral vehicles; and secondly, because it is the only Guatemalan political organization during the democratic period that has been an electorally and legislatively relevant "party" over a considerable period, that is, a span of seventeen years (2003–20) and counting. For the purposes of this book and beyond, Guatemala constitutes an important case study because, arguably, in no other Latin American polity has the party concept been stretched so profusely and widely. Misclassifying electoral vehicles – mistaking them for full-fledged parties – can easily overstate their autonomy and power qua actors, while hindering the identification of the true central political actors. Only by understanding that Guatemala lacks political parties worthy of the name can we begin to come to grips with the country's empirical regularities, its anemic electoral democracy, and the unchanging nature of its political balance of power.

It is well known that electoral vehicles in Guatemala are short-lived (Sánchez 2008). The UNE stands as an exception. This raises the question of what has afforded the UNE its long endurance, which no other Guatemalan electoral vehicle has equaled during the country's thirty-five-year democratic era. The answer lies in the UNE's incipient party brand, a well-cultivated, on-the-ground party organization, as well as a base of clients in rural Guatemala who benefited from UNE-initiated conditional cash transfer (CCTs) programs and remained loyal to the organization. The UNE's longevity, however, does not necessarily grant it the status of a political party, as defined by Luna et al. in this volume. Indeed, an empirical evaluation of the UNE's horizontal coordination and vertical interest aggregation capabilities reveals that, as an organization, it fails along both dimensions. UNE party architects certainly intended to create a lasting political party, and for that purpose set out to accomplish three tasks: endow the party with an ideology, train and form new party cadres, and build on-the-ground organization. This ambition and vision of the future superseded that of all previous founders of electoral vehicles in Guatemala (except for the Democracia Cristiana Guatemalteca – Guatemalan Christian Democracy). In this, the UNE's origins were unique. However, the quest for power and the attendant imperatives of pragmatism, the individual political ambitions of some party heavy-weights, the incoherent internal configuration of the organization, and constraining structural factors specific to Guatemala all would soon transform the founders' original dreams into something much more prosaic, rendering the UNE an entity similar to the modal Guatemalan electoral vehicle, that is, "independents" (Luna et al. Introduction this volume). The UNE's horizontal coordination capacity was very limited, not least because its electoral competitiveness depended on instrumental arrangements with autonomous local caudillos (see Piñeiro, Rosenblatt, and Toro Maureira this volume). In Congress, the organization's ability to act as a cohesive, unified actor across time was low. In terms of vertical interest aggregation, the UNE mobilized the collective interests of the underprivileged in a general sense, but it did not intermediate social demands, whether in or out of the Executive. While it developed a loyal following in rural Guatemala and small urban environs via clientelist dynamics and an incipient party brand, its supporters had no input into, or ability to constrain, UNE policies. Thus UNE voters did not meet the standard of a bona fide constituency as defined in this volume.

THE ORIGINS AND EARLY TRAJECTORY OF THE UNE

The key political figure in the origins and early development of the UNE is Álvaro Colom Caballeros. Colom enjoyed independent political capital due to his family heritage: he was the nephew of the country's great symbol of social democracy and arguably its most salient political leader of the second half of the twentieth century, Manuel Colom Argueta, who was killed in 1979 by the high command of the military regime. This family lineage generated sympathy and natural support for Colom among social sectors and voters with left-wing inclinations. Colom had no organic links with the armed guerillas. He was an entrepreneur in the maquila business and a government functionary. Another biographical element in Álvaro Colom's professional trajectory that also served him well politically and electorally as he entered the national political stage was his time as director of the Fondo Nacional para la Paz (National Fund for Peace, FONAPAZ), the key agency entrusted with supervising the implementation of the historic 1996 Peace Accords. His stint at FONAPAZ – straddling the governments of Jorge Serrano, Ramiro de Leon Carpio, and Álvaro Arzú – enabled Colom to travel widely throughout the national territory and establish personal relationships and linkages with indigenous ancestral communities, labor unions, domestic NGOs, and social movements (Figueroa Ibarra 2010, 77–78). By all accounts, he proved an effective leader of the agency and a good manager of FONAPAZ programs. He established bonds of trust with the communities and organizations he dealt with, an outcome helped by his affable personality and his well-known consensus-driven approach to solving problems.

Colom first ran for president in 1999 as head of the Alianza Nueva Nación (New Nation Alliance, ANN), an alliance of left-wing political parties, which included the Unidad Revolucionaria Nacional Guatemalteca (Guatemalan National Revolutionary Unity, URNG). The ANN placed third in those general elections, the best showing for the political left in Guatemala's post-1985 democracy (Lehoucq 2002). It was at this juncture that Colom – cognizant of the debilitating divisions that plagued the four factions that composed the ANN – decided to create his own political organization: the UNE. In 2000, Colom made the political calculation that, in the context of a polarized and politically conservative country, running for the presidency atop an alliance of niche left-wing parties hindered his ambitions. Starting a new party could liberate him from the old feuds within the Left and its electoral liabilities. In that year, he announced publicly that he wanted to build a party that was "inclusive and participatory" (ASIES 2004).

The UNE was thus born in 2001 as a congressional splinter faction of the ANN, and throughout 2001 and 2002, it included lawmakers from Rios-Montt's Frente Republicano Guatemalteco (Guatemalan Republican Front), Álvaro Arzú's Partido Unionista (Unionist Party), and the ex-guerilla URNG. The UNE was built with political cadres from the old revolutionary party, former Christian democrats, and a potpourri of left-wing politicians, most of whom had substantial political experience. UNE party notables, with Colom at the head, sought to build a party with territorial organization, but also one that had a sectoral component that included peasants, women's movements and the indigenous population (personal interviews: Bolaños 2019, Núñez 2019; see Appendix).

The UNE's original architects were rather novel in the Guatemalan context in one important respect: they aimed to construct an organization with a real claim to representation and institutional longevity, as well as one endowed with programmatic content. For these purposes, a party institute was created to train future party cadres in public administration and socialize them into the main ideas of social democracy, with a view to the 2003 general election. In total, an estimated 5,000 trainees received a political education at UNE institutes by the 2007 general election. Citizenship party councils were created as part of the UNE organizational structure with a view to representing different sectors (women councils, peasants, Mayan/indigenous communities, cooperativists). The party aimed to eventually have an organized presence in all 330 of the country's municipal districts (personal interview: Monzón 2019). After 2003, intellectual Luis Zurita Tablada, a former candidate of the leftist Partido Socialista Democrático (Democratic Socialist Party, PSD) for the vice-presidency and author of the book *El ABC de la Socialdemocracia* (Zurita Tablada 2016), was integrated into the UNE with the task of developing the party's programmatic content. At a meeting in Escuintla, all the party delegates (more than 200) voted in favor of officially giving the party a social-democratic programmatic identity.

The UNE also sought to learn from foreign social-democratic parties. For example, some UNE party leaders traveled to Costa Rica and Spain to meet social-democratic politicians from the Partido Liberación Nacional (National Liberation Party, PLN) and the Partido Socialista Obrero Español (Spanish Socialist Workers´ Party, PSOE), respectively, in order to study their programmatic tenets and learn from their political experience.

In the 2003 general election, the UNE placed second, with over 26 percent of the vote, while earning thirty-two seats in Congress, the third-largest party in the chamber. It lost the second round of the presidential election to Oscar Berger's Gran Alianza Nacional (Grand National Alliance, GANA) (Azpuru 2005; Gálvez Borrell 2004). Unlike other party formations, the UNE's activities did not come to a halt after the general elections. The party established workshops and courses, which lasted from 2003 to 2008, with the aim of training future UNE congressional representatives and city mayors. Some of those who enrolled in the courses later became secretaries of state, mayors, and mid-level state administrators (personal interviews: Monzón 2019, Alejos 2019).

The results of the 2007 general elections confirmed the UNE's ascendant trajectory, with the party earning 28.2 percent of the vote in the first round, enough to advance to the second round. Álvaro Colom won the presidency in 2007 with 52.8 percent of the vote in the runoff, and the UNE obtained a sizable fifty-one-seat plurality in Congress. The geographic distribution of the UNE's support extended to all of the rural and poorest provinces of Guatemala, while the Partido Patriota (Patriot Party, PP) won decisively in the capital (Sabino 2007). The UNE's victory was novel in that no other party had previously won the presidency by earning the support of rural constituencies while losing the Ciudad de Guatemala metropolitan area (comprising about 25 percent of registered voters) (Azpuru and Blanco 2008, 231). Thereafter, elections in 2011, 2015, and 2019 confirmed the UNE's status as a systemic player, displaying a level of intertemporal electoral stability (both congressional and presidential) previously unseen in Guatemala's democracy. Indeed, what distinguishes the UNE from other electoral vehicles in Guatemala is its political longevity as a systemic electoral vehicle. Since 2003, the UNE has always placed among the top three vote getters in presidential elections, and, because of its loyal supporters, it has advanced to the runoff no fewer than four times (see Table 13.1). It won the presidency in 2007. Its performance in congressional elections has been similarly consistent: the party has enjoyed one of the three largest congressional caucuses in the 2003–19 period. The UNE currently comprises the largest congressional caucus in the 2020–4 legislature. However, the UNE's consistent electoral performance was achieved despite enormous deficiencies in its ability to coordinate and maintain the loyalty of its congressional caucuses and regional representatives over time. Figure 13.1 compares the UNE's electoral trajectory with that of the most important parties to have populated the Guatemalan landscape in terms of their intertemporal electoral strength: the Partido Democrata Cristiano Guatemalteco (Guatemalan Christian Democratic Party), the Partido de Avanzada Nacional (National Advancement Party), the Frente Republicano Guatemalteco (Guatemalan Republican Front, FRG), and the Partido Patriota (Patriot Party).

HORIZONTAL COORDINATION IN THE UNE

The following sections seek to elucidate the degree to which the UNE has been able to enforce horizontal coordination in different arenas: candidate

TABLE 13.1 *Electoral performance of the UNE, 2003–2019*

	2003	2007	2011[1]	2015	2019
Presidential first round	707,635 (26%)	926,236 (28%)	–[2]	948,809 (17%)	1,122,909 (26%)
Presidential runoff	1,046,744 (46%)	1,449,533 (53%)	–[3]	1,328,342 (32%)	1,384,112 (42%)
Congressional elections	457,308 (20%)	720,285 (22%)	985,610 (22%)	676,080 (15%)	724,517 (18%)
Seats in Congress	32 (20%)	51 (32%)	48 (30%)	32 (20%)	52 (32%)
Local governments	37 (11%)	103 (31%)	94 (28%)	62 (18%)	107 (31%)

1 UNE competed in an electoral alliance with Gran Alianza Nacional (Grand National Alliance, GANA).
2 UNE did not have a presidential candidate.
3 No runoff.
Sources: Informe analítico proceso electoral ASIES 2004, 2007, 2011; Memoria electoral Tribunal Supremo Electoral 2015; Tribunal Supremo Electoral preliminary results website 2019.

selection for mayoral races and congressional seats, the articulation of coordinated political and electoral strategy between the center and local governments, and party discipline in Congress.

UNE's Candidate Selection: Personalistic and Clientelistic Dynamics

Parties with high levels of horizontal coordination are capable of monopolizing candidate selection, which implies that they authorize party nominations at all levels and prospective candidates accept the results of those processes. Effective party monopoly can result from institutional variables, such as district magnitude and list type (Carey and Shugart 1995), reelection rules, geographic organization, as well as contextual variables such as the degree of party centralization, party organization, and campaign finance models (Siavelis and Morgenstern 2008b).

In Guatemala, the candidate selection process is shaped by the institutional weakness and permissiveness inherent in the formal rules established by the Ley Electoral y de Partidos Politicos (Electoral and Political Parties Law), which have incentivized Guatemalan electoral vehicles to create informal institutions to suit their interests qua organizations. A first overarching objective of the electoral law in Guatemala is to foster party

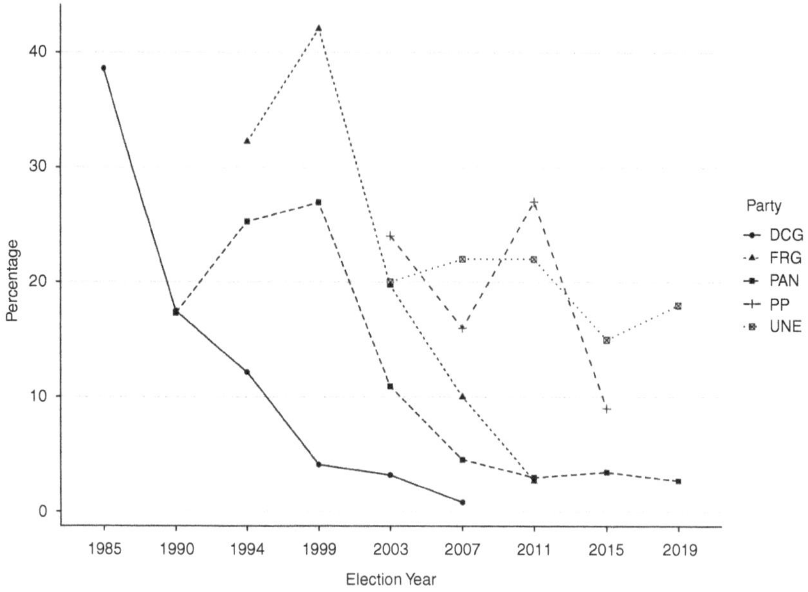

FIGURE 13.1 Votes in congressional elections, 1985–2019
Source: Tribunal Supremo Electoral.

nationalization, that is, to aid the formation of parties with presence throughout the national territory. A second general objective of the legal framework is to foster internal party democracy via a bottom-up candidate selection mechanism (personal interview: García Cuyún 2013). Guatemalan electoral vehicles' interests dovetail with the first objective, but not with the second one. To accomplish party nationalization, which furthers electoral competitiveness, large parties in Guatemala make use of a substitutive informal institution, defined as one that "enables actors to achieve goals that formal institutions were designed, but fail, to achieve" (Levitsky 2012, 92). This substitutive informal institution is a franchise-type arrangement with local strongmen. These arrangements help lower the prohibitive costs of pursuing party nationalization using the party's resources alone. The cost of nationalization is lowered by delegating the task and cost of grassroots organization to local and regional strongmen (see Abente Brun this volume, and Piñeiro Rodríguez, Rosenblatt, and Toro Maureira this volume).

Parties in Guatemala are uninterested in implementing internal democracy mechanisms, as mandated by the law. They effectively establish competing informal institutions that actively encourage the subversion of the formal rules. The Electoral and Political Parties Law establishes the procedure that all parties must follow to pick candidates. The selection of candidates is supposed to take place in assemblies: municipal assemblies that elect candidates for local governments (Article 47 b, c); departmental assemblies elect candidates for congressional district list; and national assemblies elect candidates for president and for the congressional party national list (Article 47e). In order to participate in elections, parties in Guatemala are expected to register a minimum of fifty municipal assemblies, out of a total of 340 municipalities; and they must register twelve departmental assemblies, out of the country's twenty-two departments (Article 49c). But, regardless of the letter and spirit of the formal rules, informal dynamics end up partially centralizing candidate selection in the hands of party elites. This occurs partly because the electoral law is ineffective, but also because it is permissive, in that it leaves room for national committees to directly pick candidates for local governments and Congress in those municipalities and departments where there is no formally registered committee (Electoral Law Article 29d, Brolo 2012).

Most political parties in Guatemala do not go much beyond the minimum number of municipal committees needed to meet legal requirements (Jones 2011; Lemus 2012). According to Brolo (2013), for the 2011 election, the twenty-nine registered political parties recorded an average of eighty-one organized municipal committees. By this measure, the UNE performed slightly better than other parties. In 2011, the UNE registered the third-largest number of official municipal committees with 104 (Brolo 2013), out of a total of 304. In 2019, the UNE had the most municipal organizations of any party in the country: it registered 107 municipal committees (Figueroa 2019). While these municipal committees purportedly enjoy autonomy, national party leaders regularly and informally become involved in candidate selection (Barreda 2013). The UNE, like other parties, used tactics such as registering new members in a municipal assembly to oppose the local candidate, appealing candidate registration to the Electoral Tribunal,[1] or negotiating a new arrangement in which the initial candidate agrees to take a different position in the party lists (personal interview: Barreda 2013). These regularly employed tactics constitute competing informal institutions that directly contravene the

[1] "Rechazan recurso de UNE: diputado de edecanes buscará la reelección." (Soy502, July 13, 2015). https://www.soy502.com/articulo/diputado-edecanes-si-podra-buscar-reeleccion (last accessed May 22, 2020).

formal legal framework. These informal institutions include sanctions such as social exclusion or the restriction of access to goods and services (Lauth 2015). The UNE candidates who did not go along with these informal arrangements faced both types of sanctions.

Candidate selection is also shaped by contextual factors, as Siavelis and Morgenstern (2008b) suggest. The key contextual factor in Guatemala is the entrenchment of "politico-economic networks"[2] at the local level, to use CICIG's (2015) terminology. Notwithstanding the ability of parties to circumvent the spirit and letter of the electoral law, effective candidate selection monopoly in the UNE is seriously undermined because its national leaders actively engage in the common practice of hiring local caudillos. When deciding on candidates, the party has searched for leaders at the department level, preferably district congressmen who, in turn, recruit candidates for mayor.[3] Because national leaders seek to decrease the costs of fulfilling the legal requirements of party territorial presence, they search for departmental and municipal leaders who will assume these costs; in exchange, the local leaders obtain an electoral vehicle to participate in elections (Lemus 2013; Waxenecker 2019). This is the mutually beneficial transaction that Lemus (2013) has conceptualized as the franchise party model. All large parties in Guatemala partake in these transactional arrangements, including the UNE. The deliberate inclusion of politically resourceful local caudillos into the UNE accelerated during Álvaro Colom's presidency (2007–11). These strongmen had little in common with the party's ideology, nor had they graduated from the UNE's training workshops.[4] The reason Álvaro Colom and his circle welcomed them into the UNE rested upon the fact that these caudillos provided the most sought-after political resources: a ready-made pool of clientelistic networks and autonomous political financing. Notwithstanding internal tensions and disagreements about the decision, Álvaro Colom considered these caudillos "a necessary evil," as he put it in private, in order to win elections and remain electorally competitive

[2] The CICIG describes these networks as follows: "Guatemala's politico-economic networks involve politicians, functionaries of the state, judges, lawyers, military officials, and businessmen who together establish ties to engage in illicit criminal activity and ensure impunity. ... Their infiltration in the institutions of the state allow these networks to extract public resources, particularly by becoming state contractors" (CICIG 2015). All direct quotes that appear in the chapter were translated from Spanish by the authors.

[3] Personal communication with Oscar Argueta, September 4, 2019.

[4] "UNE y el caudillo de Alta Verapaz, la sombra de la alcaldesa Lilian García." (*RepúblicaGT*, July 14, 2017). http://republica.gt/2017/07/24/une-y-el-caudillo-de-alta-verapaz-la-sombra-de-la-alcaldesa-lilian-garcia/ (last Accessed May 22, 2020).

(personal interview: Bolaños 2019). Thus, the path of the UNE's convergence with other Guatemalan parties – mercantilist in nature, and ruthlessly pragmatic in its modus operandi – was forged. The implication of this discussion is that parties' prospects for monopolizing candidate selection, the UNE included, are seriously undermined by the indispensability of some local caudillos.

Scant Coordination between Center and Local UNE Governments

The electoral vehicles that populate the Guatemalan landscape tend not to employ formal mechanisms to coordinate either electoral strategy during campaigns or their relationship with mayors between elections. In this respect, as in many others, the UNE does not differ from its competitors. During the 2007 campaign, the UNE tried to coordinate their candidates for Congress and local governments by establishing some informal rules. According to Roberto Alejos (personal interview: 2019), former UNE member at the time, "the leaders of the Training Institute worked very hard to spread party ideas to local leaders and recruit candidates and unify our campaign messages." There was a government plan, called "The Green Book" (in allusion to the party's color), which contained all the public policies promoted by Álvaro Colom. Furthermore, the party established an informal requirement, namely, only billboard ads featuring the UNE's presidential candidate were allowed in the campaign. However, candidates for Congress with ample personal financial resources, such as Eduardo Meyer or Manuel Baldizón, did not respect such rules and deployed a large amount of self-promoting publicity on the streets (personal interview: Alejos 2019).

The UNE candidates for local government and for Congress employ mixed campaign strategies. On the one hand, they follow a programmatic party line emphasizing the return of social programs; on the other hand, they follow a clientelistic appeals strategy, catering to local basic needs (Dalmasso 2019).[5] The coordination of electoral strategies across territories and levels of government has been weak throughout UNE's history. The micromanagement leadership style and concentration of power in the person of Sandra Torres after 2011, as well as the introduction of the social programs, may have improved coordination. Local candidates

[5] See also "Video de edecán de la UNE causa indignación en las redes sociales" (Soy502, April 16, 2015). www.soy502.com/articulo/video-edecan-une-causa-indignacion-redes-sociales (last accessed May 22, 2020).

followed the programmatic party line with respect to social programs, but they retained freedom to carry out personalistic campaign strategies, alongside a staple of Guatemalan campaigns: clientelism.[6] In sum, the UNE has improvised informal and ephemeral coordination mechanisms of campaign strategy, but with limited success and no means of enforcement. The operational and political autonomy of many UNE local caudillos has granted them plenty of latitude to fashion their own campaigns and conduct politics as they see fit.

Party Discipline in Congress

The legislature is yet another arena where the UNE's inability to enforce horizontal coordination is laid bare. Like other large electoral vehicles in Guatemala, it has been beset by high levels of party switching. The literature identifies an array of institutional factors that shape legislative party discipline, including, chiefly, electoral systems, rules governing reelection, party system institutionalization, internal party rules, and internal legislative rules (Morgenstern and Nacif 2002). Guatemala's institutional framework contains elements that alternatively facilitate and hinder party discipline in Congress (Novales 2015). The electoral system provides incentives for party discipline: plurinominal districts and close lists, and candidate selection mechanisms; decision-making can be exclusive and centralized. However, three other institutional factors hinder party discipline: congressmen have no legal impediments preventing them from forming a caucus inside Congress without a party (only prohibited after the 2016 reforms); rules allow for reelection; and there is ample opportunity for congressional candidates to obtain private funding.

High levels of party discipline in the Guatemalan Congress are reported by Fortín (2010) and Jones (2011). In addition, the median Rice Score for Guatemalan parties stands at 0.96 for the 1996–9 period, 1.00 for the years 2000–3, and 0.98 for the 2004–7 period, indicating a very high level of party discipline.[7] However, these authors also agree that these indicators are artificially inflated due to the frequency with which congressmen switch parties. In other words, the very meaning and measurement of

[6] See also "Así Funciona el clientelismo, con Ejemplos de UNE y VAMOS" (Gustavo Herrarte, Plaza Pública, August 7, 2019); "Sandra Torres visita Chiantla y ofrece programas sociales" (Daniel Tzoc, *PubliNews*, July 27, 2019). www.publinews.gt/gt/noticias/2019/07/27/sandra-torres-chiantla-huehuetenango.html (last accessed May 22, 2020).

[7] See Piñeiro Rodríguez, Rosenblatt, and Toro Maureira this volume for more details on the Rice Index.

party discipline is highly diluted when electoral vehicles regularly lose a large portion of their legislative caucuses. A standard rational choice explanation yields much insight into the pervasive party switching seen in Guatemala (Fortín 2010; Jiménez Badillo 2018), which exhibits one of the highest rates in the world. In the context of extremely high vote volatility, Guatemalan representatives have every incentive to switch parties in order to increase their probabilities of being reelected. The fact that UNE representatives have not behaved differently than other party lawmakers pours cold water on the notion that the party's social-democratic ideology or its professed vocation to be a durable organization would help the party's horizontal coordination in the legislature. In practice, UNE legislators have behaved as free agents.

In order to illustrate the historical inability of the UNE to elicit party loyalty in the legislature, Figure 13.2 briefly outlines the key junctures as regards the electoral vehicle's internal dynamics, divisions, and splits, from its creation to the present day. The UNE suffered from party switching shortly after entering the legislature, and was crippled by *en masse* defections (twenty-six members) while in government, and later suffered an even larger parliamentary exodus (forty-one members) when two key party notables exited to create their own parties. The prevalence of party switching over time constitutes the best indicator of the UNE's inability to maintain loyalty and coordination among its office-seeking members in Congress.

VERTICAL AGGREGATION

Mobilization of Collective Interests

The early leaders of the UNE described the party as having aspirations to become a democratic platform and a "channel of expression of popular sectors" (ASIES 2004, 122). Among its declared ambitions was the reconstruction of Guatemala's social fabric, the promotion of participatory development, such that those who had never been able to participate in political life because of their low social status could do so (ASIES 2004, 122). In his inaugural address, President Colom declared that he came to the presidency with "the purpose of converting Guatemala into a social democratic country, but with a Maya face, and the smell of corn" (*El País* 2008).[8]

[8] "El "rostro maya" sigue ausente en el Gobierno de Guatemala." (*El País*, March 6, 2008). https://elpais.com/internacional/2008/03/07/actualidad/1204844405_850215.html (last accessed May 25, 2020).

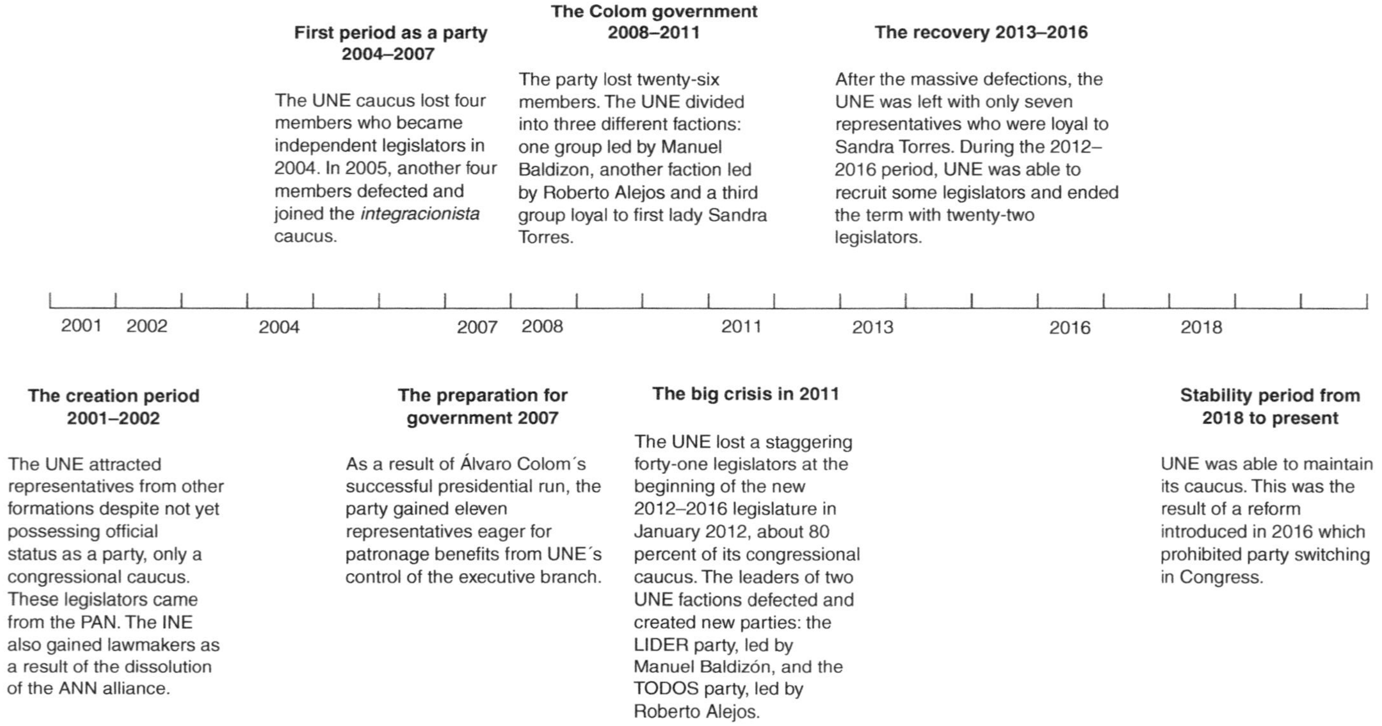

The Colom government 2008–2011
First period as a party 2004–2007
The recovery 2013–2016
The UNE caucus lost four members who became independent legislators in 2004. In 2005, another four members defected and joined the *integracionista* caucus.
The party lost twenty-six members. The UNE divided into three different factions: one group led by Manuel Baldizon, another faction led by Roberto Alejos and a third group loyal to first lady Sandra Torres.
After the massive defections, the UNE was left with only seven representatives who were loyal to Sandra Torres. During the 2012–2016 period, UNE was able to recruit some legislators and ended the term with twenty-two legislators.
2001
2002
2004
2007
2008
2011
2013
2016
2018
The creation period 2001–2002
The preparation for government 2007
The big crisis in 2011
Stability period from 2018 to present
The UNE attracted representatives from other formations despite not yet possessing official status as a party, only a congressional caucus. These legislators came from the PAN. The INE also gained lawmakers as a result of the dissolution of the ANN alliance.
As a result of Álvaro Colom´s successful presidential run, the party gained eleven representatives eager for patronage benefits from UNE´s control of the executive branch.
The UNE lost a staggering forty-one legislators at the beginning of the new 2012–2016 legislature in January 2012, about 80 percent of its congressional caucus. The leaders of two UNE factions defected and created new parties: the LIDER party, led by Manuel Baldizón, and the TODOS party, led by Roberto Alejos.
UNE was able to maintain its caucus. This was the result of a reform introduced in 2016 which prohibited party switching in Congress.

FIGURE 13.2 Key moments in UNE party switching, 2001–2019

But once in office those promises were promptly forgotten. While the indigenous vote was essential in delivering the presidency to the UNE, the Colom government's public policy "ignored substantive indigenous concerns" either "in the form of funding or legislative attention" (Isaacs 2010, 117). In important respects, the UNE treated the indigenous community as a clientelistic base ripe for electoral co-optation, chiefly via cash transfer programs. It did not invest in creating a much-needed programmatic linkage with indigenous constituencies.

In the exercise of executive power, UNE leaders developed the idea of constructing a voter constituency, one focused on rural spaces as well as intermediate-sized cities (so called *ciudades departamentales*), which are demographically fed by internal rural migrants. This targeted group of low-income and poor Guatemalans would be politically cultivated via social spending programs. These programs were coordinated by the Consejo de Cohesion Social (Social Cohesion Council), which First Lady Sandra Torres created and managed, by all accounts with a view toward building a loyal voting base that could be leveraged to serve her future presidential ambitions (Fuentes Knight 2011 and personal interview: Robles 2019). She and other UNE operatives aimed to make women the subject of conditional cash transfer funds and place women at the center of social policy. Women were underrepresented in the electoral roster: in 2003, women represented only 46 percent of the roster but 52 percent of the overall Guatemalan population. The UNE, from its early days, sought to not only cultivate the female rural vote but also to register female voters. A UNE-sponsored electoral reform in 2006 created the Registro Nacional de las Personas (National People's Registry, RENAP) and a new document that citizens needed in order to enroll in the national roster. The UNE's tireless and successful efforts to enhance women's representation in the national voting registry was reflected in the 2007 election, by which time women composed 51 percent of the registry, a sizable increase in four years. The reforms expanded political rights and citizenship rights and promoted gender equity, while they concurrently aligned with the UNE's politico-electoral interests. The new potential voters and recipients of cash transfer programs constituted a large prospective pool of electoral support for the UNE. Moreover, female electoral registration correlated with levels of participation. Lehoucq and Wall (2004, 497) showed that in Guatemala "municipalities with larger numbers of registered female voters have higher turnout rates than those with fewer women registered to vote."

The flagship social program created by the UNE was a conditional cash transfer (CCT) scheme called Mi Familia Progresa (My Family Progresses,

MIFAPRO). The political importance of this program for understanding the UNE's trajectory is threefold. First, it solidified a base of electoral and political support for the party in Guatemala's rural districts. Second, it endowed the party with an incipient socio-cultural party brand, whereby the UNE became the "party of the poor" in the collective imagination. Third, it gave the UNE qua organization added political value in the eyes of local leaders and strongmen. MIFAPRO and Bolsa Solidaria (Solidarity Bag) were intended to augment the UNE's electoral performance in the 2011 general elections and beyond, while burnishing the party's leftist credentials.

MIFAPRO began as a form of programmatic mobilization on the part of the UNE, but it became more clientelistic over time. The program was particularly politicized in the targeting of additional beneficiaries and clientelistic vote buying (Sandberg and Tally 2015). As the most comprehensive examination of MIFAPRO concludes:

> [The program] stands out as an aggravated case of politicization due to the blatant vote-buying, the threats of expulsion from the program based on electoral outcomes, and the fact that benefit-payment events were turned into outright political rallies. (Sandberg and Tally 2015, 513)

The UNE was successful in associating the CCT with the UNE in rural voters' minds. This politicization of the conditional cash transfer programs paid off for the party. Fortin and Naveda (2012) find evidence that the social programs had a positive effect on the UNE's 2011 regional vote patterns, consistent with other scholarly findings that conclude that beneficiaries of CCTs vote for incumbents at higher rates in subnational areas with higher CCT coverage (De La O 2013). The fact that the succeeding right-wing PP government dismantled MIFAPRO and created a new CCT program, Mi Bono Seguro (My Security Bonus), which offered a much lower level of benefits (around one-third of the MIFAPRO budget) to far fewer recipients, helped entrench the UNE's party brand as the "party of the poor" among former MIFAPRO recipients.

Early evidence demonstrating that the social programs had created an important constituency for the UNE came in the 2011 general elections. Sandra Torres was not allowed to participate as a candidate because of a Constitutional Court ruling, but the statistical data shows a direct relationship between the district beneficiaries of MIFAPRO and null votes in the first round of the 2011 election, following UNE appeals to cast null ballots (Fortin and Naveda 2012). The social programs helped create what became the UNE's core constituency: rural female voters and their families.

The stability in the electoral performance of the UNE post-2011, after its tenure in government, has been unprecedented in Guatemala's democratic period. Incumbency has constituted a lethal electoral liability for all governmental parties, with the UNE as the sole exception. After four years in office, the Colom administration had a poor showing on standard measures of governmental performance: crime and other measures of citizen insecurity did not improve, nor did the economy experience significant GDP growth (Rosal 2012). Cases of corruption occurred during the Colom administration, leading to the ouster of several tainted ministers and "a high rotation in the cabinet contributing to a deterioration in public administration" (Rosal 2012, 179). Moreover, the high profile of the Rosemberg scandal – which involved accusations of presidential involvement in the assassination of a businessman, later proven false – permanently eroded the government's legitimacy. In line with previous administrations, the popularity of the Colom government (2007–11) declined rather dramatically after a few months in office, showcasing once more the "incumbent disadvantage" phenomenon by which state weakness contributes to lackluster governmental performance in public goods delivery (Klašnja 2016; Sánchez-Sibony 2016). Therefore, governmental performance cannot account for the UNE's notably good 2011 legislative electoral results or for its high electoral competitiveness in the post-Colom era.

The self-styled leftist UNE developed a core constituency among underprivileged rural communities not because of programmatic voting. Comparative evaluations reveal Guatemala to exhibit one of the lowest levels of program-based voting in Latin America both before and after the UNE's administration (2007–11). The UNE did not move Guatemala toward stable programmatic political competition; clientelistic, valence-based, and personalistic political dynamics continue to dominate. But the UNE did activate class-based voting, as it emerged as a viable left-wing electoral option. The UNE's electoral platform included not only the promise of more inclusive representation, but also the general basic need demands of poor rural and poor urban dwellers.

The available empirical evidence shows that the UNE's organizing strategy from 2003 to 2007, during the organization's formative years, worked in activating class-based voting: Colom fared much better among the poorest voters in the 2007 election in comparison to the 2003 election (Mainwaring, Torcal, and Somma 2016) – when he did only somewhat better than the opposition in attracting poor voters. The UNE's core constituency was forged as a result of a (segmented) appeals strategy that promised to represent the politically invisible, poor, and marginalized social groups; and secondly, as a result of UNE-initiated social programs and their politicization. It is often overlooked that clientelism "can be an important means of stabilizing electoral competition" (Mainwaring and Torcal 2006, 210). The clientelistic implementation of MIFAPRO and Solidarity Bag programs helped forge a rather durable linkage between the UNE and their voters that has lasted to the present day. The results and geographic distribution of the vote in the general elections of 2007, 2011, 2015, and 2019 demonstrated that UNE's intertemporal vote stability emanated from voter loyalty in rural districts and medium-sized urban centers. In conclusion, the UNE did electorally mobilize collective interests, both by means of its electoral platform (however general in nature) and by developing a core constituency. However, it is a constituency that had little voice in, or capacity to constrain, party decisions.

The UNE in Power: The Nonintermediation of Social Demands

All manner of Guatemalan social organizations, after many years of neglect, derision, and even repression by successive conservative governments, expected that the UNE's putative left-of-center government would be receptive to their demands and grievances. Peasants, who had been discriminated against by the policies of the Berger government (2003–7), including suffering arbitrary expulsion from various lands and the multiplication of unresolved land conflicts, also placed high hopes on the UNE government. The Mayan community expected that Colom's "Mayan face" government would respond to their greviances (personal interview: Lux de Coti 2019). Cooperativist groups and labor unions publicly threw their support behind the UNE in the 2007 elections. The UNE enjoyed good relations with the Unidad de Accion Sindical y Popular (Popular and Union Action Unity, UASP), the country's flagship labor union, and the Asamblea Nacional del Magisterio (Teachers' National Assembly), the largest teachers' union. The Colectivo de Organizaciones Sociales (Social Organizations Collective, COS) granted its tacit support to the UNE in the 2007 elections, and two of its leaders, Orlando Blanco and Jairo Flores, joined Colom's cabinet. Because this was the first leftist government of the post-1985 era, and because its programmatic agenda contained progressive elements, lower-class sectors had reason to believe a UNE government would constitute a departure from previous administrations. But the hopes that social sectors placed upon the Colom government were thoroughly dashed. The political honeymoon with the social sectors was short-lived.

One of the most prominent developments in the evolution of Guatemala's postwar civil society is the increased number of indigenous communities that organized to defend their territories and natural resources (Bastos and Brett 2010). Protests mounted by these communities have burgeoned in tandem with the large increase in extractive economic activity. Large scale mining projects have multiplied in Guatemala since the early 2000s (Almeida 2014), resulting in a 1,000 percent increase (ten-fold) in mining contracts and licenses issued between 1998 and 2008 to multinational firms with operations in Guatemala (Dougherty 2011). Many popular consultations convoked by rural Mayan communities in the municipalities situated in San Marcos, Quiche, Huehuetenango, and Solola have systematically rejected open mining operations (Véliz and Yagenova 2009). Organized grassroots protests against large hydroelectricity and mining projects are examples of Guatemalans' growing popular rejection of an extractive model of economic development based on the exploitation of commodities, a model that alters labor relations and damages land property rights. The UNE came to power in this context of fraught relations between, on one hand, the Guatemalan state and extractive multinationals, and, on the other, affected communities.

The UNE's first year in office revealed that the party would not promote redress of its constituents' most pressing grievance, namely, extractive economic activity. A plethora of ongoing or new extractive projects generated organized social opposition during the first months of the UNE's government, including open mining in the Department of San Marcos; resistance to the construction of a hydroelectric plant in Xalala; protests by peasant communities in Livingston due to agrarian problems; resistance against the forced expulsion of peasants and forced buying of lands by MNCs investing in sugar cane and African palm oil in Peten and Alta Verapaz; protests against mining in the region of Huehuetenango and in other regions (UDEFEGUA 2008). In these and other cases, the rhetoric of the Colom government obviated the legitimate concerns articulated in the protests. Moreover, it often stigmatized the social organizations that orchestrated them. Prominent among such organizations leading the resistance to extractivist activity were peasant federations such as the Comité de Unidad Campesina (Peasants' Unity Committee, CUC), the Coordinadora Nacional Indígena y Campesina (National Indigenous and Peasants Coordinator, CONIC), and the Coordinadora Nacional de Organizaciones Campesinas (National Coordinator of Peasants Organizations, CNOC). These organizations fought against forced resettlements, environmental contamination, and repressive acts by multinational corporations. Many mayors and local leaders also fought against these practices. Organized municipal resistance, embodied in the Consejos Municipales de Desarrollo Urbano y Rural (Municipal Councils of Urban and Rural Development, COMUDE) also ensued during the UNE's period in government. Previous Guatemalan governments had resorted to criminalizing social protests to delegitimize them. To the chagrin of civil society actors which hoped the UNE government could effectively mediate these state-society conflicts, President Colom also criminalized protests – as denounced by several social sector organizations (Samayoa 2008; UDEFEGUA 2008). The government often responded to peaceful societal contestation with repression, using the police, marines, and the army. In some regions, the government declared a state of emergency to bring protestors to heel, as in San Juan de Saquetepez.[9] The International Labor Organization Convention 169, which enshrines indigenous and tribal peoples' right of consultation, was ratified by the Guatemalan Congress in 1996. However, "in practice Indigenous consultation in Guatemala has been reduced to a simple exercise in community dialogue carried out by municipal governments" (Elias and Sánchez 2014). The UNE government, in line with its predecessors, awarded licenses to the extractive industry without consulting affected indigenous communities, brazenly violating Guatemalan law.

One of the sole areas where the UNE government showcased some vertical interest aggregation functions concerned human rights and historical accountability for past crimes. The Colom government ordered the declassification of some military archives, while it also increased reparations payments to survivors of the civil conflict (1954–96) made by the previous administrations.[10] President Colom also officially asked for forgiveness for the Guatemalan state's offenses during the civil war.[11] In his official speeches, the UNE's leader championed the 1944 Revolution and the progressive legacy of President Jacobo Arbenz interrupted by the

[9] See also: "Protesta contra Cementera tensa ambiente antiminero" (Inforpress, 1755, June 6, 2008).

[10] "Payments and Apologies for Victims of Guatemala's Civil War" (Anne-Marie O'Connor, *Washington Post*, May 6, 2009).

[11] "Presidente pide perdón a víctimas de conflicto armado en Quiche" (*Gobierno de Guatemala*, August 28, 2008).

1954 coup. These symbolic gestures were a departure from previous democratic Guatemalan governments. In political terms, they were a low-cost way for the UNE to represent social demands and burnish its (otherwise tarnished) leftist credentials.

Beyond an agency-centered analysis of the UNE's modus operandi, it is germane to contextualize its actions within the broader setting: there are important structural factors inherent to the Guatemalan political landscape that constrain any party's potential to act as a vehicle for aggregating interests and demands. An important structural factor limiting vertical accountability is the exceedingly weak and fragmented nature of Guatemala's civil society. Even the largest organizations that purportedly represent sectors such as peasants, Mayans, cooperatives, labor unions, and others are very small and possess weak links with those in whose name they claim to speak (Fonseca 2004; Pallister 2013). For example, the Mayan social movement exhibits a dispersed pattern of social mobilization and bewildering levels of fragmentation (Pallister 2013). Some of the most well-known organizations are NGOs sponsored and financed by western donors, rather than organizations that have organically emerged bottom-up from Guatemalan society. As a result, the absence of large, representative, and organic mobilizing structures in Guatemala hampered the UNE's ability to serve as a conduit of lower-class political demands. Moreover, the UNE judged that incorporating social organizations into party decision-making structures did not endow the party with the political capital necessary to confront the private sector in pushing for left-of-center policy initiatives (personal interviews: Bolaños 2019, Robles 2019). In other words, even to the extent that some of the UNE's leading cadres were committed to the representation of social sectors, they were cognizant of the severe political limitations, and scant party benefits inherent in expending political capital to fight for the interests of such sectors. In this assessment, the UNE, notwithstanding its left-of-center representative aspirations, made the same political calculus as all other major Guatemalan parties in the post-1985 democratic era.

A second structural factor that explains the inability of Guatemalan political parties to respond to social sectors, underprivileged groups, and neglected minorities, is the central role of money. Securing campaign contributions from millionaires "has become the critical factor for accessing political power" (González 2014, 403) in Guatemala. On a cost-per-capita basis, Guatemalan elections rank alongside those of the United States as the most expensive in the Western Hemisphere.[12] The absence of programmatic politics and loyal constituencies further enhances the role of money in winning elections, for a priori electoral loyalty cannot be counted upon in a marketplace of floating voters. Conservative and right-wing parties are the natural beneficiaries of private funding. During electoral campaigns, leftist party formations are systematically outspent by right-wing competitors by many orders of magnitude (Acción Ciudadana 2012). Colom, Sandra Torres, and their inner circle were highly cognizant of such structural conditions hobbling left-wing parties. In their efforts to promote the UNE's electoral competitiveness, they displayed enormous (unprincipled) pragmatism: to buttress party coffers, the UNE sought financing from corrupt businessmen hailing from the emerging sector (most prominently pharmaceutical businessman Gustavo Alejos, who became Colom's powerful chief of staff), and from entrepreneurs operating in illicit economies (Solano 2007).[13] The CICIG later documented that the UNE had exceeded legal campaign spending limits by orders of magnitude and concealed the lion's share of its financing in the 2007, 2011, and 2015 elections. Because the UNE had proved its electoral competitiveness in the 2003 general elections, it had little problem in obtaining finance from the private sector (the G-8 great bourgeoisie excepted) despite its leftist bona fides. But in accepting this Faustian bargain, the president and his coterie all but ensured that during the UNE administration the private sector would be overwhelmingly privileged over the lower classes, very much in line with previous administrations. The traditional, oligarchic private sector always viewed the UNE with skepticism (personal interview: Fuentes Knight 2019). But it soon concluded that the ruling party posed little threat to the reigning neoliberal paradigm, and that its left-wing ideological zeal was more rhetorical than substantive. The pink tide came and left Guatemala without attracting much notice. While other countries in Latin America governed by the political Left – whether contestatory or moderate – introduced notable social and economic policy changes (Weyland, Madrid, and Hunter 2010), Guatemala under the UNE witnessed continuity with its neoliberal orientation.

[12] See Edgar Gutierrez, "Las Elecciones más caras" (*El Periódico*, October 11, 2011).

[13] See also Carolina Gamazo, "Gustavo Alejos y los Negociantes de la Salud" (*Plaza Pública*, October 28, 2015).

CONCLUSIONS

The UNE has been the most successful electoral vehicle in Guatemala since the country's military-led restoration of democracy in the mid-1980s. The UNE's longevity as a key player in Guatemalan party politics is unprecedented. It also stands apart in the party-building and ideology-centered ambitions of its architects. The UNE was born with a mission to create a representative and substantive political party, a mission that virtually all other political entrepreneurs in Guatemala have lacked. However, notwithstanding its proven longevity, by the standard of the stated objectives of Álvaro Colom, Sandra Torres, and their original coterie of party builders, the project failed. In terms of the new typology developed in this volume, the UNE qualifies as an electoral vehicle of "independents." Its ability to monopolize candidate selection is very incomplete, and its half-hearted attempt to coordinate the behavior of its local leaders or harmonize campaign strategies via informal institutions proved inadequate to the task. Nor was it able to coordinate behavior in Congress and command the intertemporal loyalty of its representatives. The UNE did develop a core constituency of poor voters in rural Guatemala, who have stayed loyal to the organization through the years. Election after election, the UNE has shown the capacity to electorally mobilize these rural voters via an electoral platform that promises to continue and build upon CCT programs such MIFAPRO. But party decisions have not been constrained by these voter-clients at all, nor did the UNE channel or intermediate the demands and interests of its voters, either while it held the presidency or at any other time as an opposition party.

Endogenous factors precluded vertical interest aggregation as well as horizontal coordination. The UNE's ability to fulfill its avowed purpose to represent the lower social classes and sectors and to become a worthy exemplar of the social-democratic tradition was truncated by endogenous conditions, that is, those that pertain to the party's key decisions, its internal composition, and its traits qua organization. The UNE leadership's deliberate decision in its formative years to integrate into the party a broad array of actors and *poderes facticos*, including financers with shady backgrounds, emergent capitalists, hidden powers, military operators, and others, fatally undercut its potential to create a true, coherent social-democratic party, as well as its ability to represent social sectors. Within the party's internal structures, those party notables representing the center-left wielded the least de facto political power. Colom's failure to provide firm navigation and consistent presidential support for center-left public policies during his administration undermined the morale and loyalty of social-democratic party notables and cabinet members. The UNE under Sandra Torres became even more pragmatic and deliberatively made a political voyage to the political right. Its range of political alliances became even more incongruous and contradictory than during the Colom administration. The social programs (CCTs) initiative that gave the UNE its identity and incipient party brand as the "party of the poor," was not conceived by Sandra Torres as part of a broader plan to endow the UNE with programmatic identity; rather, it was aimed at launching her political career via establishing clientelistic exchanges with poor dwellers in rural Guatemala, which entailed the deliberate politicization of the CCT programs. The UNE in power proved a strong defender of large-scale investments by multinationals with few strings attached, to the detriment of UNE-voting rural communities whose demands went unheeded and whose protests were actively repressed. Another factor endogenous to the UNE also precluded it from enforcing horizontal coordination: excessive personalization. Torres' abrasive and authoritarian manners coupled with the UNE's lack of institutionalization of accepted rules for internal conflict resolution contributed to important party splits: defections by key party strongmen and their respective caucuses of UNE lawmakers spawned repeated, debilitating *en masse* party-switching episodes. Personality-driven factionalism, party splits, and widespread party switching in Congress have afflicted the UNE as much as other large Guatemalan parties, past and present. While the organization devised ad hoc and informal methods of horizontal coordination, these proved short-lived and ineffective, undercut by stronger political currents and the intertemporal incentives of free agents. Most UNE mayors, lawmakers, and high-level public officials joined the party for instrumental reasons and, as is true of other vehicles, displayed little party loyalty. In addition, the UNE did not filter out ideologically incongruous or corrupt newcomers, following the same pragmatic streak that informs all other electoral vehicles.

Party-specific characteristics and behaviors aside, exogenous conditions have also limited the UNE's capacity for vertical interest aggregation and horizontal coordination; these conditions emanate from Guatemala's politico-economic structural environment and shape the parameters within which every Guatemalan electoral vehicle operates. Horizontal coordination is constrained by the inescapable reality that autonomous politico-economic networks control much of Guatemala's local politics. Strongmen spearheading these networks have undermined the UNE's central-to-local party coordination, campaign strategy harmonization, and party loyalty in the legislature (via lawmakers who are beholden to such strongmen). Exogenous factors limiting the UNE's vertical interest aggregation potential include the extreme fragmentation and feebleness of civil society, as well as the increasing cost of launching competitive electoral campaigns, which entices electoral vehicles to link up either with emergent capitalists, the traditional private sector (oligarchy), or illegal actors (including narcos). The upshot is that the UNE only represented social sectors in selected (symbolic) issue areas that entailed a low political cost and that did not contravene the private sector's material interests. Indeed, the UNE's time in power empirically demonstrated that nominally left-of-center parties face formidable structural obstacles in piercing through the nonrepresentative nature of Guatemalan democracy.

The UNE has operated in an environment inimical for party building writ large. Guatemala's severe state weakness, among the most pronounced in the Western hemisphere, has hobbled the prospects of all electoral vehicles to have held the presidency, chiefly because it produces serial malperformance in office. Peru is the country in Latin America that most closely resembles Guatemala in terms of its party nonbuilding trajectory under democracy. Both Peru and Guatemala are afflicted by what may be termed a "negative legitimacy environment" characterized by an electorate of floating voters, the prevalence of negative identities and personal brands, and a priori voter bias in favor of newcomers (itself a type of negative legitimacy) (Sanchez-Sibony 2022). In such environments, independents wield, to a large degree, a negative legitimacy form of political capital, which is much more ephemeral than standard positive legitimacy – almost by definition. Additionally, in both countries the legacies of civil conflict and the ravages of counterinsurgency efforts yielded a barren sociopolitical terrain for party building, particularly for the political Left. Beyond differences in nation-level historical legacies, both Guatemala and Peru show that partyless democracies contain many self-reproducing mechanisms that impede the advent of a bona fide party system and render successful party building very unlikely. Some of these self-reproduction mechanisms relate to conditions extraneous to diminished-type electoral vehicles, others are intrinsic to them. Independent electoral vehicles, given their constitutive traits, are especially vulnerable to laws of political entropy – manifested in schisms, myopic short-termism, defections, errors of political agency, and others – that seal their fate, often sooner rather than later. These two country cases teach us in stark fashion that electoral democracy and repeated electoral cycles need not produce political parties as defined in this volume. On the contrary, elite and voter behavior can interact to reproduce indefinitely personalist-based politics detached from party norms. Insofar as the trend toward party system deinstitutionalization across Latin America has unquestionably become generalized and powerful undercurrents continue to move the region in that direction, there are empirical (and theoretical) reasons to think that Guatemala and Peru may be alarming precursors for part or much of the hemisphere, with dreadful consequences upon democratic governance.

APPENDIX: LIST OF INTERVIEWEES

Alejos, Roberto. Former President of Congress and UNE legislator. September 3, 2019.

Barreda, Carlos. UNE Lawmaker and President of the Economic Commission in Congress. March 18, 2013.

Bolaños, Raúl. Founding Member of UNE. August 10, 2019.

Fuentes Knight, Juan Alberto. Former Minister of Finance under Alvaro Colom administration. August 5, 2019.

García Cuyún, Francisco. Former director of the department of political organizations at Tribunal Supremo Electoral in Guatemala. 2013.

Lux de Coti, Otilia. Social leader for Indigenous rights. Former Minister of Culture under Portillo administration. August 17, 2019.

Nuñez, Eduardo. Director of National Democratic Institute. August 7, 2019.

Robles, Ronaldo. 2019. Former Secretary of Communication of Álvaro Colom Government. August 14, 2019.

14

Conclusions

Juan Pablo Luna, Rafael Piñeiro Rodríguez, Fernando Rosenblatt, and Gabriel Vommaro

Analysts agree that political parties are facing a crisis, especially in terms of their inability to produce democratic representation. Some seminal works have analyzed this crisis of representation in relation to its modern concept (Manin 1997). However, the party crisis has not led to renewed reflection on the function of parties and their link with democracy. The result is a relative lack of consensus about what we can expect parties to do. Various scholars have noted the complex causal relation between actually existing electoral vehicles and democratic representation (Hicken 2009; Kitschelt and Wilkinson 2007; Lawson and Merkl 1988; Levitsky 2003; Luna 2014; Luna and Zechmeister 2005; Mainwaring 2018; Mainwaring and Scully 1995; Piñeiro Rodríguez and Rosenblatt 2020; Roberts 2014b). Not all electoral vehicles provide democratic representation. Some electoral vehicles facilitate democratic representation, while others are less connected with demands and interests that emanate from society. The party politics literature regarding Latin America has observed a great deal of variation among organizations that compete in elections. However, this literature has not provided a conceptual discussion that theorizes the existence of diminished political party subtypes. This edited volume sought to help fill this conceptual gap and provide an empirical analysis of different electoral vehicles in Latin America.

We have proposed a definition of *political party* based on an organization's capacity to produce democratic representation. Two crucial dimensions were defined: horizontal coordination and vertical aggregation of interests and demands. These dimensions allow parties to provide voters a coherent and legible offer, channeling social groups' demands and interests and transforming them into policies. A thorough conceptualization of diminished subtypes, based on the two constitutive dimensions of political parties, improves the analytical value of the study of political parties and of other forms of electoral political organizations in terms of their role in democracy. Our typology of political party diminished subtypes is based on the presence or absence of two primary attributes: horizontal coordination among ambitious politicians during electoral campaigns and while in office and vertical aggregation to electorally mobilize collective interests and to intermediate and channel collective demands.

Different problems for democracy arise when parties are unable to channel demands from society, but are still able to horizontally coordinate ambitious politicians. These *unrooted parties* look like traditional parties, can be electorally stable, and can coordinate their members' actions between elections, but they do not connect with any relevant social group or interest. As an institution, this kind of diminished subtype does a poor job of incorporating social demands in stable and predictable ways in the political process. In the extreme case, they are detached from society and are unable to remedy social conflicts or civil unrest. In our typology, the mirror image of unrooted parties are *uncoordinated parties*, which vertically aggregate collective interests or demands but cannot coordinate political elites during or between elections. This diminished subtype expresses social cleavages but has difficulties performing instrumental and representative functions (Lipset and Rokkan 1967). Uncoordinated parties are not suited to "strike bargains and to stagger demands" (Lipset and Rokkan 1967, 5). Finally, some political organizations, which we call *independents*, do not perform either function. These electoral vehicles do little to coordinate the actions of their leaders either between or during elections; as with the uncoordinated party type, internal conflicts and lack of legislative discipline hinder collective action. The party is not able to induce collective action through selective incentives that moderate free riding. Common positions or electoral strategies result from the convergence of all individuals' preferences. Additionally, as with the unrooted party type, independents do not, as a party aggregate collective interests. Individual leaders within the electoral vehicle might promote a specific programmatic agenda (or a specific issue) as part of an individual strategy of credit claiming. However, voters do not identify these agendas as part of the vehicle's platform. Thus, the electoral vehicle does not aggregate these interests.

Our edited volume has presented various cases of these diminished subtypes. The electoral vehicles discussed in the volume tend to have problems fulfilling at least one of the two political party functions and many of the cases analyzed here have difficulties in performing both functions. The empirical analysis seems to suggest that an organization that has problems fulfilling one of the functions will tend to have difficulty accomplishing the other function. For example, the inability to horizontally coordinate actions during or between elections hinders an organization's ability to act as a party that not only promotes some issues but that also interacts with and aggregates social organizations' collective demands. The Guatemalan Unidad Nacional de la Esperanza (National Unity of Hope, UNE) shows how difficulties enforcing collective action, due to the power of local *caudillos* and the pervasiveness of lawmakers' changing their party affiliation to increase their own probability of reelection, affect the capacity to aggregate interests. Conversely, there seems not to be a trade-off between investing in the two functions; improving performance along one dimension need not come at the expense of the other. The party politics literature and the conventional definition of political party posit horizontal coordination as the concept's defining attribute (Aldrich 1995; Schlesinger 1994). However, this volume surveyed Latin American electoral vehicles that horizontally coordinate but have no substantive linkages with collective organized demands and do not represent any collective interest. In the most extreme cases, electoral vehicles that achieve relative electoral success remain detached from society. The description of the Chilean Partido por la Democracia (Party for Democracy, PPD) in this volume by Piñeiro Rodríguez, Rosenblatt, and Toro highlights an electoral vehicle that is relatively successful electorally but has no ability as an organization to aggregate interests from society. This disconnect is also observed in the case of the UNE in Guatemala, where the fragmentation of social actors and the importance of private campaign financing prevent the UNE from vertically aggregating interests from its constituency (see Sanchez-Sibony and Lemus this volume).

Political parties can change over time, but they do not necessarily increase their ability to perform their functions for democracy. Parties gain or lose the ability to support horizontal coordination (during the campaign and/or between elections) or to channel and aggregate collective interests. The collapse or adaptation of parties is not the only possible response to exogenous or endogenous crises. Parties can also adopt new forms (types), which allow them to persist and maintain, in many cases, their label and electoral success. However, they might no longer perform one or both functions that, we argue, define a political party. Wills-Otero, Ortega, and Sarmiento (this volume), describe how the Colombian Partido Liberal (Liberal Party, PL) and Partido Conservador (Conservative Party, PC) gradually lost their capacity to vertically aggregate interests from society and have low degrees of horizontal coordination. However, as the authors describe, both electoral vehicles remain competitive in elections despite not representing a clearly defined constituency.

Electoral continuity (stability) both facilitates and is achieved, intertemporally, by horizontal coordination and vertical interest aggregation. Yet, observing that a particular electoral vehicle is temporally stable should not suffice for one to conclude that such a vehicle is a political party. Several electorally stable vehicles fail to provide effective horizontal coordination and vertical aggregation and should therefore be characterized as diminished subtypes of the political party concept. Moreover, political parties that satisfy both functions can change over time and cease to fulfill one or both functions. Thus, fulfillment of both functions during a given period does not necessarily imply the reproduction of the ability to perform both functions in the future. Whether a given party has the capacity to reproduce these functions is an empirical question. To answer the question, one must assess whether the conditions or political institutions that prevail for a given electoral vehicle hinder or engender the increasing returns that reinforce the reproduction of an organization's ability to perform these functions. The Frente Amplio (Broad Front, FA) case in Uruguay shows that the institutionalized participation of grassroots activists can guarantee vertical aggregation over time if the grassroots activists manage to acquire and maintain significant influence over party decisions (see Pérez Bentancur, Piñeiro Rodríguez and Rosenblatt this volume).

This conceptualization and typology allows one to analyze how changes in parties' ability to perform both functions affect institutionalization. The mere continuity of an electoral label does not ensure stable levels of coordination and/or aggregation of collective interests nor does it ensure a constant contribution to democratic representation. If we extend this logic to the system level, the institutionalization of horizontal coordination and vertical aggregation of interests in individual parties, and not simply the stability of party labels, is what should matter for assessing party system institutionalization. This reconceptualization thus questions conventional thinking on party system institutionalization (see, e.g., Mainwaring 2018).

Unpacking political parties and diminished subtypes increases the analytical capacity to differentiate cases of decay and collapse. Electoral vehicles differ in their capacity to resist and adapt to exogenous shocks. Political parties that fulfill both functions are better equipped to weather different challenges over time. Without the ability to distinguish between cases, party collapse appears as an abrupt event. The conceptualization of diminished subtypes, however, advances our analytical understanding of processes of organizational decay and the slow-moving dimensions underlying this process. This counters the bias of attributing collapse to short-term factors (Pierson 2004). A given electoral vehicle can undergo a gradual process of decay, wherein an established political party gradually loses the capacity to perform one or both functions. Different empirical chapters in this volume have addressed the gradual decay of established parties, such as the traditional parties in Colombia (see Wills-Otero et al. this volume) or the Partido Liberación Nacional (National Liberation Party, PLN) in Costa Rica (see Alfaro-Redondo and Gómez-Campos this volume).

What determines the presence or absence of a given type of electoral vehicle in a given case? There are elective affinities between electoral vehicle types and the levels at which they compete. Vehicles comprising a group of leaders who have difficulty coordinating with each other and who do not aggregate any collective interests, a group we call independents, emerge more frequently as a loose coalition of leaders at the local level. In such a context, there is less need for a stable organization to deploy a campaign and/or to establish channels for aggregating interests. The organizational development and electoral performance of a given electoral vehicle may vary across different districts. Uncoordinated parties often allow local leaders great programmatic autonomy, with the result that voting for a given label may lead to supporting different public policies in different districts. This is theoretically significant in light of the structural challenges that democracies face in unequal societies with unequal subnational levels of development (Giraudy and Pribble 2019; Niedzwiecki 2018). Also, this type of vehicle has found fertile ground in countries that have implemented decentralization reforms and that have electoral systems that grant autonomy at the subnational level (Vergara 2011), a process inverse to that described by Chhibber and Kollman (2004).

Different institutional rules facilitate (or hinder) the development of different types of electoral vehicles. For instance, electoral systems that do not allow individual candidacies or that force candidates to run under a party label in a given number of districts inhibit the emergence of independent candidates. In Congress, some institutional rules favor coordination along partisan lines, while others do not promote it (Cox and McCubbins 1993 and 2001; Weingast and Marshall 1988). This literature acquires greater theoretical significance when the effects of different rules can be linked to the dimensions of our conceptualization. The literature on the effects of particular electoral rules has highlighted how rules affect personalization (Carey and Shugart 1995) and discipline in Congress (Morgenstern and Nacif 2002), among others. Nevertheless, this literature fails to provide a comprehensive view of how these effects alter parties' capacities to perform their function for democracy. Differentiating the constitutive dimensions of the political party concept allows one to develop more nuanced theories about the effect of rules on parties.

The recent literature on party-voter linkages (Calvo and Murillo 2019; Kitschelt 2000; Kitschelt et al. 2010; Kitschelt and Wilkinson 2007; Luna 2014; Piattoni 2001; Taylor-Robinson 2010) made significant progress in detailing how parties function as agents of representation. Nonetheless, they have not articulated how this linkage works in different party organizations and how it, thus, can affect democracy in different ways. For example, clientelism interacts with how parties perform vertical interest aggregation and horizontal coordination. This occurs in different ways in different parties. Thus, clientelism does not have a unique, direct, and homogeneous effect on democratic representation. Rather, its effect depends how that interaction occurs. When particularistic resources are centrally managed by national party leaders, clientelism may distort programmatic approaches to vertical interest aggregation while, at the same time, enhancing horizontal coordination. If the same particularistic resources are decentralized in the hands of local party leaders, the party will be less able to perform horizontal coordination (even if local branches of the party can aggregate interests at the local level on the basis of those resources). In both scenarios, the party has clientelistic linkages with voters, but the party will perform differently in the two situations and clientelism will affect the democratic process differently in the two cases. In the latter scenario, the inability of party elites to horizontally coordinate their efforts hinders the capacity to build the democratic process around parties as agents of representation.

The literature that links democracy with redistribution or with the provision of public goods (Acemoglu and Robinson 2006; Ansell and Samuels 2014; Boix 2003) assumes that democracy automatically responds to median voter preferences (Meltzer and Richard 1981). However, the validity of this assumption depends on having democratic competition among parties that can vertically aggregate interests and horizontally coordinate action. Understanding the degree to which political agents fulfill one or both of these functions enables us to develop better theories about how different types of electoral vehicles engender different results in terms of redistribution and in the provision of public goods. Democracy can take different forms depending on the type of parties that exist in a given system. Political parties determine the way preferences are translated into politics. Whenever vertical interest aggregation and horizontal coordination operate effectively, the democratic process is more likely to reflect the citizens' underlying preferences.

Rethinking the concept of political parties in terms of the concept's constitutive dimensions affords the opportunity to build conceptual typologies other than the diminished subtypes typology presented here. The cases analyzed in this volume fulfill the functions of horizontal coordination and vertical interest aggregation in different ways. For example, some vehicles coordinate horizontally via strong leaders, as observed in the cases of Movimiento al Socialismo (Movement Toward Socialism, MAS) and Alianza PAIS (PAIS Alliance, AP). In Ecuador, Rafael Correa's charismatic appeal enforced horizontal coordination through a top-down structure (see Conaghan this volume). In the Bolivian MAS, Evo Morales' leadership is a source of coordination in the party's relationship with the social movements that constitute its core constituency (see Anria this volume). Other parties, however, perform this same function via the value of their party brand and the power of the party's organizational structure, as in the cases of the FA, Primero Justicia (Justice First, PJ), Voluntad Popular (Popular Will, VP), PLN, and Partido Acción Ciudadana (Citizen Action Party, PAC). Thus, parties differ as to *whether* they perform horizontal coordination (or vertical aggregation) and in *how* they perform it. Changes in the way a party performs these functions should not be seen as evidence of deterioration but, rather, as an adaptation to different contexts, available resources, and institutional incentives. In addition, a party's initial conditions (i.e., those associated with the context in which a party is born), might shape its organizational features (Panebianco 1988). Those features persist over time and induce path dependence. Likewise, party founders' particular social backgrounds might also shape party's organizational features by making specific resources available to the nascent organization. For example, leaders' social backgrounds provide access to specific social networks (e.g., church communities, social movements, business) and specific access to funding sources. These networks and funding opportunities might also shape the configuration of horizontal coordination and vertical aggregation mechanisms at the birth of a given organization. Whether, in fact, certain ways of performing horizontal coordination and vertical aggregation are more stable and self-reinforcing than other ways of doing so and how the different ways of performing the two functions affect representation and democracy are questions for future research to explore.

The Propuesta Republicana (Republican Proposal, PRO) in Argentina and Movimiento Regeneración Nacional (National Regeneration Movement, MORENA) in México (and, to a lesser extent, the PAC in Costa Rica) show that, in the early twenty-first century, it remains possible to build parties that can fulfill vertical interest aggregation and horizontal coordination. Other cases have been able to fulfill both functions over prolonged periods (e.g., the FA). However, as Levitsky et al. (2016) highlight, most prospective political parties do not endure; many, in fact, die out quickly. Moreover, we show throughout this volume that most electoral vehicles that survive do not develop into a fully fledged political party.

Becoming and enduring as a political party is difficult. The successful and unsuccessful cases in this volume teach that structural challenges (rampant inequality, social actors' fragmentation, and underdevelopment) set high, sometimes enormous, barriers to building and sustaining mature, nationwide political parties. Yet, the contrast between the successful and unsuccessful cases in Latin America also indicates that there are ways for politicians and the general population to overcome such challenges. A party's willingness to empower people seems to be a key ingredient of success. The successful case of the MAS in Bolivia and the unsuccessful case of the UNE in Guatemala, two equally poor, highly unequal countries that both have large indigenous populations, show the importance of activating electoral bases in a bottom-up process of party building. At the same time, the successful case of the FA in Uruguay and the decay of the PLN in Costa Rica, the region's two most equal countries, highlight the importance of bottom-up politics for reproducing a fully developed party over time.

We have sought in this volume to overcome a theoretical gap in the party politics literature. As Stokes (1999) claimed, the literature has not developed a theoretical link between political parties and democracy. We agree with her observation and attribute this void to the prevalence of an approach that at least tacitly stresses the electoral competition dimension of democracy. In keeping with the view expressed by Dahl, who conceived democracy as the continuous correspondence between citizens' preferences and government actions, we emphasize the functions that parties must fulfill, if they are to have a positive effect on the democratic process. Parties must coordinate action among their cadres and leaders on a permanent ongoing basis and need to be permanently engaged in an ongoing process of aggregating changing needs and demands from society in interaction with civil society organizations. The existence of organizations that perform the above functions is a necessary, though not sufficient, condition for effective democratic representation.

Improved concepts and, more crucially, improved attribute definitions enhance our capacity to develop useful theories. It is precisely in the relationship between attributes of different concepts that we build theories (Goertz 2006). A well-developed concept of political party that includes the attributes that link parties with the functioning of democracy is necessary not only to empirically assess parties but, more importantly, to understand how parties can promote or hinder democracy.

Our concept is not without limitations. Before closing the volume, we address two major shortcomings and outline areas through which future research can contribute conceptual and empirical improvements. The first limitation relates to the level of analysis. Party-system-level variance is important and has been theoretically and empirically associated with relevant outcomes (Kitschelt et al. 2010; Mainwaring 2018). However, the conceptualization we propose is not readily amenable to party-system-level assessments. The way we have chosen to conceptualize and operationalize the concept requires in-depth knowledge of individual party characteristics and dynamics. This is so because we do not measure parties' institutional attributes or formal documents such as internal rules or electoral manifestoes; instead, we propose to observe and measure electoral agents' actual behavior and organizing. To adequately observe and gauge such behavior, measurement efforts require intense fieldwork, which, in turn, renders multiparty and broad comparative assessments more demanding. Moreover, inferring party-system characteristics from individual party traits risks missing the mark, particularly given the levels of heterogeneity and volatility observed in contemporary systems.

A second limitation relates to the different ways through which vertical interest aggregation and horizontal coordination can be achieved. Nonprogrammatic political mobilization (e.g., clientelistic or charismatic/personalistic mobilization) can produce high levels of vertical interest aggregation and horizontal coordination. In this regard, not all political organizations that fulfill both functions and are, thus, consistent with our notion of political parties, necessarily contribute to democracy in the same manner.

We think future research could eventually address both shortcomings through empirical work. Empirical applications of our framework can explicitly be deployed to develop system-level indicators. Systematic analyses of specific cases can reveal how different mechanisms of vertical interest aggregation and horizontal coordination are used and (eventually) combined by different types of contemporary political parties. On that basis, for instance, the predominance of top-down or bottom-up types of interest aggregation could be identified, as well as the effects the different mechanisms have on democracy in each case.

The increasingly frequent collapse of established party systems was one of the main drivers of our work. Using both functions (i.e., vertical interest aggregation and horizontal coordination) to trace the processes through which political parties decay and eventually collapse might advance understanding of such processes. This work would also provide fruitful opportunities to consider how important concepts in the literature, such as policy switching or brand dilution, interact with parties' capacity to successfully carry out each type of function. Moreover, future research could systematically explore how electoral-institutional change, social-structural transformations, and processes of state reform might shape electoral organizations' long-term capacity to sustain both functions. Change in these three broad arenas shapes incentives, constraints, and opportunities for electoral organizations that, in turn, have important implications for the evolution of mobilization strategies, organizational patterns, and financing. Institutional and societal changes thus shape political organizations' capacity to fulfill vertical interest aggregation and horizontal coordination.

References

Abente Brun, Diego. 1989. "The Liberal Republic and the Failure of Democracy." *The Americas* 45 (4):525–546.

Abente Brun, Diego. 1995. "A Party System in Transition: The Case of Paraguay." In *Building Democratic Institutions: Party Systems in Latin America*, edited by Scott Mainwaring and Timothy Scully, 298–320. Stanford, CA: Stanford University Press.

Abente Brun, Diego. 2014. "Introduction." In *Clientelism, Social Policy, and the Quality of Democracy*, edited by Diego Abente Brun and Larry Diamond, 1–14. Baltimore, MD: Johns Hopkins University Press.

Acción Ciudadana. 2012. *¿Cuánto Costó la Campaña Electoral? Analisis del Gasto y Rendicion de Cuentas en el proceso electoral Guatemala 2011*. Guatemala City: Magna Terra Editores.

Acción Ciudadana Partido. 2019. Estatuto Orgánico. San José: Partido Acción Ciudadana.

Acemoglu, Daaron, and James Robinson. 2006. *Economic Origins of Dictatorship and Democracy*. New York: Cambridge University Press.

Acuña, Santiago, Rafael Piñeiro Rodríguez, and Cecilia Rossel. 2018. "¿Quién Maneja la Caja? Financiamiento Político y Estructuras Partidarias en Uruguay." *Colombia Internacional* 95:55–77.

Adams, James. 2001. *Party Competition and Responsible Party Government*. Ann Arbor: University of Michigan Press.

Aguirre Bayley, Miguel. 2001. *1971–5 de Febrero–2001: 30 Años de Compromiso con la Gente*. Montevideo: La República.

Albarracín, Juan, Laura Gamboa, and Scott Mainwaring. 2018. "Deinstitutionalization without Collapse: Colombia's Party System." In *Party Systems in Latin America. Institutionalization, Decay and Collapse*, edited by Mainwaring Scott, 227–254. New York: Cambridge University Press.

Aldrich, John H. 1995. *Why Parties? The Origin and Transformation of Political Parties in America*. Chicago: University of Chicago Press.

Alfaro-Redondo, Ronald. 2006. "Elecciones Nacionales 2006 en Costa Rica y la Recomposición del Sistema de Partidos Políticos." *Revista de Ciencia Política* 26 (1):125–137.

Almeida, Mónica, and Ana Karina López. 2017. *El Séptimo Rafael*. Quito: Aperimus Ediciones.

Almeida, Paul. 2014. *Mobilizing Democracy: Globalization and Citizen Protest*. Baltimore, MD: Johns Hopkins University Press.

Altman, David. 2010. *Direct Democracy Worldwide*. New York: Cambridge University Press.

Anria, Santiago. 2013. "Social Movements, Party Organization, and Populism: Insights from the Bolivian MAS." *Latin American Politics and Society* 55 (3):19–46.

Anria, Santiago. 2018. *When Movements Become Parties: The Bolivian MAS in Comparative Perspective*. New York: Cambridge University Press.

Anria, Santiago, and Jennifer Cyr. 2017. "Inside Revolutionary Parties: Coalition-Building and Maintenance in Reformist Bolivia." *Comparative Political Studies* 50 (9):1255–1287.

Anria, Santiago, and Evelyne Huber. 2018. "The Key to Evo Morales' Political Longevity: Why He's Outlasted Other Latin American Left-Wing Leaders." *Foreign Affairs*, February 14, 2018. www.foreignaffairs.com/articles/bolivia/2018-02-14/key-evo-morales-political-longevity.

Ansell, Ben, and David Samuels. 2014. *Inequality and Democratization: An Elite-Competition Approach*. New York: Cambridge University Press.

Arditi, Benjamín. 1993. "Del Granito al Archipiélago: El Partido Colorado sin Stroessner." In *Paraguay en Transición*, edited by Diego Abente Brun, 161–172. Caracas: Editorial Nueva Sociedad.

Arellano, Diana. 2004. *Movimiento 14 de Mayo: Memorias de No Resignación*. Posadas: EDUNaM.

Arriondo, Luciana. 2015. "De la UCeDe al PRO: Un Recorrido por la Trayectoria de los Militantes de Centro Derecha de la Ciudad de Buenos Aires." In *Hagamos equipo PRO y la Construcción de la Nueva Derecha en Argentina*, edited by Gabriel Vommaro and Sergio Morresi, 203–230. Los Polvorines: Ediciones UNGS.

ASIES. 2004. *Informe Analítico Proceso Electoral 2003*. Guatemala City: Asociación de Investigación y Estudios Sociales.

Astori, Danilo. 2001. "Estancamiento, Desequilibrios y Ruptura, 1955–1972." In *El Uruguay del Siglo XX: La Economía*, edited by Benjamín Nahum, 65–94. Montevideo: Instituto de Economía-Ediciones de la Banda Oriental.

Auyero, Javier. 2001. *Poor People's Politics: Peronist Survival Networks and the Legacy of Evita*. Durham, NC: Duke University Press.

Azpuru, Dinorah. 2005. "The General Elections in Guatemala, November–December 2003." *Electoral Studies* 1 (24):143–149.

Azpuru, Dinorah, and Ligia Blanco. 2008. "Guatemala 2007: Un Año de Contrastes para la Democracia." *Revista dde Ciencia Política* 28 (1):217–244.

Bargsted, Matías A. , and Luis Maldonado. 2018. "Party Identification in an Encapsulated Party System: The Case of Postauthoritarian Chile." *Journal of Politics in Latin America* 10 (1):29–68.

Barrero, Fredy, and Fabián Acuña. 2015. "Cuando Ganar es Perder un Poco: Selección de Candidatos de los Partidos Políticos Colombianos, Elecciones Presidenciales 2014." In *Elecciones en Colombia, 2014: ¿Representaciones Fragmentadas?*, edited by Fredy Barrero and Margarita Batlle, 117–141. Bogota: Konrad- Adenauer-Stiftung.

Bartolini, Stefano. 2000. *The Political Mobilization of the European Left, 1860–1980: The Class Cleavage*. Cambridge: Cambridge University Press.

Basabe-Serrano, Santiago. 2016. "Asociación Cívica y Desinstitucionalización de los Partidos Políticos en Ecuador: Rupturas y Continuidades, 1979–2014." *Política y Sociedad* 53 (3):937–960.

Basabe-Serrano, Santiago, and Julián Martínez. 2014. "Ecuador: Cada Vez Menos Democracia, Cada Vez Más Autoritarismo...Con Elecciones." *Revista de Ciencia Política* 34 (1):145–170.

Bastos, Sebastián, and Roderick Leslie Brett. 2010. *El Movimiento Maya en la Década Después de la Paz*. Guatemala City: F&G Editores.

Batlle, Margarita. 2011. "La Difícil Tarea de Seleccionar un Candidato: Cambios y Continuidades en las Estrategias de Selección de Candidatos en los Partidos Colombianos (1990–2010)." In *Elecciones 2010: Partidos, Consultas y Democracia Interna*, edited by Yann Basset, Margarita Batlle, Paola Montilla, and Margarita Marín, 51–105. Bogota: Universidad Externado de Colombia.

Batlle, Margarita, and José Ricardo Puyana. 2011. "El Nivel de Nacionalización del Sistema de Partidos Colombiano: Una Mirada a Partir de las Elecciones Legislativas de 2010." *Colombia Internacional* 74:27–57.

Benavides Vásquez, Wilson Rodrigo. 2012. "La Construcción Política del Correismo: Una Mirada al Movimiento País." MA Thesis, Facultad Latinoamericana de Ciencias Sociales, Sede Ecuador.

Benítez, Justo P. 1988 (1932). *Ensayos sobre el Liberalismo Paraguayo*. Asunción: El Gráfico.

Bergara, Mario. 2015. *Las Nuevas Reglas de Juego en Uruguay: Incentivos e Instituciones en una Década de Reformas*. Montevideo: dECON, Facultad de Ciencias Sociales, Universidad de la República - Fin de Siglo.

Bermeo, Nancy. 2016. "On Democratic Backsliding." *Journal of Democracy* 27 (1):5–19.

Bidegain Ponte, Germán. 2013. "Uruguay: ¿El Año Bisagra?" *Revista de Ciencia Politica* 33 (1):351–374.

Boix, Carles. 2003. *Democracy and Redistribution*. Cambridge: Cambridge University Press.

Bolívar Meza, Rosendo. 2014. "Morena: El Partido del Lopezobradorismo." *Polis* 10 (2):71–103.

Bolleyer, Nicole, and Saskia P. Ruth. 2018. "Elite Investments in Party Institutionalization in New Democracies: A Two-Dimensional Approach." *The Journal of Politics* 80 (1):288–302.

Borges, Julio. 2012. Primero Justicia: *¡De dónde venimos y a dónde vamos!* Caracas: Primer Justicia.

Bourscheid, Junior Ivan. 2018. "La Ideología Colorada: El Papel de los Intelectuales para la Permanencia del Liderazgo del Bloque Hegemónico

Paraguayo." *Revista Mexicana de Ciencias Políticas y Sociales* 63 (232):181–218.
Bowen, James D. 2010. "Ecuador's 2009 Presidential and Legislative Elections." *Electoral Studies* 29 (1):186–189.
Brezzo, Liliana M. 2010. "Reconstrucción, Poder Político y Revoluciones (1870–1920)." In *Historia del Paraguay*, edited by Ingacio Telesca, 199–224. Asunción: Taurus.
Bril Mascarenhas, Tomás 2007. "El Colapso del Sistema Partidario de la Ciudad de Buenos Aires: Una Herencia de la Crisis Argentina de 2001–2002." *Desarrollo Económico* 47 (187):367–400.
Brolo, Javier. 2012. "Organización Partidaria en Guatemala." In *Partidos Políticos Guatemaltecos: Dinámicas Internas y Desempeño*, edited by ASIES, 31–40. Guatemala City: Asociación de Investigación y Estudios Sociales.
Brolo, Javier. 2013. "Escasa Organización y Afiliación Partidaria en Guatemala." In *Partidos Políticos Guatemaltecos: Cobertura Territorial y Organización Interna*, edited by Jonatán Lemus and Javier Brolo, 1–26. Guatemala City: Asociación de Investigación y Estudios Sociales.
Brownlee, Jason. 2007. *Authoritarianism in an Age of Democratization.* New York: Cambridge University Press.
Bruhn, Kathleen. 1997. *Taking Goliath: The Emergence of a New Left Party and the Struggle for Democracy in Mexico.* University Park: Pennsylvania State University Press.
Bruhn, Kathleen. 2013. "El PRD y los Movimientos Populares en el Distrito Federal." In *El PRD: Orígenes, Itinerarios, Retos*, edited by Jorge Cadena-Roa and Miguel A. López Leyva, 115–187. México City: Ficticia.
Buquet, Daniel, Daniel Chasquetti, and Juan Andrés Moraes. 1998. *Fragmentación Política y Gobierno en Uruguay: ¿Un Enfermo Imaginario?* Montevideo: Facultad de Ciencias Sociales.
Buquet, Daniel, and Rafael Piñeiro. 2014. "La Consolidación de un Nuevo Sistema de Partidos en Uruguay." *Revista Debates* 8 (1):127–148.
Burbano de Lara, Felipe 2017. "Ciudadanía, Dominación Estatal y Protesta en la "Revolución Ciudadana" en Ecuador (2007–2016)." *Iberoamericana* 27 (65):179–200.
Burgess, Katrina, and Steven Levitsky. 2003. "Explaining Populist Party Adaptation in Latin America: Environmental and Organizational Determinants of Party Change in Argentina, Mexico, Peru, and Venezuela." *Comparative Political Studies* 36 (8):881–911.
Bushnell, David, ed. 2016. *Colombia: Una Nación a Pesar de Sí Misma*. Bogota: Planeta.
Caballero Aquino, Ricardo, and Lorenzo N. Livieres Banks. 1993. *Los Partidos Políticos en América Latina: El Sistema Político Paraguayo*. Asunción: Konrad-Adenauer-Stiftung.
Caballero Carrizosa, Esteban. 1993. "Los Partidos Políticos de Oposición en el Paraguay: El Caso del Partido Liberal Radical Auténtico." In *Paraguay en Transición*, edited by Diego Abente Brun, 182–185. Caracas: Nueva Sociedad.

Caballero Carrizosa, Esteban. 2003. "Partidos Políticos y Sistema Electoral." In *Cultura Política, Sociedad Civil y Participación Ciudadana*, edited by A. Vidal, 255–284. Asunción: CIRD.

Caballero, Víctor. 2019. *Mototaxi: Auge y Caída de Fuerza Popular*. Lima: Penguin Random House.

Cadena-Roa, Jorge. 2003. "State Pacts, Elites, and Social Movements in Mexico's Transition to Democracy." In *States, Parties, and Social Movements*, edited by Jack Goldstone, 107–143. New York: Cambridge University Press.

Cadena-Roa, Jorge, and Miguel A. López Leyva. 2013. "Introducción: Consideraciones sobre un Partido que Puede Ser Democrático, de Izquierda y Enraizado en la Sociedad." In *El PRD: Orígenes, Itinerarios, Retos*, edited by Jorge Cadena-Roa and Miguel A. López Leyva, 21–37. México City: Ficticia.

Cadenas Sangronis, Mariana Eva. 2005. "Primero Justicia: De ONG a Partido Político: Reportaje Interpretativo sobre la Evolución del Partido Político Primera Justicia contado por sus Actores." Undergraduate Thesis, Universidad Católica Andrés Bello.

Caetano, Gerardo, and Gustavo De Armas. 2011. "Diez Años del Informe de Coyuntura. Del Uruguay de la Crisis a las Posibilidades y Exigencias de Desarrollo." In *Política en Tiempos de Mujica. En Busca del Rumbo: Informe de Coyuntura N° 10*, edited by Gerardo Caetano, María Ester Mancebo and Juan Andrés Moraes, 11–41. Montevideo: Estuario Editora.

Calderón, Marco A. 1994. *Violencia Política y Elecciones Municipales*. Zamora, Michoacán: El Colegio de Michoacán/Instituto Mora.

Calvo, Ernesto, and Maria Victoria Murillo. 2019. *Non-policy Politics: Richer Voters, Poorer Voters, and the Diversification of Electoral Strategies*. New York: Cambridge University Press.

Cameron, Maxwell A. 1994. *Democracy and Authoritarianism in Peru: Political Coalitions and Social Change*. London: Palgrave Macmillan.

Carey, John. 2002. "Parties, Coalitions, and the Chilean Congress in the 1990s." In *Legislative Politics in Latin America*, edited by Scott Morgenstern and Benito Nacif, 222–253. Cambridge: Cambridge University Press.

Carey, John M. 2007. "Competing Principals, Political Institutions, and Party Unity in Legislative Voting." *American Journal of Political Science* 51 (1):92–107.

Carey, John, and Matthew S. Shugart. 1995. "Incentives to Cultivate a Personal Vote: A Rank Ordering of Electoral Formulas." *Electoral Studies* 14 (4):417–439.

Castellani, Ana. 2018. "Cambiemos SA" Exposición a los Conflictos de Interés en el Gobierno Nacional: Los Funcionarios con Participación en Empresas Privadas a Junio de 2018. In *Observatorio de las Elites Argentinas*. Informe de Investigación No. 5 Parte 1. Buenos Aires: IDAES- Universidad Nacional de San Martín.

Cawthorne, Andrew. 2017. "Hardline Party on Front Line of Venezuelan Political War." *Reuters*, January 23, 2017, www.reuters.com/article/us-venezuela-polit ics-party/hardline-party-on-front-line-of-venezuelan-political-war-idUSKB N15718T (last accessed January 18, 2021).

Centurión, Carlos R. 1947. *Historia de las Letras Paraguayas, Tomo II*. Asunción: Editorial Ayacucho.

Chang, Paul Y. 2008. "Unintended Consequences of Repression: Alliance Formation in South Korea's Democracy Movement (1970–1979)." *Social Forces* 87 (2):651–677.

Chartrain, François. 1973. *La République du Paraguay*. Vol. 1. Paris: Berger-Levrault.

Chernick, Marc W. 1989. "Reforma Política, Apertura Democrática y el Desmonte del Frente Nacional." In *La Democracia en Blanco y Negro: Colombia en los Años Ochenta*, edited by Patricia Vásquez de Urrutia, 285–320. Bogota: Ediciones Uniandes.

Chhibber, Pradeep, and Ken Kollman. 2004. *The Formation of National Party Systems: Federalism and Party Competition in Canada, Great Britain, India, and the United States*. Princeton, NJ: Princeton University Press.

CICIG. 2015. *Informe: El Financiamiento de la Política en Guatemala*. Guatemala City: Comisión Internacional contra la Impunidad en Guatemala.

Collier, David, and Steve Levitsky. 1997. "Democracy with Adjectives: Conceptual Innovation in Comparative Research." *World Politics* 49 (3):430–451.

Combes, Hélène. 2011. *Faire Parti, Trajectoires de Gauche au Mexique*. Paris: Karthala.

Combes, Hélène. 2013. "Un Analisis del PRD desde sus Dirigentes Multi-Posicionados." In *El PRD: Orígenes, Itinerarios, Retos*, edited by Jorge Cadena-Roa and Miguel A. López Leyva, 115–187. México City: Ficticia.

Combes, Hélène. 2018. "Foyers Contestataires à Mexico. Du Plánton à Morena (2006–2018). Pour une Sociologie de l'Engagement: un Regard Latino-Américaniste." Habilitation à diriger des recherches. PSL/Ecole normale supérieure.

Combes, Hélène. Forthcoming. *Foyers Contestataires à Mexico*. Paris: Le Croquant.

Combes, Hélène, Sergio Tamayo, and Michael Voegtli, eds. 2015. *Pensar y Mirar la Protesta*. México City: Universidad Autónoma Metropolitana.

Conaghan, Catherine. 1995. "Politicians against Parties: Discord and Disconnection in Ecuador's Party System." In *Building Democratic Institutions: Party Systems in Latin America*, edited by Scott Mainwaring and Timothy Scully, 434–458. Stanford, CA: Stanford University Press.

Conaghan, Catherine. 2000. "The Irrelevant Right: Alberto Fujimori and the New Politics of Pragmatic Peru." In *Conservative Parties, the Right, and the Democracy in Latin America*, edited by Kevin Middlebrook, 255–284. Baltimore, MD: Johns Hopkins University Press.

Conaghan, Catherine. 2005. *Fujimori's Peru: Deception in the Public Sphere*. Pittsburgh, PA: University of Pittsburgh Press.

Conaghan, Catherine. 2016. "Delegative Democracy Revisited: Ecuador Under Correa." *Journal of Democracy* 27 (3):109–118.

Conaghan, Catherine. 2017. "Contra-Associational Strategy in a Hybrid Regime: Ecuador, 2007–2015." *Bulletin of Latin American Research* 36 (4):509–525.

Conaghan, Catherine. 2018. "From Movements to Governments. Comparing Bolivia's MAS and Ecuador's PAIS." In *Reshaping the Political Arena in Latin America. From Resisting Neoliberalism to the Second Incorporation*, edited by Eduardo Silva and Federico Rossi, 222–250. Pittsburgh, PA: University of Pittsburgh Press.

Congreso Visible. 2014. Balance de la Tercera Legislatura del Congreso Colombiano: Julio de 2012 a Junio de 2013, https://congresovisible.uniandes.edu.co/media/uploads/boletines/Resumen_Tercera_Legislatura.pdf.

Coppedge, Michael. 2001. "Political Darwinism in Latin America's Lost Decade." In *Political Parties and Democracy*, edited by Larry Diamond and Richard Gunther, 173–205. Baltimore, MD: Johns Hopkins University Press.

Cordero Cordero, Maria Virginia. 2016. "Alianza País: El Movimiento Político como Campo Multi-Organizacional." MA Thesis, Facultad Latinoamericana de Ciencias Sociales, Sede Ecuador.

Corrales, Javier. 2015. "The Authoritarian Resurgence: Autocratic Legalism in Venezuela." *Journal of Democracy* 26 (2):37–51.

Cox, Gary W., and Mathew D. McCubbins. 1993. *Legislative Leviathan: Party Government in the House*. Los Angeles: University of California Press.

Cox, Gary, and Matthew McCubbins. 2001. "Introduction: Political Institutions and the Determinants of Public Policy." In *Presidents, Parliaments, and Policy*, edited by Stephan Haggard and Matthew D McCubbins, 1–20. Cambridge: Cambridge University Press.

Cyr, Jennifer. 2013. "Que Veinte Años No es Nada: Hugo Chávez, las Elecciones de 2012 y el Continuismo Político Venezolano." *Revista de Ciencia Política* 33 (1):375–391.

Cyr, Jennifer. 2017. *The Fates of Political Parties: Crisis, Continuity, and Change in Latin America*. New York: Cambridge University Press.

Cyr, Jennifer, and Carlos Meléndez. 2016. "Una Exploración de la Identidad (y la Anti-Identidad) Política a Nivel Subnacional: El Fujimorismo y el Chavismo en Perspectiva Comparada." In *Representación Política en América Latina: Partidos Políticos, Elecciones y Reglas*, edited by Fernando Tuesta Soldevilla, 211–228. Lima: Jurado Nacional de Elecciones.

Cyr, Jennifer, and Iñaki Sagarzazu. 2014. "Sistemas de Partido Multinivel y el Colapso del Sistema de Partidos en Venezuela: Congruencia, Incongruencia y Volatilidad." In *Territorio y Poder: Nuevos Actores y Competencia Política en los Sistemas de Partidos Multinivel en América Latina*, edited by Flavia Freidenberg and Julieta Suárez Cao, 339–365. Salamanca: Ediciones Universidad de Salamanca.

Dahl, Robert. 1971. *Polyarchy: Participation and Opposition*. New Haven, CT: Yale University Press.

Dalmasso, Simone. 2019. "El Mitin." *Plaza Publica*, August 9, www.plazapublica.com.gt/content/el-mitin-0 (last accessed May 22, 2020).

Dargent, Eduardo, and Paula Muñoz. 2013. "¿Democracia Contra Partidos? Desinstitucionalización del Sistema de Partidos en Colombia." *Politai: Revista de Ciencia Política* 4 (7):51–72.

Dávila Ladrón de Guevara, Andrés, and Natalia Delgado. 2002. "La Metamorfosis del Sistema Político Colombiano: ¿Clientelismo de Mercado o Nueva Forma de Intermediación?" In *Degradación o Cambio, Evolución del Sistema Político Colombiano*, edited by Francisco Gutierrez, 319–356. Bogota: Grupo Editorial Norma.

De Belaunde, Alberto. 2019. *¡No Retiro Nada!* Lima: Planeta.

De La O, Ana. 2013. "Do Conditional Cash Transfers Affect Electoral Behavior? Evidence from a Randomized Experiment in Mexico." *American Journal of Political Science* 57 (1):1–14.

De la Torre, Carlos. 2013. "El Tecnopopulismo de Rafael Correa ¿Es Compatible el Carisma con la Tecnocracia?" *Latin American Research Review* 48 (1):24–43.

De los Santos, Tomás. 1984. *La Revolución de 1922*. Vols. 1 and 2. Asunción: El Lector.

della Porta, Donatella, Joseba Fernández, Hara Kouki, and Lorenzo Mosca. 2017. *Movement Parties against Austerity*. Cambridge: Polity Press.

Di Tella, Torcuato S. 1971. "La Búsqueda de la Fórmula Política Argentina." *Desarrollo Económico* 11 (42–44):317–325.

Dietz, Henry A., and David J. Myers. 2007. "From Thaw to Deluge: Party System Collapse in Venezuela and Peru." *Latin American Politics & Society* 49 (2):59–86.

Dirección General de Estadística, Encuestas y Censos. 2018. *Principales Indicadores de Empleo: 2017*. Asunción: Dirección General de Estadísticas, Encuestas y Censos.

Dix, Robert. 1987. *The Politics of Colombia*. New York: Praeger.

Došek, Tomáš, Liliana Rocío Duarte Recalde, and Marcos Pérez Talia. 2016. "Elecciones Municipales de 2015 en Paraguay: Cambios Simbólicos y Continuidades Sustanciales." *Revista Uruguaya de Ciencia Política* 25 (1):137–156.

Dougherty, Michael L. 2011. "The Global Gold Mining Industry, Junior Firms, and Civil Society Resistance in Guatemala." *Bulletin of Latin American Research* 30 (4):403–418.

Downs, Anthony. 1957. *An Economic Theory of Democracy*. New York: Harper and Row.

Duverger, Maurice. 1954. *Political Parties*. London: Methuen.

Echt, Leandro. 2016. "Los Think Tanks Partidarios: Entre el Conocimiento y la Política. El caso de la Fundación Pensar y PRO en Argentina." Maestría en Políticas Públicas y Gerenciamiento del Desarrollo: Universidad Nacional de San Martín and Georgetown University.

Eichorst, Jason, and John Polga-Hecimovich. 2014. "The 2013 Ecuadorian General Elections." *Electoral Studies* 34 (1):361–365.

Elias, Silvel, and Gisselle Sánchez. 2014. "Country Study: Guatemala." *Americas Quarterly*. www.americasquarterly.org/issue/consulta-previa-and-investment/.

Etchemendy, Sebastián. 2019. "The Rise of Segmented Neo-Corporatism in South America: Wage Coordination in Argentina and Uruguay (2005–2015)." *Comparative Political Studies* 52 (10):1427–1465.

Ferreira Pérez, Saturnino. 1986. *Proceso Político del Paraguay 1943–1947: Una Visión desde la Prensa*. Asunción: El Lector.

Figueroa Ibarra, Carlos. 2010. *¿En el Umbral del posneoliberalismo? Izquierda y Gobierno en America Latina*. Guatemala City: F&G Editores.

Figueroa, Sonny. 2019. "Partido Todos No es el Más Grande como Dijo su Secretario General." *Confirmado*. www.confirmado.org/2019/02/partido-todos-no-es-el-mas-grande/ (last accessed May 22, 2020).

Filártiga Callizo, Camilo. 2016. "La Estabilidad del Sistema de Partidos de Paraguay (1989–2015)." In *Los Sistemas de Partidos en América Latina 1978–2015. Tomo 2: Cono Sur y Países Andinos*, edited by Flavia Freidenberg, 193–234. Mexico City: Universidad Nacional Autonoma de Mexico.

Fonseca, Marco. 2004. *Entre la Comunidad y la República: Ciudadanía y Sociedad Civil en Guatemala*. Guatemala City: F&G Editores.

Fortín, Javier. 2010. "Transfuguismo Parlamentario en Guatemala: Un Caso de Altos Costos de Asociación, Monopolio Partidario y Bajos Costos de Transacción." *América Latina Hoy* 54:141–166.

Fortin, Javier, and Enrique Naveda. 2012. "¿Inciden las Transferencias Condicionadas en las Elecciones?" *Espacios Políticos* 5 (6):27–48.

Fox, Jonathan. 1994. "The Difficult Transition from Clientelism to Citizenship: Lessons from Mexico." *World Politics* 46 (2):151–184.

Freidenberg, Flavia. 2012. "Ecuador 2011: Revolución Ciudadana, estabilidad política y personalismo político." *Revista de Ciencia Política* 32 (1):129–150.

Fuentes Knight, Juan Alberto. 2011. *Rendición de Cuentas*. Guatemala City: F&G Editores.

Fuerza Popular. 2016. *Plan de Gobierno de Fuerza Popular: Al Perú*. Lima: Fuerza Popular.

Funk, Robert. 2006. *El Gobierno de Ricardo Lagos: La Nueva Vía Chilena hacia el Socialismo*. Santiago: Ediciones Universidad Diego Portales.

G25. 2014. *Anuario 2013*. Buenos Aires: G25.

G25. 2015. *Anuario 2014*. Buenos Aires: G25.

Gálvez Borrell, Víctor. 2004. "Guatemala: Riesgos de Reversión Autoritaria y Retorno de los Empresarios." *Nueva Sociedad* 191:4–15.

Gandhi, Jennifer, and Ora John Reuter. 2013. "The Incentives for Pre-electoral Coalitions in Non-democratic Elections." *Democratization* 20 (1):137–159.

Garcé, Adolfo. 2007. Partidos Políticos y Think Tanks en América Latina. London: Overseas Development Institute.

Garcé, Adolfo, and Jaime Yaffé. 2005. *La Era Progresista*. Montevideo: Editorial Fin de Siglo.

García Linera, Álvaro, Marxa Chávez León, and Patricia Costa Monje. 2004. *Sociología de los Movimientos Sociales en Bolivia*. La Paz: Plural Editores.

Garretón, Manuel Antonio. 1989. *The Chilean Political Process*. Winchester, MA: Hyman.

Gaxie, Daniel. 1977. "Économie des Partis et Rétributions du Militantisme." *Revue Française de Science Politique* 27 (1):123–154.

Gehring, Huber. 2016. *Partidos Políticos en Colombia: Evolución y Prospectiva*. Bogota: Fundación Konrad-Adenauer-Stiftung.

George, Alexander L., and Andrew Bennett. 2005. *Case Studies and Theory Development in the Social Sciences*. Cambridge: MIT Press.

Gibson, Edward L. 1996. *Class and Conservative Parties: Argentina in Comparative Perspective*. Baltimore, MD: Johns Hopkins University Press.

Gibson, Edward L., and Julieta Suárez-Cao. 2010. "Federalized Party Systems and Subnational Party Competition: Theory and an Empirical Application to Argentina." *Comparative Politics* 43 (1):21–39.

Gilens, Martin. 2012. *Affluence and Influence: Economic Inequality and Political Power in America*. Princeton, NJ: Princeton University Press.

Giraudy, Agustina, and Jennifer Pribble. 2019. "Rethinking Measures of Democracy and Welfare State Universalism: Lessons from Subnational Research." *Regional & Federal Studies* 29 (2):135–163.

Godoy, Juan Alejandro. 2021. *El Último Dictador: Vida y Gobierno de Alberto Fujimori*. Lima: Debate.

Goertz, Gary. 2006. *Social Science Concepts: A User's Guide*. Princeton, NJ: Princeton University Press.

Gómez-Campos, Steffan. 2015. "La Organización Partidaria Importa: Una Aproximación a los Partidos Políticos Costarricenses." *Revista de Derecho Electoral* 20 (3):276–308.

Gómez-Campos, Steffan. 2020. "El Votómetro: Exploración de las Identidades Políticas en la Decisión Electoral." In *Elecciones 2018 en Costa Rica: Retrato de una Democracia Amenazada* edited by Ronald Alfaro Redondo and Felipe Alpízar Rodríguez, 150–177. San José: CONARE-PEN.

Gómez Albarello, Juan Gabriel, and Juan Carlos Rodríguez-Raga. 2007. "Competencia Electoral en Grandes Circunscripciones: El Caso del Senado Colombiano." In *Entre la Persistencia y el Cambio: Reconfiguración del Escenario Partidista y Electoral en Colombia*, edited by Diana Hoyos, 49–83. Bogota: CEPI.

Gómez Florentín, Carlos. 2013. *El Paraguay de la Post Guerra (1870–1900)*. Asunción: El Lector.

González, Fernán. 1997. "Aproximación a la Configuración Política en Colombia." In *Para Leer la Política: Ensayos de Historia Política de Colombia*. Vol. I, edited by Fernán González, 21–70. Bogota: CINEP.

González, Luis Eduardo. 1991. *Political Structures and Democracy in Uruguay*. Notre Dame, IN: University of Notre Dame Press.

González, Pablo. 2014. "Guatemala." In *Handbook of Central American Governance*, edited by Diego Sánchez-Ancochea and Salvador Martí i Puig, 400–419. New York: Routledge.

Grandinetti, Juan. 2015. "'Mirar para Adelante'. Tres Dimensiones de la Juventud en la Militancia de Jóvenes PRO." In *Hagamos Equipo: PRO y la Construcción de la Nueva Derecha en Argentina*, edited by Gabiel Vommaro and Sergio Morresi, 231–263. Los Polvorines: Ediciones UNGS.

Greene, Keneth. 2007. *Why Dominant Parties Lose: Mexico's Democratization in Comparative Perspective*. New York: Cambridge University Press.

Grisaffi, Thomas. 2018. *Coca Yes, Cocaine No: How Bolivia's Coca Growers Reshaped Democracy*. Durham, NC: Duke University Press.

Gunther, Richard, and Larry Diamond. 2003. "Species of Political Parties: A New Typology." *Party Politics* 9 (2):167–199.

Gutiérrez Sanín, Francisco. 2006. "¿Más partidos?" In *En la Encrucida. Colombia en el Siglo XXI*, edited by Francisco Leal, 147–172. Bogota: Ediciones Uniandes.

Gutiérrez Sanín, Francisco. 2007. *¿Lo que el Viento se Llevó? Los Partidos Políticos y la Democracia en Colombia 1958–2002*. Bogota: Grupo Editorial Norma.

Guzmán Campos, Germán. 1962. "La Quiebra de las Instituciones Fundamentales." In *La Violencia en Colombia. Estudio de un Proceso Social*, edited by Germán Guzmán, Orlando Fals Borda and Eduardo Umaña Luna, 239–286. Bogota: Ediciones Tercer Mundo.

Hale, Michelle. 2009. "Kirchheimer's French Twist: A Model of the Catch-All Thesis Applied to the French Case." *Party Politics* 15 (5):592–614.

Han, Hahrie. 2014. *How Organizations Develop Activists: Civic Associations and Leadership in the 21st Century*. New York: Oxford University Press.

Handlin, Samuel. 2013. "Social Protection and the Politicization of Class Cleavages during Latin America's Left Turn." *Comparative Political Studies* 46 (12):1582–1609.

Harnecker, Marta. 2011. *Ecuador: Una Nueva Izquierda en Busca de la Vida en Plenitud*. Barcelona: El Viejo Topo.

Hartlyn, Jonathan. 1988. *The Politics of Coalition Rule in Colombia*. New York: Cambridge University Press.

Hazan, Reuven, and Gideon Rahat. 2010. *Democracy within Parties: Candidate Selection Methods and Their Political Consequences*. Oxford: Oxford University Press.

Hermet, Guy, Alain Rouquié, and Juan José Linz. 1978. *Des Élections pas Comme les Autres*. Bordeaux: Presses de la Fondation Nationale des Sciences Politiques.

Hernández Naranjo, Gerardo. 2001. "Tendencias Electorales y Sistema de Partidos en Costa Rica." In *La Democracia de Costa Rica ante el Siglo XXI*, edited by Jorge Rovira Mas, 255–275. San José: Editorial de la Universidad de Costa Rica.

Hernández Naranjo, Gerardo 2007. "Dinámicas del Sistema de Partidos Políticos y del Cambio Institucional en el Régimen Electoral de Costa Rica 1952–2002." Tesis de Doctorado, Centro de Estudios Sociológicos, El Colegio de México.

Hernández, Virgilio, and Fernando Buendía. 2011. "Ecuador: Avances y Desafíos de Alianza País." *Nueva Sociedad* 234 (July–August):129–142.

Herrera Llive, Klever Vinicio. 2017. "Las Organizaciones de Base de Alianza Pais: El Papel de los Comités de la Revolución Ciudadana en la Movilización Política." *Análisis Político* 30 (91):96–109.

Hicken, Allen. 2009. *Building Party Systems in Developing Democracies*. New York: Cambridge University Press.

Hilgers, Tina. 2008. "Causes and Consequences of Political Clientelism: Mexico's PRD in Comparative Perspective." *Latin American Politics and Society* 50 (4):123–153.

Hirschman, Albert. 1970. *Exit, Voice, and Loyalty: Responses to Decline in Firms, Organizations, and States*. Cambridge, MA: Harvard University Press.

Holland, Alisha C. 2016. "Insurgent Successor Parties: Scaling Down to Build a Party after War." In *Challenges of Party-Building in Latin America*, edited by

Steven Levitsky, James Loxton, Brandon Van Dyck and Jorge Domínguez, 273–304. New York: Cambridge University Press.
Hoskin, Gary. 1998. "Elecciones Presidenciales, 1998." In *Elecciones y Democracia en Colombia 1997–1998*, edited by Ana María Bejarano and Andrés Dávila Ladrón de Guevara, 361–399. Bogota: Fundación Social, Departamento de Ciencia Política Universidad de los Andes, Veeduría Ciudadana a la Elección Presidencial.
Huber, Evelyne, and John D Stephens, eds. 2012. *Democracy and the Left: Social Policy and Inequality in Latin America*. Chicago: University of Chicago Press.
Hunter, Wendy. 2010. *The Transformation of the Workers' Party in Brazil, 1989–2009*. New York: Cambridge University Press.
Huntington, Samuel. 1968. *Political Order in Changing Societies*. New Haven, CT: Yale University Press.
Immigration and Refugee Board of Canada. 2016. Memo: "Venezuela: Information on the Political Party Justice First (Primero Justicia), Including Membership Procedures, Structure and Leadership at the National Level and in Maracaibo (2014–May 2016)." www.refworld.org/docid/591612444.html (last accessed October 15, 2019).
Isaacs, Anita. 2010. "Trouble in Central America: Guatemala on the Brink." *Journal of Democracy* 21 (2):108–122.
Jiménez Badillo, Margarita. 2018. "Transfuguismo Legislativo entre Gobierno y Oposición en Guatemala." *América Latina Hoy* 79 (1):153–187.
Jiménez, Maryhen. 2018. "Challenging the Autocrat: Opposition Responses to Regime Repression in Venezuela." XXXVI International Congress of the Latin American Studies Association, Barcelona, May 23–26.
Jones, Mark P. 2011. "Weakly Institutionalized Party Systems and Presidential Democracy: Evidence from Guatemala." *International Area Studies Review* 14 (4):3–30.
Jones, Mark P., and Wonjae Hwang. 2005. "Party Government in Presidential Democracies: Extending Cartel Theory beyond the US Congress." *American Journal of Political Science* 49 (2):267–282.
Kattán Hervas, Sharvelt Raphael. 2018. "La Apropiacion del Concepto "Patria" en Ecuador. Análisis Semiótico de la Campaña Electoral Audiovisual de Rafael Correa en 2013." Tesis Licenciatura en Comunicación, Escuela de Comunicación, Pontifícia Universidad Católica del Ecuador.
Katz, Richard S., and Peter Mair. 1995. "Changing Models of Party Organization and Party Democracy: The Emergence of the Cartel Party." *Party Politics* 1 (1):5–28.
Keck, Margaret E. 1992. *The Worker's Party and Democratization in Brazil*. New Haven, CT: Yale University Press.
Kirchheimer, Otto. 1966. "The Transformation of the Western European Party System." In *Political Parties and Political Development*, edited by Joseph LaPalombara and Myron Weiner, 177–200. Princeton, NJ: Princeton University Press.
Kitschelt, Herbert. 1989. *The Logics of Party Formation: Ecological Politics in Belgium and West Germany*. Ithaca, NY: Cornell University Press.

Kitschelt, Herbert. 1994. *The Transformation of European Social Democracy.* New York: Cambridge University Press.

Kitschelt, Herbert. 2000. "Linkages between Citizens and Politicians in Democratic Polities." *Comparative Political Studies* 33 (6–7):845–879.

Kitschelt, Herbert. 2006. "Movement Parties." In *Handbook of Party Politics*, edited by Richard Katz and William Crotty, 278–290. London: Sage.

Kitschelt, Herbert, Kirk Hawkins, Juan Pablo Luna, Guillermo Rosas, and Elizabeth Zechmeister. 2010. *Latin American Party Systems.* New York: Cambridge University Press.

Kitschelt, Herbert, and Steven Wilkinson, eds. 2007. *Patrons, Clients and Policies: Patterns of Democratic Accountability and Political Competition.* New York: Cambridge University Press.

Klašnja, Marko. 2016. "Increasing Rents and Incumbency Disadvantage." *Journal of Theoretical Politics* 28 (2):225–265.

Lachi, Marcello, and Raquel Rojas Scheffer. 2018. *Correligionarios: Actitudes y Prácticas Políticas del Electorado Paraguayo.* Asunción: Arandurã Editorial.

Lanzaro, Jorge. 2004. "La Izquierda se Acerca a los Uruguayos y los Uruguayos se Acercan a la Izquierda: Claves de Desarrollo del Frente Amplio." In *La izquierda uruguaya entre la oposición y el gobierno*, edited by Jorge Lanzaro, 13–107. Montevideo: Fin de Siglo-FESUR.

Lanzaro, Jorge. 2008. "La Socialdemocracia Criolla." *Nueva Sociedad* 217:40–58.

Lauth, Hans-Joachim. 2015. "Formal and Informal Institutions." In *Routledge Handbook of Comparative Political Institutions*, edited by Jennifer Gandhi and Rubén Ruiz-Rufino, 56–69. New York: Routledge.

Lawson, Kay, and Peter H. Merkl, eds. 1988. *When Parties Fail: Emerging Alternative Organizations.* Princeton, NJ: Princeton University Press.

Le Cour, Romain. 2017. "Pueblo Chico, Infierno Grande. Territorialidad e Intermediación Política: Las Autodefensas de Michoacán." In *La inseguridad en Michoacán*, edited by Salvador Maldonado Aranda, 153–178. Zamora: Colegio de Michoacán.

Leal Buitrago, Francisco, and Andrés Dávila Ladrón de Guevara. 1990. *Clientelismo: El Sistema Político y su Expresión Regional.* Bogota: Instituto de Estudios Políticos y Relaciones Internacionales.

Leal, Diego, and David Roll. 2013. "Tanques de Pensamiento y Partidos Políticos en Colombia: El Caso de las Reformas Políticas de 2003 y 2009." *Ciencia Política* 8 (16):89–112.

LeBas, Adrienne. 2013. *From Protest to Parties: Party-Building and Democratization in Africa.* New York: Oxford University Press.

Lehoucq, Fabrice. 2002. "The 1999 Elections in Guatemala." *Electoral Studies* 21 (1):107–114.

Lehoucq, Fabrice. 2012. *The Politics of Modern Central America: Civil War, Democratization, and Underdevelopment.* New York: Cambridge University Press.

Lehoucq, Fabrice, and David L. Wall. 2004. "Explaining Voter Turnout Rates in New Democracies: Guatemala." *Electoral Studies* 23 (3):485–500.

Leiras, Marcelo. 2007. *Todos los Caballos del Rey: La Integración de los Partidos Políticos y el Gobierno Democrático de la Argentina, 1995–2003*. Buenos Aires: Prometeo.

Lemus, Jonatán. 2012. "Democracia Interna de los Partidos Políticos Guatemaltecos: un Desafío Pendiente." In *Partidos Políticos Guatemaltecos: Dinámicas Internas y Desempeño*, edited by ASÍES, 1–30. Guatemala City: Asociación de Investigación y Estudios Sociales.

Lemus, Jonatán. 2013. "Partidos Franquicia: La Distorsión del Modelo de Organización de la Ley Electoral y de Partidos Políticos." In *Partidos Políticos Guatemaltecos: Cobertura Territorial y Organización Interna*, edited by Jonatán Lemus and Javier Brolo, 25–53. Guatemala City: Asociación de Investigación y Estudios Sociales.

León Trujillo, Jorge. 2012. "Correa: Dinámica de la Concentración de Poder y la Modernización Conservadora." In *Balance de la Revolución Ciudadana*, edited by Sebastián Mantilla and Santiago Mejía, 373–400. Quito: Editorial Planeta del Ecuador.

Levitsky, Steven. 2001. "Inside the Black Box: Recent Studies in Latin American Party Organizations." *Studies in Comparative International Development* 36 (2):92–110.

Levitsky, Steven. 2003. *Transforming Labor-Based Parties in Latin America: Argentine Peronism in Comparative Perspective*. New York: Cambridge University Press.

Levitsky, Steven. 2012. "Informal Institutions and Politics in Latin America." In *Routledge Handbook of Latin American Politics*, edited by Peter Kingstone and Deborah Yashar, 88–100. New York: Routledge.

Levitsky, Steven, and Maxwell Cameron. 2003. "Democracy without Parties? Political Parties and Regime Change in Fujimori's Peru." *Latin American Politics & Society* 45 (3):1–33.

Levitsky, Steven, James Loxton, Brandon Van Dyck, and Jorge Domínguez. 2016. *Challenges of Party-Building in Latin America*. New York: Cambridge University Press.

Levitsky, Steven, and Kenneth Roberts, eds. 2011. *The Resurgence of the Latin American Left*. Baltimore, MD: Johns Hopkins University Press.

Levitsky, Steven, and Lucan Way. 2010. *Competitive Authoritarianism: Hybrid Regimes After the Cold War*. New York: Cambridge University Press.

Levitsky, Steven, and Mauricio Zavaleta. 2016. "Why No Party-Building in Peru?" In *Challenges of Party Building in Latin America*, edited by Steven Levitsky, James Loxton, Brandon Van Dyck and Jorge Dominguez, 412–439. New York: Cambridge University Press.

Lewis, Paul H. 1988. "The Ideological Origins of the Paraguayan Parties." XIV International Congress of Latin American Studies Association, New Orleans, March 17–19.

Lewis, Paul H. 1993. *Political Parties and Generations in Paraguay's Liberal Era, 1869–1940*. Chapel Hill: University of North Carolina Press.

Liberación Nacional Partido. 2017. *Estatuto Orgánico*. San José: Partido Liberación Nacional.

Linz, Juan. 1964. "An Authoritarian Regime: Spain." In *Cleavages, Ideologies and Party Systems: Contributions to Comparative Political Sociology*, edited by Erik Allardt and Littunen Yrjö, 291–341. Helsinki: Westermarck Society.

Lipset, Seymour M., and Stein Rokkan. 1967. "Cleveage Structures, Party Systems, and Voter Aligments: An Introduction." In *Party Systems and Voter Aligments: Cross-National Perspectives*, edited by Seymour Martin Lipset and Stein Rokkan, 1–64. New York: Free Press.

Loaeza, Soledad. 1999. *El Partido Acción Nacional, la Larga Marcha, 1939–1994: Oposición Leal y Partido de Protesta*. México City: Fondo de Cultura Economica.

Londoño, Juan Fernando. 2009. "Partidos Políticos y Think Tanks en Colombia." In *Dime a Quién Escuchas ... Think tanks y partidos en América Latina* edited by Enrique Mendizabal and Kristen Sample 127–156. Lima: IDEA & ODI.

López Cariboni, Santiago, and Rosario Queirolo. 2015. "Class Voting versus Economic Voting: Explaining Electoral Behavior before and after the 'Left turn' in Latin America." 8ª Congreso Latinoamericano de Ciencia Política, ALACIP, Lima, Perú, July 22–24, 2015.

López Leyva, Miguel Armando. 2007. *La encrucijada entre la protesta social y la participación electoral*. México: Plaza y Valdés.

Loxton, James. 2016. "Authoritarian Successor Parties and the New Right in Latin America." In *Challenges of Party Building in Latin America*, edited by Steven Levitsky, James Loxton, Brandon Van Dyck and Jorge Dominguez, 245–272. New York: Cambridge University Press.

Luján, Diego, and Juan A. Moraes. 2017. "Why Fusions? The Role of Electoral Coordination in the Frente Amplio's Formation." Working paper. Montevideo: Departamento de Ciencia Política, Universidad de la República, Uruguay.

Luna, Juan P., and Elizabeth J. Zechmeister. 2005. "Political Representation in Latin America: A Study of Elite-Mass Congruence in Nine Countries." *Comparative Political Studies* 38 (4):388–416.

Luna, Juan Pablo. 2004. "Shaky Foundations? The Transformation of Party-Society Relations in Contemporary Chile." Annual Meeting of the Midwest Political Science Association, Chicago.

Luna, Juan Pablo. 2007a. *Cultura Política de la Democracia en Chile: 2006*. Santiago: Instituto de Ciencia Política.

Luna, Juan Pablo. 2007b. "Frente Amplio and the Crafting of a Social Democratic Alternative in Uruguay." *Latin American Politics and Society* 49 (4):1–30.

Luna, Juan Pablo. 2010. "Segmented Party Voter Linkages in Latin America: The Case of the UDI." *Journal of Latin American Studies* 42 (2):325–356.

Luna, Juan Pablo. 2014. *Segmented Representation: Political Party Strategies in Unequal Democracies*. Oxford: Oxford University Press.

Luna, Juan Pablo, and David Altman. 2011. "Uprooted but Stable: Chilean Parties and the Concept of Party System Institutionalization." *Latin American Politics & Society* 53 (2):1–28.

Luna, Juan Pablo, and Rodrigo Mardones. 2010. "Chile: Are the Parties Over?" *Journal of Democracy* 21 (3):107–121.

Luna, Juan Pablo, and Rodrigo Mardones. 2017. "Introducción: Estado, Partidos y Sociedad en Chile pre 1973 y post 1990." In *La Columna Vertebral*

Fracturada: Revisitando Intermediarios Políticos en Chile, edited by Juan Pablo Luna and Rodrigo Mardones, 15–32. Santiago: PUC-RIL.

Luna, Juan Pablo, and Fernando Rosenblatt. 2012. "¿Notas para una Autopsia? Los Partidos Políticos en el Chile Actual." In *Democracia con Partidos. Informe para la Reforma de los Partidos Políticos en Chile*, edited by Francisco J. Díaz ; Lucas Sierra, 115–268. Santiago: CEP-CIEPLAN.

Luna, Juan Pablo, and Fernando Rosenblatt. 2017. "Las Organizaciones Partidarias Antes y Después de 1973." In *La Columna Vertebral Fracturada: Revisitando Intermediarios Políticos en Chile*, edited by Juan Pablo Luna and Rodrigo Mardones, 33–56. Santiago: PUC/RIL editores.

Lupu, Noam. 2014. "Brand Dilution and the Breakdown of Political Parties in Latin America." *World Politics* 66 (04):561–602.

Lupu, Noam. 2016. *Party Brands in Crisis: Partisanship, Brand Dilution, and the Breakdown of Political Parties in Latin America*. New York: Cambridge University Press.

Madrid, Raúl L. 2012. *The Rise of Ethnic Politics in Latin America*. New York: Cambridge University Press.

Magaloni, Beatriz. 2006. *Voting for Autocracy: Hegemonic Party Survival and its Demise in Mexico*. New York: Cambridge University Press.

Mainwaring, Scott, ed. 2018. *Party Systems in Latin America: Institutionalization, Decay, and Collapse*. New York: Cambridge University Press.

Mainwaring, Scott, Ana María Bejarano, and Eduardo Pizarro. 2006. *The Crisis of Democratic Representation in the Andes*. Stanford, CA: Stanford University Press.

Mainwaring, Scott, and Aníbal Perez Liñán. 1997. "Party Discipline in the Brazilian Constitutional Congress." *Legislative Studies Quarterly* XXII:453–481.

Mainwaring, Scott, and Timothy Scully, eds. 1995. *Building Democratic Institutions: Party Systems in Latin America*. Stanford, CA: Stanford University Press.

Mainwaring, Scott, and Mariano Torcal. 2006. "Party System Institutionalization and Party System Theory After the Third Wave of Democratization." In *Handbook of Party Politics*, edited by Richard S. Katz and William Crotty, 204–227. Thousand Oaks, CA: Sage.

Mainwaring, Scott, Mariano Torcal, and Nicolás Somma. 2016. "The Left and the Mobilization of Class Voting in Latin America." In *The Latin American Voter: Pursuing Representation and Accountability in Challenging Contexts*, edited by Ryan Carlin, Matthew Singer and Elizabeth Zechmeister, 69–98. Ann Arbor: University of Michigan Press.

Mainwaring, Scott, and Edurne Zoco. 2007. "Political Sequences and the Stabilization of Interparty Competition." *Party Politics* 13 (2):155–178.

Mair, Peter. 1997. *Party System Change: Approaches and Interpretations*. Oxford: Oxford University Press.

Malamud, Andrés. 2011. "Ni Mucho Gobierno de la Opinión Pública ni Tanto Regreso a la Voluntad: Bipartidismo Recargado." In *En La política en tiempos de los kirchner*, edited by Andrés Malamud and Miguel De Luca, 105–114. Buenos Aires: Eudeba.

Mangonnet, Jorge, María Victoria Murillo, and Julia María Rubio. 2018. "Local Economic Voting and the Agricultural Boom in Argentina, 2007–2015." *Latin American Politics and Society* 60 (3):27–53.

Manin, Bernard. 1997. *The Principles of Representative Government*. New York: Cambridge University Press.

Martínez-Escobar, Fernando. 2015. "El Sistema de Partidos del Paraguay a través de la Distribución del Poder y las Reglas del Juego 1989–2013." *Revista Paraguaya de Sociología* 52 (147):99–126.

Martuccelli, Danilo. 2015. *Lima y sus Arenas: Poderes Sociales y Jerarquías Culturales*. Lima: Cauces Editores.

Martz, John D. 1966. *Acción Democratica: Evolution of a Modern Political Party in Venezuela*. Princeton, NJ: Princeton University Press.

Mauricio Vargas, José P. 2015. "Informality in Paraguay: Macro-micro Evidence and Policy Implications." Working Paper. Washington: International Monetary Fund.

Mayorga, Fernando. 2019. *Antes y Después del Referendum: Política y Democracia en el Estado Plurinacional*. Cochabamba: UMSS-CESU.

Mejia Acosta, Andres, and Karla Meneses. 2019. "Who benefits? Intergovernmental Transfers, Subnational Politics and Local Spending in Ecuador." *Regional & Federal Studies* 29 (2):219–247. doi: 10.1080/13597566.2018.1556644.

Meléndez, Carlos. 2014. "Is There a Right Track in Post-Party System Collapse Scenarios? Comparing the Andean Countries." In *The Resilience of the Latin American Right*, edited by Juan Pablo Luna and Cristóbal Rovira Kaltwasser, 167–193. Baltimore, MD: Johns Hopkins University Press.

Melo, Jorge Orlando. 2018. *Historia Mínima de Colombia: La Historia de un País que ha Oscilado entre la Guerra y la Paz, la Pobreza y el Bienestar, el Autoritarismo y la Democracia*. México: Colegio de México/Ediciones Turner.

Meltzer, Allan H, and Scott F Richard. 1981. "A Rational Theory of the Size of Government." *Journal of Political Economy* 89 (5):914–927.

Michels, Robert. 1999 (1911). *Political Parties: A Sociological Study of the Oligarchical Tendencies of Modern Democracy*. New Brunswick, NJ: Transaction Publishers.

Middlebrook, Kevin J., ed. 2000. *Conservative Parties, the Right and Democracy in Latin America*. Baltimore, MD: Johns Hopkins University Press.

Mizrahi, Yemile. 2003. *From Martyrdom to Power: the Partido Acción Nacional in Mexico*. South Bend, IN: University of Notre Dame Press.

Monestier, Felipe. 2011. *Movimientos Sociales, Partidos Políticos y Democracia Directa desde Abajo en Uruguay: 1985–2004*. Buenos Aires: Consejo Latinoamericano de Ciencias Sociales.

Monestier, Felipe. 2017. "Formas de Actuación Política de las Élites Económicas. Argentina, Chile y Uruguay en Perspectiva Comparada." Doctor en Ciencia Política, Instituto de Ciencia Política, Pontificia Universidad Católica de Chile.

Montero, Mariano D. 2019. *Agapito Valiente. Stroessner Kyhyjeja*. Asunción: Arandurá.

Montilla, Paola. 2011. "La Democracia Interna y su Influencia en la Cohesión de Partido: El Caso de Colombia." In *Elecciones 2010: Partidos, Consultas y Democracia Interna*, edited by Yann Basset, Margarita Batlle, Paola Montilla and Margarita Marín, 107–159. Bogota: Universidad Externado de Colombia.

Moraes, Juan Andrés, and Diego Luján. 2015. "The Heft of the Uruguayan Left: A Case of Party Adaptation without Moderation." Paper Prepared for the Project "Reforming Communism: Cuba in Comparative Perspective."

Moreira, Constanza. 2000. "Las Paradojales Elecciones del Fin de Siglo Uruguayo: Comportamiento Electoral y Cultura Política." In *Elecciones 1999/2000*, edited by Oscar A. Bottinelli et al., 87–110. Montevideo: Ediciones de la Banda Oriental.

Moreira, Constanza. 2004. *Final de Juego: Del Bipartidismo Tradicional al Triunfo de la Izquierda en Uruguay*. Montevideo: Ediciones Trilce.

Moreira, Constanza, and Andrea Delbono. 2016. "Diferenciación Social, Generacional y Geográfica del Voto del Frente Amplio en las Elecciones Nacionales de 2014: Revisando la Hipótesis del Policlasismo de los Partidos Políticos Uruguayos." In *Permanencias, Trancisiones y Rupturas: Elecciones en Uruguay 2014/15*, edited by Adolfo Garcé and Niki Johnson, 119–139. Montevideo: Editorial Fin de Siglo.

Morgan, Jana. 2011. *Bankrupt Representation and Party System Collapse*. University Park: Pennsylvania State University Press.

Morgenstern, Scott, and Benito Nacif, eds. 2002. *Legislative Politics in Latin America*. Cambridge: Cambridge University Press.

Morínigo, José Nicolás. 2005. "La Práctica del Orekuete como Matriz de la Discriminación Política." In *Discriminaciones*, edited by Line Bareiro, 147–166. Asunción: CDE, UNFPA, Comisión de Equidad, Género y Desarrollo Social de la Cámara de Senadores, la Comisión de Equidad Social y Género de la Cámara de Diputados, la Comisión de Derechos Humanos y Asuntos Indígenas de la Cámara de Diputados.

Morínigo, José Nicolás. 2008. "Clientelismo y Padrinazgo en la Práctica Patrimonialista del Gobierno en el Paraguay." *Revista Paraguaya de Sociología* 132/133:203–224.

Morresi, Sergio, and Gabriel Vommaro. 2014. "Argentina: The Difficulties of the Partisan Right and the Case of Propuesta Republicana." In *The Resilience of the Latin American Right*, edited by Juan Pablo Luna and Cristóbal Rovira Kaltwasser, 319–342. Baltimore, MD: Johns Hopkins University Press.

Muñoz, Paula, and Eduardo Dargent. 2016. "Patronage, Subnational Linkages and Party-Building: The Cases of Colombia and Peru." In *Challenges of Party-Building in Latin America*, edited by Steven Levitsky, James Loxton, Brandon Van Dyck and Jorge Dominguez, 187–216. New York: Cambridge University Press.

Murakami, Yusuke. 2007. *Perú en la Era del Chino: La Política No Institucionalizada y el Pueblo en Busca de un Salvador*. Lima: Instituto de Estudios Peruanos.

Murillo, Maria Victoria. 2001. *Labor Unions, Partisan Coalitions, and Market Reforms in Latin America*. New York: Cambridge University Press.

Mustillo, Thomas J. 2007. "Entrants in the Political Arena: New Party Trajectories During the Third Wave of Democracy in Latin America." PhD Thesis in Political Science, The University of North Carolina at Chapel Hill.

Nahum, Benjamin, Ana Frega, Móncia Marona, and Ivette Trochón. 1993. *Historia Uruguaya: El Fin del Uruguay Liberal. Tomo 8 1959–1973.* Montevideo: Ediciones de la Banda Oriental.

Navarro, Melissa. 2011. "La Organización Partidaria Fujimorista a 20 años de su Origen." Licenciatura en Ciencia Política y Gobierno, Pontificia Universidad Católica del Perú.

Nichols, Byron. 1968. "Las Expectativas de los Partidos Políticos en el Paraguay." *Revista Paraguaya de Sociología* 13:37–59.

Niedzwiecki, Sara. 2018. *Uneven Social Policies: The Politics of Subnational Variation in Latin America.* New York: Cambridge University Press.

Norris, Pippa, and Ronald Inglehart. 2019. *Cultural Backlash: Trump, Brexit, and Authoritarian Populism.* New York: Cambridge University Press.

Novales, Hugo. 2015. *Análisis de la Unidad Partidaria en el Congreso de Guatemala.* Guatemala City: Asociación de Investigación y Estudios Sociales.

Núñez Muñoz, Ingrid, and Nury Pineda Morán. 2003. "Nuevos Partidos, Nuevos Liderazgos: Primero Justicia." *Cuestiones Políticas* 30:45–74.

O'Donnell, Guillermo. 1977. "Estado y Alianzas en la Argentina, 1956–1976." *Desarrollo Económico* 16 (64):523–554.

Observatorio Legislativo. 2013. *Vigilancia Ciudadana a la Asamblea Nacional.* Quito: Observatorio Legislativo.

Observatorio Legislativo. 2015. *Vigilancia Ciudadana a la Asamblea Nacional.* Quito:Observatorio Legislativo.

Offerlé, Michel. 2011. *Perímetros de lo Político: Contribuciones a una Socio-Historia de la Política.* Buenos Aires: Antropofagia.

Olivares, Alejandro. 2017. "La Conformación de Gabinetes y Supervivencia de Ministros en Chile y Uruguay Durante los Períodos Pre y Post Golpes de Estado." Doctorado en Ciencias Sociales, Tesis de Doctorado Universidad de Chile.

Ortega y Gasset, José. 1921. *España Invertebrada: Bosquejos de Algunos Pensamientos Históricos.* Madrid: Calpe.

Ortiz Crespo, Santiago, and Agustín Burbano de Lara. 2017. *Comicios en Ecuador: Victoria Electoral de Alianza Pais, Disputa Hegemónica en Ciernes.* Quito: Friedrich-Ebert-Stiftung–ILDIS.

Pachano, Simón. 2006. "Ecuador: Fragmentation and Regionalization of Representation." In *The Crisis of Democratic Representation in the Andes*, edited by Scott Mainwaring, Ana María Bejarano and Eduardo Pizarro Leongómez, 100–131. Stanford, CA: Stanford University Press.

Pachano, Simón. 2010. "Ecuador: El Nuevo Sistema Político en Funcionamiento." *Revista de Ciencia Política* 30 (2):297–317.

Pachón, Mónica, and Matthew S. Shugart. 2010. "Electoral Reform and the Mirror Image of Inter-Party and Intra-Party Competition: The Adoption of Party Lists in Colombia." *Electoral Studies* 29 (4):648–660.

Padrón, Álvaro, and Achim Wachendorfer. 2017. Trade Unions in Transformation – Uruguay: Building Trade Union Power. *Trade Unions in Transformation.* Berlin: Friedrich-Ebert-Stiftung. http://library.fes.de/pdf-files/iez/13845.pdf.

Pallister, Kevin. 2013. "Why No Mayan Party? Indigenous Movements and National Politics in Guatemala." *Latin American Politics and Society* 55 (3):117–138.

Palma, Esperanza. 2011. "El PRD en 2009: Crisis, Centralización de los Métodos de Selección de Candidatos y Reclutamiento Legislativo." In *Partidos y Elecciones Intermedias 2009: Problemas para la Construcción de Mecanismos de Representación y Participaión en México*, edited by Esperanza Palma, 39–59. México City: UAM Cuajimalpa/Miguel Ángel Porrúa.

Panebianco, Angelo. 1988. *Political Parties: Organization and Power*. New York: Cambridge University Press.

Partido Liberal. 1987. *Resolución No. 07 Por la cual la Dirección Nacional Liberal Promulgó los Presentes Estatutos*. Bogota: Partido Liberal.

Partido Por la Democracia. 1989. *La Democracia que Anhelamos: Programa del Partido por la Democracia*. Santiago: Interamericana.

PEN – Programa Estado de la Nación. 2017. *Informe Estado de la Nación 2017*. San José: Programa Estado de la Nación.

PEN – Programa Estado de la Nación. 2019. *Informe Estado de la Nación 2019*. San José: Programa Estado de la Nación.

Pérez Baralt, Carmen. 2004. "Primero Justicia: Dificultades para la Consolidación de un Nuevo Partido." In *Los Partidos Políticos Venezolanos en el Siglo XXI*, edited by José Enrique Molina Vega and Ángel Eduardo Álvarez Díaz, 263–277. Caracas:Vadell Hermanos Editores.

Pérez Bentancur, Verónica, Rafael Piñeiro Rodríguez, and Fernando Rosenblatt. 2020. *How Party Activism Survives: Uruguay´s Frente Amplio*. New York: Cambridge University Press.

Pérez Bentancur, Verónica, Rafael Piñeiro Rodríguez, and Fernando Rosenblatt. 2019. "Efficacy and the Reproduction of Political Activism: Evidence from the Broad Front in Uruguay." *Comparative Political Studies* 52 (6):838–867.

Pérez Talia, Marcos. 2017. "La Institucionalización Partidista y su Relación con la Calidad de la Democracia: Paraguay y Uruguay en Perspectiva Comparada." *Revista Mexicana de Ciencias Políticas y Sociales* 62 (229):299–330.

Pérez, Verónica, and Rafael Piñeiro. 2016. "Uruguay 2015: Los Desafíos de Gobernar por Izquierda cuando la Economía se Contrae." *Revista de Ciencia Politica* 36 (1):339–363.

Persello, Ana Virginia. 2007. *Historia del Radicalismo*. Buenos Aires: Edhasa.

Piattoni, Simona, ed. 2001. *Clientelism, Interests, and Democratic Representation: The European Experience in Historical and Comparative Perspective*. Cambridge: Cambridge University Press.

Pierson, Paul. 2004. *Politics in Time: History, Institutions, and Social Analysis*. Princeton, NJ: Princeton University Press.

Piñeiro, Rafael, and Jaime Yaffé. 2004. "El Frente Amplio por dentro: Las Fracciones Frenteamplistas 1971–1999." In *La izquierda uruguaya entre la oposición y el gobierno*, edited by Jorge Lanzaro, 297–319. Montevideo: Fin de Siglo/FESUR.

Piñeiro Rodríguez, Rafael, and Fernando Rosenblatt. 2020. "Stability and Incorporation: Toward a New Concept of Party System Institutionalization." *Party Politics* 26 (2):249–260.

Pitkin, Hanna Fenichel. 1967. *The Concept of Representation*. Berkeley: University of California Press.

Pitkin, Hanna Fenichel. 2004. "Representation and Democracy: Uneasy Alliance." *Scandinavian Political Studies* 27 (3):335–342.

Pizarro Leongómez, Eduardo. 2006. "Giants with Feet of Clay: Political Parties in Colombia." In *The Crisis of Democratic Representation in the Andes*, edited by Scott Mainwaring, Ana María Bejarano and Eduardo Pizarro Leongómez, 78–99. Stanford, CA: Stanford University Press.

Pizzorno, Alessandro. 1970. "An Introduction to the Theory of Political Participation." *Social Science Information* 9 (5):29–61.

Pluá Cedeño, María Lorena. 2014. "Enlace Ciuidadano: Dispositivo de la Revolución Ciudadana." MA Thesis, Facultad Latinoamericana de Ciencias Sociales, Sede Ecuador.

PNUD-Congreso de la República. 2009. Indicadores de Gobernabilidad Democrática en Paraguay. Asunción: Congreso de la República and PNUD.

Polga-Hecimovich, John. 2013. "Ecuador: Estabilidad Institucional y la Consolidación de Poder de Rafael Correa." *Revista de Ciencia Política* 33 (1):135–160.

Poole, Keith T., and Howard Rosenthal. 1985. "A Spatial Model for Legislative Roll Call Analysis." *American Journal of Political Science* 29 (2):357–384.

Poole, Keith T., and Howard Rosenthal. 2000. *Congress: A Political-Economic History of Roll Call Voting*. New York: Oxford University Press.

Pribble, Jennifer. 2013. *Welfare and Party Politics in Latin America*. New York: Cambridge University Press.

Prud'homme, Jean-François. 1996. El PRD: Su Vida Interna y sus Elecciones Estratégicas. Working paper, edited by División de Estudios Políticos del CIDE. México: CIDE.

Przeworski, Adam, Susan Stokes, and Bernard Manin. 1999. *Democracy, Accountability, and Representation*. Cambridge: Cambridge University Press.

Przeworski, Adam, and Henry Teune. 1970. *The Logic of Comparative Social Inquiry: Comparative Studies in Behavioral Science*. New York: Wiley-Interscience.

Rahat, Gideon, and Reuven Hazan. 2001. "Candidate Selection Methods: An Analytical Framework." *Party Politics* 7 (3):297–322.

Rejas, Milagros. 2015. "Conflictos Internos y Construcción Partidaria del Partido Fujimorista en el Período 2006–2014." Licenciatura en Ciencia Política y Gobierno, Pontificia Universidad Católica del Perú.

Rice, Stuart A. 1925. "The Behavior of Legislative Groups: A Method of Measurement." *Political Science Quarterly* 40 (1):60–72. http://doi.org/10.2307/2142407.

Roberts, Kenneth. 2002. "Social Inequalities without Class Cleavages in Latin America's Neoliberal Era." *Studies in Comparative International Development* 1 (36):3–33.

Roberts, Kenneth. 2006. "Populism, Political Conflict, and Grass-Roots Organization in Latin America." *Comparative Politics* 38 (2):127–148.

Roberts, Kenneth. 2014a. *Changing Course in Latin America: Party Systems in the Neoliberal Era*. New York: Cambridge University Press.

Roberts, Kenneth. 2019. "Parties, Populism, and Democratic Decay: A Comparative Perspective on Political Polarization in the United States." In *When Democracy Trumps Populism: European and Latin American Lessons for the United States*, edited by Kurt Weyland and Raúl Madrid, 132–153. New York: Cambridge University Press.

Roll, David. 2002. *Rojo Difuso, Azúl Pálido: Los Partidos Tradicionales en Colombia entre el Debilitamiento y la Persistencia*. Bogota: Unibiblos.

Rosal, Lautaro. 2012. "Escenarios de Fragilidad Política, Balance Político: Guatemala 2010–2011." *Revista de Ciencia Política* 32 (1):171–191.

Rosenblatt, Fernando. 2018. *Party Vibrancy and Democracy in Latin America*. New York: Oxford University Press.

Rossel, Cecilia. 2016. "De la Heterogeneidad Productiva a la Estratificación de la Protección Social." In *Hacia un Desarrollo Inclusivo: El caso del Uruguay*, edited by Verónica Amarante and Ricardo Infante, 103–164. Santiago: Comisión Económica para América Latina y el Caribe (CEPAL).

Sabino, Carlos. 2007. "Elecciones Presidenciales en Guatemala." *ARI* 119/2007. Real Instituto Elcano.

Samayoa, Claudia. 2008. "Cuando se Pasa la Frontera en la Lucha." *El Observador: Análisis Alternativo sobre Política y Economía* 3 (11–12):77–78.

Samuels, David. 2004. "From Socialism to Social Democracy: Party Organization and the Transformation of the Workers' Party in Brazil." *Comparative Political Studies* 37 (9):999–1024.

Samuels, David. 2006. "Sources of Mass Partisanship in Brazil." *Latin American Politics & Society* 48 (2):1–27.

Samuels, David, and Matthew Shugart. 2010. *Presidents, Parties, and Prime Ministers: How the Separation of Powers Affects Party Organization and Behavior*. New York: Cambridge University Press.

Sanchez-Sibony, Omar. 2022. *Democracy without Parties: The Case of Peru*. New York: Palgrave Macmillan.

Sánchez-Sibony, Omar. 2016. "Guatemala's Predicament: Electoral Democracy without Political Parties." In *Guatemala: Gobierno, Gobernabilidad, Poder Local y Recursos Naturales*, edited by Gemma Sánchez Medero and Ruben Sánchez Medero, 123–152. Valencia: Editorial Tirant Humanidades.

Sánchez, Francisco, and John Polga-Hecimovich. 2019. "The Tools of Institutional Change under Post-Neoliberalism: Rafael Correa's Ecuador." *Journal of Latin American Studies* 51 (2):379–408. http://doi.org/10.1017/S0022216X1800072X.

Sánchez Garrido, Tania. 2011. "Las Adelitas: Subalternidad y Problemas en la Edificación Democrática del Espacio Público." *Espacialidades: Revista de Temas Contemporáneos sobre Lugares, Política y Cultura* 1 (1):153–178.

Sánchez, Gonzalo, and Donny Meertens. 1983. *Bandoleros, Gamonales y Campesinos: El Caso de la Violencia en Colombia*. Bogota: El Áncora Editores.

Sánchez, José T. , Ignacio González-Bozzolasco, and Fernando Martínez-Escobar. 2015. "Paraguay y las trayectorias de la izquierda desde 1989." In *Desde sus Cenizas: Las izquierdas en América Latina a 25 Años de la Caida del Muro de*

Berlin, edited by Daniel Keersffeld, 375–396.Quito: Friedrich-Ebert-Stiftung–Universidad Andina Simón Bolívar.

Sánchez, Marco Aurelio. 1999. *PRD, la Élite en Crisis: Problemas Organizativos, Indeterminación Ideológica y Deficiencas Programáticas*. México City: Plaza y Valdés.

Sanchez, Omar. 2008. "Transformation and Decay: The De-institutionalisation of Party Systems in South America." *Third World Quarterly* 29 (2):315–337.

Sánchez, Omar. 2008. "Guatemala's Party Universe: A Case Study in Underinstitutionalization." *Latin American Politics and Society* 50 (1):123–151.

Sandberg, Johan, and Engel Tally. 2015. "Politicisation of Conditional Cash Transfers: The Case of Guatemala." *Development Policy Review* 33 (4):503–522.

Sartori, Giovanni. 1970. "Concept Misinformation in Comparative Politics." *American Political Science Review* 64 (4):1033–1053.

Sartori, Giovanni. 1976. *Parties and Party Systems: A Framework for Analysis*. New York: Cambridge University Press.

Sawicki, Frédéric. 1997. *Les Réseaux du Parti Socialiste: Sociologie d'un Milieu Partisan*. Paris: Belin.

Scarrow, Susan. 2015. *Beyond Party Members: Changing Approaches to Partisan Mobilization*. Oxford: Oxford University Press.

Schattschneider, Elmer. 1942. *Party Government*. New York: Holt, Rinehart and Winston.

Schatz, Sara. 2001. "A Difficult Birth: Dissent, Opposition, and Murder in the Rise of Mexico's Partido de la Revolución Democrática (PRD)." In *Political Opportunities, Social Movements, and Democratization*, edited by Patrick G. Coy, 255–295. Amsterdam: Elsevier Science.

Schlesinger, Joseph A. 1994. *Political Parties and the Winning of Office*. Ann Arbor: University of Michigan Press.

Schneider, Ben Ross. 2004. *Business Politics and the State in Twentieth-Century Latin America*. New York: Cambridge University Press.

Schwartz, Mildred A. 1990. *The Party Network: The Robust Organization of Illinois Republicans*. Madison: University of Wisconsin Press.

Seawright, Jason. 2012. *Party-System Collapse: The Roots of Crisis in Peru and Venezuela*. Stanford, CA: Stanford University Press.

Segovia, Carolina. 2009. "¿Crisis de la política en Chile? Percepciones y Valoraciones sobre los Partidos." In *La Sociedad de la Opinión: Reflexiones sobre Encuestas y Cambio Político en Democracia*, edited by Rodrigo Cordero, 197–224. Santiago: Ediciones Universidad Diego Portales.

Senatore, Luis, Natalia Doglio, and Jaime Yaffé. 2004. "Izquierda Política y Sindicatos en Uruguay (1971–2003)." In *La Izquierda Uruguaya entre la Oposición y el Gobierno*, edited by Jorge Lanzaro, 251–295. Montevideo: Fin de Siglo.

Senatore, Luis, and Gustavo Méndez. 2011. "La Política Salarial en el Bienio 2010–2011." In *Política en Tiempos de Mujica: En Busca del Rumbo: Informe de Coyuntura N° 10*, edited by Gerardo Caetano, María

Ester Mancebo and Juan Andrés Moraes, 113–123. Montevideo: Estuario Editora.

Serafin Castro, Alexei. 2018. "Uso del Sorteo, Participación Política y Democracia: Una Lección para México." VI Congreso Nacional de Ciencias Sociales San Luis Potosí, 19–23 March.

Siavelis, Peter M., and Scott Morgenstern, eds. 2008a. *Pathways to Power: Political Recruitment and Candidate Selection in Latin America*. University Park: Pennsylvania State University Press.

Siavelis, Peter, and Scott Morgenstern. 2008b. "Political Recruitment and Candidate Selection in Latin America: A Framework for Analysis." In *Pathways to Power: Political Recruitment and Candidate Selection in Latin America*, edited by Peter Siavelis and Scott Morgenstern, 3–37. University Park: The Pennsylvania State University Press.

Silva, Eduardo. 2017. "Reorganizing Popular Sector Incorporation: Propositions from Bolivia, Ecuador, and Venezuela." *Politics & Society* 45 (1):91–122.

Silva, Eduardo, and Federico Rossi. 2018. *Reshaping the Political Arena in Latin America: From Resisting Neoliberalism to the Second Incorporation*. Pittsburgh, PA: University of Pittsburgh Press.

Sivak, Martín. 2010. *Evo Morales: The Extraordinary Rise of the First Indigenous President of Bolivia*. New York: Palgrave.

Soifer, Hillel, and Alberto Vergara. 2019. *Politics after Violence: Legacies of the Shining Path Conflict in Peru*. Austin: University of Texas Press.

Solano, Luis. 2007. "Los Financistas del PP y de la UNE. ¿Quien Gobernará?" *El Observador: Analisis Alternativo sobre Politica y Economia* 2 (9):31–48.

Sonnleitner, Willibald. 2012. *Elecciones Chiapanecas: del Régimen Posrevolucionario al Desorden Democrático*. México City: El Colegio de México.

Stokes, Susan. 1999. "Political Parties and Democracy." *Annual Review of Political Science* 2 (1):243–267.

Stokes, Susan C. 2001. *Mandates and Democracy: Neoliberalism by Surprise in Latin America*. Cambridge: Cambridge University Press.

Stoll, Heather. 2013. *Changing Societies, Changing Party Systems*. New York: Cambridge University Press.

Strom, Kaare. 1990. "A Behavioral Theory of Competitive Political Parties." *American Journal of Political Science* 34 (2):565–598.

Tato, María Inés. 2013. "El Conservadurismo Argentino: ¿Una Categoría Evanescente?" Actas del Tercer Taller de Discusión Las derechas en el Cono Sur, Siglo XX, Los Polvorines.

Tavera Fenollosa, Ligia. 2013. "El Movimiento Urbano Popular y el Frente Democrático Nacional: Campo Organizacional y Liderazgos." In *El PRD a Veinte Años de su Fundación*, edited by Jorge Cadena-Roa and Miguel A. López Leyva, 105–131. México City: Universidad Nacional Autonoma de Mexico.

Tavits, Margit. 2005. "The Development of Stable Party Support: Electoral Dynamics in Post-Communist Europe." *American Journal of Political Science* 49 (2):283–298.

Tavits, Margit. 2008. "Party Systems in the Making: The Emergence and Success of New Parties in New Democracies." *British Journal of Political Science* 38 (1):113–133.

Tavits, Margit. 2013. *Post-Communist Democracies and Party Organization*. New York: Cambridge University Press.

Taylor-Robinson, Michelle M. 2010. *Do the Poor Count? Democratic Institutions and Accountability in a Context of Poverty*. University Park: Pennsylvania State University Press.

Tejera, Héctor, and Diana Castañeda. 2017. "Estructura Política, Redes Político-Clientelares y Oscilaciones Electorales en la Ciudad de México." *Perfiles Latinoamericanos* 25 (50):227–246.

Thachil, Tariq. 2014. "Elite Parties and Poor Voters: Theory and Evidence from India." *American Political Science Review* 108 (2):454–477.

Tilly, Charles. 2006. *Regimes and Repertoires*. Chicago: The University of Chicago Press.

Tönnies, Ferdinand. 1957 (1887). *Community and Society: Gemeinschaft und Gesellschaft*. East Lansing: Michigan State University Press.

Toro Maureira, Sergio. 2007. "Conducta Legislativa ante las Iniciativas del Ejecutivo: Unidad de los Bloques Políticos en Chile." *Revista de Ciencia Política* 27 (1):23–41.

Torre, Juan Carlos. 2003. "Los Huérfanos de la Política de Partidos sobre los Alcances y la Naturaleza de la Crisis de Representación Partidaria." *Desarrollo Económico* 42 (168):647–665.

Trujillo, Jorge León, and Susan Spronk. 2018. "Socialism without Workers? Trade Unions and the New Left in Bolivia and Ecuador." In *Reshaping the Political Arena in Latin America: From Resisting Neoliberalism to the Second Incorporation*, edited by Eduardo Silva and Federico Rossi, 129–156. Pittsburgh, PA: University of Pittsburgh Press.

UDEFEGUA. 2008. "La Tendencia Creciente de la Criminalizacion del Movimiento Social Guatemalteco." *El Observador: Análisis Alternativo sobre Política y Economía* 3 (14):22–30.

Urrutia, Adriana. 2011. "Que la Fuerza (2011) esté con Keiko: El Nuevo Baile del Fujimorismo. El Fujimorismo, su Organización y sus Estrategias de Campaña." In *Poscandidatos: Guía Analítica de Supervivencia Hasta las Próximas Elecciones*, edited by Carlos Meléndez, 91–120. Lima: Mitin Editores.

Valenzuela, Arturo. 1977. *Political Brokers in Chile: Local Government in a Centralized Polity*. Durham: Duke University Press.

Van Cott, Donna Lee. 2005. *From Movements to Parties in Latin America: The Evolution of Ethnic Politics*. New York: Cambridge University Press.

Van Dyck, Brandon. 2016. "The Paradox of Adversity: New Left Party Survival and Collapse in Brazil, Mexico, and Argentina." In *Challenges of Party-Building in Latin America*, edited by Brandon Van Dyck, James Loxton, Jorge I. Domínguez and Steven Levitsky, 133–158. Cambridge: Cambridge University Press.

Van Dyck, Brandon. 2017. "The Paradox of Adversity: The Contrasting Fates of Latin America's New Left Parties." *Comparative Politics* 49 (2):169–192.

Vargas Cullell, Jorge. 2007. "Costa Rica: Fin de una Era Política." *Revista de Ciencia Política* 27 (EE):113–128.
Vargas Cullell, Jorge. 2008. "Costa Rica: Una Decisión Estratégica en Tiempos Inciertos." *Revista de Ciencia Política* 28 (1):147–169.
Vázquez, Melina, Dolores Rocca Rivarola, and Alejandro Cozachcow. 2018. "Compromisos Militantes en Juventudes Político-Partidarias (Argentina, 2013–2015)." *Revista Mexicana de Sociología* 80 (3):519–548.
Velásquez, Claudio, and Renato Angulo Aponte. 2019. *La Historia de una Guerra Civil (1922–1923)*. Asunción: El Lector.
Vélez, Cristina, Juan Pablo Ossa, and Paula Montes. 2006. "Y se Hizo la Reforma ... Condiciones que Permitieron el Trámite Exitoso de la Reforma Política del 2003." In *La Reforma Política de 2003. ¿La Salvación de los Partidos Políticos Colombianos?*, edited by Gary Hoskin and Miguel García Sánchez, 1–32. Bogota: Uniandes - CESO.
Véliz, Rodrigo J, and Simona Violetta Yagenova. 2009. *Capital y Luchas: Breve Ználisis de la Protesta y el Conflicto Social Actual, Cuadernos de Debate*. Guatemala City: FLACSO.
Verdesoto Custode, Luis Fernando. 2014. *Los Actores y la Producción de la Democracia y la Política en Ecuador 1979–2011*. Quito: Ediciones Abya-Yala.
Vergara, Alberto. 2011. "United by Discord, Divided by Consensus: National and Sub-national Articulation in Bolivia and Peru, 2000–2010." *Journal of Politics in Latin America* 3 (3):65–93.
Vergara, Alberto. 2014. "The Fujimori Regime Through Tocqueville's Lens: Centralism, Regime Change, and Peripheral Elites in Contemporary Peru." In *Peru in Theory*, edited by Paul Drinot, 19–47. New York: Palgrave Macmillan.
Vergara, Alberto, and María Claudia Augusto. 2020. "Explorando el Fujimorismo en el Ámbito Subnacional: Los Gobiernos Regionales de Ica, Pasco y San Martín (2014–2018)." *Argumentos* 1 (1):33–57.
Villarreal Vásquez, José Antonio. 2015. "La Intermediación como Práctica Sociopolítica de los Sectores Urbanos Marginales de Guayaquil en el Contexto de la Revolución Ciudadana." MA Thesis, Facultad Latinoamericana de Ciencias Sociales, Sede Ecuador.
Vivero-Ávila, Igor. 2006. *Desafiando al Sistema: La Izquierda Política en México*. México: UAEM-Porrúa.
Vommaro, Gabriel. 2017. *La Larga Marcha de Cambiemos*. Buenos Aires: Siglo XXI Editores.
Vommaro, Gabriel, and Hélène Combes. 2016. *El Clientelismo Político: desde 1950 hasta Nuestros Días*. Buenos Aires: Siglo XXI Editores.
Vommaro, Gabriel, and Mariana Gené. 2019. "Party-building and Supporting Coalitions: Construction of the Political Bases for a Promarket Program in Argentina (2015–2018)." Paper prepared for the REPAL 2019 Annual Meeting, Tulane.
Vommaro, Gabriel, and Sergio Daniel Morresi. 2014. "Unidos y Diversificados: La Construcción del Partido PRO en la CABA." *Revista SAAP* 8 (2):375–417.
Vommaro, Gabriel, and Sergio Morresi. 2015. *Hagamos Equipo: PRO y la Construcción de la Nueva Derecha en Argentina*. Buenos Aires: Universidad Nacional de General Sarmiento.

Vommaro, Gabriel, Sergio Morresi, and Alejandro Bellotti. 2015. *Mundo PRO: Anatomía de un Partido Fabricado para Ganar*. Buenos Aires: Planeta.

Warren, Harris Gaylord. 1985. *Rebirth of the Paraguayan Republic: The First Colorado Era, 1878–1904*. Pittsburgh, PA: University of Pittsburgh Pres.

Waxenecker, Harald. 2019. *Redes Ilícitas y Crisis Política: La Realidad del Congreso Guatemalteco*. Guatemala City: Fundación Myrna Mack, Comisión Internacional contra la Impunidad en Guatemala, Nómada.

Weingast, Barry, and William Marshall. 1988. "The Industrial Organization of Congress." *Journal of Political Economy* 96 (1):132–163.

Weyland, Kurt, Raúl Madrid, and Wendy Hunter, eds. 2010. *Leftist Governments in Latin America: Successes and Shortcomings*. New York: Cambridge University Press.

Wills-Otero, Laura. 2015. *Latin American Traditional Parties, 1978–2006*. Bogota: Universidad de los Andes, Facultad de Ciencias Sociales, Departamento de Ciencia Política, Ediciones Uniandes.

Wills-Otero, Laura. 2016. "The Electoral Performance of Latin American Traditional Parties, 1978–2006: Does the Internal Structure Matter?" *Party Politics* 22 (6):758–772.

Wolff, Jonas. 2018a. "Ecuador after Correa: The Struggle over the 'Citizens' Revolution.'" *Revista de Ciencia Política* 38 (2):281–302.

Wolff, Jonas. 2018b. "Political Incorporation in Measures of Democracy: A Missing Dimension (and the Case of Bolivia)." *Democratization* 25 (4):692–708.

World Bank. 2018. *Ecuador: Systematic Country Diagnostic*. Washington, DC: World Bank Group.

Yaffé, Jaime. 2005. *Al Centro y Adentro: La Renovación de la Izquierda y el Triunfo del Frente Amplio en Uruguay*. Montevideo: Linardi y Risso.

Zavaleta, Mauricio. 2014. *Coaliciones de Independientes: Las Reglas no Escritas de la Política Electoral*. Lima: Instituto de Estudios Peruanos.

Zavaleta, Mauricio, and Paulo Vilca. 2017. "Partidos Nacionales, Políticos Locales: Una Mirada a las Candidaturas Parlamentarias desde el Sur del Perú." In *Perú: Elecciones 2016: Un País Dividido y un Resultado Inesperado*, edited by Fernando Tuesta, 309–336. Lima: Fondo Editorial Pontificia Universidad Católica del Perú.

Zegada, María Teresa, and Jorge Komadina. 2014. *El Espejo de la Sociedad: Poder y Representación en Bolivia*. La Paz: CERES/Plural.

Zuazo, Moira. 2010. "¿Los Movimientos Sociales en el Poder? El Gobierno del MAS en Bolivia." *Nueva Sociedad* 227 (May–June):120–135.

Zurita Tablada, Luis. 2016. *El ABC de la Socialdemocracia: Una Perspectiva Guatemalteca y Mundial*. Guatemala City: Magna Terra Editores.

Name Index

Organization Index

Subject Index

Ingram Content Group UK Ltd.
Milton Keynes UK
UKHW010701250423
420667UK00009B/29